T0338209

Machine Learning for Risk Calculations

Founded in 1807, John Wiley & Sons is the oldest independent publishing company in the United States. With offices in North America, Europe, Australia and Asia, Wiley is globally committed to developing and marketing print and electronic products and services for our customers' professional and personal knowledge and understanding.

The Wiley Finance series contains books written specifically for finance and investment professionals as well as sophisticated individual investors and their financial advisors. Book topics range from portfolio management to e-commerce, risk management, financial engineering, valuation and financial instrument analysis, as well as much more.

For a list of available titles, visit our Web site at www.WileyFinance.com.

Machine Learning for Risk Calculations

A Practitioner's View

I. RUIZ

M. ZERON

Foreword by P. Karasinski

WILEY

Registered Office
John Wiley & Sons Ltd, The Atrium, Southern Gate, Chichester, West Sussex, PO19 8SQ, UK

Editorial Office
The Atrium, Southern Gate, Chichester, West Sussex, PO19 8SQ, UK

For details of our global editorial offices, customer services, and more information about Wiley products visit us at www.wiley.com.

Wiley also publishes its books in a variety of electronic formats and by print-on-demand. Some content that appears in standard print versions of this book may not be available in other formats.

Library of Congress Cataloging-in-Publication Data

Names: Ruiz, Ignacio, 1972- author. | Laris, Mariano Zeron Medina, author.
Title: Machine learning for risk calculations : a practitioner's view /
    Ignacio Ruiz, Mariano Zeron Medina Laris.
Description: Hoboken, New Jersey : Wiley, [2022] | Includes index.
Identifiers: LCCN 2021036694 (print) | LCCN 2021036695 (ebook) | ISBN
    9781119791386 (hardback) | ISBN 9781119791393 (adobe pdf) | ISBN
    9781119791409 (epub)
Subjects: LCSH: Machine learning. | Financial risk management.
Classification: LCC Q325.5 .R855 2022 (print) | LCC Q325.5 (ebook) | DDC
    332.10285/631—dc23
LC record available at https://lccn.loc.gov/2021036694
LC ebook record available at https://lccn.loc.gov/2021036695

Cover image: © korkeng/Shutterstock
Cover design: Wiley

SKY9D71FD69-5470-4D80-A625-379722B1B4E1_111021

To my sister Cristina, a beautiful soul around us, an inspiration in my life.

To my parents, for their unwavering support.

Contents

PART FOUR
Applications

Acknowledgements

This book has been significantly benefited from the support and input of a whole range of individuals whom we want to thank. In particular, we would like to thank our friend Emilio Viúdez, who directly contributed to many of the chapters in this book. Most importantly, he has been an extraordinary companion in the journey of which this book is one of the results.

We would also like to thank (in no particular order of importance) Jesus Alonso, Andrew Aziz, Dimitra Bampou, Russell Barker, Assad Bouayoun, Juan Antonio Burgos, Paul Burnett, Pablo Cassatella, Justin Chan, Lucia Cipolina, Alex Daminoff, Matthew Dear, Piero Del Boca, Thomas Devereux, Alberto Elices, Eduardo Epperlein and his group at NOMURA, Andrew Green, Stephen Hancock, Brian Huge, Marc Jeannin, Akshay Jha, Paul Jones, Christian Kappen, Piotr Karasinski, Gordon Lee, Udit Mahajan, Navneet Mathur, Adolfo Montoro, Cesar Mora, Rubén Moral, Yacine Moulay-Rchid, Laura Müller, Stuart Neil, Maria Nogueiras, Yogi Patel, Jose María Pesquero, Maxim Petrashev, Carlos Rioja, Samir Saurav, Joaquín Seco, Naimish Shah, Anton Simanenka, Jono Simpson, Takis Sironis, John Sleath, Robert Smith, Theo Stampoulis, Lauri Tamminen, Alok Tiwari, Alessandro Vecci, Satya Vemireddy and Hernan Zúñiga for the time and patience they had with us in different occasions.

The reader can find further resources on the topics of this book at

mocaxintelligence.org

and on the YouTube channel

youtube.com/mocax

Foreword

I met Mariano and Ignacio at the Quantitative Finance 2019 Rome conference. Mariano gave a presentation on the joint work with Ignacio on the Chebyshev Tensors techniques for CVA pricing and FRTB capital. After the talk I went to speak to Mariano, as I had found the results he had shown quite remarkable. That was the beginning of my productive relationship with both of them.

The 2008 banking crisis changed profoundly the derivatives industry. Before it, the derivatives business was driven by the creation of exotic trades. After the crisis, the paradigm changed and computing the risks carried in the balance sheets became central to a degree not seen before. Being able to compute accurately these risk numbers in a timely and cost-effective manner is now the main driver of the business.

This has been achieved historically mostly by increasing the amount of hardware used for the computation in conjunction with only a few limited algorithmic solutions. This route has become increasingly less economical, as computational needs have further increased due to regulation and market demand. Mariano and Ignacio offer in this book a family of algorithmic solutions that substantially reduce the need for increased computational power, as well as solutions for some calculations that are very difficult to do without them.

This text applies the mathematics behind the Chebyshev Tensors combined with Deep Learning within the specific contexts of many of the risk calculations that banks, hedge funds and other financial institutions need to do on a constant basis, with the aim of reducing the computational demand of these calculations, while retaining the required accuracy. This is done in a robust manner, using as a starting point the mathematical properties of the techniques involved, but not forgetting that at times some well understood heuristics are needed to potentiate the applicability of the mathematical methods chosen.

This thinking process is applied to a number of practical applications presented in the final chapters of the book, ranging from counterparty credit risk (CCR), market risk, portfolio optimisation, and several others. The results presented in this book have the potential to be disruptive for the industry. I hope that the quantitative finance community will enjoy and benefit from the ideas put forward in this text.

Piotr Karasinski

Motivation and aim of this book

The world of risk analytics has had an ever growing demand for computing capacity since the early 2000s. When one of the book's authors started working in this field, he was asked to work on the CCR engine at Credit Suisse for the new Basel II regulation and IMM capital calculation. At the time, it was the latest big thing in the industry. The IMM-related calculations were one of the most (if not the most) complicated calculations the bank had done up to that point. A few hundred CPUs were bought and installed in a state-of-the-art grid computing farm. The belief was that such grid would be able to do any CCR calculation. However, it did not take much time for the team to realise that more computing power was needed to match the computational requirements of new calculations being requested. Over the years, we have experienced a world in which, regardless of how much computing power is available with the latest technologies, soon it is insufficient to meet the new demands and needs to be upgraded only a few years later.

Indeed, the world of banking, and in particular the business of derivatives, has become a technology race (like many other industries, it must be said). As P. Karasinski says in his Foreword to this book, it used to be about creating and selling the new exotic product. Now it is about computing prices and increasingly sophisticated risk metrics in a prompt and efficient manner — partly as a result of regulations that have become more stringent since the 2008 crisis, partly as a result of the higher standards for risk management the industry has developed. That is where the differentiation between different broker-dealers resides and where the source of profitability lies at present.

Until recently, the computational cost associated with the calculation of risk numbers has been mostly addressed by throwing brute computing capacity at it, that is, buying more and better hardware. It is known that many tier-one banks have farms of several tens of thousand of CPUs and GPUs. Also banks are now leasing cloud computing capability from external vendors. This is, of course, at a considerable cost, which needs to be managed. Obviously, this cannot continue increasing forever without denting the profitability of the business.

Part of the reason why financial institutions have opted for more hardware is down to Moore's second law that states that the computing capacity of transistor chips per dollar of capital expenditure grows exponentially.[1] This has certainly been true up to recently. However, this increase in computing capacity was driven by the constant miniaturisation of the basic elements of chips (semiconductor transistors, magnetic memory bits, etc.). Now that we are reaching the 10 nanometer range for

---

[1] Moore's first law relates to the capacity of processors. Moore's second law relates to the monetary cost of processors.

semiconductor transistors, the rate of growth stated in Moore's Laws is stalling in commercial computers. This is illustrated by the fact that 10 years ago, the processing capability of a new computer was massively superior compared to the processing capacity of computers only a few years before; at present, it is only marginally better. The reason is that the size of one atom is, roughly, around 0.1 nanometers, and when we decrease the size of transistors below a few tens of nanometers, quantum effects start to appear and temperature becomes a problem. The subject of quantum computing — a most interesting topic — is well outside the scope of this book, but the reality is that, for now and for the foreseeable future, hardware will only be able to offer limited increased computing capacity. As a result, the paradigm has changed from creating more computing power via hardware to developing algorithmic solutions that optimise calculations.

In parallel, there has been a lot of work done by the quantitative analytics community to create algorithmic methods that accelerate the calculations and decrease their hardware need. A notorious example has been the family of Adjoint Algorithmic Differentiation (AAD) solutions in the world of XVA pricing, which in its general version can compute as many XVA sensitivities as needed with the added cost of (roughly) 10 XVA pricing runs. Seen from the perspective of the times when computing one CVA run for a few netting sets was already a challenge, this improvement is remarkable. However, it comes at a considerable price: the implementation effort is most significant. This is particularly the case if one already has a functioning XVA platform and wants to adapt it to AAD. This task can be so daunting that many banks do not consider it a viable option.

This book is based on the belief that the optimal solution to many of the computational challenges in finance lies in the union of algorithmic solutions, and appropriate software implementation of these, run on powerful hardware. The aim of this book is to review how some numerical mathematical methods, when applied thoughtfully, taking into account the specific characteristics of the calculations we want to improve, can create substantial computational enhancements. Indeed, the book is the direct result of the experience the authors have had, over the past few years, while trying to solve difficult calculations (sometimes seemingly impossible) in real-life settings within financial institutions.

The solutions proposed throughout this book apply mainly to existing risk engines within operating financial institutions. Some of these risk engines have been developed over many years by different business units and with different goals in mind. This has produced, in many cases, an amalgamation of risk engines that is suboptimal from an efficiency standpoint. Although starting new engines from scratch may correct the shortcomings of the legacy systems, this requires not only a lot of time and money but also enormous projects in many cases. In fact, a number of banks have reportedly started and stopped the development of global pricing and risk systems from the ground up due to the scale of the job. Quite often, it makes more sense, from a practical perspective, to upgrade existing engines, improving what already exists, using the increasingly demanding business needs and regulatory environment as guidelines, instead of developing a new one. With this in mind, the solutions proposed in this book are highly pragmatic.

Also, we keep in mind that for a solution to be implemented, budgets need to be approved by someone usually high up in the pyramid. Therefore, small(ish) incremental changes with tangible benefits are more likely to succeed than big open ambitious projects. However, to be noted, this does not mean that the solutions put forward in the book cannot be implemented in a system being built from the ground up; in fact, in some cases this would be the optimal approach. All we say is that having the option of incremental changes that are easy to manage is always a bonus to not lose sight of.

One of the common threads in all solutions discussed in the book is that they are grounded on mathematically robust results. Ideally, we would like everything to be based on solid theoretical frameworks. However, as the reader will soon learn, sometimes heuristic rules need to be used in conjunction with mathematical theories. The right combination of mathematical theories and heuristics, partly determined by the context of the problem (for example, the characteristics of the systems being used), is what delivers the most effective outcome. When such heuristic rules are used or discussed, we make the point clear, indicating its range of validity and limitations, so the quantitative analyst can make use of them safely.

Many of the computational problems that banks encounter are the result of having to evaluate a given function a large number of times under (only slightly) different inputs, together with the fact that such functions are costly to compute. Examples of these functions are Over-the-Counter derivative pricing functions, that need to be evaluated from several hundreds to millions of times in risk calculations. From a computational standpoint, these computations tend to be the bottleneck in risk calculations. Our approach is to find a way to take advantage of the specifics in the risk calculation so that a very accurate and fast-to-compute replica of the pricing function can be generated. As a consequence, one computes the same risk metrics in practice, but more efficiently. Also, similar replication methods are applied to other computational challenges for model calibration, for example, leading to significant improvements, too. Furthermore, the techniques presented in this book open the door for a new family of computations that, without them, seem impossible to achieve in many cases, like balance sheet optimisations.

BOOK OUTLINE

As just said, the solutions discussed in this book are rooted in identifying computationally expensive functions to evaluate — which create computational bottlenecks in calculations — and creating replicas of these problematic functions that can be efficiently computed while at the same time giving essentially the same results.

We start off in Part I with a general overview of Machine Learning techniques. Then we focus on two of the most effective methods to replicate functions: Deep Neural Nets (DNNs) and Chebyshev Tensors (CTs). In mathematical terms, we delve into *function approximation* because the goal is to create a mathematical object, which comes with a computational architecture, that closely approximates the original function. In our case, we look for techniques that deliver replicas that can be evaluated substantially faster than the function they approximate and that can be calibrated with reasonable computational effort. At this point, discussions are mostly theoretical and few comments are made regarding their applications. The goal is to provide a solid mathematical background we can leverage from subsequent chapters.

Once the fundamental approximation methods have been established, we present, in Part II, a number of tools that will enable the optimal utilisation of the approximation methods in the applications of interest. We see these tools as the equivalent of nuts, bolts and spanners used to assemble the different components of a car: essential tools without which we cannot build the vehicle. A number of mathematical and computational tools will be discussed, these being the Composition Technique, Tensor Extension Algorithms, Sliding Techniques and Jacobian Techniques.

Then, Part III explains how the approximation methods from Part I and the tools in Part II can be combined to create solutions. In particular, we focus on how to use the toolkit with DNNs and with CTs, as well as how to use DNNs and CTs together in order to achieve a hybrid approximation method.

Following all the previous discussions, the book comes to life in Part IV. In it, the theoretical solutions are applied to real computational problems that financial institutions face. We cover the fundamental calculations in CCR (XVAs, IMM capital, PFE); XVA sensitivities (hedging and CVA capital); Market Risk (VaR and FRTB); dynamic simulation of portfolio sensitivities in a Monte Carlo simulation — with a special focus on its application to the simulation of Initial Margin (XVAs, IMM capital, PFE and CVA capital); we discuss computational techniques that enable the efficient calibration of sophisticated pricing models (Front Office pricer calibration); we also see how the fundamental approximation techniques can be used in the context of implied volatility evaluation (ultra-fast computations); stable computations of sensitivities for exotic derivatives is covered (Front Office hedging); we also discuss how to use the techniques presented in the previous part of the book in the context of balance sheet and portfolio optimisation problems (profitability maximisation); and we elaborate on an originally unintended but positive side effect of the methods: how a pricing function can be "cloned" from one IT system to another (IT systems interaction).

The different software packages used to generate the results presented (mainly) in Part IV are referenced in a chapter toward the end of the book, along with the websites where they can be downloaded from. The software package that implements most of the Chebyshev machinery used in this book, the MoCaX suit (developed by us), has dedicated sections in that chapter with examples of how to use it. We trust the readers will find it useful.

Some of the methods discussed in this book fall under the scope of a patent. At the time of this book going to press, the patent holders are happy to provide a license to anyone interested in using them. For further information, please contact the authors.

We hope that the quantitative community finds this book interesting and useful, and we encourage anyone working in this field to get in touch with us. We very much enjoy collaboration frameworks. We can be reached via LinkedIn, for example.

# One

Fundamental Approximation Methods

CHAPTER 1

Machine Learning

The aim of this chapter is to present in the clearest possible manner the main concepts behind Machine Learning (ML) models. This will set a unified framework under which the approximation methods — which constitute the spearhead of the solutions used to tackle the computational problems in Part IV — are presented.

The main ideas presented in this chapter will be particularly relevant to Chapter 2, where DNNs are introduced. Without them, a good number of ideas in Chapter 2 will not be as easy to digest.

The chapter starts with a quick introduction to the field of ML. We then touch upon its history, briefly describe the main areas in ML and mention the applications we are most interested in.

Then we delve into the core of the chapter, which is the presentation of the main concepts underpinning most ML models. These will be treated either in relation to the concept of training and predicting with an ML model — considering both the frequentist and the Bayesian approach — or in relation to the idea of model complexity.

Along the way, we will use the standard Linear Model to introduce and illustrate the main concepts. Despite its simplicity, the standard Linear Model shares the key ML concepts with most other models. It therefore makes sense to use it as a guiding thread.

1.1 INTRODUCTION TO MACHINE LEARNING

Artificial Intelligence (AI), the field that studies the intelligence of machines — as opposed to natural intelligence, which is displayed by humans and animals — has been one of the most successful and thriving areas of study in the last few decades. Among its many branches, ML is the one that is concerned with algorithms that automatically improve through experience. This is a fundamental component of AI, as it enables learning from the structures and patterns of data, allowing non-human agents to make decisions.

An often-quoted formal definition of ML is the following:

> "A computer program is said to learn from experience E with respect to some class of tasks T and performance measure P if its performance at tasks in T, as measured by P, improves with experience E" ([57]).

Intuitively speaking, this says that ML consists of a collection of methods and algorithms that automatically extract patterns from data with the purpose of performing predictive tasks.

1.1.1   A brief history of Machine Learning Methods

Even though the term Machine Learning was coined in 1959 by Arthur Samuel — a leading figure in the fields of computer gaming and AI — some of the most basic and common ML algorithms predate the second half of the 20th century, the period with which ML is normally associated.

For example, the origins of Linear Regression can be traced to the beginning of the 19th century through the works of Legendre and Gauss ([70]). This technique was designed to determine the orbit of bodies around the sun by using astronomical data. Calculations would have been made by hand. Also, the amount of data collected would have been small (minuscule by today's standards). Yet, the technique proved successful even under these circumstances.

Other ML models were also developed decades before the advent of computers. For example, Principal Component Analysis (PCA), a well-known dimensionality reduction technique — used on a regular basis still today — was first developed in 1901 by Karl Pearson.

Also, the main ideas underpinning decision trees — the main constituent in random forests, one of the most powerful ML models — have existed, in some form or another, for centuries. Clustering techniques — a common technique employed in ML and data science these days — were used in psychology and anthropology as early as the 1930s.[1]

However, the models just mentioned did not develop into the form they have today until the second half of the 20th century. There were two key elements that helped change the landscape. The first was an unprecedented increase, throughout the 20th century, in the sophistication of statistical modelling. The second and probably most fundamental was the development of the computer as we know it today in the 1950s.

Before the advent of the computer, thinking of asking a machine to perform the tasks we nowadays do on a regular basis would have been unthinkable to the vast majority of scientists. Having access to a computer meant that computations with data sets could take place in a very short period of time. Also, it enabled researchers to consider larger and more complex data sets. This, alongside a larger appetite for more complex statistical models, led to the enhancement of old models and the creation of new.

For example, all sorts of bells and whistles were added to the 19th century version of Linear Regression to make it much more flexible, robust and capable of learning from non-linear data. Also, decision trees gave rise to random forests. At the same time, new models — some of the most powerful in ML today — were developed, such as support vector machines and Neural Nets.

---

[1]The idea of a hierarchical arrangement used to make decisions has not only been of important philosophical importance, but has been used in practical settings for centuries.

Linear Regression still relevant today

It is worth mentioning that, despite the large number of new models developed over the last few decades, the Linear Model — as mentioned before, one of the oldest — is still used with great success to this day. Moreover, it has been one of the main building blocks for other, more sophisticated models. Despite its simplicity, it shares its main characteristics with pretty much all other ML models. As such, it will be, in coming sections, the example we use to illustrate the main facets of ML models and in particular those of DNNs.

In the first few years, even decades, of the ML era, the range of applications was limited. This was not just due to the simplicity of the models and the small number of people working with them but also to the fact that computers were only found in specialised research centres. As computers have become more powerful and ubiquitous — not only in a good number of industries but also as a tool for personal use — the range and number of applications has grown substantially.

Nowadays, Machine Learning models are used in a wide range of applications: in forecasting, such as in weather and stock market prediction; in anomaly detection, for example, fraud detection; for classification, for example, to identify patients with specific medical conditions; for ranking tasks, as search engines do when recommending websites; for summarising, for example, sentiment analysis in social media; for decision-making in robotics. And the list goes on.

1.1.2 Main sub-categories in Machine Learning

As was mentioned in Section 1.1, ML consists of a set of models that automatically learn patterns from data and use these patterns to perform some task. These methods are typically divided into three sub-categories: *supervised* learning, *unsupervised* learning and *reinforcement* learning.

Supervised learning

Models and algorithms that fall into the category of supervised learning are those that learn from input and output data. Denote the input data by X. This consists of a set of vectors $(x_1, \ldots, x_m)$, where each vector x_i, for $i = 1, \ldots, m$, lives in $\mathbb{R}^n$, for some $n \in \mathbb{N}$. The variables in these vectors are typically called *features* or *attributes* of the set X. They can be discrete or continuous. The output data, denoted by Y, consists of a set of vectors $(y_1, \ldots, y_m)$ — typically real values — that represent a *response* or *target* variable. Again, this variable can be discrete or continuous.

Each element x_i in X pairs up with y_i. The data used to train the algorithm therefore consists of data points $\mathcal{D} = \{(x_i, y_i)\}_{i=1}^n$. The model learns patterns from $\mathcal{D}$ subject to this pairing; the idea being that once these patterns are learnt, the model can, with a high degree of accuracy, assign a value y to any new data point x.

One of the implicit assumptions in supervised learning is that the features from the data set X are powerful enough to the target variable y. For example, if we want to predict whether it will rain we should consider features that are related to the chance of raining. One should not choose the amount of oil being extracted in Saudi Arabia as a feature to predict the chance of rain in Buenos Aires, but rather measurements such as atmospheric pressure, humidity and wind around Buenos Aires.

There is a vast number of situations where supervised learning has been applied over the years. We make use of it on a regular basis in things such as email spam detection, image and speech recognition, fraud detection, weather prediction, medical diagnosing and so on.

Unsupervised learning

By contrast, in unsupervised learning the data set $\mathcal{D}$ consists of only the input set X. The goal is to find patterns in X that are not subject to a target variable. This is, of course, a problem that opens up a range of options in terms of how one should train the algorithms.

Although not used as often as supervised learning, the range of applications nowadays is anyway vast. It is used for clustering, anomaly detection, information compression, density estimation and latent variable learning. These techniques can help assign labels to data that are otherwise unlabelled. It can also help reduce the size of the feature space in data sets, making it more portable and in some cases reducing the complexity of the data set (something that can make supervised algorithms perform better).

There is a type of unsupervised learning algorithm that is of particular relevance to this book. This encompasses all dimensionality reduction algorithms, such as Principal Component Analysis. Not only have they been used in finance for a long time and in a wide range of cases, but they constitute an important part of the Sliding Technique presented in Chapter 7.

Reinforcement learning

The third main sub-category in ML is reinforcement learning. This field deals with the ways in which a software agent ought to make decisions within an environment, where the aim is to maximise a predefined notion of gain or reward. Under this ML paradigm, there is no input/output data available to train from the beginning. The model learns through interaction with the environment. The data from which it learns are constantly generated and depend on the model used. Reinforcement learning models have become popular in applications such as self-driving cars, reducing energy costs in different industries, and famously helping train a machine to beat the number one player in the world at Go.[2] It also has become important in hyper-parameter optimisation, a very important aspect that comes up when working in real-life applications with many ML models. We discuss this topic in more detail in Section 1.4.3.

---

[2]We refer to https://deepmind.com/research/case-studies/alphago-the-story-so-far for more details on how ML algorithms were used to beat the Go world champion.

1.1.3 Applications of interest

The applications of interest in this book are presented in Part IV. These essentially consist of resolving the computational bottleneck associated with the repeated call of functions in risk calculations. We explain the specifics of applications to CCR, market risk, model calibration, balance sheet optimisation, volatility surfaces and risk metric optimisation exercises. Although the main ML model used in recent years to tackle these problems is based on DNNs, more general (and basic) ML models have been used for a long time to tackle closely related problems.

Linear regression has been used for years in many areas of finance. In fact, one of the most popular techniques in the last 20 years, used to speed up the pricing of exotic products and the computation of risk calculations, is Longstaff-Schwartz (least-squares Monte Carlo), which essentially relies on the repeated application of Linear Regression in a Monte Carlo simulation. This was first presented in [52] and opened up new avenues of research. Alongside Linear Regression, dimensionality reduction techniques, such as PCA, have been used for a long time in many areas of finance. People often think of ML as a set of techniques recently developed, involving much more complex and expensive algorithms than the ones underpinning Linear Regression and PCA. However, both Linear Regression and PCA perfectly satisfy the conditions to be ML algorithms.

For a long time, the ML models and algorithms used in finance were of the simpler kind. But with the advent of powerful computing capabilities, a range of well implemented and easy to use DNNs packages in the most common programming languages, practitioners have begun to increasingly use DNNs.

In particular, risk calculations, risk optimisation and calibration of pricing functions — all exercises that demand large computational capabilities — stand to gain a lot from the use of approximating techniques. This book elaborates on two of the most powerful ones that we know of: DNNs and Chebyshev Tensors (CTs). Chapter 2 sets the theoretical framework for DNNs, and Chapter 3 does so for CTs.

Focusing on DNNs, there is a growing body of literature addressing the computational bottleneck of risk calculations using DNNs, examples of which are [25] in CCR and [41] in pricing function calibration. The core idea is to replace functions that are called thousands of times in a particular process by a DNN. Once the approximation has been achieved — through proper training — the DNN is used instead of the function. Because DNNs are fast to evaluate — unless they are too large, amounting to little more than simple linear algebra operations — the process that was once problematic from a computational point of view is reduced to a manageable computation.

1.2 THE LINEAR MODEL

This section presents the core elements of Linear Regression. Linear Regression (more generally, Linear Models) is very important in ML. Mathematically, it is one of the simplest and easiest to understand. A big advantage is that it can be solved analytically; meaning, it is easy to use and quick to deploy, features that many other models do not have. However, despite their simplicity, Linear Models are used on a regular basis in a wide range of contexts with success. Not only that, but Linear Models also constitute important modules or building blocks for more complex models. Finally — and of particular importance for this chapter — the fundamental concepts and characteristics of a huge range of ML models can be found in the Linear Model. As the latter is simpler, it makes sense to start there.

1.2.1 General concepts

Consider the following example. A real estate company is interested in having an effective way of pricing houses in different areas of a city. Assume they have access to the surface area of the properties and the average household income of each post code. Moreover, assume they have the price for n of these properties. This means, in terms of input/output data $\mathcal{D} = \{X, Y\}$, that they have input data $X = (x_{1i}, x_{2i})_{i=1}^{m}$, where i represents a property, x_{1i} its corresponding surface area, and x_{2i} the average income of the post code where the property is located, and output data $y = (y_i)_{i=1}^{m}$, where y_i is the price of the i-th property.

The question we ask is whether the data $\mathcal{D} = \{X, Y\}$ can be used to obtain a function f with which we can predict the price of properties. In particular, can we obtain a function f, such that given any pair (x_1, x_2), not necessarily in $\mathcal{D}$, — where x_1 is the surface area of the property and x_2 the average income of its post code — the value $f(x_1, x_2)$ is a good proxy to the real price of the property? That is, can we *learn* the patterns present in $\mathcal{D}$ and capture them in a function f?

Notice that as an ML problem, this example belongs to the supervised learning category. The covariates or predictors are the surface area of the property and the average income of the property's post code. They define a 2-dimensional space from which we have the data set $(x_{1i}, x_{2i})_i$, where $1 \leq i \leq m$. The target variable is the price of the property, for which we have the data set y_i, again where $1 \leq i \leq m$. These data would typically look like those in Table 1.1.

Choice of model

Given that we are in search of a function f, the first thing to consider is the space of functions $\mathcal{F}$, where the search takes place. The larger the space $\mathcal{F}$, the more choices available. However, the larger $\mathcal{F}$, the more difficult the search typically becomes. It is often a question of how much model flexibility we want in exchange of model tractability. The question of which model to choose — essentially determining the family of functions $\mathcal{F}$ where we search — is one of the most important and challenging ones in ML, a recurring theme throughout this chapter and intricately related to model complexity briefly discussed in Section 1.4.

TABLE 1.1   Table showing an example of data to train on.

Data point	1	2	3	$\cdots$	m
Surface area m^2 (x_1)	105	95	150	$\cdots$	45
Avg. income postal area $ (x_2)	1500	950	2000	$\cdots$	1200
Property price $ (y)	85000	50000	85000	$\cdots$	75000

The typical spaces of families considered in regression problems — for reasons that will become clear — are parametrised by a set of real vectors W. This means that each function f considered in this family depends on a vector w. To make this dependency clear, we denote such functions by f_w.

To make the problem of finding suitable functions f_w more tractable, conditions are imposed on the form these functions can take. One of the most basic examples of $\mathcal{F}$ consists of linear functions given by the following expression

$$\begin{aligned} f_w(x) &= w_0 + w_1 x_1 + \cdots + w_n x_n \\ &= w^T x, \end{aligned} \tag{1.1}$$

where $w = (w_0, w_1, \ldots, w_n)$ and $x = (1, x_1, \ldots, x_n)$. Notice the vector x is considered as vector of length $n + 1$ to incorporate the displacement component into the inner product and simplify notation.

Learning and predicting

The function f_w in Equation 1.1 depends on two families of variables. The first are the predictor variables $x = (x_1, \ldots, x_n)$ in $\mathbb{R}^n$. The second are vectors $w = (w_0, w_1, \ldots, w_n)$ in $\mathbb{R}^{n+1}$, normally called *weights*. It helps to think of the function in Equation 1.1 as a function in terms of x, parametrised by w, $f_w(x)$.

Learning essentially consists of exploring the space of functions $\mathcal{F}$ by changing w in search for a function f_w that accurately returns target values y, given feature vectors x.[3] In our real estate example, $n = 2$, and the function f we are after is a function defined by a fixed $w = (w_0, w_1, w_2)$.

As mentioned, the search for a suitable w is what is known as *learning* or *training*.[4] If we manage, through training, to find a function f_w that is a good fit to the data $\mathcal{D}$, we say the family of functions $\mathcal{F}$ has learned the data. Moreover, if it predicts the price of houses that were not in the data set $\mathcal{D}$, to a high degree of accuracy, then we say f_w *generalises* well.

Generalising well is the main goal of ML models. In our real estate example, obtaining such a function f_w gives us a tool that enables us to predict, with a high degree of accuracy, the price of any given property, based on the surface area of the property and average income of its post code, regardless of whether that property was in the data set $\mathcal{D}$ or not.

The example of regression function considered in Equation 1.1 admits a nice geometric interpretation of what it means to train. Notice the function f_w in Equation 1.1 describes a hyper-plane in $\mathbb{R}^{n+1}$. For our running real estate example, where $n = 2$, the data $\mathcal{D}$ can be seen as points in $\mathbb{R}^3$, since each vector $x = (x_1, x_2)$ is in $\mathbb{R}^2$, and its corresponding value y is in $\mathbb{R}$, which means that (x_1, x_2, y) lives in $\mathbb{R}^3$. Therefore, for this

---

[3]How the space $\mathcal{F}$ is explored is a fundamental part of learning. However, to avoid getting sidetracked, we address this question in Section 1.3.

[4]This refers to learning under the frequentist approach, described in Section 1.3.1. The other main learning approach is the Bayesian one, described in Section 1.3.2.

example, the image of f_w can be seen as a plane in $\mathbb{R}^3$, and the data $\mathcal{D}$ as points in $\mathbb{R}^3$. This is shown in Figure 1.1. Learning, in this context, consists of finding the tilt and intercept of the plane that best fits the data $\mathcal{D}$. The data $\mathcal{D}$ used for training is marked with disks in Figure 1.1. We will have generalised well if the plane obtained at the learning stage fits unseen data. Unseen data are marked by triangles in Figure 1.1.

The cost function

But how do we measure the accuracy or (equivalently) the error of the chosen f_w? Intuitively, we want $f_w(x)$ to be as close as possible to y, where x is a feature vector that corresponds to the target value y. One of the most common ways of measuring this error is through *mean squared error*

$$\phi(w; X, Y) = \frac{1}{m} \sum_{i=1}^{m} (f_w(x_i) - y_i)^2. \tag{1.2}$$

From an intuitive point of view, the formula presented in Equation 1.2 makes sense as we are taking the average of the squares of the distances, between the prediction made by f_w on x_i, and the actual value y_i, using all data points (x_i, y_i) in the data set $\mathcal{D}$. However, there is a reason why this particular expression is used. We will touch upon this in Section 1.3.1. Any function or formula used to measure the error, such as the one in Equation 1.2, is known as *cost*, *loss* or *energy* function.

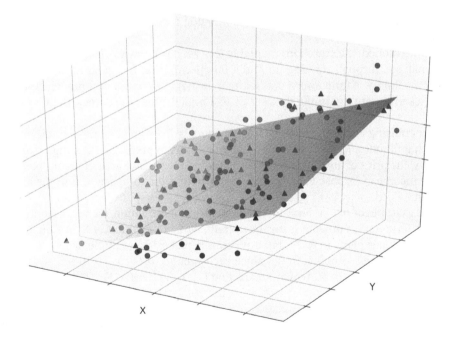

FIGURE 1.1   Linear Regression fit to points in dimension 3. Filled in circles represent data used for training, while filled in triangles represent data for testing (unseen data).

Notice that although the expression in Equation 1.2 makes explicit reference to the data set $\mathcal{D}$, it can also be used on data that was not used for training. As long as we have input and output vectors — given by x and y, respectively — the function can be used.

Equation 1.2 presents one of the most common cost functions used. However, others may be considered. In fact, in some cases, the choice of cost function is very important. Which cost function to use given a particular problem is an active area of research.

Model complexity

In the example presented so far, we have restricted our attention to learning the patterns in the data $\mathcal{D}$, while restricting our attention to the family of functions $\mathcal{F}$, given by Equation 1.1. However, no reason was given for such choice.

In any ML problem, a model must be chosen before training. Deciding which model to use on a given set of data $\mathcal{D}$ is not always a straightforward thing. Once a choice of model is made, there is an implicit assumption — or hope — that the model will fit the data and generalise well. However, there is no guarantee that such a thing will happen.

There are several factors that determine whether this happens or not, for example, the flexibility of the model and the amount and quality of the data available. Sometimes the data are such that less flexible models can perform very well with little data. This is, for example, the case of Linear Regression in certain contexts. Other models are more flexible and effective at finding more complex relationships in the data. These, however, tend to need larger data sets and training can often — as we will see — be more complicated. This is the case of DNNs.

The ability to choose the right model for the given data is a challenging one and often determines the success or failure of the task in hand. We discuss in more detail the question of model complexity (Section 1.4) and how to tune it when we discuss regularisation and hyper-parameter optimisation.

Regression problem of interest

Let us now take a look at the regression problem that is relevant to many of the applications presented in Part IV. We start with a pricing function P. Pricing functions take variables x as input and return real values y. Let us call the input variables of P risk factors. The values y returned by P are prices. The function P establishes a relationship between x and y. Moreover, it can be used to generate data by calling P at a collection of vectors x within its domain.

Note that in the real estate example we started with just data; no function was available a priori. These data are then used to produce a function f_w that fits it. This constitutes the typical ML problem. With pricing functions, we have two possibilities. In the Longstaff-Schwartz regression method, for example, we do not have the function P, but we have estimates of sets of points (x, y), so we try to find the best possible f_w that fits those estimates. In other applications discussed later in this book, we start with a function P, we generate data with it and we use the data to find a function f_w that fits it.

What we are doing here is finding a proxy f_w to P. Working with f_w instead of P can be very useful in certain contexts since pricing functions can be very expensive to work with, computationally speaking. Finding an accurate proxy f_w to P with much faster evaluation times has considerable advantages. This will be exemplified through all the applications presented in Part IV.

1.2.2 The standard linear model

In this section we give the definition of the basic Linear Model for regression. Although this was used as the example in the previous section (1.2.1), here we give the formal definition and set the scene for the subsequent sections where we touch upon the main concepts and properties of the model, shared also with more complex ones, such as DNNs.

Linear Regression is a supervised learning type of ML model. It considers feature vectors $x = (x_1, \ldots, x_n)$ in $\mathbb{R}^n$, and target variables y in $\mathbb{R}$. The target variable y is assumed random and expressed as the sum of a deterministic and a random component. The deterministic component is given by the inner product of the feature vector x with weights w, both in $\mathbb{R}^n$, plus a displacement w_0. The random component ε is modelled by $\mathcal{N}(0, \sigma^2)$, the normal distribution centred at 0 with variance σ^2. The relationship just described is expressed as follows

$$
\begin{aligned}
y &= \sum_{i=0}^{n} w_i x_i + \varepsilon \\
&= w^T x + \varepsilon,
\end{aligned}
$$

(1.3)

where $w = (w_0, w_1, \ldots, w_n)$ and $x = (1, x_1, \ldots, x_n)$.

Note that, strictly speaking, the variable y represents a collection of random variables. That is, for every fixed vector x, the expression $\sum_{i=0}^{n} w_i x_i + \varepsilon$ defines a random variable given by $\mathcal{N}(\sum_{i=0}^{n} w_i x_i, \sigma^2)$. The distributions of two of these random variables y can be seen in Figure 1.2. These are Gaussian distributions around the points marked with an **X**, where this point is given by $\sum_{i=0}^{n} w_i x_i$.

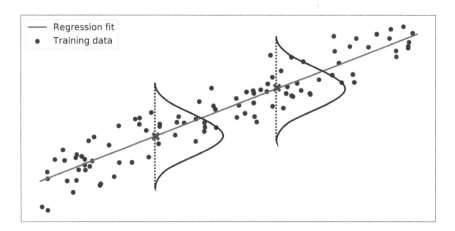

FIGURE 1.2 Linear regression fit (denote by regression fit) to given data (denote by training data). Two points are marked with an **X**. These are the predictions of the model at the corresponding points on the domain. At each of these predictions there is a Gaussian distribution that represent the random variable y at those points.

Model assumptions

There are several assumptions made in this model. The first and directly clear from Equation 1.3 is that the mean of the target variables y is a linear combination of w and x. That is

$$\mathbb{E}[y|x] = \sum_{i=0}^{n} w_i x_i = w^T x. \tag{1.4}$$

Notice that the expression in Equation 1.4 does not involve any random component. This is important as it will be the basis for defining the function f_w with which predictions are made under one of the most important learning approaches in ML: the frequentist approach, discussed in Section 1.3.1.

Second, y is a collection of random variables while x is not. The latter is also known as weak *exogeneity* and essentially means that x is assumed to contain no noise or errors. Third, the target variables given by y have the same variance σ^2; this is known as *homoscedasticity*. Fourth, the errors of the random variables represented by y are uncorrelated. Finally, none of the predictor variables can be linearly expressed in terms of the others with a high degree of accuracy; this is known as lack of *perfect multicollinearity*.

It is very important to highlight that the assumptions just stated rarely hold in real-life data. This applies to most ML models. Model characteristics are chosen for their ability to describe processes, but also for their mathematical tractability. Without some of these assumptions, one would rarely have the nice properties that allow us to work with them. It is a balance one has to live with as a practitioner. For example, even when some of the characteristics mentioned rarely hold in real-life data, without them, the Linear Model would not have some of the properties that have made it so popular, such as having an analytic solution to the problem of learning, as we show in Section 1.3.

One further note on Equation 1.3. Notice the expression assumes a one-dimensional variable y. There is nothing stopping us from considering multidimensional variables y; one simply uses an expression like the one in Equation 1.3 for each dimension. In what follows, by working with one-dimensional target variables y, we do not lose any degree of generality. Most of the applications of interest in this book relate to the approximation of functions that return real values, such as pricing functions. Hence, there will be no need to consider multidimensional target variables.

Generalisations

It is very common for models to have variants. This has advantages and disadvantages. On the one hand it provides flexibility. This can be useful as it helps adapt the model to the given data and potentially improve results. On the other hand, this opens up the problem of which variant of the model to choose — a question of model complexity that can be very tricky to deal with in some cases.

There is always a trade-off between simplicity and power that the ML practitioner needs to learn how to balance. This issue has already been mentioned in Section 1.1.2.

We will delve into it in more detail in Section 1.4, where we cover regularisation and hyper-parameter optimisation.

There are several generalisations of the Linear Regression Model (Equation 1.3). One such extension is given by the following

$$y = \sum_{i=0}^{l} w_i \phi_i(x_1, \ldots, x_n) + \varepsilon$$

$$= w^T \phi + \varepsilon.$$

(1.5)

The functions ϕ_i, where $1 \leq i \leq l$, define a function $\phi = (\phi_1, \ldots, \phi_l)$ that takes vectors x in $\mathbb{R}^n$ and returns vectors in $\mathbb{R}^l$. It transforms the n-dimensional data X into l-dimensional data. The inner product that characterises Linear Regression takes place in $\mathbb{R}^l$, after X has been transformed. As such, this model is considered to be part of the family of linear models. The linearity makes reference not to the functions ϕ_i but to the fact that the target variable y is modelled by an inner product plus some noise.

Note that if $l = n$ and ϕ_i is the i-th projection, that is, if $\phi_i(x_1, \ldots, x_n) = x_i$, then we recover Linear Regression as in Equation 1.3. This means the expression in Equation 1.5 is genuinely a generalisation of the one in Equation 1.3.

The extra flexibility introduced by ϕ lets the practitioner model data that Equation 1.3 cannot. For example, consider the data set in Figure 1.3. These data are one-dimensional and cannot be modelled using Linear Regression as defined in Equation 1.3. However, by using $\phi = (\phi_0(x) = 1, \phi_1(x) = x, \ldots, \phi_4(x) = x^4)$, we are able to learn from these data.

The example presented in Figure 1.3 shows how the model in Equation 1.3 becomes more powerful with the introduction of ϕ. However, using the model in Equation 1.5 opens up issues around the choice of complexity in the model, for example, which ϕ to use when presented with some data. Do we consider polynomials up to order 2, 3 or some other order? This is a model complexity issue directly related to the question of hyper-parameter optimisation that we describe in Section 1.4.3.

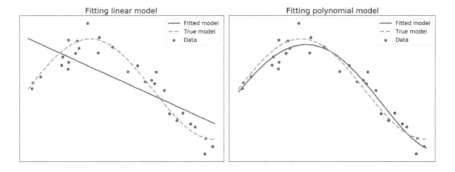

FIGURE 1.3 Left pane shows how the basic model of Linear Regression is not powerful enough to fit the data. Right pane uses polynomial regression to fit the data to a higher lever of accuracy.

1.3 TRAINING AND PREDICTING

As with all ML exercises, before any model is considered, we start with a data set $\mathcal{D} = \{X, Y\}$. Notice that, as we are concerned with a supervised learning problem, we have both input data X and target data Y.

A model must then be considered for training. There are different ways of choosing a model. We will explore ways of doing this when we discuss model complexity in Section 1.4. For the time being, we assume one has been chosen — for example, after inspecting the data and using previous experience that tells us which data characteristics lend well to which models. In any case, whatever model is chosen, it is chosen with the implicit believe that it will be capable of learning the relationships between X and Y — that is, the relationships embedded in the data.

We are currently concerned with the Linear Model, hence assume the model chosen is the one described in Equation 1.3. The variable x represents the feature vectors X in the data, and y represents data values Y.

Notice, from Equation 1.3, that for each point x, the corresponding variable y is given by the normal distribution $\mathcal{N}(f_w(x), \sigma^2)$. It therefore makes sense, if what we are after is reducing the difference between prediction and values of y, to take the mean of this normal distribution as an estimate for y.[5] This is what is marked with an **X** in Figure 1.2, when the model chosen is Linear Regression.

Therefore, a candidate function to makes predictions with is

$$f_w(x) = \sum_{i=0}^{n} w_i x_i = w^T x. \tag{1.6}$$

Examples of functions used to predict can be seen in Figure 1.2, where such function is labelled as "regression fit", and in Figure 1.3, where two such functions are labelled as "fitted model".

From this perspective, learning (or training) from the data $\mathcal{D}$ consists of finding parameters w, which in turn define a function f_w that predicts the variable y accurately upon a given vector x, where high or low levels of accuracy are determined depending on the context.

What we just described is the *frequentist* approach to learning, details of which will be covered in Section 1.3.1. There is another important learning framework that we consider: the *Bayesian* framework, discussed in Section 1.3.2. Whenever faced with the need to make a choice for illustration purposes, we opt for the frequentist approach, still to this day the most common approach in Machine Learning — although the Bayesian is rapidly gaining ground — and the one used in the applications presented in Part IV.

Cost function and optimisation

The consistency with which an ML model predicts with accuracy — in this case, values for y, given new values for x — is what distinguishes both the right choice of model and

---

[5]It is a property of the normal distribution that the point in its domain that minimises the mean squared error taken over the whole distribution is its mean.

the quality of the training on the given data $\mathcal{D}$. There are two questions that naturally come up at this point. The first is how to measure the accuracy of the predictions made by f_w. The second is how to find a suitable w that consistently gives a level of accuracy that is deemed appropriate. As we will see, both questions are related through the *cost function*.

The error between f_w and y on a given data set $\mathcal{D} = \{X, Y\} = \{x_i, y_i\}_{i=1}^m$ can be measured in different ways. Typically, this is done — for reasons that will be explained in Section 1.3.1 — using the *mean squared error*, given by the following

$$\phi(w; X, Y) = \frac{1}{m} \sum_{i=1}^m (f_w(x_i) - y_i)^2. \tag{1.7}$$

As said previously, the function in Equation 1.7 is usually called the *cost function*. Notice that the cost function depends on the parameter w and data $\mathcal{D}$. Given the latter is fixed, w is the only variable in Equation 1.7. Therefore, the problem of increasing the accuracy of the chosen f_w is equivalent to the problem of finding w that minimises ϕ. This is an optimisation problem that can be stated as follows

$$w^* = \underset{w \in W \subset \mathbf{R}^n}{argmin} \ \phi(w; X, Y). \tag{1.8}$$

Notice that the model in Equation 1.3 assumes the variable y is random. As predictions are done using the deterministic function f_w, the difference between the prediction $f_w(x)$ and target value y should in theory capture the noise ε in Equation 1.3. In light of Equation 1.7, increasing the accuracy of prediction is equivalent to reducing the variance of this random component.

The solution to the optimisation problem presented in Equation 1.8 depends on the characteristics of the ML model chosen, in particular on the characteristics of f_w. In the case of Linear Regression, optimisation can be solved analytically. This means that the value of w that defines the global minimum of the cost function in Equation 1.7 can be expressed in terms of the data $\mathcal{D}$.

The reason is that when the expression in Equation 1.6 is used in the cost function in Equation 1.7, one obtains a quadratic equation, such as the one presented in Figure 1.4. The dependence of f_w on w is linear and hence the gradient (i.e. vector of partial derivatives) is easy to compute. Therefore, critical points can be found analytically. As there is a single critical point for the cost function in the case of Linear Regression, the following expression can be obtained

$$w^* = (A^T A)^{-1} A^T B, \tag{1.9}$$

where A is the matrix obtained from the data points X in $\mathcal{D}$ (each element in X conforming a row in A), and B the matrix obtained in the same way as A but using the data points Y in $\mathcal{D}$.

For other models — including DNNs — the optimisation becomes a more difficult task. The function to minimise is no longer as well behaved as the one in Figure 1.4. In the case of DNNs, the loss function could be something as in Figure 1.5. Explicit formulas for w are not available and one must resort to optimisation routines.

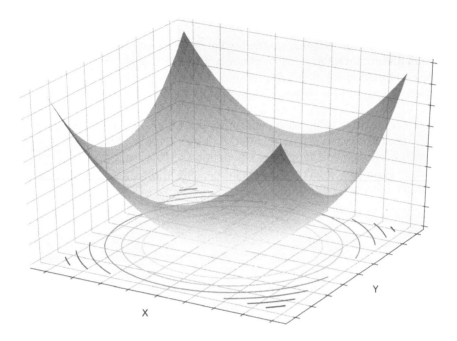

FIGURE 1.4   Surface of loss function for basic Linear Regression.

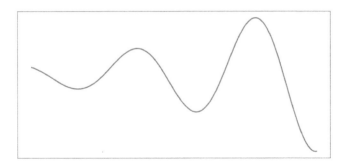

FIGURE 1.5   Cross-section of cost function for DNN.

The importance of the gradient

We will cover the details of such optimisations in Section 2.4. What is important to bear in mind is that the gradient of the cost function plays a crucial role. The gradient of a function gives, at each point of its domain, the direction of steepest ascent, while its corresponding negative value the direction of steepest descent. The mechanism for learning in this case consists of following the opposite direction of the gradient, thus exploring areas within the domain of the cost function that reduce the error measured by the cost function (Equation 1.7).

1.3.1   The frequentist approach

In the previous section, training was defined through Equation 1.8. It says that training consists of finding parameters w that minimise the cost function in Equation 1.7. Notice that the cost function is expressed in terms of the square of the differences between the predictions $f_w(x_i)$ and the values y_i. Minimising this function reduces the prediction error.

In principle, there is no reason why other ways of measuring the prediction error cannot be used to define the cost function. However, there is a framework that justifies the use of the cost function as defined in Equation 1.7. This framework is the frequentist approach to parameter inference in statistics — one of the most important paradigms in statistical inference.

An example

Let us examine the frequentist approach to parameter estimation using an example. Say we are given a data set of real values $\mathcal{D} = \{y_i\}_{i=1}^m$. Suppose there are good reasons to assume $\mathcal{D}$ has been obtained from a random variable that follows a normal distribution $\mathcal{N}(\mu, \sigma^2)$ but we do not know the values of the parameters μ and σ. In this type of situation, the aim is to estimate μ and σ using the data set $\mathcal{D}$.

Intuitively, if $\mathcal{D}$ follows a normal distribution, we should be able to say something about where $\mathcal{N}(\mu, \sigma^2)$ is located (that is, the value of μ) and the width of such distribution (the value of σ). Take a look at Figure 1.6. Notice where the data $\mathcal{D}$ (dots) lie on the line and compare this to the two examples of normal distributions, A and B, shown in the Figure 1.6. It should be intuitively clear that distribution A stands a much smaller chance of randomly generating the data set $\mathcal{D}$ compared to distribution B. The idea behind the frequentist approach is to find the values of μ and σ that define a normal distribution that best fits the data.

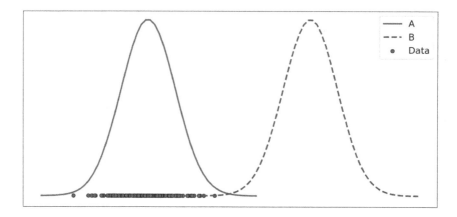

FIGURE 1.6   Probability density functions of normal distribution.

The intuition just described is expressed mathematically in the following way. The normal distribution $\mathcal{N}(\mu, \sigma^2)$ has the following probability density function

$$f(y \mid w) = \frac{1}{\sigma\sqrt{2\pi}} \exp\left(-\frac{1}{2}\left(\frac{y-\mu}{\sigma}\right)^2\right), \tag{1.10}$$

where $w = (\mu, \sigma)$.

One of the model assumptions we have made so far is that each element y_i is generated by a random variable $\mathcal{Y}_i$ with distribution $\mathcal{N}(\mu, \sigma^2)$. Moreover, we also assume that all random variables $\mathcal{Y}_i$ are independent of one another. In this case, we say the collection $Y = \{\mathcal{Y}_i\}_{i=1}^m$ of random variables are *independent and identically distributed*. Under this assumption, the probability density function of the joint probability distribution of the random variables Y is given by the product of the probability density functions of each random variable. Since they are all identical, we have

$$f(y_1, \ldots, y_m \mid w) = \prod_{i=1}^m f(y_i \mid w)$$

$$= \left(\frac{1}{\sigma\sqrt{2\pi}}\right)^m \exp\left(-\frac{1}{2\sigma^2}\sum_{i=1}^m (y_i - \mu)^2\right). \tag{1.11}$$

Equation 1.11 is called the *likelihood* function of the random variables $\{Y_i\}_{i=1}^m$. Notice it is a function in terms of two families of variables: the y_i variables that take the randomly generated values of $\{Y_i\}_{i=1}^m$ and $w = (\mu, \sigma)$, which are the parameters that define the random variables. Also notice that for a fixed data set, such as $\mathcal{D}$, the value of the likelihood function increases as we centre and adjust the width (by varying μ and σ, respectively) of the normal distribution around the values of $\mathcal{D}$.

Indeed, parameter estimation under the frequentist approach consists of finding the μ and σ that maximise the value of the likelihood function (Equation 1.11) for the given data set $\mathcal{D}$. The likelihood function is therefore often denoted as a function of the parameters only, $like(w) = f(y_1, \ldots, y_m \mid w)$. The estimator obtained as results of this maximisation process (Equation 1.12) is known as the *maximum likelihood estimator*, one of the most powerful and widely used estimators there is.[6]

$$w^* = \underset{w \in w \subset \mathbf{R}^2}{argmax} \; like(w). \tag{1.12}$$

Frequentist Machine Learning

In ML we can apply the same maximum likelihood principle to obtain estimates for the parameters w in the model of choice. In the case of Linear Regression, y_i is a random variable given by $\mathcal{N}(\sum_{i=0}^n w_i x_i, \sigma^2)$. Notice that the mean μ from the example

---

[6]For a more thorough presentation of maximum likelihood estimators, we refer the reader to [36].

is now $\sum_{i=0}^{n} w_i x_i$; that is, for each element $x = (1, x_1, \ldots, x_n)$, we have a corresponding $\mu = \sum_{i=0}^{n} w_i x_i$, which defines a random variable y. Therefore, using Equation 1.11, the likelihood function takes the following form

$$f(Y \mid X, w, \sigma) = \left(\frac{1}{\sigma\sqrt{2\pi}}\right)^m \exp\left(-\frac{1}{2\sigma^2} \sum_{i=1}^{m} (y_i - f_w(x_i))^2\right), \qquad (1.13)$$

where $f_w(x_i) = \sum_{i=0}^{n} w_i x_i$ is, as in Equation 1.6, the deterministic part of the Linear Model.

Now we show how Equation 1.13 leads to the cost function presented in Equation 1.7. Maximising Equation 1.13 is the same as maximising its logarithm.[7] The logarithm of Equation 1.13 is also known as the *log-likelihood*, a very common function often considered as it simplifies calculations. As a result of this transformation, and due to the basic properties of logarithms, we obtain

$$\log(f(y \mid x, w, \sigma)) = \frac{m}{2}\log(2\pi) + \frac{m}{2}\log(\sigma^2) - \frac{1}{2\sigma^2} \sum_{i=1}^{m} (y_i - f_w(x_i))^2. \qquad (1.14)$$

Notice that even when σ is also a parameter of the model (which can be estimated), to define our prediction function f_w, we only need to estimate w, which is exclusively present in the last term of Equation 1.14. Therefore, maximising Equation 1.14 is equivalent to minimising the negative of the last term, which is equivalent to minimising the cost function in Equation 1.7.

This concludes how training in ML is done using the frequentist approach. From what we have seen in this section, the use of maximum likelihood estimators in ML is equivalent to the optimisation problem of the cost function in Equation 1.7. Once values for w are estimated, a predicting function f_w is obtained.

Taking the logarithm of the likelihood

The logarithm function is often applied to the likelihood function in Equation 1.13. As mentioned before, one of the reasons for doing this is to simplify expressions. But, more importantly, in practical settings where calculations are done on a computer, the logarithm solves a very common problem: arithmetic underflow.

Arithmetic or floating point underflow refers to the situation when a calculation, performed on a computer program, gives a result that is smaller, in absolute value, than what can be represented in memory on its CPU.

The likelihood function is expressed as the product of terms. Each term represents a probability, hence taking a value between 0 and 1. This means the product quickly becomes very small, increasing the chances of underflows. The logarithm changes the product to addition, correcting this issue.

---

[7]This holds as the logarithm is a monotone-increasing function.

1.3.2 The Bayesian approach

In this section, we present a different way of obtaining a predicting function through training. The frequentist approach presented in Section 1.3.1 makes use of maximum likelihood estimators to estimate the parameters of the ML model. The values estimated w are then used to produce the predicting function f_w.

One of the main assumptions underlying the frequentist approach is that the parameters w are not random. The Bayesian approach looks at this from a different perspective. Philosophically, the Bayesian paradigm for statistical inference constitutes a very different approach to the frequentist one. It assumes that parameters are random quantities and, hence, instead of estimating fixed values for these parameters, it estimates parameter distributions.

Partly due to its intensive computational requirements, it has rarely been the default approach in ML. However, as computer power and data mining techniques have improved, practitioners have found more and more contexts where the Bayesian approach is more effective than the frequentist approach. There are many examples within bioinformatics and healthcare, for example, where the Bayesian approach has become prominent.

Note that all applications presented in this book (Part IV) only make use of the frequentist approach to train DNNs. This is not to say that Bayesian inference cannot be used. Indeed, there may be applications not covered in this book where the Bayesian approach may give better results. We leave these for future projects. However, for the sake of completeness and the ever increasing relevance of Bayesian techniques within ML, we cover the essential elements involved in the Bayesian approach.

Bayes' Theorem

Any Bayesian technique relies on Bayes' Theorem. First postulated by Reverend Thomas Bayes in the 18th century, it constitutes one of the most important rules of reasoning there are. This theorem gives a way of expressing or presenting the probability of an event, call it A, subject to the knowledge of a prior event, say B, which is relevant to A. Mathematically, this is expressed as follows.

Bayes' Theorem

$$P(A \mid B) = \frac{P(B \mid A)P(A)}{P(B)} \tag{1.15}$$

The probability of event A subject to event B is equal to the product of the probability of B given A, times the probability of A, divided by the probability of B.

The probability $P(A)$ is often called the *prior probability*, while $P(A \mid B)$ is called the *posterior probability*. This reflects the core of Bayes' rule. We may have information on the probability of event A happening, but this probability changes when subject to another event, in this case B, which is relevant to A.

An important note to make is that Bayes' Theorem can also be expressed in terms of distributions and not just events. This is particularly relevant to Bayesian Machine Learning, where models are given in terms of distributions. Instead of talking about the prior and posterior probabilities, we talk of prior and posterior distributions.

An example

Let us give a simple example of the applicability and power of Bayes' rule. Say there is a fatal condition we are interested in detecting in patients but it is very rare; only 1 in 100,000 have it in the general population. Moreover, assume there is a test such that if the patient has the disease, the test comes out positive 99% of the times. Likewise, if the patient does not have the disease, the test comes out negative 99% of the times. Say we apply the test to a patient and it comes out positive. The question is, what is the probability that the patient has the disease given that the test came out positive — should the patient be concerned?

Note we do not have any a priori knowledge of whether the patient has the disease or not. We are using the data available — accuracy of test knowing whether the patient has the disease and proportion of population that has it — to estimate the probability of having the disease given that the test came out positive.

In our case, A is the event of having the disease and B testing positive. In terms of the probabilities involved in Bayes' Theorem, this means

$$P(A) = 0.00001, \qquad P(B \mid A) = 0.99$$

and

$$p(B \mid A^C) = 1 - P(B^C \mid A^C) = 1 - 0.99 = 0.01,$$

where A^C and B^C denote the complements of A and B, respectively, that is, not having the disease and not testing positive, respectively.

The only probability missing to use Bayes' Theorem is $P(B)$, the probability of testing positive. By basic probability

$$P(B) = P(B \mid A)P(A) + P(B \mid A^C)P(A^C).$$

Putting it all together, we get

$$P(A \mid B) = \frac{P(B \mid A)P(A)}{P(B)} = \frac{0.99 \cdot 0.00001}{0.99 \cdot 0.00001 + 0.01 \cdot 0.99999} = 0.00099$$

The result surprises many people. Despite the apparent accuracy of the test (99% to both detect when the patient has the disease and when they do not), the actual probability of having the disease given that the patient tested positive is minute: only 0.099%. This highlights the importance of considering all the events involved, in this case the probability of event A and the prevalence of the disease in the general population. In our example, the prevalence is so small that even a test which may be considered to be very accurate fails at detecting the disease if we do not know whether the patient has the disease.

Notice how the result depends on the prior distribution. Had the disease been much more prevalent, say 1 in 100, the probability of having the disease given a positive test would be a very different 50%.

The application of Bayes' Theorem in examples such as the one presented here is one that is often ignored. Even medical professionals can sometimes get it wrong. Unfortunately, this important rule of reasoning is seldomly taught and one can be misled very easily.

This is not unique to the medical profession. In other fields such as law, this rule of reasoning has been considered, at times, to be too complicated. In 2011, there was a famous court case in the UK where the judge deemed the use of Bayes' Law too complicated for the jury. This, unfortunately, can have disastrous effects, as it increases the chances of a miscarriage of justice (see [65]).

Bayesian Machine Learning

Let us now see how Bayes' Theorem is applied in ML. The starting assumption is that the parameters of the model are a random variable. As such, we have a probability distribution $p(w)$. This plays the role of $P(A)$ in Equation 1.15.

A note on prior distributions

The prior distribution is chosen by the practitioner. The choice is sometimes based on experience or knowledge of the particular problem; sometimes it is conveniently taken from a family of well-known distributions that make the problem mathematically tractable. As such, it has a degree of subjectivity that is often the focus of Bayesian inference critique. As the example on disease detection shows, Bayes' Theorem can be very sensitive to the prior distribution. Choosing this sensibly is therefore an important part of Bayesian inference.

Then we have the data $\mathcal{D} = \{X, Y\}$, with which we want to train an ML model. The assumption is that the data $\mathcal{D}$ is random and generated by the model of choice. For example, in the case of Linear Regression, the model is given by Equation 1.3. In general, the dependence of the data $\mathcal{D}$ on the parameter w is encapsulated by the distribution $P(y \mid x, w)$. Note this is the function that gives rise to the likelihood function (Equation 1.13 in the case of Linear Regression) and the one that is maximised in the frequentist approach to obtain values of w, which are used to produce the predictive function f_w.

With these two distributions, Bayes' rule takes the following form:

$$P(w \mid x, y) = \frac{P(y \mid x, w)P(w)}{P(x, y)}. \tag{1.16}$$

As we just mentioned, $P(y \mid x, w)$ is given by the model. The prior distribution $P(w)$ is be selected given the context. The distribution of the data $\mathcal{D}$, independent of the parameters w, given by $P(x, y)$, has not yet been addressed. If available, then Bayes' Theorem gives us the distribution of the parameters w subject to the data collected $\mathcal{D}$. That is, an updated distribution of w, which takes into account the data available.

The reader will recognise this as learning something about the parameters of a model given a data set $\mathcal{D}$. This is one of the stepping stones in ML. The difference with respect to the frequentist approach is that we do not find a value for the parameters w, but we learn a distribution of these parameters.

In the frequentist approach, the values of w obtained through the maximum likelihood estimator — that is, the maximisation of $P(y \mid x, w)$ — are used to define the function to predict with. One simply uses these values to specify f_w from Equation 1.6. However, in the Bayesian approach, we do not have a single value for w, but a range of them. There are a few things one can do with the resulting distribution of w to obtain a predicting function f^*. For example, take the mean or the median of the distribution to define a predictive function. However, using the whole distribution is generally considered to be the most Bayesian thing to do. This is done as follows.

Consider the model chosen. The distribution of the model is given by $P(y \mid x, w)$. Notice the distribution describes the variables x and y that give rise to the data $\mathcal{D}$ in terms of w — at least that is the implicit assumption when we choose a model. What Bayes' Theorem gives us is a posterior distribution of w. Intuitively, the Bayesian approach consists of taking an average of all possible functions f_w, defined by the values w that come from the distribution $P(w \mid \mathcal{D})$.

Mathematically, this average is obtained by considering the following integral

$$f^*(y \mid x, \mathcal{D}) = \int_w P(y \mid x, w) P(w \mid \mathcal{D}). \tag{1.17}$$

As Equation 1.17 shows, integrating over w removes it from the equation, leaving a function $f^*(y \mid x, \mathcal{D})$ that we can use to predict.

We still have not addressed how to compute $P(x, y)$, which is an important part of Equation 1.16. By definition,

$$P(x, y) = \int_w P(y \mid x, w) P(w).$$

The problem with this integral is that often, it is very difficult to compute. In some cases, there is an analytic solution. This can happen for certain choices of the prior $P(w)$ — in fact, this often determines the choice of $P(w)$. When there is no analytic solution, the integral must be approximated numerically. This problem also applies to the integral in Equation 1.17.

Algorithms such as Markov Chain Monte Carlo — one of the most important algorithms in the 20th century — are often used for such purposes. We will not go into the details of how it is used in this context. The main point is that computing the relevant integrals for Bayesian inference in ML often relies on algorithms that require a lot of data and computational power — one of the main reasons why the Bayesian approach was not used much in the beginning.

1.3.3 Testing – in search of consistent accurate predictions

In Section 1.3, we saw that the accuracy of prediction is typically measured using the cost function shown in Equation 1.7. One of the aims of training is to minimise this error; this is particularly clear in the frequentist approach where training is directly expressed in terms of the minimisation of the cost function (Equation 1.8). However, another very important aspect is consistency: we want the model not just to give accurate predictions on the data on which is was trained, but on unseen data as well. That is, we want the model to *generalise* beyond the training data set. Next, we see how this is done.

We start with a given data set $\mathcal{D}$. Regardless of whether we opt for the frequentist or the Bayesian approach, the aim is to find a function f^* that predicts with a high degree of accuracy. Given that f^* is generated using the data $\mathcal{D}$, reducing the error on $\mathcal{D}$ does not guarantee good results on unseen data.[8]

The following heuristic approach is what is used to look for consistency. The data set $\mathcal{D}$ is split into three subsets. The first set is called the *training set*. This is used to find the function f^* to predict with. The second set is called the *validation set*. This is used to validate the accuracy (typically using the cost function in Equation 1.7) of f^* on unseen data for a particular set of model hyper-parameters — notice the validation set was not used to generate f^*.[9] As hyper-parameters vary (for example, model architecture), the values of the cost function obtained on training and validation sets vary. The third set, called the *testing set*, is used to provide an unbiased value of the cost function of the final model fit.

There is no set rule for how training, validation and testing sets should be chosen given a data set $\mathcal{D}$. The heuristic rule, however, is that 60% of the data is used for training, while 20% for validation and the remaining 20% for testing. Of course, this can change from case to case. Also, it is common to be in situations where data are not abundant or where hyper-parameters are not adjusted. In these cases, it is not rare to split the data into only two sets: training and validation. Validation sets in these cases are also used to report the final metrics of the fitted model.

It is important to bear in mind that even if we get accurate predictions on the testing set, this does not guarantee predictions will always be consistently accurate. This is just a heuristic rule designed to give us evidence that perhaps the model chosen has captured the underlying trends of the data and is generalising well.

1.3.4 Underfitting and overfitting

In this section, we cover the different scenarios that can arise after we train our models. The aim is to achieve high levels of accuracy at both training and validation. However, if this is not the case, there are some adjustments that can be made to improve the situation. Next we describe what are the main scenarios to identify and what they mean in terms of the data and model chosen to train on it. They also introduce us to the

---

[8]If the data are generated by the model itself, then we would expect the model to learn from the data without much trouble. More often than not, practitioners deal with real-life noisy data that have not been generated by a model.

[9]See Section 1.4.3 for a discussion on hyper-parameters and how these are adjusted.

important topic of model complexity and two important ways in which it can be controlled: regularisation and hyper-parameter optimisation, which are covered in Section 1.4.

One possibility is that the error on the training set is too high. This normally means the chosen model lacks the required power — or flexibility — to capture the relevant characteristics of the data. In this case, we get what is known as *underfitting* or high *bias*. The left pane in Figure 1.7 shows an example of underfitting.

The data are clearly not linear, hence polynomial regression with degree 1 — that is, basic Linear Regression as defined in Equation 1.3 — cannot capture this trend. The problem is typically corrected by increasing the model's complexity, in this case, the degree of polynomials used. In some cases, this may be enough. In other cases, we may need to change the model altogether and opt for one that is more powerful.

On the opposite side of the spectrum, the model chosen may prove to be too powerful for the trends on the data set. In this case, the model is powerful or flexible enough that it models the noise rather than the underlying trend — for example, ε in Equation 1.3 rather than f_w in Equation 1.6. This phenomenon is known as *overfitting* or high *variance*. It usually manifests itself with low errors at training but high at validation (see Table 1.2). Graphically, overfitting displays the behaviour seen on the right pane of Figure 1.7. In this example, the function fitted follows every training data point (blue dots) too closely, giving small errors at training. However, as Table 1.2 shows, the error on unseen data (green crosses) is much higher.

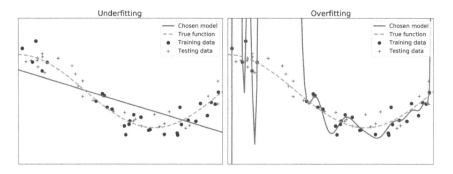

FIGURE 1.7   Figure showing underfitting and overfitting phenomenon. The plot on the left shows how the basic linear model underfits the data, giving poor training and validation accuracy. The plot on the right shows how polynomial regression with too much complexity overfits the data, giving high accuracy at training but poor at validation.

TABLE 1.2   Underfitting and overfitting accuracy, measured using mean squared error (MSE) on training and validation data.

Polynomial regression	Degree 1	Degree 20
Training error (MSE)	0.257	0.222
Testing error (MSE)	0.018	775.047

There are a few things that can be done to correct this problem. One is to increase the amount and quality of the data one is working with. A different approach consists of adjusting the complexity of the model using regularisation and hyper-parameter optimisation, techniques presented in Sections 1.4.1 and 1.4.3, respectively.

Bias-variance trade-off

Underfitting and overfitting normally pull in opposite directions: the greater the bias (underfitting), the smaller the variance (overfitting) and vice versa. This is known as the *bias-variance trade-off*.

If the bias is too great then we usually lack accuracy and we need to increase the power of the model. However, a model that is too powerful normally results in high variance, giving poor predictions. When either of these things happens, one is confronted with increasing the amount of data, improving its quality or both. In some cases, one will have to grapple with the problem of adjusting the complexity of the model. The latter is a crucial and often difficult point in applied ML — one for which little rigorous mathematical theory exists and mostly depends on heuristics. In the following sections, we discuss some of the ways in which the question of model complexity can be dealt with.

1.3.5   *K*-fold cross-validation

In Section 1.3.3, we explained that a way of detecting if a model has been properly trained is by splitting the data set $\mathcal{D}$ into different subsets. Normally, three subsets are created: one (usually the largest) for training, another for validating the trained model and a final third for testing.[10] This data split can help us identify problems with the model such as underfitting and overfitting (see Section 1.3.4), which in turn helps us assess whether the model should be changed.

However, if the data split is done differently, we may get very different results. This means that a single data split only gives partial information on the actual performance of the model given the data $\mathcal{D}$ available.

The idea behind k-fold cross-validation is to obtain a more complete picture of how well the model is trained given the data set $\mathcal{D}$. This form of cross-validation (note we will see a different one in Section 1.4.2) systematically trains and evaluates a model on multiple subsets of $\mathcal{D}$. The result is a distribution of cost values for training and validation from which we can extract more information. For example, we can compute the average and standard deviation of these distributions, which in turn help us find confidence intervals for the performance of the model.

There is no rule for how many times a model should be trained in k-fold validation. Common values, however, oscillate between 5 and 10. Say we choose to train the model five times. To do this, the data set $\mathcal{D}$ is split into five subsets of equal size (or as close as

---

[10]If the size of the data set is small considering the needs of a particular model, we may just take training and validating subsets.

possible). Say we order the subsets $S_1, \ldots, S_5$. We first train the model using $S_1, \ldots, S_4$, leaving S_5 for validation. Then we train the model using S_1, S_2, S_3, S_5, leaving S_4 for validation. As we rotate the validation subset, we end up with five different trained models. In this way, every data point will have been used to train and we end up with a distribution of cost values for training and validation.

Note that k can in principle be any positive integer. In some applications, it makes sense to use a low value of k while in others a high one. In some extreme cases, one may even perform cross-validation, considering all the different possible ways in which a data set can be divided into a training and validation set.

In general, k-fold cross-validation (and generalisations of it) gives us a more nuanced picture of the performance of the model. This in turn makes model reporting more complete and allows for better model comparison.

The possible downside is that the model must be trained k number of times. If the training of the model takes a substantial amount of time, k-fold cross-validation may be problematic in practice.

1.4 MODEL COMPLEXITY

So far, we have been discussing how a given model learns from a given data set. A crucial problem practitioners face on a regular basis is, given a data set, what model should be chosen to train?

There are mathematical frameworks that give learning a solid foundation. We have covered two of them: the frequentist and the Bayesian approach to learning (Sections 1.3.1 and 1.3.2, respectively). However, the choice of model lacks an equivalent mathematical framework. Practitioners mostly rely on heuristics when forced to make decisions.

What are the tools available to practitioners when having to choose a model? Inspecting the data set is normally the first thing to do. Some models require huge amounts of data to be trained, while others do not. Some models are sensitive to outliers (noise in the data), while others are more robust. Knowing the strengths and weaknesses of models, the amount of data available and its characteristics can often help rule out certain options.

Over the years, more and better visualisation tools have been developed. Better than ever before, we can inspect the data and identify trends that can help choose or rule out which model to train. In addition, statistical tests and metrics (for example, the correlation between features) can be computed from the data giving the practitioner further insight.

At this point, it may be possible to choose a model. As we have mentioned before, there is the implicit belief — perhaps hope — that the model will learn from the data and predict accurately with consistency.

Once the model has been trained, it is important to examine whether underfitting or overfitting has happened, as explained in Section 1.3.4. If results are not good, then the following question should be asked: should the model be replaced for a different one, or will an adjustment of the current model suffice to get the prediction accuracy we are after?

The latter point is very important in practice and highlights a few crucial ideas, some of which have already been touched upon. As we saw in Section 1.2.2, the Linear Regression model has variants. The choice of function ϕ in Equation 1.5 introduces a way of altering the complexity of the model. An example of this, polynomial regression, is presented in Section 1.2.2.

The characteristic of being able to alter a model's complexity is one shared by most ML models. In Section 2, we will see, for example, that DNNs have many parameters that play this role. These parameters are normally called *hyper-parameters* to distinguish them from the weights or parameters w determined at training.

Hyper-parameters give each model the needed flexibility to adapt to a given data set. The question of how practitioners go about modifying these hyper-parameters to improve results is discussed in Section 1.4.3. But before we embark on hyper-parameter optimisation, we discuss another common and powerful way of adjusting the complexity of a model: regularisation.

1.4.1 Regularisation

As we have mentioned before, regularisation is a technique designed to control the complexity of a model. We will see how this technique was developed, what it corrects and how it fits within the learning framework we have covered so far.

Learning with the Linear Model reduces down to the analytic expression presented in Equation 1.9. Despite the advantage of having an easy formula to work with, evaluating this expression on a computer sometimes gives rise to numerical problems. Inverting the matrix $X^T X$, in Equation 1.9, relies on computing its eigenvalues. If these are too small, numerical instabilities creep in. This is a common problem that is often solved by adding a small positive value to the diagonal of the matrix.

Back in the 1970s, engineers used this trick to solve the numerical problems when calculating the expression in Equation 1.9. The resulting, numerically more stable equation is

$$w = (X^T X + \lambda I_d)^{-1} X^T Y \qquad (1.18)$$

where λ is the (small) positive value added to the diagonal for stability.

This trick solved the numerical instabilities. But more important, engineers noticed that by varying λ, the accuracy of the trained model could also be adjusted. In a way, what they found was a way of giving Linear Regression a certain degree of flexibility and, with it, increase its power so that it could be applied to a wider range of data sets.

We know that the cost function for Linear Regression (Equation 1.7) has a unique solution given by Equation 1.9, obtained by computing the gradient of the cost function and finding the weights that equate it to zero. Therefore, engineers tried to work backwards, starting from the solution in Equation 1.18, to find a cost function with a minimisation solution that corresponds to Equation 1.18. What they found was the following cost function:

$$\phi_{reg}(w, X, Y) = \frac{1}{m} \sum_{i=1}^{m} (f_w(x_i) - y_i)^2 + \lambda \parallel w \parallel_2^2 . \qquad (1.19)$$

This is known as the cost function of *regularised regression* or *ridge regression*. The parameter λ is called the *regulariser*.

Note the similarities between the cost functions for ordinary regression and ridge regression. The first term in Equation 1.19 is the same as Equation 1.7. The difference is given by the second term in Equation 1.19. This term consists of the norm of the vector of weights w, scaled by λ, the value that parametrises ridge regression.

In ridge regression, from the point of view of optimisation, we are no longer just finding the weights $w = (w_0, \ldots, w_n)$ that minimise the prediction error captured by the ordinary cost function (Equation 1.7), but we are simultaneously minimising this error, subject to a penalty on the size of the vector w. The regulariser λ controls the degree to which the size of w is penalised. Each λ value gives a constraint. Each constraint gives a different solution. If λ is zero, we recover the ordinary cost function — this means ridge regression is a generalisation of ordinary regression. However, as we increase the value of λ, we increase the penalisation on the size of the weights w_i.

One of the strengths of regularisation is that by varying the value of λ one adjusts the complexity of the model. Lower values of λ allow for higher entry values in w and, hence, greater sensitivity to changes in the values of the features. However, increasing the value of λ penalises the values in w, making them less sensitive to changes in the features, and with it, making the model more rigid and less prone to overfit.

The next couple of sections give an example where ridge regularisation can be used and how it is used in practice.

An example

Take the following simple yet illustrative example. Consider the data in Figure 1.8. Say we are interested in learning from it using Linear Regression. As we explained in Section 1.3.3, just by looking at the data, we can eliminate standard Linear Regression. Say we have reasons to believe (could be from just looking at the data or some other reason) that polynomial regression will do a good job. When working with polynomial regression one must specify certain hyper-parameters before it can be used, for example, the degree of the polynomial must be chosen before training.

One possibility is to test a collection of polynomial degrees. For each degree, we have an instance of polynomial regression and for each we would have to train the model and test it. This is a perfectly valid approach that falls under the category of hyper-parameter optimisation covered in Section 1.4.3. This is essentially what Figure 1.3 shows. Normally a range of different polynomial degrees are tested to see which fits the data best. Figure 1.3 only shows two different degrees. However, the important thing to notice about it is that by adjusting hyper-parameters — in this case the polynomial degree — we are able to obtain a better fit.

Alternatively, one can consider ridge regression for a given polynomial degree. That is, we fix an instance of the polynomial we want to work with and adjust the complexity of this model by introducing a regulariser into the cost function as in Equation 1.19.

For example, Figure 1.8 shows how polynomial regression can be made to work better with the use of a regulariser. The function used to generated the data is the same as the one in Figure 1.7. The left pane shows a fit done with polynomial regression of degree 20. This is the same degree used in Figure 1.7 to illustrate the phenomenon

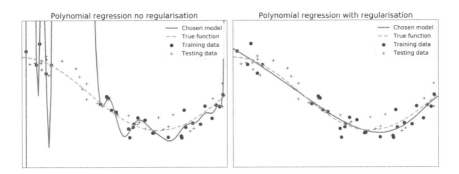

FIGURE 1.8 Figure showing how regression fit improves with regularisation. The left pane shows polynomial regression of degree 20 overfitting the data. The right pane shows polynomial regression of degree 20 with regularisation.

of overfitting. The pane on the right-hand side shows the fit obtained with the same degree but using a regulariser. It can clearly be seen that the regulariser penalises the magnitude of the regression weights, allowing for a more accurate fit.

It is important to highlight adding a regulariser will not always improve the fit of a model. Whether we get a better fit or not depends on the combination of data set and initial model chosen.

There is no right or wrong approach to model complexity tuning. Regularisation and hyper-parameter optimisation are two different techniques used, in this case, for the same purpose: adjusting the model trained to the given data set with the aim of predicting with high accuracy on data points that have not yet been seen.

1.4.2 Cross-validation for regularisation

As we said before, each possible value for λ gives a different solution in ridge regression. The question then is how to find the most appropriate value of λ. The most common way of addressing this problem is through *cross-validation*. This consists of taking a discrete set of values for λ. Then for each, train the model and obtain cost values for the training and testing sets.

In Section 1.3.3, we explained how to test a model once trained. The main purpose is to obtain a consistently accurate function to predict with. To achieve this, the data set is split into training, validation and testing subsets. Once trained on the training set, the result of the model fitted is validated using the validation set. With ridge regression we do the same, but we repeat this exercise for each of the λ values chosen. Therefore, a list of training and validation cost values are obtained. Based on these, a decision must be made regarding the value of λ that best suits the problem in hand.

Table 1.3 shows an example of a collection of λ values with its corresponding training and validation errors measured using the root mean squared errors.

The values in Table 1.3 were taken from a collection of 100 different λ values used for cross-validation applied to the function in Figure 1.8. The different training and validation errors are shown in Figure 1.9.

TABLE 1.3 Table showing train and validation errors for different values of regulariser λ.

Regulariser λ	1.5×10^{-13}	4×10^{-8}	1×10^{-2}	1	3.5×10^3
Train error	0.036	0.042	0.045	0.136	0.487
Validation error	0.154	0.053	0.055	0.126	0.643

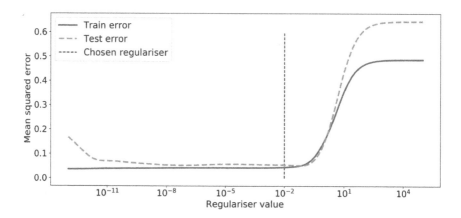

FIGURE 1.9 Figure showing the different values for training and validation errors as the value of λ changes.

The degree of the polynomial used for regression is 20. With no regularisation we obtain the fit displayed on the left pane of Figure 1.8. Clearly the degree of overfitting is considerable. This is essentially the result obtained when very small values of λ are used. This is indeed reflected on the left-hand side of Figure 1.9, where a λ value of 1.5×10^{-13} gives a small training error of 0.036 and high validation error (in comparison to training) of 0.154 (see Table 1.3).

As the value of λ increases, the size of the weights w is penalised and the validation errors decrease. Figure 1.9 shows how training errors remain low for λ values of up to 0.1. For these same λ values, the validation error decreases, reaching similar values to the training error.

For values of λ greater than 0.1, both training and validation error increase due to an excessive penalisation from the regulariser. This corresponds to underfitting. Actual numbers for representative λ values are found in Table 1.3.

There is no strict rule as to what value of λ should be chosen given the results shown in Figure 1.9. The aim is to predict with accuracy, not just on the data trained on, but on data the model has not yet seen. Therefore, the rule of thumb is to opt for a λ that gives a good accuracy balance between training and validation cost values. Given this, in our example, one may choose λ equal to 0.01, which is marked by the vertical dashed line in Figure 1.9. However, this is by no means an unequivocal answer; depending on the application and objectives, one may choose other values.

Using other norms

Ridge regression is not only good at adjusting the power of the model, but it can also be used to identify the features in predictor variable x that explain the relationship between predictors x and target variable y.

When we start with a data set $\mathcal{D} = \{X, Y\}$, we do not know if all the features in X are needed in the training of a given model. Varying the regulariser can help identify this. As the regulariser increases in value, the penalisation on w increases, hence each weight w_i will tend to reduce in size. However, not all weights will decrease at the same rate. The ones that decrease quicker tend to be less relevant and can, in some cases, be discarded. The ones that do not decrease as quickly tend to be the weights corresponding to the features in X that drive the relationship between predictor variable x and target y.

This can be very important in some applications, especially in those where we benefit a lot from identifying causes for certain outcomes. For example, we may be interested in predicting a certain medical condition based on a set of metrics taken from the patient's blood. We may get good results using the whole set of metrics. However, we would benefit substantially from knowing which of these metrics are relevant at predicting the condition and which are not. In this case, changing the regulariser λ can help identify the metrics we are after.

Identifying how the weights decrease in value as the regulariser increases is known as *weight decay*. A further refinement in weight decay is introduced by changing the norm in the penalisation term for w. So far we had only considered the 2-norm.[11] To reference the fact that we are using the 2-norm, we call this L_2 regularisation. This norm can be replaced, for example, by some other more punitive one, such as the 1-norm, which gives rise to L_1 regularisation.[12] By doing this we force the weights w_i to decay faster.

1.4.3 Hyper-parameter optimisation

We have mentioned several times that ML models have variants. For example, Linear Regression as described in Equation 1.5 encompasses a range of *model instances*. The different instances represented by Equation 1.5 are given by the different choices of function ϕ.

The range of options offered by ϕ gives the model flexibility. When ϕ is the identity function, we recover the standard Linear Regression model. This is not able to capture trends such as the ones shown in Figure 1.3. However, polynomials can. As ϕ can be defined using polynomials, the model in Equation 1.5 enjoys the necessary flexibility to adapt to data sets, such as the one shown in Figure 1.3, that the standard linear model cannot.

However, even when this degree of flexibility confers more power to the model, it introduces the problem of deciding, for example, which ϕ to use. Remember that in

---

[11] If $w = (w_1, \ldots, w_n)$, the 2-norm is given by $\left(\sum_{i=1}^{n} |w_i|^2 \right)^{1/2}$.

[12] If $w = (w_1, \ldots, w_n)$, the 1-norm is given by $\sum_{i=1}^{n} |w_i|$.

order to train, we must specify an instance of the model. In this case, we must decide which ϕ to use. Parameters such as ϕ, which determine model instances, are called *hyper-parameters*.

They are called hyper-parameters to distinguish them from the internal parameters of the model (so far denoted by w). Notice one key difference: parameters w are found by the learning process whereas hyper-parameters are specified before the learning process.

The standard Linear Regression model (Equation 1.3) is one of the simplest models and does not have hyper-parameters. There are no possible adjustments and tweaks that can be made. If it is to learn and generalise from the data available, we are bound to find out soon. Other models, such as DNNs, have many more hyper-parameters (we will see them in Section 2). This makes DNNs very powerful but introduces the often problematic issue of choosing the hyper-parameters that determine the instance to train.

Remark 1.4.1 It is important to note that having more or fewer hyper-parameters does not make a model better or worse. The use or applicability of a model should be assessed case by case. There are data sets for which Linear Regression will give consistently accurate predictions. In these cases, there is no need to opt for a more complex and difficult to use model — simplicity should always be a choice when presented with otherwise equal options. However, there will be data sets for which Linear Regression falls short. For these cases, other, more flexible and powerful models should be considered; their extra flexibility and power means that in certain situations we will end up with trained models capable of predicting accurately in a consistent manner.

Grid search

Hyper-parameter optimisation is the problem of choosing the optimal hyper-parameters for an ML model. Several approaches to this problem can be considered. If the number of hyper-parameters is not too great, one may consider an exhaustive search through the space of hyper-parameters. This is normally knows as *grid search*. This is done by taking a discrete collection of values for the hyper-parameters and testing all possible combinations.

Notice this is exactly what we do in cross-validation when using regularisation. In fact, one can think of the regulariser as a particular example of hyper-parameter. The reason this is sometimes given a different status is that regularisation can be applied to a model instance. That is, once the hyper-parameters of a model have been fixed and an instance is ready to be trained, regularisation opens an extra degree of freedom or dimension over which the complexity of the model can be adjusted.

Smarter approaches to hyper-parameter optimisation

The problem with grid search is that the combinations of hyper-parameter grows exponentially as the number of hyper-parameters increases. This is yet another example of the curse of dimensionality, a condition that is touched on throughout the book. A single hyper-parameter usually causes no problem; one takes between 5 and 10 discrete values, giving rise to between 5 and 10 training routines, something that is normally manageable. However, just 3 hyper-parameters, each with 5 discrete values, give rise to $5^3 = 125$ combinations of hyper-parameters. Given that — at least for models such as DNNs — a training and testing routine can take several minutes and in some cases even hours, the number of combinations becomes a problem; we may be waiting several hours for the grid search to finish. If the number of hyper-parameters grows to 10 — something far from outlandish — we are looking at years of computation. Clearly, for some of these situations, alternative options to grid search must be considered.

The area of hyper-parameter optimisation is an active area of research. Alternative options to grid search go from random sampling the hyper-parameter space to Bayesian optimisation techniques, gradient-based optimisers and evolutionary algorithms. These are essentially clever ways of exploring the space of hyper-parameters in search of the optimal configuration. The problem is that even some of the most advanced algorithms struggle to search the vast domain of hyper-parameters and may take a long time to complete.

There are applications where there are no time constraints and one can run these optimisations for a long time. However, there are others where one cannot afford such luxury. Given that the latter is often the case, practitioners opt for rules of thumb that have been learned through experience and the hyper-parameter optimisation problem is rarely fully addressed.

Future research

The problem of hyper-parameter optimisation is a difficult one for the reasons just outlined. One part of the problem is the exponential growth of the grids used to cover the space of hyper-parameters that needs to be explored. The other is that testing each hyper-parameter (even without k-fold cross-validation) can be costly — essentially a training and validating exercise, which in some cases can take hours to run.

The exercise of finding the right hyper-parameters is an optimisation problem. Optimisations normally involve trial-and-error exercises where the function to optimise is called at every iteration. In the case of the hyper-parameter optimisation problem, the function to be optimised consists of training the model with a chosen set of hyper-parameters and evaluating the cost function using the trained model on the validation data. Using the notation of the cost function in Equation 1.7, the function to optimise is

$$\phi(\lambda; \omega(\lambda), X, Y). \tag{1.20}$$

Note that this function depends on the hyper-parameter configuration defined by λ, the parameters ω obtained after training, plus the training and validation sets, which remain fixed throughout the optimisation. Our goal is to find the hyper-parameter configuration λ^* that delivers the minimal validation cost $\phi(\lambda^*; \omega(\lambda^*), X, Y)$.

The methods normally employed to tackle the problem of hyper-parameter optimisation (mentioned in the previous section) belong to two families: either the space of hyper-parameters is explored randomly or the hyper-parameters at each trial are determined based on the results obtained in the previous iteration. Since each iteration or trial is expensive to run (computationally speaking), the algorithms used in the latter approach aim at minimising the number of times the function has to be called.

In this section, we propose a different method to reduce the computational cost involved in exploring the space of hyper-parameters. This is based on approximating the function to optimise with CTs, which are presented in Chapter 3.

What we propose is very similar to some of the solutions presented in Part IV of this book. For example, in Chapter 20, we want to maximise a function that depends on the balance sheet of a bank. This function is computationally costly to run and hence finding its maximum is a computationally expensive exercise. What we do is replicate this function using an approximation method that can replicate it with a minimal number of calls while achieving a high degree of accuracy. If this approximation is fast to compute, finding its maximum is an easy exercise.

One crucial thing to note in the case of the hyper-parameter optimisation problem is the following: the computation of ϕ in Equation 1.20 at each point in its domain can be very costly. What we need is a method to explore the space of hyper-parameters that is highly efficient.

That is precisely what CTs do, as explained in detail in Chapter 3. By exploring the space as described in Chapter 3 (at predefined points, called Chebyshev points), we obtain a function that generalises over the full space of hyper-parameters with sub-exponentially convergent accuracy (sub-exponential on the number of exploration points — that is, on the size of the training set). This sub-exponential law means that a small number of sample points, especially compared to all other known methods, yields an approximation to the original function that is very accurate.

By using CTs we aim to create a good and fast-to-compute replica of the cost function in Equation 1.20. As this function depends on the hyper-parameters λ, we can then use the CT to find the optimal set of hyper-parameters λ^*.

For this approach to work effectively, we must bear in mind that two conditions need to be met. First, each call of the function to optimise — the training of the model in our case — cannot be extremely expensive. Despite the sub-exponential convergence that CTs offer, the building of such tensors requires calling the function in question many times.

Second, the number of hyper-parameters cannot be too large. Estimating an upper bound on the number of hyper-parameters depends on the context. First, there is the curse of dimensionality that tensors suffer from. This says that as the dimension grows — in our case the number of hyper-parameters — the number of tensor points grows exponentially. The problem with this is that the function to be approximated by CTs has to be evaluated on an exponentially growing set of points. This can be alleviated (to a degree) by the Tensor Extension Algorithms presented in Chapter 6. These algorithms extend substantially the number of dimensions we can work with. However, there is still a limit to the number of hyper-parameters we can realistically consider.

Another aspect to consider regarding the number of hyper-parameters we can handle is the shape of the function to approximate — in our case ϕ in Equation 1.20. If the function has large curvature and changes in acceleration, we will need a larger training grid. This translates into higher computational costs and hence a smaller number of hyper-parameters that we can reasonably manage. If the number of training points is small enough, then we can afford to consider a larger set of hyper-parameters.

When one cannot cover all hyper-parameters, one should choose the most important ones, leaving the rest constant. Also, if we know that a collection of hyper-parameters affects the cost function jointly in a determined manner, we could focus on exploring the variables that relate them rather than each individually, effectively reducing the dimensionality of the space to explore. This is in essence the technique exploited, for example, in Chapters 15, 16 and 17.

Let us summarise the main ideas presented in this section. The key point is to exploit the highly efficient way CTs have to explore multidimensional spaces, aided (if necessary) by the Tensor Extension Algorithms. This can be applied in the context of hyper-parameter optimisation, where the replica of the cost function in Equation 1.20, obtained via CTs, can then be used to find the hyper-parameter configuration that minimises Equation 1.20.

At the moment of this book going to press, the approach described in this section has not been fully tested and constitutes future research. However, we believe it can help some instances of the problem of hyper-parameter optimisation.

## CHAPTER 2

Deep Neural Nets

D NNs are one of the many families of mathematical models and algorithms within ML that have become prominent in a wide range of applications, both in academia and in industry. In finance in particular, there is a growing body of literature showing the potential they have of alleviating the computational burden associated with some of the applications presented in Part IV.

In this chapter, we cover what DNNs are, how they work and why they are good function approximators, which ultimately justifies their use in the applications presented in Part IV.

First, we introduce the necessary concepts to define a DNN. In doing so, the model's flexibility will be highlighted along with the features that can be modified and give rise to hyper-parameters.

The main elements involved in training a DNN for which a fixed set of hyper-parameters have been chosen is then discussed. Both the frequentist and Bayesian approach will be considered. However, we will mainly focus on the former as it is the one used to obtain the results found in Part IV and the most commonly found in the literature for the type of problems relevant to this book. As we will see, an immediate consequence of training is the specification of the function used for predictions.

Particular attention will be paid to one of the main strengths DNNs have: their flexibility. This is the result of the range of hyper-parameters they have. However, this is also the source of one of its main problems: hyper-parameter optimisation. We will also touch upon the bias-variance trade-off and regularisation for DNNs.

Whenever we can, we will make use of the material covered for the Linear Model in Chapter 1. As we mentioned in Section 1.2, many of the fundamental notions about the Linear Model are equally relevant to DNNs. Whenever there are differences, we will point them out, specifically when it comes to the ones that make DNNs so special.

2.1 A BRIEF HISTORY OF DEEP NEURAL NETS

As mentioned in Section 1.1.1, the range of ML models and algorithms developed over the last few decades is significant. Different models address different problems. There is not a single model that fits all. However, among all models, one that stands out — at least for the range and power of its applications in recent years — is DNNs.

Neural Nets — and their evolved cousin DNNs — have an interesting history. The first example of a neural net was defined in 1943 by Warren McCulloch and Walter Pitts ([55]). They decided to create a model using an electrical circuit based on biological neurons. However, the first example of an artificial neural network was given by Frank

Rosenblatt in 1957 ([62]). It was initially designed for image recognition and was called a *Perceptron*.

A Perceptron is a binary classifier. It is essentially a function that takes vector inputs, given by $(1, x_1, \ldots, x_n)$ in Figure 2.1, and determines whether that input belongs to one of two possible classes (classes 1 and 2 in Figure 2.1).

Initially, the Perceptron seemed promising and high expectations were raised around the possibility that the "Perceptron may eventually be able to learn, make decisions, and translate languages."[1] However, its limitations soon became evident. In particular, a very famous book titled *Perceptrons: An Introduction to Computational Geometry*, published by Marvin Minsky and Seymour Papert in 1969 ([56]), proved that the Perceptron was not able to learn even basic functions. This gave the misleading idea that nothing interesting could be done with it.

The effects of this book were devastating. Expectations had been raised very high and limitations underestimated. This led to severe criticisms, and subsequent funding cuts, and the field went through what is known as the winter of Artificial Intelligence in the 1970s and part of the 1980s.

Even though it was known by some that clustering Perceptrons together — forming a Neural Net — created models capable of recognising more complex patterns, this was simply a theoretical possibility more than an actual practical one; the amount of data and computer power needed to make any of these work was not available at the time.

It was not until the 1990s that these ideas were picked up with greater enthusiasm within academic circles and specialised industries. Finally, one of the main blocking points — computational power and data — were reaching the levels required to make Neural Nets work effectively. Since then, the development of hardware — such as more powerful CPUs, the invention of GPUs and more recently Deep Learning Processors such as TPUs — improved ways of data collection and increased storage capabilities, meaning that DNNs, which for a long time could scarcely be used, are now — and have been for more than two decades — a genuine possibility.

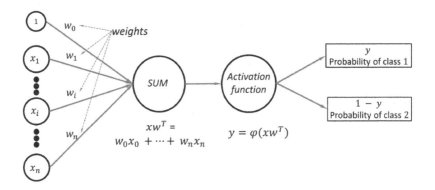

FIGURE 2.1   Diagram of a Perceptron.

---

[1] Famous quote typically attributed to Frank Rosenblatt.

But what distinguishes DNNs from other ML algorithms? One of the most important characteristics — at least from the point of view of function approximation — is embodied by the Universal Approximation Theorem. We will explore the statement of a version of such Theorem in Section 2.3. Essentially, the Theorem says that as long as the function f to be approximated is well behaved, increasing the number of neurons in a Neural Net — either in a single layer, or across layers — guarantees convergence with the function. This makes Neural Nets (and DNNs) a clear candidate to approximate functions. More so, the dimension of the domain of the function f does not affect the convergence of the Neural Net. That is, we can always find a DNN that can approximate a function f, as long as it is well behaved, regardless of its dimension.

Another advantage of DNNs comes from their architecture. DNNs are composed of neurons (covered in Section 2.2). Neurons can be put together to produce a DNN in many ways. This flexibility lets DNNs adapt to different problems, making them powerful classifiers and regressors.

This flexibility, however, comes with costs, the main one being the amount of data needed, in some cases, to train the DNN. In addition, each application may require its own architecture; some architectures yield very good results for a given problem, while others do not. Moreover, it is not always clear which architecture is needed to achieve a certain degree of accuracy — the Universal Approximation Theorem only says that there is a DNN that approximates a function f to a given degree of accuracy, but not how to obtain it.

The question of determining the right architecture for a given problem — and other variants that can be incorporated into the model, which we will see in subsequent sections — is an instance of a wider problem known as hyper-parameter optimisation, discussed in Section 1.4.3. This problem represents, in some cases, the biggest hurdle when training an ML algorithm. Unfortunately, DNNs, given their flexibility, require substantial heuristic knowledge in some applications, to determine the hyper-parameters that give good results. In a nutshell, the degree of flexibility that DNNs benefit from can also be its Achilles heel.

However, when these issues are circumvented, the impact DNNs have can be substantial. In recent years, DNNs have been used with success in all sorts of fields, for example, in data compression — more generally dimension reduction — image and speech recognition, film recommendations, filling in missing data, anomaly detection, credit scoring, medical diagnosing, and the list goes on.

2.2 THE BASIC DEEP NEURAL NET MODEL

The main constituent component of a DNN is a neuron. In what follows, we describe what a neuron is and how a collection of neurons come together to form DNNs.

2.2.1 Single neuron

A neuron is best described by the diagram in Figure 2.2. If the neuron takes input data that consists of vectors $x = (x_1, \ldots, x_n)$, for some natural number n, then it comes equipped with a vector of weights $w = (w_0, w_1, \ldots, w_n)$ in $\mathbb{R}^{n+1}$. The neuron processes

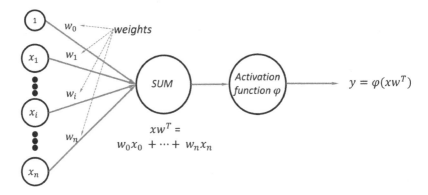

FIGURE 2.2   Diagram of an artificial neuron.

the data vectors x by taking the inner product of x with w. Notice the length of the vectors considered so far is not exactly the same; to match them we extend the vector x to $(1, x_1, \ldots, x_n)$. From now on, whenever we consider input data x, we assume its first entry $x_0 = 1$. Given the dimension of the vectors involved, we say the neuron has dimension n.

The inner product of x with w constitutes the first operation done by the neuron. Notice that so far it does the same as the linear model in Equation 1.3. The result obtained is then transformed by the function φ, generally called *activation function*.

The activation function is a key characteristic of the neuron. Its main role is to introduce non-linearity. This lets neurons learn from non-linear data that the Linear Model in Equation 1.3 cannot. Notice that if the activation function is the identity function, we recover the Linear Model. Therefore, a neuron is a generalisation of the Linear Model presented in Equation 1.3.

The range of activation functions that can be used is enormous. Some are suited better for regression problems while others for classification. We will not discuss activation functions in detail but give a couple of examples highlighting their strengths.

Activation functions

Some of the most commonly used activation functions are shown in Figure 2.3. These are the sigmoid function, the hyperbolic tangent function, the rectified linear unit and the leaky rectified linear unit function.

The activation function used in a neuron is an example of a hyper-parameter that needs to be determined before a neuron is trained.

The different activation functions developed over the years have advantages and disadvantages. The sigmoid function, for example, was one of the first to be used due to the fact that it returns values between 0 and 1, naturally covering the range of a probability space. Also, its derivative — essential for training as we will see in Section 2.4 — is very easy to compute. However, it suffers from the vanishing gradient problem, which means training grinds to a halt.

To solve the problem of vanishing gradients, activation functions such as ReLU were developed. This is one of the most popular activation functions nowadays. However, although it solves the problem of vanishing gradients, it tends to become inactive (the dying ReLU neuron problem), making training difficult in some cases. In turn, the leaky ReLU function was designed to solve this problem.

In general, as with many other hyper-parameters, the choice of activation function depends on the problem at hand.

Just as with the Linear Model, one of the main assumptions is that the model takes input data x in n dimensions and returns random samples of a random variable y. This is represented mathematically, under the frequentist approach, as

$$y = \varphi\left(\sum_{i=0}^{n} w_i x_i\right) + \varepsilon$$

$$= \varphi(w^T x) + \varepsilon,$$

(2.1)

where ε is given by the standard normal distribution $\mathcal{N}(0, 1)$.

Comparison with biological neurons

The first artificial neuron was the Threshold Logic Unit presented in 1943 ([55]). It was originally conceived as a mathematical model of biological neuron, hence the name *artificial neuron*.

Figure 2.4 shows an image of a biological neuron. The dendrites of the neuron are the channels through which the cell receives input signals, for example, from other neurons. The input signals are represented by the input vectors x in the case of the artificial neuron. Each dendrite weights its corresponding input x_i with its weight w_i. These are all then added up in the soma. This corresponds to adding all values $x_i w_i$ in the artificial neuron, that is, the inner product. The combination of dendrite signals are then processed through the axon. This is represented by the activation function in the artificial neuron. The resulting signal is then channelled to the terminals at the other end of the neuron to be transferred to other neurons.

2.2.2 Artificial Neural Net

A collection of neurons constitutes a Neural Net or *Artificial Neural Net* (ANN). Here we cover how to build an ANN out of artificial neurons.

The easiest way to see how they come together is via a diagram such as the one in Figure 2.5. A collection of neurons is assembled in what is known as a layer (presented vertically in Figure 2.5). The vector $x = (x_1, \ldots, x_n)$ is the input for the ANN. Clearly, all neurons need to have the same dimension as x. If there are m neurons, we say the

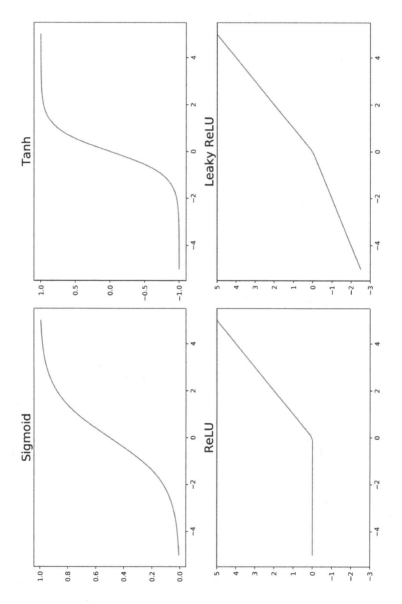

FIGURE 2.3 Some of the most popular activation functions.

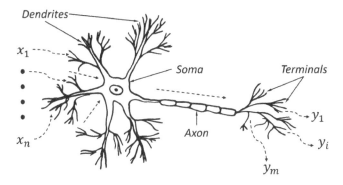

FIGURE 2.4   Biological neuron.

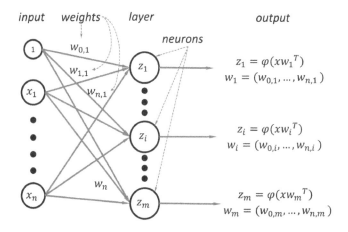

FIGURE 2.5   Artificial neural network with multidimensional output.

layer has *width m*. Note that transforming x by all neurons yields a vector z in $\mathbb{R}^m$, the entries of which are given by the different values z_i under output in Figure 2.5.

There are several things that can happen to the output vector z. First, this vector can be the output of the ANN. In this case, the ANN defined takes inputs x in $\mathbb{R}^n$ and returns vectors in $\mathbb{R}^m$. This type of ANN is represented by Figure 2.5. Another option is to use a single neuron of dimension m, placed after the layer of neurons, that takes vectors z as input and returns a single real value y. The layer plus the single neuron define an ANN such as the one in Figure 2.6.

The applications of interest presented in Part IV revolve around the approximation of functions (most often pricing functions) which take input values x in $\mathbb{R}^n$ and return real values. Therefore, the type of ANNs of interest to us are the ones represented by Figure 2.6.

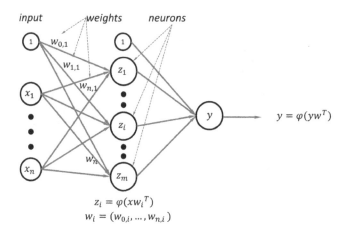

$$z_i = \varphi(xw_i{}^T)$$
$$w_i = (w_{0,i}, \dots, w_{n,i})$$

FIGURE 2.6   Artificial neural network with output of dimension 1.

Under the frequentist approach and assuming the configuration in Figure 2.6, the model for the ANN takes the following form:

$$y = \varphi\left(\sum_{i=0}^{m} w_i z_i\right) + \varepsilon$$

$$= \varphi(w^T z) + \varepsilon, \tag{2.2}$$

where $w = (w_0, \dots, w_m)$ are the weights of the neuron on the right in Figure 2.6, ε is given by $\mathcal{N}(0,1)$, φ is an activation function and z_i is the output of i-th neuron within the single layer of the ANN, which is given by

$$z_i = \varphi\left(\sum_{j=0}^{n} w_{ji} x_j\right). \tag{2.3}$$

Note we have used φ for the activation function in every neuron of the ANN. This does not mean all activation functions have to be the same. One is free to use whichever. However, in practice, the same activation function is used for all neurons in the layer. The output neuron, however, most often uses the identity function when used for regression.

2.2.3   Deep Neural Net

A DNN consists of several layers of neurons joined together. If an ANN consists of a layer of neurons, a DNN is just an ANN with more than one layer, hence the name "deep". Figure 2.7 shows an example of such a net. The dimension of the input vector x is n, there are k layers and if j represents the j-th layer, then it has l_j neurons. In this case, the *depth* of the DNN is k.

As can be seen from Figure 2.7, the output (real value) of every neuron on the $(j-1)$-th layer serves as input to every neuron in the j-th layer. This is an example of a *totally connected* DNN. For the layers to fit, the dimension of each neuron in the j-th layer must be equal to the number of neurons in the $(j-1)$-th layer. As it has already been mentioned, we will primarily focus on DNNs with a one-dimensional output. Therefore, we append a single neuron after the last layer as shown in Figure 2.7.

The model of a totally connected DNN, such as the one in Figure 2.7, can be expressed, under the frequentist approach, as follows:

$$y = \varphi \left(\sum_{i=0}^{l_k} w_i z_i^k \right) + \varepsilon, \tag{2.4}$$

Just like the ANN model, $w = (w_0, w_1, \ldots, w_m)$ are the weights of the last neuron, φ the activation function (typically the identity in the final layer when used for regression) and ε is given by $\mathcal{N}(0, 1)$. The variables z_i^k are the outputs of the neurons in the last layer. Notice these in turn will be obtained through Equation 2.3, which in the case of a DNN, is expressed in terms of the weights of the layer in question and the outputs of the previous layer.

Equation 2.4 has has a deterministic component f_w, which plays a central role in training

$$f_w = \varphi \left(\sum_{i=0}^{l_k} w_i z_i^k \right), \tag{2.5}$$

Notice that each layer adds a composition of functions to the function defined in Equation 2.4. This will become an important element to consider in the training of DNNs (Section 2.4).

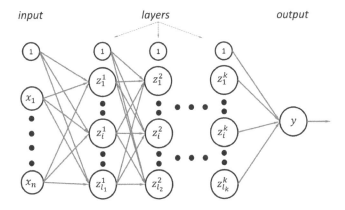

FIGURE 2.7 A Deep Neural Net with input dimension n, k layers and the j-th layer has l_j neurons, where $1 \le j \le k$.

2.3   UNIVERSAL APPROXIMATION THEOREMS

By construction, DNNs have a lot of flexibility. They are built out of neurons arranged in layers. The number of layers, the size of each layer and the type of activation function constitute examples of hyper-parameters. In Figure 2.7, we show a DNN that is totally connected. However, DNNs do not need to be totally connected. The DNN model allows for a wide range of configurations, each configuration determining an instance of a Neural Net. In Section 2.5, we will see examples of different DNN architectures that have proven to be effective for particular applications.

The architectural flexibility of DNNs lies at the heart of their approximation power. This is formally expressed through a range of theorems called *Universal Approximation Theorems*. Intuitively, they say that as long as the function f to approximate is well-behaved (say continuous), then, given any degree of accuracy ε, we can always find a DNN that approximates f to that degree of accuracy, by either adjusting the width or the depth of the DNN. The version we present in Theorem 2.3.1 ([48]) is from 2020.

Universal Approximation Theorem for DNNs

Theorem 2.3.1 *Let $f : \mathbb{R} \to \mathbb{R}$ be any non-affine continuous function which is continuously differentiable at at least one point, with nonzero derivative at that point. Denote by $C(K; \mathbb{R}^m)$ the space of real vector-valued continuous functions on K, a compact subset of $\mathbb{R}^n$. Let $\mathcal{N}$ be the space of Neural Nets with input dimension n, output dimension m, and an arbitrary number of hidden layers each with $n + m + 2$ neurons. Moreover, assume that every hidden neuron has activation function φ, while the neurons in the last layer have the identify function as activation function. Then, $\mathcal{N}$ is dense in $C(K; \mathbb{R}^m)$. That is, for every $\varepsilon > 0$, and $f \in C(K; \mathbb{R}^m)$, there is a Neural Net $\mathcal{F} \in \mathcal{N}$ such that*

$$\|\mathcal{F} - f\|_\infty < \varepsilon. \tag{2.6}$$

There are many versions of the theorem just presented. The first appeared in 1989 in [16] and is stated in terms of varying width, hence it applies to Neural Nets of a single layer. Since then, many different versions have appeared in the literature, some generalising the results in [16] by considering more general architectures and activation functions (for example, [51]).

Theorem 2.3.1 provides clear evidence that the flexibility DNNs have from construction lie at the heart of their ability to approximate any function. However, one common theme across these theorems is that they do not specify the width or depth needed to approximate a given function f. In some cases, the size of the Neural Net may be too large to work with in practice. Even in cases where the Neural Net is feasible, there is no way of knowing what configuration works.

This gives rise to the hyper-parameter optimisation or tuning problem: given a function f to approximate, how many layers, how many neurons in each layer and which activation function should we use to obtain good results? In some cases, simple configurations suffice. In some others, several combinations must be tested before obtaining good results. It may well be that no good results are obtained from among the configurations tested within the time and computational power constraints.

Although the Universal Approximation Theorems give no insight into the architecture of the DNN needed to approximate a given function f, there are results that establish a relationship between error of approximation and the architecture of the DNN. Specifically, the following result, found in [4], for single-layered DNNs, says that the error of approximation can be split into the following two components:

$$\mathcal{O}\left(\frac{C}{k}\right) + \mathcal{O}\left(\frac{kd}{n}\log(n)\right). \tag{2.7}$$

The first involves a constant C (the first absolute moment of the Fourier magnitude distribution of f) and the number of neurons k in the only layer of the Neural Net. The size of this component is controlled completely by k — the larger the number of neurons, the smaller the error — and hence only depends on the architecture of the Neural Net.

The second component involves the dimension d of the input domain of f (which is fixed), the number of neurons k and the size of the data set n. This component increases with the number of neurons and decreases as the size of the data set n increases. We can think of this component as the one that captures the variance of the model. That is, how much it overfits — the larger the number of neurons k, the more likely a model is to overfit, which is reflected in an increase in the second component. The way to control it is by increasing the amount of data to train with — that is, increase n.

2.4   TRAINING OF DEEP NEURAL NETS

In Sections 1.3.1 and 1.3.2, we covered the main two approaches to training the Linear Model: the frequentist and the Bayesian approach. For DNNs we have the same situation. In what follows we focus on the frequentist, as this is the one used in all applications in Part IV.

As presented in Section 1.3.1, training through the frequentist approach reduces down to solving Equation 1.8. This is equivalent to minimising the cost function, which in the case of the Linear Model is given by Equation 1.7. In the case of DNNs, the cost function takes the same general form, the only difference being the definition of the function f_w:

$$\phi(w; X, Y) = \frac{1}{m} \sum_{i=1}^{m} (f_w(x_i) - y_i)^2. \tag{2.8}$$

Using a different function f_w makes little difference conceptually. However, in practice, it changes the way in which the minimisations of the cost function is done. At this point, we are forced to depart from the simplicity of the Linear Model.

2.4.1 Backpropagation

One of the main advantages of the Linear Model is that the minimisation of Equation 1.7 can be solved analytically. This means there is a formula in terms of the data $\mathcal{D} = \{X, Y\}$ that gives the values of w. Specifically, if A is the matrix obtained from the data points X in $\mathcal{D}$ (each element in X conforming a row in A), and B the matrix obtained in the same way as A but using the data points Y in $\mathcal{D}$, then w is given by

$$w^* = (A^T A)^{-1} A^T B. \tag{2.9}$$

In the case of DNNs, the story changes. Computing the gradient of f_w is much more complicated as f_w is defined as the composition of the different layers of neurons in the DNN, each of which has variables in w. Moreover, the cost function is no longer convex. Global solutions are hence much more difficult to find. Overall, the minimisation of the cost function becomes a more complicated task.

Therefore, other ways to minimise the cost function in Equation 2.8 must be considered. Normally, this is done using optimisation algorithms. There is a wide range of optimisation algorithms. Two categories among them stand out: optimisation algorithms that depend on the gradient of the function to optimise and the ones that do not. The main advantage of the former is that they are very efficient — assuming the gradient is already available. The gradient points in the direction of greatest descent — if you want to learn fast, follow the gradient.[2]

Although gradient-free optimisers have been garnering a lot of attention in recent times in a wide range of fields, they have not been incorporated as standard methods for the minimisation of Equation 2.8.

One of the main drawbacks of gradient-based optimisers is the computation of the corresponding gradient. As a quick reminder, the gradient of a function ϕ, with respect to a set of variables w (using the notation in Equation 2.8), is the vector that consists of the partial derivatives $\partial \phi / \partial w_i$, where w_i is a variable in ϕ. In some cases, the computation of the gradient is straightforward; in some others it is very inefficient. The complexity depends on the definition of the function ϕ in terms of the variables w.

The function to optimise in the training of DNNs is the cost function in Equation 2.8. The dependence of such function on w is captured by the dependence of f_w on w. Therefore, the challenge is to compute the gradient of f_w and apply the chain rule.

Note that if we want to train the DNN with a regulariser parameter, the cost function takes the following form:

$$\phi_{reg}(w, X, Y) = \frac{1}{m} \sum_{i=1}^{m} (f_w(x_i) - y_i)^2 + \lambda \, \|w\|_2^2. \tag{2.10}$$

However, computing the gradient of the regulariser component of ϕ with respect to w is straightforward. The complicated part is the computation of the gradient of f with respect to w. Therefore, this will be the focus from now on.

---

[2]Strictly speaking, the gradient points in the direction of greatest ascent. Its negative points in the direction of greatest descent, which is what is followed when minimising a function.

The most efficient method to compute the gradient of f_w in the case of DNNs is called *backpropagation*. Conceptually it is just the application of the chain rule from calculus to the computation of partial derivatives. However, this is done in such a way that redundant calculations are avoided. In the next section, we use a simple DNN to illustrate the main characteristics of backpropagation.

2.4.2 Backpropagation example

Learning under the frequentist approach is the process through which we try to find the weights or parameters w of the network that minimise the cost function (Equation 2.8). In the case of DNNs, this is done using gradient-based optimisers. To compute the gradient at each point of the parameter domain, we make use of the chain rule.

The chain rule

As an illustration of how the chain rule is applied, we use a two-dimensional function $f(x, y)$. The partial derivatives of f are simply $\partial f / \partial x$, $\partial f / \partial y$. Assume, however, that x and y depend on some variables u, v. This means, there are functions $x(u, v)$, $y(u, v)$ and the following composition may be considered $f(x(u, v), y(u, v))$.

The previous composition expresses the function f in terms of u, v. The chain rule says that as long as the functions involved are differentiable (f, x and y), then the partial derivatives of f with respect to u and v can be obtained from the partial derivatives of f with respect to x, y, and the partials of x, y with respect to u, v. Specifically, in the case of the partial derivative of f with respect to u, this means

$$\frac{\partial f}{\partial u}(u_0, v_0) = \frac{\partial f}{\partial x}(x(u_0, v_0), y(u_0, v_0)) \cdot \frac{\partial x}{\partial u}(u_0, v_0) + \frac{\partial f}{\partial y}(x(u_0, v_0), y(u_0, v_0)) \cdot \frac{\partial y}{\partial u}(u_0, v_0). \tag{2.11}$$

The cost function in Equation 2.8 depends on the variables w through f_w. In a DNN, there are at least two layers of neurons. This means f_w can be seen as the composition of functions. This nested inter-dependence of the variables involved is why the chain rule is a natural way of computing the partial derivatives of f_w with respect to the variables in w — that is, the gradient of f_w. However, the direct or naive application of the chain rule in this context is inefficient, as intermediary partials (such as $\partial f / \partial x$ in Equation 2.11) are computed several times.

When the number of layers in a DNN increases (something we might want to do to improve the accuracy of the DNN; see Theorem 2.3.1), the number of function compositions that define f_w increases, and with it, the inefficiency of the chain rule.

Backpropagation is an algorithm (or families of algorithms) designed to eliminate this inefficiency from the chain rule by storing the partials computed at each step of the process and reusing them in future steps.

A common misconception is to talk of backpropagation as the training of DNNs. Although at the heart of training, backpropagation only computes the gradient.

To a degree, it is the algorithm that makes the application of gradient-based optimisers feasible in the training of DNNs.

We illustrate how backpropagation works using the DNN in Figure 2.8. Although simple, this DNN has all the elements needed to illustrate the main characteristics of backpropagation and how it applies to any number of layers and neurons per layer. Also notice the algorithm describes how to compute the gradient (in this case of f_w) at a given parameter point $(w_1, \ldots, w_n)$. Learning using gradient-based optimisers will require the gradient at thousands of points. Backpropagation is applied the same way regardless of the point.

As we have already mentioned, to learn we need the gradient of the cost function ϕ (Equation 2.8) with respect to the parameters w. As the function ϕ depends on w through f_w, the focus will be the computation of the gradient of f_w. The gradient of ϕ can then be recovered by a trivial use of the chain rule. Moreover, this allows us to simplify the exposition by assuming we only deal with one single data points (x_1, x_2).

Figure 2.8 represents a DNN with a two-dimensional input domain, two layers each with two neurons. There is a total of 10 weight parameters. Parameters w_9 and w_{10} belong to the last neuron, the one with no activation function. Therefore, the function that represents the evaluation of the DNN in Figure 2.8 is given by

$$f_w(x_1, x_2) = w_9 z_3 + w_{10} z_4. \tag{2.12}$$

Parameters w_5, w_6, w_7 and w_8 belong to the second layer. Finally, w_1, w_2, w_3 and w_4 correspond to the first. The objective is to compute $\partial f_w / \partial w_i$, for $i = 1, \ldots, 10$, where x_1 and x_2 are fixed values from the data set used for training. Moreover, notice $\partial f_w / \partial w_i$ means the partial of f_w with respect to the i-th parameter, evaluated at a fixed value in the parameter domain w, that is, the gradient ∇f_w at some point $(w_1, \ldots, w_{10})$.

Notice that the neurons used in this example do not have translation term — for example, the output of the first neuron is $\varphi(w_1 x_1 + w_2 x_2)$ and not $\varphi(w_0 + w_1 x_1 + w_2 x_2)$, as has been the case up to this point in the chapter. We did this to reduce the number of parameters in the example and make the exposition clearer.

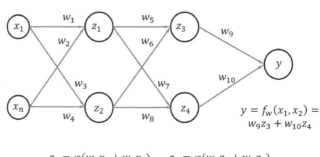

$$z_1 = \varphi(w_1 x_1 + w_2 x_2) \qquad z_3 = \varphi(w_5 z_1 + w_6 z_2)$$

$$z_2 = \varphi(w_3 x_1 + w_4 x_2) \qquad z_4 = \varphi(w_7 z_1 + w_8 z_2)$$

FIGURE 2.8 Forward pass in backpropagation.

To compute the gradient with backpropagation, there are two processes that need to be considered. The first is called the *forward pass*, which is depicted in Figure 2.8. The second, the *backward pass*, is presented in Figure 2.9. The forward pass consists of evaluating f_w at the point $(w_1, \ldots, w_{10})$, using the data set given by (x_1, x_2), keeping track of the result at each stage. That is, given the point $(w_1, \ldots, w_{10})$, we compute z_i, for $i = 1, \ldots, 4$.

The variables z_1 and z_2 are expressed as

$$z_1 = \varphi(w_1 x_1 + w_2 x_2), \tag{2.13}$$

$$z_2 = \varphi(w_3 x_1 + w_4 x_2). \tag{2.14}$$

Finally, variables z_3 and z_4 are expressed as

$$z_3 = \varphi(w_5 z_1 + w_6 z_2), \tag{2.15}$$

$$z_4 = \varphi(w_7 z_1 + w_8 z_2). \tag{2.16}$$

The reason for computing these values will become evident when we compute the partials of f_w with respect to the parameters w, using the chain rule.

There are two types of variables we need to identify in the backward pass. The partials of f_w with respect to both will appear when we use the chain rule. The first consists of the parameters w. The second of the variables z keep track of the values in the network as we do a forward pass.

Let us now compute the partials of f_w with respect to the parameters in w. This is done layer by layer, starting from the last and working our way back — hence backward pass. The partials with respect to the parameters on the last layer (single neuron) are trivial to compute. Given Equation 2.12, the partial, for example, with respect to w_9 is $\partial f_w / \partial w_9 = z_3$. If the forward pass has been completed, we obtain the result for this partial as it is z_3.

Take the partial of f with respect to a parameter in the second layer, say w_5. By the chain rule

$$\frac{\partial f}{\partial w_5} = \frac{\partial f}{\partial z_3} \cdot \frac{\partial z_3}{\partial w_5}. \tag{2.17}$$

Notice the first partial corresponds to a partial on the single neuron (last layer) with respect to a z variable, that is, $\partial f_w / \partial z_3$. Its expression must be evaluated at the corresponding point obtained with the forward pass. The second partial sits in the second layer as the partial is computed with respect to a parameter, in this case w_5.

The partial with respect to w_6 is computed essentially in the same way we just did for w_5. For the other parameters on the same layer (w_7, w_8), one uses $\partial f_w / \partial z_4$ instead of $\partial f_w / \partial z_3$.

Notice that one of the things done so far is compute the partial of f_w with respect to each of the z variables on this layer. A very important aspect of backpropagation is that partials with respect to the variables z computed at each step (so far the ones corresponding to the single neuron) will be used in subsequent steps. Any implementation of backpropagation should be taking this into account.[3]

Let us now compute the partials with respect to the parameters in the first layer. This time we will see how some of the values obtained in the previous step can be reused. Take as an example w_1. By the chain rule, the partial of f_w with respect to w_1 is

$$\frac{\partial f}{\partial w_1} = \frac{\partial f}{\partial z_3} \cdot \frac{\partial z_3}{\partial z_1} \cdot \frac{\partial z_1}{\partial w_1}$$
$$+ \frac{\partial f}{\partial z_4} \cdot \frac{\partial z_4}{\partial z_1} \cdot \frac{\partial z_1}{\partial w_1}.$$

$$(2.18)$$

Notice $\partial f_w/\partial z_3$ and $\partial f_w/\partial z_4$ have already been computed in the previous step of the backward pass. The partials that correspond to the current step of the backward pass are $\partial z_3/\partial z_1$ and $\partial z_4/\partial z_1$. Given that we have already done a forward pass, their expressions can be evaluated. The final partial needed is z_1 (output variable of current layer), with respect to the corresponding w parameter w_1.

The DNN used in this illustrative example only has two layers (not counting the last neuron). If there were more layers, the partials computed so far would be carried over for the next step of the backward pass.

However, notice the common pattern that emerges. At each step of the backward pass, we compute the partial of the z variables, which are outputs of the layer in question, with respect to the z variables that serve as inputs to the same layer, for example, z_4 with respect to z_1 in the last layer of the DNN in Figure 2.9. The remaining partials needed in the chain rule have either been computed already (previous steps) or are the partials of z variables with respect to parameters w, for example, $\partial z_4/\partial w_7$ in the last layer of the DNN in Figure 2.9. Therefore, backpropation needs three things at each layer: the values of the z variables from the forward pass, the partial of the z output variable with respect to the input z variables and the partial of the z output variable with

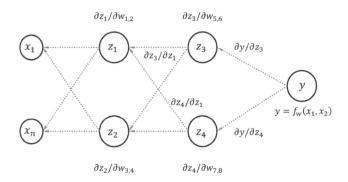

FIGURE 2.9 Backward pass in backpropagation.

---

[3]Indeed, a good number of software packages for DNNs implement backpropagation this way.

respect to the w parameters. With these three things at each layer, the gradient of the cost function at a point $(w_1, \ldots, w_n)$ can be computed without too much effort.

2.4.3 Optimisation of cost function

In this section, we see how the gradient of the function to minimise (for example, the cost function in Equation 2.8) can be used by a typical gradient-based optimiser in the training of DNNs.

Let us first start with what it is about the gradient that optimisers exploit. The main characteristic of the gradient, which optimisation algorithms make use of, is that the negative of the gradient points in the direction of greatest negative change (when the function in question is smooth). This is the same as the direction of greatest descent.

Let us gain some intuition of how the optimisation takes place. Consider a function ϕ to optimise. If the domain of this function is in $\mathbb{R}^n$ and it returns values in $\mathbb{R}$, then its image can be thought of as a surface in $\mathbb{R}^{n+1}$. For example, in the simple case when $n = 2$, the image can be thought of as the surface of a mountain range in dimension 3.

At each point of the domain in $\mathbb{R}^n$, the gradient shows us the direction of greatest descent (by considering its negative value). In the example of the mountain surface ($n = 2$), this would be the direction, at each point on the mountain, where the mountain has the steepest descent. If the aim is to locate the point where the mountain range reaches its lowest value as efficiently as possible, it makes sense, at least intuitively, to walk in the direction of steepest descent.

Notice that by following the path of greatest descent, there is no guarantee of reaching a global minimum. The hope is that we get to a point that is sufficiently low. This is a common characteristic of gradient-based optimisers; one forfeits the guarantee of finding a global minimum in the hope of finding, in an efficient manner, a domain point that gives a good-enough result. In our context, a good-enough result translates into finding values for w that define a function f_w that generalise or predict with accuracy (a notion that of course depends on the context) on a consistent basis.

There are many different algorithms that rely on the gradient of f_w to explore its domain in search of appropriate values of w. The one in Equation 2.19 is called *gradient descent* and is one of the most basic and commonly used ones. Mathematically, it is expressed as follows:

Gradient Descent Algorithm

Say we want to optimise a function ϕ. Denote the gradient of ϕ by $\nabla \phi$. Gradient descent consists of taking repeated steps, each in the direction of greatest descent, which is given by the negative of the gradient.

Each step taken must be of a certain size. At the k-th step this is controlled by λ_k.

$$w_{k+1} = w_k - \lambda_k \nabla \phi(w_k; X, Y) \tag{2.19}$$

(continued)

(*continued*)

Note that λ_k admits a different value per iteration. However, it is very common to use the same step size for all iterations.

Also, it is worth pointing out that the value of λ can have a big effect on the effectiveness of the algorithm. In some cases, a small step size will prevent us from quickly reaching a minimum for ϕ. In others, a large step value may cause us to miss the minimum. The value of λ is yet another example of a hyper-parameter, one which may need to be tweaked in some cases to improve results.

When ϕ is the cost function in Equation 2.8, gradient descent takes the form

$$w_{k+1} = w_k - \lambda_k \frac{1}{m} \sum_{i=1}^{m} \nabla (f_w(x_i) - y_i)^2 \qquad (2.20)$$

Note that this expression involves the computation of as many gradients as data points for each iteration. Depending on the size of the data set, this may become a computational bottleneck. In the following sections, we present ways of reducing this computational cost.

An illustration of what gradient descent does can be seen in Figure 2.10.

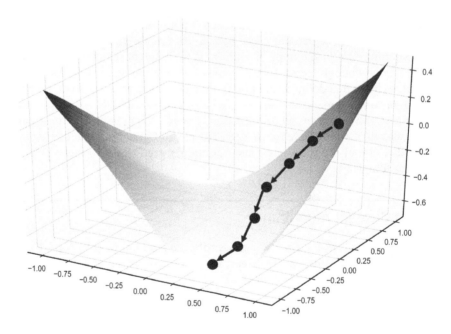

FIGURE 2.10   Surface representing the cost function for which gradient descent finds a minimum. The dots represent each step in gradient descent. The arrow starting at each dot points in the direction of greatest descent.

There are many elements of a practical nature that need to be considered when using gradient descent. One of them, the size of the step at every iteration, has already been mentioned. But there are others too, such as how to choose the first set of values for the weights w to start the algorithm and how to decide when to stop gradient descent.

All of these can be thought of as examples of hyper-parameters that need to be chosen every time we train. Sometimes, the choice of these hyper-parameters does not affect the outcome significantly. Unfortunately, there are cases when it does. Different heuristic rules, which vary depending on the context, have been developed over time. The details of these heuristics are beyond the scope of this book. However, it is very important to be aware of the problems that can come as a result of poorly choosing some of these hyper-parameters.

Although gradient descent comes with the issues just mentioned, it is important to see why it has become the default choice (along with its variants, for example, Sections 2.4.4 and 2.4.5) to train DNNs. First, it is easy to implement. Second, one can considerably reduce its computational cost by using backpropagation, making the training of DNNs viable in many applications. Third, it applies to a wide range of cost functions. Finally, the memory requirements for the family of gradient descent algorithms is manageable.

Many others algorithms that find the minimum of a function exist. However, we will not discuss them, in order to keep the text focused. For the purposes of this book, it suffices to know that DNNs are generally trained by algorithms that efficiently explore the domain of the cost function, making use of the latter's gradient, which is obtained by backpropagation.

Optimisation and the Hessian

Some gradient-based optimisation algorithms also make use of the Hessian of the function ϕ to optimise. The Hessian is defined as the second-order derivative of ϕ. While the gradient indicates the direction of greatest descent, the Hessian gives information about the curvature of ϕ. This information is exploited by some optimisation algorithms to improve the way in which the domain of ϕ is explored. A well-known algorithm that uses the Hessian for optimisation is the Newton Conjugate Gradient Algorithm.

2.4.4 Stochastic gradient descent

Gradient descent as presented in Equation 2.20 requires computing, for each iteration of the algorithm, the gradient of f_w as many times as there are data points. If the data set is large, this becomes a considerable computational task. Say we have 100,000 data points and we run gradient descent for 1,000 iterations, both realistic situations when training a DNN. Using gradient descent would require 100,000,000 gradient calculations, something that can be problematic.

Stochastic gradient descent is an algorithm designed to bypass this problem. It essentially consists of choosing a subset of data points at each iteration of gradient descent. Therefore, instead of computing the gradient m times — where m is the number of data points in Equation 2.20 — we compute it only on a batch of data of size l, where $l < m$. If l is considerably lower than m, this can reduce the computational load at training considerably. Equation 2.20 changes to

$$w_{k+1} = w_k - \lambda_k \frac{1}{l} \sum_{j=1}^{l} \nabla(f_w(x_{i_j}) - y_{i_j})^2. \tag{2.21}$$

Stochastic gradient descent has two main advantages. The first and most important is that each iteration is done faster than with the standard gradient descent. The second is that it allows for updating the model with continuously incoming data. One does not need to wait for a huge amount of data to train the model; one can use a small data set and update the model trained so far with newly incoming data.

The disadvantages are that as we reduce the size of the data set we get noise in the training. At one iteration we may have a reduction in error while at the next an increase. Another disadvantage is that stochastic gradient descent tends to be more sensitive to the choice of the step size, making hyper-parameter optimisation more challenging in some cases.

Practitioners normally distinguish between two types of stochastic gradient descent. The first is called *online* stochastic gradient descent. This consists of using just one data point at each iteration, that is, $l = 1$. Although the fastest form of stochastic gradient descent, it is the one with the largest amount of noise. It is, however, very good at dealing with streaming data as it updates the model weights with every new data point.

The other form of stochastic gradient descent is called batch or mini-batch. This is when $1 < l < m$, as $l > 1$ one tends to observe less noise with *batch* gradient descent. Also, if l is not too large, then the computational time taken during training can be significantly smaller than with gradient descent.

2.4.5 Extensions of stochastic gradient descent

One of the main issues encountered when using gradient descent to train a DNN is the time the algorithm takes to search the space of weights of the cost function. We have already seen that stochastic gradient descent is one way of reducing this time. However, gradient descent — and its stochastic cousin — use the gradient of the cost function to find weights that reduce the error. In some cases, this is very effective, but in others, it means moving along the domain of the cost function in a very inefficient way.

Consider, for example, the cost function whose level curves are showing in Figure 2.11. This cost function has contour lines that are elliptical. We know that at every point of the domain, the gradient points perpendicularly to the contour lines. If what we want is to get to the minimum, marked with an **X**, and we follow the gradient, we may follow a path similar to the zig-zag in Figure 2.11. Clearly, if we could, we would follow a more direct path.

There are several algorithms — all extensions of gradient descent — that have been developed to alleviate this problem, their main aim being to follow a path during training that requires fewer steps. The result is more efficient training exercises.

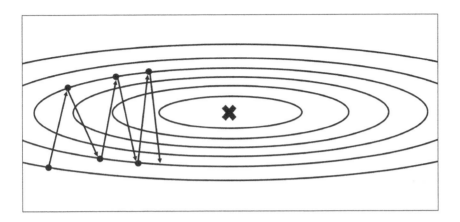

FIGURE 2.11 Level curves example for cost function. Arrows denote possible path followed by gradient descent.

Covering the full range of extensions is outside the scope of this book. However, the idea behind all these extensions is to make the steps at each iteration more efficient, either by smoothing the gradients (momentum methods) or by changing the size of the step size at each iteration (adaptive methods). A well-known momentum method is Nesterov Momentum. Good examples of iterative methods are AdaGrad ([20]), RMSProp ([40]) and the Adaptive Moment Estimation (Adam) optimiser, which is one of the most widely used extensions of gradient descent these days ([18]).

2.5 MORE SOPHISTICATED DNNs

So far we have considered fully connected DNNs. As the reader is surely aware by now, these consist of layers made of neurons, which are placed one after the other, connecting every neuron in a given layer with all the neurons in the next.

Fully connected DNNs have proved to be very useful in many areas. However, their applicability in some areas can be significantly potentiated by changing the characteristics of the layers, the way they are connected and the use of new training heuristics.

In this section, we briefly cover one of the most popular architectures. We avoid excessive detail — the purpose is only to present some of the ways in which modifications to the fully connected architecture can create models that are more powerful in specific instances. For a more in-depth presentation on the different types of Neural Net architectures and (deep learning in general), we recommend [31].

2.5.1 Convolution Neural Nets

Convolutional Neural Nets (CNNs) are one of the most popular types of DNNs. Although the central notions related to CNNs have been known since the 1980*s*, it was only in recent years, with the development of sufficiently powerful computing hardware and large data sets that their applications became mainstream, especially in the field of image recognition.

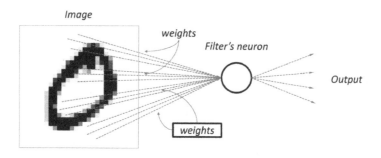

FIGURE 2.12   Image represents the incoming data point. The neuron focuses on a region of the image at a time. For each region, the neuron gives an output. After the neuron has covered the whole image, the neuron will have filtered the image.

The design of CNNs was partly inspired by the connectivity pattern between neurons in the visual cortex of animals. Research in the 1960s (for example, [17]) showed that individual cortical neurons respond only to stimuli in small regions of the visual field. These restricted regions are called *receptive fields*. The information of the full image is then captured by the overlapping receptive fields of neighbouring neurons.

Inspired by the behaviour of biological neurons just described, instead of considering artificial neurons with as many parameters as variables in the input space — as is the case with fully connected DNNs — CNNs consider filters. These are neurons with a reduced number of weights, at least compared to the number of variables in the input space. The weights in the filters are used in inner product computations with subsets of the variables in the input space. The result is then passed through an activation function. Normally, the subsets of variables considered in these inner products are contiguous sets of variables. In this way, the filter analyses a region within the given data point, exploiting local correlations. If the data point is an image, then the filter only analyses a particular region of the image a step at a time.

To cover the whole image, the filter analyses region by region of the image — this is what is known as convolution (shown in Figure 2.12) as it mimics the mathematical convolution operation.[4] In this way, the filter behaves like the cortical neurons described previously, which only process information on restricted visual fields. As the neuron scans the image region by region, one can piece together information of the whole image.

For example, if the input data points consist of 1,000 variables, these can be split into 100 contiguous regions, each with 50 variables.[5] The neuron then processes each of them separately — that is, we obtain an output using the weights and activation function of the neuron, for each of the 100 regions. The collection of outputs, 100 in this case, constitute the filtered data point.

To get a better idea of how filters behave like a set of cortical neurons, think of a fully connected layer, where each neuron has a set of non-zero set of weights in a designated

---

[4]For details on the convolution operation between functions, we refer to https://en.wikipedia .org/wiki/Convolution.

[5]In this example, we assume non-overlapping regions for simplicity. However, filtering neurons normally explore regions of the incoming data point that overlap.

set of variables. These variables define the receptive field of the neuron. If we impose that all neurons have the same weights but are assigned to different receptive fields, we end up with a collection of neurons of the same type but with varying receptive fields. In this way, each neuron is assigned a region of the image.

Notice, however, that by imposing the condition that the weights in the neurons across the layer are the same, we dramatically reduce the number of weights that need to be trained. This is one of the reasons why CNNs are effective in tasks where the dimension of the input space is too large.

Take, for example, fully connected DNNs in a task such as image recognition. Images consist of many pixels. Each pixel is a variable in the input space. If the image consists of 300 by 300 pixels (a size that is not large at all), this corresponds to incoming data with 90,000 dimensions. If we consider coloured images, this triples the number of pixels and hence the dimension of the input space. When a fully connected DNN is used, each neuron in the first layer has as many weights (plus one due to the displacement parameter) as variables in the input space. As we add layers and neurons to each layer — needed to learn the complexities of images — the number of weight parameters increases dramatically. It would not be unusual to reach the billions of parameters in a fully connected DNN, which makes training very hard.

However, by using filters, CNNs reduce the number of weights dramatically while retaining the learning properties of DNNs. For the image example given previously, a typical filter would consist of a neuron with 5-by-5 pixels (or non-zero weights). As these are shared across neurons in the layer, we have a total of 25 parameters (plus the displacement term).

Normally, a set of filters are applied one after another. If the first filter only focuses on a small region of the image at a time, the next filter focuses on small regions of the output of the first filter. This means the second filter captures larger portions of the original image. In this way, filters learn relevant features from the data in the task at hand. In the case of image recognition, a filter may learn how to identify the eyebrows of humans, or tails in cats, for example.

A set of filters stacked one after another constitutes a *convolutional* layer. This is the core building block of CNNs. However, there are other layers also used in CNNs. Another very important one is the *pooling* layer.

Pooling layers are used to further reduce the dimension of the data and control overfitting. By reducing the dimension of the data, the number of parameters to train is reduced and with it the computational load associated with training the Neural Net. To control overfitting, pooling layers return summaries of incoming data.

For example, consider Figure 2.13. On the left-hand side, we have a data point consisting of 16 variables. The values of each variable are represented by the numbers in each box (pixel, for example). Similar to what a filtering neuron does, the pooling neuron only focuses on a region of the data point at a time. In this example, the pooling neuron computes the maximum of all the values in each 4-by-4 region. Note that in Figure 2.13 we assume the regions to be passed through max pooling to be disjoint; therefore a total of 4 regions are processed.[6]

---

[6] Another common choice of pooling is defined by the mean of the values in each region.

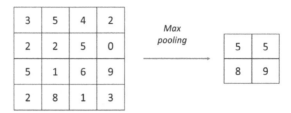

FIGURE 2.13 Max pooling.

For example, the first region, consisting of the 2-by-2 square on the top left-hand-corner, with the values 3, 5, 2, 2, becomes 5 after max pooling has been applied. By doing this we lose some information, such as the variation of the numbers along with their location. However, this makes the Neural Net more robust to variations in the position of the features.

Once a predetermined number of a few convolutional layers and pooling layers have been stacked one after another, a fully connected DNN is usually appended to the CNN.

Note that by the time the fully connected DNN is appended to the convolutional and pooling layers, the dimension of the data is such that one can train a fully connected DNN. In a way, what filters and pooling layers do is remove the high degree of granularity often present in high-dimensional data sets. Once this has been done, one stands a much higher chance of learning the filtered features with the power of a fully connected DNN.

Having discussed the strengths that CNNs bring, it must be said that such architectures are bound to present problems at training. Indeed, training CNNs is not always trivial. The number of hyper-parameters, to begin with, is substantial. There is the number and size of filters, the pooling type and its size, the type of activation function, the number of layers ... just to name a few. With such a number of different choices, we gain flexibility on the one hand. On the other hand, however, more flexibility usually means we need to be aware of possible underfits and overfits. For the latter, a very useful heuristic technique was developed, called *dropout* ([59]).

Dropout

Typically, all the weights in a Neural Net are updated at each iteration of (stochastic) gradient descent. However, in some cases, this makes the Net more prone to overfit. Dropout consists of keeping the weights in a collection of neurons at each iteration of the training process fixed (i.e. dropping them out), which in turn reduces overfitting. This is a very simple and easy way to prevent overfitting, not just in CNNs, but for Neural Nets in general.

Applications

The areas where CNNs have had the most impact are those that involve image recognition tasks as an important component of its processes. For over 10 years, larger and more sophisticated CNNs have been reducing the best reported errors associated with image recognition challenges. For example, the best results to date, in competitions such as the ImageNet Large Scale Visual Recognition Challenge, have been obtained with CNNs.[7]

Although image recognition tasks have been the training ground for CNNs, these have also been successfully applied in other areas, too. For example, CNNs have been used in drug discovery, health risk assessment, Natural Language Processing and even in board game competitions such as Go. In particular, CNNs have been an important component of the AlphaGo software that was able to defeat the best Go player in the world in 2016.

In the realm of finance, CNNs have also been showing promising results. Although not thought to be initially the best choice to analyse financial time series (Recurrent Neural Nets are generally considered a better choice for time-parametrised data), recently they have been shown to give good results ([75]). Also, and of particular relevance to this book, CNNs have been used for pricing model calibration ([26]), an application which we delve into in Chapter 18.

It is important to note that training some of the most sophisticated CNNs today is a computational challenge. Despite their lack of connectivitiy, which helps keep the number of weight parameters low, some of these CNNs take days to train with some of the most powerful hardware available. Clearly, using fully connected DNNs for these tasks would be futile. However, the fact that CNNs with all sorts of particular architectural characterisics have been designed over the years is testament to the flexibility and power that Neural Nets bring.

2.5.2 Other famous architectures

Covering the range of different Neural Net architectures that have proved useful in different areas (in the last decade or so) is outside the scope of this book. However, given the impact these have had in recent years (and will surely continue to have), it is only natural to mention a few.

Recurrent Neural Nets (RNNs) are Neural Nets that incorporate a temporal component into their architecture. The features associated with the temporal component that is sometimes present in data can be missed by Neural Nets. Not capturing these features can be detrimental in some cases. RNNs are designed to learn these features, making them ideal in contexts such as time series prediction, speech recognition, grammar learning, music composition, and so on.

---

[7]The ImageNet Large Scale Visual Recognition Challenge is an annual competition organised by the ImageNet project, where participants put forward their software programs to see which achieves the highest level of accuracy at classifying and detecting objects.

Another type of DNN that has gained a lot of attention in recent years is the Generative Adversarial Net (GAN). It consists of two Neural Nets (often CNNs) that compete against one another within a defined set of rules. The objective is to generate new data that share the same characteristics as the original training set, making them ideal in image and voice generation.

For the type of problems addressed in this book (Part IV), fully connected DNNs and slight variants of these suffice. In fact, up to now, most of the literature that uses Deep Learning in applications, such as the ones considered here, rarely use Neural Nets that are not fully connected. However, we believe it is only a matter of time before other architectures find their way into a wide range of applications, not just in the applications considered in this book, but in finance more generally.

2.6   SUMMARY OF CHAPTER

- **Approximation power**. Given a continuous function f and a degree of accuracy specified, we know that there exists a DNN configuration that will approximate f to the specified degree of accuracy.
- **Efficient and stable evaluation**. The evaluation of DNNs boils down to simple matrix multiplications and the evaluation of activation functions that are fast to compute. In practical settings, this means that as long as the architecture of the DNN is not too large, thousands of evaluations can be performed in a fraction of a second.
- **Architecture flexibility**. Neural Nets, by design, have high degrees of flexibility. This makes DNNs very adaptable. In particular, they can deal with input data of high dimensions. The downside is that if the architecture of the DNN becomes too complex, the amount of training data may be too large for some applications.

CHAPTER 3

Chebyshev Tensors

This chapter presents the main mathematical results behind CTs and interpolants as function approximators. These constitute the mathematical backbone that justifies the use of these objects in practical settings such as the ones presented in Part IV.

An interesting aspect of polynomial interpolation is that it has enjoyed a bad reputation for quite a long time. In fact, for a good part of the 20th century the belief amongst many numerical analysts was that when it came to approximating functions, one should stay away from polynomial interpolation, even for well-behaved functions. In fact, the literature is littered with comments along those lines.

There are reasons why such a reputation was built, partly due to results that appeared at the beginning of the 20th century that seemed to give a strong indication that polynomial interpolation was ill-behaved. This was compounded by the fact that the results that showed their potential as function approximators within practical applications remained largely ignored for a long time.

This chapter will show that the bad reputation just mentioned is unwarranted. In fact, quite the opposite is true. We bring to the fore the results (some of which have been known for a long time), which show that in everyday applications, polynomial interpolation is practically unbeatable.

3.1 APPROXIMATING FUNCTIONS WITH POLYNOMIALS

Polynomial functions are a well-understood family of functions used in various areas of mathematics. One of their uses has been to approximate arbitrary continuous functions. There is evidence of it that goes back as far as 1885 ([76]), when Weierstrass showed that for any given continuous function, there exists a polynomial that approximates it as closely as needed.

Theorem 3.1.1 (Weierstrass Approximation Theorem) *Let f be a continuous function on $[-1, 1]$ and let ϵ be an arbitrary real value greater than zero. There is a polynomial p such that*

$$\|f - p\|_\infty \leq \epsilon.$$

This result, however, does not give a recipe for how to find p, given f, at least not one that can be used in numerical computing within a context where ease and practicality are paramount.

There are two things to bear in mind when deciding what polynomial p to use as a proxy. On the one hand, accuracy. On the other hand, particularly in applications like the ones that concern this book, evaluating the polynomial or approximating objects as efficiently as possible on a computer.

Often, these two aims pull in different directions. Generally, the higher the accuracy requirements, the more complex the evaluation becomes. Let us express this more concretely.

Filtration of spaces of polynomials

Denote the space of polynomials by $\mathcal{P}$. Consider its canonical filtration

$$\mathcal{P} = \bigcup_{n \in \mathbb{N}} \mathcal{P}_n, \tag{3.1}$$

where $\mathcal{P}_n$ is the space of polynomials of degree at most n. The higher the n, the more polynomials available to choose from. If it is not possible to find a polynomial p in $\mathcal{P}_n$ that approximates the function f sufficiently well, we need to look for polynomials in $\mathcal{P}_m$ where $m > n$. The higher the m, the higher the degrees of the polynomials. However, the higher the degree m, the longer it takes to evaluate.

We want a systematic way to find, for low values of n, polynomials in $\mathcal{P}_n$ that approximate f to the degree we need. This is central to the applications presented in this book. It is in this sense that the theory of Chebyshev projections provides an extraordinary balance between the two, as will be seen in the following sections.

3.2   CHEBYSHEV SERIES

The previous section presented the Weierstrass Approximation Theorem (3.1.1). It says that continuous functions can be approximated by polynomials to any degree of accuracy. The problem is that it does not give a recipe of how to find such polynomials. Chebyshev Series give a way of obtaining such polynomials for a particular sub-class of continuous functions.

In what follows in this section, for ease of explanation and as a building block, the functions considered are one-dimensional and defined on the closed bounded interval $[-1, 1]$. If the function in question f is defined on a generic interval $[a, b]$, it can be pre-composed with a linear scaling function that takes the interval $[-1, 1]$ to $[a, b]$. Doing this gives a function g defined on the interval $[-1, 1]$. Every result stated from now on valid for g will also be valid for f. This section will only focus on results that apply to dimension 1. In coming sections, we will extend definitions and results to higher dimensions.

The results that constitute the core of the theory of Chebyshev approximation are valid for continuous functions that enjoy a certain degree of smoothness. Though in principle restrictive, this turns out to be particularly useful in our context, as functions in finance are often not only piece-wise continuous but piece-wise differentiable and, indeed, in most cases, piece-wise analytic, if not globally analytic.

Analytic functions

The notion of an analytic function is one of paramount importance for the remainder of this book. Therefore, it is worthwhile reminding the reader of the definition of an analytic function.

Definition 3.2.1 *A function f is analytic if for every point x in its domain, the Taylor Series of f at x exists and converges to the value f(x).*

Note that, in particular, analytic functions are infinitely differentiable. Although, strictly speaking, being analytic is a stronger property than being infinitely differentiable (that is, there are infinitely differentiable functions that are not analytic), in most practical instances, being infinitely differentiable is the same as being analytic.

As we mentioned before, some of the results that constitute the mathematical backbone of many of the solutions to the practical problems presented in Part IV rest on the assumption that the functions we work with enjoy high degrees of smoothness and in most cases are analytic or piece-wise analytic. As we argue later on in the book, in Section 13.1, this is a reasonable assumption to make. Moreover, the numerical results presented in Part IV back this assumption empirically.

It is also important to note that quantitative analysts often speak of analytic functions (or analytic solutions) as those that can be expressed with a formula. This is in contrast to those that are evaluated via numerical methods — for example, with Monte Carlo simulations. It is to be noted that this use of the term 'analytic' often used by quants refers to the method of evaluation on a computer, not to the mathematical properties we refer to in Definition 3.2.1. It is indeed true that even when the values of a function may be obtained (approximated) via Monte Carlo simulations, this does not mean the function is not analytic. From now on, whenever we say a function is analytic, we assume that Definition 3.2.1 holds, regardless of whether the function can or cannot be expressed through a formula, and regardless of how it is evaluated on a computer.

3.2.1 Lipschitz continuity and Chebyshev projections

A Lipschitz continuous function is a function that, in addition to being continuous, has a bounded variation between any two generic points.

Definition 3.2.2 *A real-valued function f* : $\mathbb{R} \to \mathbb{R}$ *called Lipschitz continuous if there exists a positive real constant K such that, for all real x_1 and x_2*

$$|f(x_1) - f(x_2)| \leq K|x_1 - x_2|.$$

The following polynomials constitute the basis of approximation we use throughout this book. These are the *Chebyshev polynomials*, sometimes also referred to in the literature as Chebyshev polynomials of first kind.

Definition 3.2.3   *The k-th Chebyshev polynomial is defined as*

$$T_k(x) = \cos(k\theta)$$

where

$$\theta = \cos^{-1}(x)$$

The polynomials defined in Definition 3.2.3 are also known as Chebyshev polynomials of the first kind. There is such a thing as Chebyshev polynomials of the second kind. Although the latter also enjoy interesting properties, we will only focus on the former. Chebyshev polynomials of the first kind suffice for the type of applications we are interested in — Part IV of this book. Examples of the first 4 Chebyshev polynomials are shown in Figure 3.1.

The following results are central in the theory of Chebyshev approximation theory. Proof of the following theorems can be found in in Chapters 3, 7 and 8 of [72].

The first of these theorems says that if the function enjoys mild smoothness conditions (such as being Lipschitz continuous), then the Chebyshev Series converges uniformly and absolutely. Essentially, terms in the series can be re-ordered and changed to their absolute values and convergence can still take place with respect to the uniform norm, which is the maximum error of approximation.

Convergence for Lipschitz continuous functions

Theorem 3.2.4 *If f is Lipschitz continuous on* $[-1, 1]$, *it has a unique representation as a Chebyshev Series,*

$$f(x) = \sum_{k=0}^{\infty} a_k T_k(x), \tag{3.2}$$

which is absolutely and uniformly convergent. The coefficients are given for $k \geq 1$ *by the formula*

$$a_k = \frac{2}{\pi} \int_{-1}^{1} \frac{f(x) T_k(x)}{\sqrt{1 - x^2}} \tag{3.3}$$

If $k = 0$, *the above formula is divided by 2.*

Theorem 3.2.4 gives a way of approximating Lipschitz continuous functions using polynomials that result from truncating Equation 3.2. Given a natural number n, the truncation of the Chebyshev Series up to its n-th degree is defined by

$$f_n(x) = \sum_{k=0}^{n} a_k T_k(x). \tag{3.4}$$

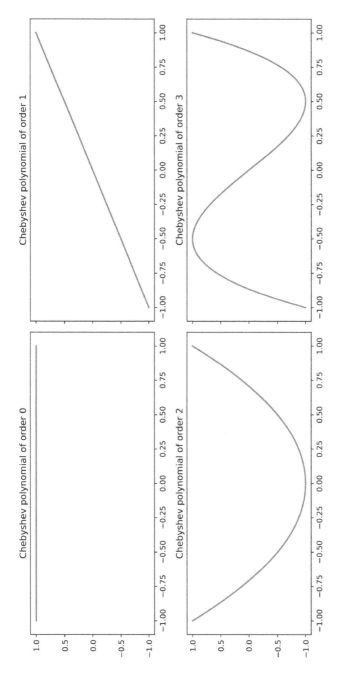

FIGURE 3.1 Chebyshev polynomials from degree 0 to degree 3.

Each vector space $\mathcal{P}_n$ from the filtration presented in Equation 3.1 can be endowed with an inner product induced by

$$\langle T_k, T_l \rangle = \frac{2}{\pi} \int_{-1}^{1} \frac{T_k(x) T_l(x)}{\sqrt{1 - x^2}}$$

where T_k and T_l are the Chebyshev polynomials of degree k and l, respectively, and where $k, l \leq n$. The truncation f_n is also called the *Chebyshev projection* of degree n because, with respect to this inner product, the n-th degree Chebyshev truncation is the projection onto the vector space of polynomials $\mathcal{P}_n$.

3.2.2   Smooth functions and Chebyshev projections

So far, the convergence of the Chebyshev Series for Lipschitz continuous functions has been established. This is a good starting point, but we need to make sure the desired degree of accuracy is obtained with the smallest possible n. Otherwise, the computational effort to evaluate f_n could be too high for it to be useful in contexts where speed and precision are critical. Therefore, it is important to use polynomials with the smallest degree possible. As we will see, the Chebyshev Series enjoys phenomenal convergence rates for a substantial class of functions. For these classes of functions, the projections used have the smallest possible degree (i.e. n is small).

The following theorem establishes that for functions that are not only Lipschitz continuous but differentiable, such n is smaller.

Convergence for differentiable functions

Theorem 3.2.5 *For an integer $m \geq 0$, let f and its derivatives up to and including f^{m-1} be absolutely continuous on $[-1, 1]$. Furthermore, suppose the m-th derivative f^m is of bounded variation V. Then for any $n > m$, its Chebyshev projections satisfy*

$$\|f - f_n\|_\infty \leq \frac{2V}{\pi m (n - m)^m} \tag{3.5}$$

For full details on this theorem, we refer to [72].

There is a further refinement of the previous theorem. If the class of functions is restricted even further, convergence rates improve. The class of functions for which the strongest results are obtained is the class of analytic function.

3.2.3   Analytic functions and Chebyshev projections

The following theorem is a strengthening of Theorem 3.2.5. It says that if the function in question is analytic, then the convergence of the Chebyshev Series is the highest rate of convergence one can expect in practice, that is, *exponential convergence*.

Convergence for analytic functions

A function *f* is analytic if for every point *x* in its domain, the Taylor Series of *f* at *x* exists and converges to the value $f(x)$.

It is a well-known fact that when a function is analytic on $[-1, 1]$ it can be analytically extended to a neighbourhood in the complex plane around $[-1, 1]$. The regions of interest where analytic functions are extended to are ellipses with foci at -1 and 1, called Bernstein ellipses. The following theorem first appeared in [6]. For a more thorough discussion on the following theorem, we refer to [72].

Theorem 3.2.6 *Let f be an analytic function on the interval* $[-1, 1]$. *Consider its analytical continuation to the open Bernstein ellipse* E_ρ, *of radius* ρ, *where it satisfies* $|f(x)| \leq M$, *for some M. Then, for each* $n \geq 0$

$$\|f - f_n\|_\infty \leq \frac{2M\rho^{-n}}{\rho - 1}$$

where f_n *is the Chebyshev projection of degree n.*

It is worth pointing out that in pure areas of study such as classical analysis, a lot of attention is paid to exceptional cases. For example, will the Chebyshev Series converge if Lipschitz continuity is replaced by a weaker condition? Fascinating as questions of this type may be, most real-world applications involve functions that enjoy high degrees of smoothness (outside a finite collection of points) and we do not need to worry about pathological cases.

For the purposes of this book, Theorem 3.2.6 is completely relevant as many of the financial functions we deal with in coming chapters are analytic (see Section 13.1). In fact, this is often the underlying assumption made about these functions when they are approximated with their Greeks, a type of approximation seen very often. For these functions, Theorem 3.2.6 says that Chebyshev projections of small degree give very good degrees of approximation.

Remark 3.2.7 The following point is worth highlighting. Although the properties of Chebyshev projections have remained somewhat hidden, the properties of Fourier approximations of periodic functions have not. Many of the results valid in the Fourier setting have their exact counterparts in the setting of function approximation with Chebyshev polynomials. Indeed, it suffices to note the definition of Chebyshev polynomials given in Definition 3.2.3, where these are expressed in terms of cosines, themselves the basis for Fourier approximation. Therefore, a problem stated in terms of Chebyshev polynomials can often be presented as a problem in the Fourier context.

3.3 CHEBYSHEV TENSORS AND INTERPOLANTS

As is evident from Theorems 3.2.4, 3.2.5 and 3.2.6, Chebyshev projections offer a very attractive way of approximating piece-wise analytic (or even differentiable) functions. However, evaluating such projections may be tricky as the coefficients in Equation 3.3 involve solving the integral in question. Such integrals usually involve evaluating the function to be approximated, $f(x)$, many times. We remind the reader that the evaluation of f is precisely what we aim to avoid in the range of applications presented in later chapters.

Fortunately, there are polynomial interpolants that enjoy the same convergence rates present in Theorems 3.2.4, 3.2.5 and 3.2.6. Moreover, these interpolants have expressions that are much easier to obtain and evaluate.

3.3.1 Tensors and polynomial interpolants

A tensor is a very basic mathematical object that will play an important role in what remains in this book. They are closely related to polynomial interpolants and will constitute the objects with which we approximate the functions relevant to the applications presented in later chapters.

Definition 3.3.1 *A tensor consists of a grid of points in Euclidean space along with a collection of real values, one per point in the grid.*

For example, a set of points $x_0, \ldots, x_n$ on the real line and a set of real values $v_0, \ldots, v_n$, where x_i is associated with v_i, for all i, $0 \le i \le n$, constitutes a tensor T of dimension 1. An example is given in Figure 3.2.

Polynomial interpolants are intimately related to tensors.

Definition 3.3.2 *Let T be a tensor. That is, a set of points $x_0, \ldots, x_n$ in Euclidean space with associated real values $v_0, \ldots, v_n$. A polynomial interpolant to T is a polynomial p such that $p(x_i) = v_i$, for all i, such that $0 \le i \le n$.*

FIGURE 3.2 Tensor of dimension 1. Grid given by balls. Values on grid points by stars.

It is a well-known result that not only are there polynomial interpolants to T, as defined in Definition 3.3.2, but there is a unique polynomial interpolant to T of degree at most n.[1]

The tensors and polynomial interpolants of relevance to this book are the ones obtained from functions. Obtaining a tensor given a function f is straightforward. Given a function f and set of points $x_0, \ldots, x_n$ on its domain, consider the tensor defined by $x_0, \ldots, x_n$ and the values $f(x_0), \ldots, f(x_n)$. As mentioned before, this tensor has a unique polynomial interpolant of degree at most n. Therefore, given a function f and a grid of points $x_0, \ldots, x_n$, there is a tensor and a corresponding polynomial interpolant that can potentially be used as a proxy for f.

Given a function f, the aim is the following: as the number of grid points $x_0, \ldots, x_n$ increases, a sequence of polynomial interpolants p_n is defined. The question is whether this sequence converges to f and if so, at what rate.

If there is a way of defining a sequence of interpolants that converges to f exponentially with respect to the number of grid points, then evaluating f on a few selected points yields a polynomial that can be used as a very accurate proxy for f. This has tremendous advantages, as it bypasses the main computational bottleneck, which is the overhead of calling financial functions f many times.

There are two main factors that determine whether the sequence of polynomial interpolants p_n, as just defined, converges to f, and if so, at what rate. The first is the geometry of the grid points $x_0, \ldots, x_n$. This is critical. For some geometries, the results can be disastrous.

There are two results that date back to the beginning of the 20th century that are partly responsible for the bad reputation polynomial interpolants have. The first one is due to Runge, who gave an example of a one-dimensional analytic function for which equidistant interpolation diverges exponentially [63].

Analytic functions, by definition, enjoy a high degree of smoothness. Equidistant points are a natural choice for interpolation if there is no a priori information to say otherwise. This example shows how polynomial interpolation, if not done properly, can have terrible consequences even on well-behaved functions.

Figure 3.3 shows the exponential divergence that characterises the Runge phenomenon. As the number of grid points increases, there is a clear difference between the Runge function and the polynomial interpolants defined on equidistant grids. This is particularly notorious toward the endpoints where the distance between the polynomial interpolants and the Runge function increases dramatically as the number of grid points increases.

The second result, due to Faber, says that there is no interpolation scheme that guarantees convergence for the set of continuous one-dimensional functions [24]. That is, there is no generic way of defining interpolants that works for all continuous one-dimensional functions.

3.3.2 Misconception over polynomial interpolation

Results such as these cemented a belief that using polynomial interpolants as approximators of functions (even analytic ones) is not appropriate. Even a good proportion of

---

[1]This is known as the interpolation theorem. For details we refer to [78].

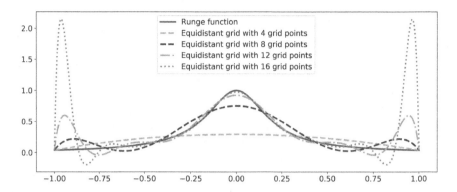

FIGURE 3.3   Exponential divergence from Runge function by polynomial interpolants on equidistant points.

the textbooks in the subject of function approximation, written in the second half of the 20th century, warn against the use of polynomial interpolants. For example,

---

Misleading quotes

Polynomial interpolants rarely converge to a general continous function (1989).

Interpolation is a notoriously tricky problem from the point of view of numerical stability (1990).

    As we will see in this book, these two statements are very misleading, especially when restricted to functions normally encountered in practical settings.[2]

    What has often been missed, even by the wider community of numerical analysts, is that interpolation on carefully selected points makes polynomial interpolation perfectly stable and efficient in most practical cases. At the heart of this confusion lies the lack of awareness of the barycentric interpolation formula, which will be described in Section 3.6.

3.3.3   Chebyshev points

The geometry of points for the tensors and associated polynomial interpolants considered henceforth is the one determined by the Chebyshev points. The reason will become evident in this and coming sections.

---

[2]For more examples and an in-depth discussion on the misleading nature of such statements, we refer to the appendix in [72] and [73].

Definition 3.3.3 *Let $\{z_j\}_{j=0}^{2n-1}$ be the 2n-roots of unity, that is, the 2n equidistant points on the unitary circle. These are the points on the complex plane that satisfy the equation $z = z^{2n}$ and are explicitly given by*

$$z_j = \exp\left(\frac{j\pi i}{n}\right) = \cos\frac{j\pi}{n} + i\sin\frac{j\pi}{n}, \qquad j = 0, 1, \ldots, 2n - 1.$$

The Chebyshev points associated with the natural number n are the real part of the points z_j

$$x_j = \operatorname{Re}(z_j) = \frac{1}{2}(z_j + z_j^{-1}).$$

Equivalently, Chebyshev points can be defined as

$$x_j = \cos\left(\frac{j\pi}{n}\right), \qquad 0 \le j \le n.$$

These points are the result of projecting equidistant points on the upper half of the unitary circle onto the real line. Figure 3.4 shows the Chebyshev points for $n = 12$.

The definition of Chebyshev points is given for an interval $[-1, 1]$. This, however, can be extended to any interval $[a, b]$ by mapping $[-1, 1]$ to $[a, b]$, with the aid of a linear transformation followed by a translation.

The following definition shows how to extend Chebyshev grids to dimensions greater than one.

Definition 3.3.4 *Let A be a hyper-rectangle in $\mathbb{R}^n$. That is, A is defined as the Cartesian product of one-dimensional closed and bounded intervals I_i, $A = I_1 \times \cdots \times I_n$. Let χ_i be Chebyshev points corresponding to the interval I_i; for all i, $1 \le i \le n$. We define the grid of Chebyshev points on A generated by $\chi_1, \ldots, \chi_n$ as the Cartesian product of the sets χ_i, $\chi = \chi_1, \times \cdots \times \chi_n$.*

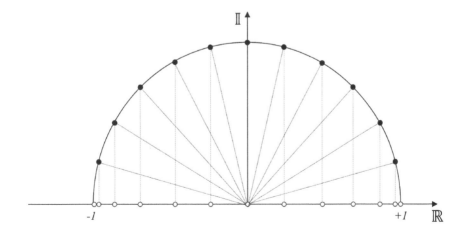

FIGURE 3.4 Chebyshev points in one dimension.

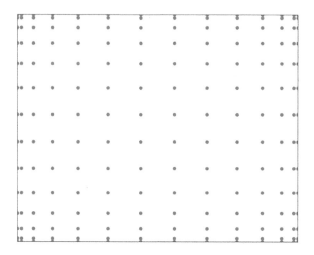

FIGURE 3.5 Chebyshev grid in two dimensions.

Using the notation in Definition 3.3.4, if the number of Chebyshev points in χ_i is m_i, then the number of points on the multidimensional Chebyshev grid is $m_1 \cdots m_n$. Figure 3.5 shows an example of a two-dimensional mesh.

Chebyshev points as defined in this section give rise to *CTs*. As the reader may suspect, these are tensors where the grid of points is given as defined in Definition 3.3.4.

3.3.4 Chebyshev interpolants

One of the main advantages of working with Chebyshev points is that polynomial interpolation on Chebyshev points has the same convergence properties as Chebyshev projections.

Denote the polynomial interpolant to a continuous function f on the first $n + 1$ Chebyshev points by p_n. Such a polynomial lies in $\mathcal{P}_n$, the space of polynomials of degree at most n. As such, it may be expressed as a linear combination of the first $n + 1$ Chebyshev polynomials (indeed, as the linear combination of any basis for $\mathcal{P}_n$):

$$p_n(x) = \sum_{k=0}^{n} c_k T_k(x). \tag{3.6}$$

Remark 3.3.5 One of the main properties of Equation 3.6 is that it can be obtained very easily. As it is shown in [58], one can compute the coefficients c_k from the values of f on Chebyshev points by using the Fast Fourier Transform. This has important consequences as the Fast Fourier Transform can be applied in only $\mathcal{O}(n\log(n))$ operations.

This property is very useful when computing with Chebyshev polynomials; we do not incur big overheads trying to compute the coefficients that determine p_n. As long as we have access to evaluating f, all we need is to apply the Fast Fourier Transform. Contrast this with the difficulty of computing the coefficients a_k in Equation 3.4.

3.3.5 Aliasing phenomenon

Easily obtaining the coefficients c_k that define the expression in Equation 3.6 is a good start. However, for the purposes of this book, this is of use only if the expression approximates its corresponding function f to a high degree of accuracy for low values of n. Fortunately, the coefficients c_k from Equation 3.6 are linked to the coefficients a_k from Equation 3.3 through the phenomenon of aliasing. This phenomenon reveals some of the deep mathematical properties that Chebyshev interpolants have as function approximators.

The full details of aliasing are beyond the scope of this book. Nevertheless, we present the following theorem ([11]), which explicitly describes the relationship between the a_k and c_k coefficients and sets the stage for a very useful technique, which will be presented in Section 3.4, which helps control the error of Chebyshev interpolants in a very effective way.

Qualitatively speaking, the following theorem says that the information carried by the coefficients a_k of the Chebyshev Series can be encoded in the coefficients c_k of the Chebyshev interpolant.

Theorem 3.3.6 *Let f be Lipschitz continuous on $[-1, 1]$ and let p_n be its Chebyshev interpolant in $\mathcal{P}_n$, $n \geq 1$. Let a_k and c_k be the Chebyshev coefficients of f_n and p_n, respectively. Then*

$$c_0 = a_0 + a_{2n} + a_{4n} + \ldots,$$

$$c_n = a_n + a_{3n} + a_{5n} + \ldots,$$

and for $1 \leq k \leq n - 1$

$$c_k = a_k + (a_{2n+k} + a_{4n+k} + \ldots) + (a_{2n-k} + a_{4n-k} + \ldots).$$

3.3.6 Convergence rates of Chebyshev interpolants

The aliasing phenomenon, along with the proofs of Theorems 3.2.4, 3.2.5 and 3.2.6, yield the following theorems, fundamental in all we do for the rest of this book. Proofs and detailed discussion of these is beyond the scope of this book. We refer the interested reader to Chapters 4, 7 and 8 of [72] for further details.

Theorem 3.3.7 says that for smooth functions, Chebyshev interpolants converge in polynomial time. This is already a fast type of convergence.

Convergence for differentiable functions in dimension 1

Theorem 3.3.7 *Let f satisfy the conditions of Theorem 3.2.5. Then for any $n > m$*

$$\|f - p_n\|_\infty \leq \frac{4V}{\pi m(n - m)^m}.$$

However, Theorem 3.3.8 says that for analytic functions, convergence is exponential. This is as fast as can be expected and ideal in practical settings.

Convergence for analytic functions in dimension 1

Theorem 3.3.8 *Let f satisfy the conditions of Theorem 3.2.6. Then for any $n \geq 0$*

$$\|f - p_n\|_\infty \leq \frac{4M\rho^{-n}}{\rho - 1}.$$

Equation 3.6, along with Theorems 3.3.7 and 3.3.8, show why polynomial interpolation on Chebyshev points is a very attractive method for approximation. First, as Remark 3.3.5 points out, an explicit expression for the interpolator is easily obtained by simply evaluating the function f on Chebyshev points and applying the Fast Fourier Transform. That is, the integrals of Equation 3.3, which require the value of f at many points, are not needed. Second, the greater the number of interpolating points, the greater the accuracy. In particular, when f is analytic, the rate of convergence is exponential.

Figures 3.6 and 3.7 show two examples of how the error of approximation obtained with Chebyshev interpolants decays exponentially as we increase the number of Chebyshev points. Figure 3.6 was obtained approximating the Runge function. Note that this is the function for which equidistant interpolation diverges exponentially. By changing only the geometry of the points we get exactly the opposite kind of approximation behaviour. Figure 3.7 shows the same exponential decay with the Black-Scholes pricing function, one of the most common and well-known pricing functions in finance. Note that in both figures the y-axis is given in logarithmic scale.

Comparison with best possible approximants

Chebyshev interpolants compare very favourably even with the best possible polynomial approximants.

Denote by p_n^* the polynomial in $\mathcal{P}_n$ that minimises $\|f - q_n\|_\infty$, the distance between f and $\mathcal{P}_n$, where q_n denotes a generic polynomial in $\mathcal{P}_n$. The polynomial p_n^* is basically the best possible polynomial approximation to f of degree less than or equal to n. Such a polynomial, though in principle ideal for approximation purposes, is often difficult to compute. Not only are Chebyshev interpolants easy to compute, but as proved in [34], if p_n is the Chebyshev interpolant of degree n, $\|f - p_n\|_\infty$ cannot exceed $\|f - p_n^*\|_\infty$ by more than the factor $2 + (2/\pi)\log(n + 1)$. Moreover, if f is analytic, such a factor is only 2. This means, that in practical contexts, Chebyshev interpolants are essentially as good as best polynomial approximators.

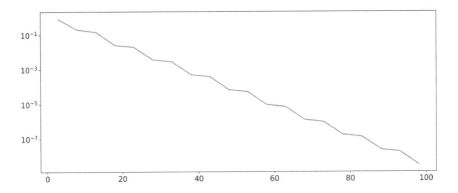

FIGURE 3.6   Chebyshev interpolants convergence to Runge function.

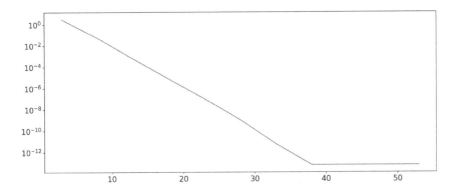

FIGURE 3.7   Chebyshev interpolants convergence error to Black-Scholes function in dimension 1.

3.3.7   High-dimensional Chebyshev interpolants

Chebyshev interpolators have high-dimensional analogues. Although the one-dimensional version has existed for more than a century, generalisations to higher dimensions were not seriously considered until recently.

There is more than one way in which one can extend the notion of Chebyshev interpolants to dimensions greater than one. The following one appears in [27].

Definition of Chebyshev interpolants in dimensions greater than one

Definition 3.3.9   *Consider the hyper-rectangle* $[-1, 1]^d$ *in* $\mathbb{R}^d$. *For each dimension consider* $n_i + 1$ *Chebyshev points, where* $1 \le i \le d$. *By Definition 3.3.4, this defines a Chebyshev grid for* $[-1, 1]^d$. *Let* $f_{(k_1, \dots, k_d)}$ *be the value of a function* f *on the Chebyshev point* $p_{(k_1, \dots, k_d)}$, *where* $0 \le k_i \le n_i$. *Then, the Chebyshev interpolant to* f *evaluated at*

(continued)

(continued)

p, where $p = (p_1, \ldots, p_d)$ is a generic point in $\in [-1, 1]^d$, is

$$\sum_{j \in J} c_j T_j(p),$$

The index j is an element of the set $J = \{(j_1, \ldots, j_d) \mid 0 \leq j_i \leq n_i\}$ and the functions T_j are defined as

$$T_j(p_1, \ldots, p_d) = \prod_{i=1}^{d} T_{j_i}(p_i).$$

The coefficients c_j are given by

$$c_j = \left(\prod_{i=1}^{d} \frac{2^{1(\{0 < j_i < n_i\})}}{n_i} \right)$$

$$\times \sum_{k_1=0}^{n_1}{}' \cdots \sum_{k_d=0}^{n_d}{}' f_{(k_1, \ldots, k_d)} \prod_{i=1}^{d} \cos\left(j_i \pi \frac{k_i}{n_i} \right), \qquad (3.7)$$

where the symbol ' in Equation 3.7 means the summation is multiplied by 0.5, when $k_i = 0, n_i$.

Note that Definition 3.3.9 relies on computing the coefficients c_j obtained through Equation 3.7. This computation increases in cost considerably as d increases. This is just one of the ways in which the curse of dimensionality appears, something which will be discussed in detail in Section 4.3.

The next theorem, published in [27], shows that when the function f is analytic, the convergence of Chebyshev interpolants is sub-exponential, which is as good as can be hoped for within a function approximation framework in high dimensions.

Convergence for analytic functions in dimensions greater than one

Theorem 3.3.10 *Let f be a d-dimensional analytic function defined on $[-1, 1]^d$. Consider its analytic continuation to a generalised Bernstein ellipse E_p, where it satisfies $\| f \|_\infty \leq M$, for some M. Then, there exists a constant $C > 0$, such that*

$$\| f - p_n \|_\infty \leq C \rho^{-m} \qquad (3.8)$$

where $\rho = min_{(1 \leq i \leq d)} \rho_i$ and $m = min_{(1 \leq i \leq d)} m_i$. The collection of values ρ_i define the radius of the generalised Bernstein ellipse E_p, and the values m_i define the size of the Chebyshev mesh (see Definition 3.3.4). For full details on Theorem 3.3.10, its proof and related results, see [27].

Remark 3.3.11 It is very important to note that all the theorems presented so far, which relate to the convergence properties of CTs and corresponding interpolants, specify a domain over which the approximation takes place. That is, once the function f to be approximated has been restricted to some domain D, the CT built to approximate it will only enjoy the properties mentioned in the statements of the theorems on D. Therefore, we cannot expect any certainty in the degree of accuracy if we evaluate the CT on a point x outside of the domain of approximation D.

There are other ways of defining interpolants on Chebyshev points. The one we find to be optimal in a practical setting builds high-dimensional interpolants using one-dimensional ones as building blocks. The following description shows how to define the two-dimensional case. The low dimension was chosen for ease of presentation. Then we generalise to higher dimensions.

Take the Chebyshev grid shown on Figure 3.8 and a function f defined over the rectangular domain covered by the grid. Each Chebyshev point along the y-axis (second dimension) defines a Chebyshev grid that runs parallel to the x-axis (first dimension). For each of these grids running horizontally, a one-dimensional Chebyshev polynomial can be built. Then, the collection of all Chebyshev interpolants defined this way constitutes the *Chebyshev interpolant of dimension* 2.

Extending this definition to higher dimensions is straightforward. Say the dimension of the Chebyshev grid is n. Forget for a second the first dimension and consider

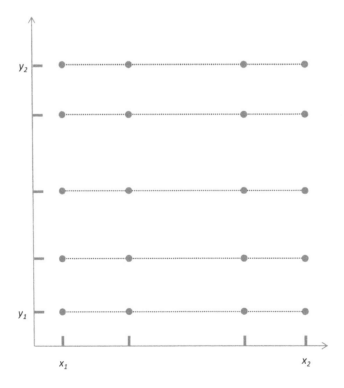

FIGURE 3.8 Chebyshev interpolant in dimension 2.

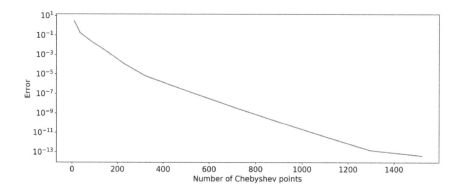

FIGURE 3.9 Chebyshev interpolants error convergence to Black-Scholes function in dimension 2 (Spot and Volatility).

points $\{x_2, \ldots, x_n\}$ in the remaining $n-1$ dimensions corresponding to Chebyshev points. That is, the point x_2 is a Chebyshev point in the second dimension, x_3 a Chebyshev point in the third dimension, and so on. Then, on the one-dimensional space defined by $\{x, x_2, \ldots, x_n\}$, where the first entry varies while the rest are fixed at Chebyshev points, one can build a one-dimensional Chebyshev interpolant. By doing this for every possible combination of Chebyshev points $\{x_2, \ldots, x_n\}$, one builds a collection of one-dimensional Chebyshev interpolants that constitute the n-dimensional interpolant for f.

The extension to higher dimensions described is the one assumed for the rest of the book and the one that has been implemented in the MoCaX Library (Chapter 24). The main advantage of this definition is its simplicity, paramount in practical applications. It leverages from the one-dimensional case allowing for quick implementation, direct extension of the operations for one dimension to higher dimensions (such as computing the derivatives of CTs, Section 3.7), while retaining great convergence properties directly inherited from the convergence properties of one-dimensional CTs.

Notice that there is no need to express the interpolant in terms of Chebyshev polynomials as is done in Definition 3.3.9. This has the added advantage of avoiding the computation of the coefficients c_j, obtained by repeatedly applying the Fast Fourier Transform, which becomes an undesired overhead as the dimension of the tensor increases.

Figure 3.9 shows how the error of approximation decays quasi-exponentially when we use Chebyshev interpolants to approximate the Black-Scholes pricing function with an input domain of dimension 2. Note that the y-axis is in logarithmic scale. The version of the CT (interpolator) used is the one described and implemented in the MoCaX Library.

3.4 EX ANTE ERROR ESTIMATION

Another important consequence of Theorem 3.3.6 is that one can estimate the error of the approximation without knowing anything about the function, other than the values of the function on Chebyshev points and the fact that it is Lipschitz continuous. This is quite a remarkable property that has important practical implications, especially in the context of heavy Monte Carlo or historical risk simulations where having an idea of the error of approximation before the simulation is launched allows for on-the-fly accuracy adjustments. This will be discussed in later chapters.

For now, the following gives a high-level description of where this error estimate comes from. In what follows, all error estimates correspond to the supremum norm — that is, the maximum error attained on the domain where a function and a tensor can be compared.[3]

Ex ante error estimation

Theorem 3.2.4 says that the Chebyshev Series is uniformly and absolutely convergent. This implies that as n tends to infinity, the absolute values of a_n tend to zero. This, coupled with the equations in Theorem 3.3.6, implies that the greater the n, the smaller the terms $(a_{2n+k} + a_{4n+k} + \dots)$ and $(a_{2n-k} + a_{4n-k} + \dots)$, which means the terms c_k and a_k get closer and closer for $1 \leq k \leq n - 1$.

On the one hand, the coefficients a_n give an idea of when we are close to converging. On the other hand, close to convergence, the coefficients c_k approximate the coefficients a_k ($1 \leq k \leq n - 1$). As the coefficients c_k are much easier to compute than the coefficients a_k (using the Fast Fourier Transform), the former can be used to identify potential convergence.

It must be noted that, strictly speaking, there is no guarantee that the series of Chebyshev interpolants has converged to the function if, say, the last few coefficients c_k are below a desired threshold. In practice, however, and especially for analytic functions such as financial functions, once the absolute value of the coefficients c_k are below a small threshold (e.g. 10^{-4}), we can be pretty sure our Chebyshev interpolant will give us at most this error. At the time of this text going to press, the authors of this book have never encountered an exception to this rule in a real-world problem.

This has practical implications as one can control the error of the approximation using only the values of the function on Chebyshev points. Therefore, if after n Chebyshev points have been sampled, the level of accuracy, estimated using the coefficients c_k, is not the one we need, we can enlarge the set of Chebyshev points, compute the new coefficients c_k and estimate the error once more. This process can be iterated until the error estimated is below a chosen level.

The advantage is that this process is very cheap as we only sample f on Chebyshev points. Moreover, the collection of Chebyshev points considered at each iteration of the process can be chosen to contain the previous grid of Chebyshev points, saving us from evaluating f on the Chebyshev points from the previous iteration. All we need is to consider Chebyshev grids of size $2^i + 1$, for $i \geq$.

---

[3]The domain over which the comparison between the function and the tensor is performed is assumed to be compact. Hence, the supremum norm is attained at some point of the domain and it corresponds to the maximum error.

The error estimation just described can be used to estimate the empirical error under the supremum norm of an already existing CT. This has been implemented within the MoCaX Library. The details of how to use it can be found in Chapter 24.

However, there is another process within the MoCaX Library where the error estimation described figures prominently. In Section 24.2.1, a MoCaX object was built by specifying the number of Chebyshev points in each dimension (Listing 4). This is a perfectly good way of doing it. However, an object can also be built by specifying the desired accuracy error. An algorithm, based on the error estimate described, determines the number of grid points needed to achieve this level of accuracy. The way to build these objects using the MoCaX Library can be found in Chapter 24.

The following plots show how effective the ex ante error estimation is at predicting the empirical error. The test was done on the Black-Scholes pricing function f in dimension 1.

The plot was obtained doing the following. Chebyshev grids with increasing number of points were considered. For each, a CT (via a MoCaX object) was built and two errors estimated. The first is the empirical error. This was estimated by evaluating f and the MoCaX object on a fine grid of points of their domain, and comparing the values. The error considered was the maximum over the absolute values of the point-wise differences.[4] The second error was obtained by running the ex ante error estimation implemented within the MoCaX Library.

As can be seen from Figure 3.10, the ex ante error estimate matches the empirical error very well. Not only do both show the expected exponential decay as the number of grid points in the Chebyshev grid increases, but up to logarithmic scale, both error estimates are pretty much indistinguishable.

The algorithm described works in dimension 1. However, there is an analogue for higher dimensions that has been implemented within the MoCaX Library. To understand how, note that high-dimensional MoCaX objects consist of collections

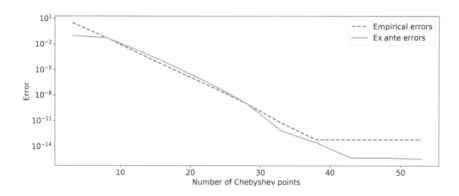

FIGURE 3.10   Empirical error versus predicted error for Black-Scholes function in dimension 1.

---

[4]This corresponds to an estimate of the error measured through the supremum norm $\| \ \|_\infty$.

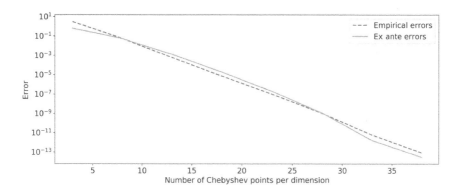

FIGURE 3.11 Empirical error versus predicted error for Black-Scholes function in dimension 2.

of one-dimensional MoCaX objects (see Section 3.3.4). The algorithm for the error estimation can be applied to each of these one-dimensional objects and the highest value taken as an estimate of the error for the multidimensional object. Note that taking the largest of all the errors makes sense as we are interested in estimating the error obtained with the supremum norm ($\| \; \|_\infty$).

Figure 3.11 shows an example of a two-dimensional function for which the empirical error and the predicted error decay together in an exponential manner as the number of Chebyshev points are increased. This plot was obtained using the Black-Scholes pricing function in dimension 2, where spot and volatility define the input domain of the function.

3.5 WHAT MAKES CHEBYSHEV POINTS UNIQUE

As was discussed in Section 3.3.1, the effectiveness of polynomial interpolation as an approximating technique relies heavily on the geometry of the grid points. The Runge function is a dramatic example of an analytic function for which equidistant interpolation (some argue a natural choice) yields exponential divergence, while Chebyshev interpolation yields exponential convergence.

Take a look at Figure 3.12. This figure shows a sequence of approximations to the Runge function using polynomial interpolation. It starts with an interpolant defined over an equidistant grid (first plot) and finishes with one over Chebyshev points, passing through two grids where the distribution of points is in between equidistant and Chebyshev. As the grid points are moved toward Chebyshev, the degree of approximation completely changes. The contrast could not be starker. The natural question is, what makes distribution of points, such as Chebyshev, so special?

There is an interesting way of looking at the role played by the geometry of points. This comes from the Hermite integral formula and the potential field associated with a collection of point charges.

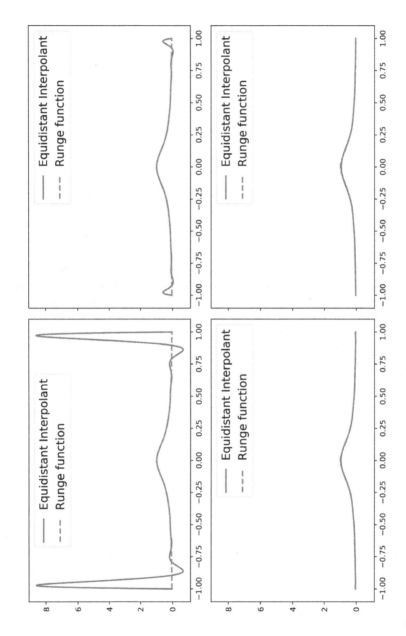

FIGURE 3.12 Approximating Runge function with different grid distributions. Starting with equidistant (top left), gradually moving grid point distribution to Chebyshev, ending with Chebyshev (bottom right).

The Hermite integral formula is one of the most powerful formulas in approximation theory. It says that the error of a polynomial interpolant is given by a contour integral, where the integrand is directly affected by the geometry of the grid points.

Hermite integral formula

Theorem 3.5.1 Hermite integral formula *Let f be an analytic function on the interval $[-1, 1]$. Let $p \in \mathcal{P}_n$ be the polynomial interpolant to f at the points $\{x_0, \ldots, x_n\}$. Let Γ be a path in the complex plane enclosing these points in the positive direction. Then, if x is a point enclosed by Γ, the error in the interpolant is given by*

$$f(x) - p(x) = \frac{1}{2\pi i} \int_\Gamma \frac{\ell(x)}{\ell(t)} \frac{f(t)}{(t-x)} dt. \tag{3.9}$$

There are a few comments worth making. The first is that this theorem is valid for analytic functions. Indeed the theorem requires f to be analytic in the area enclosed by the path Γ. Second is that the error is given for any point x; hence, if we are working with $x \in [-1, 1]$, by finding its maximum in that interval, we have a maximum error in the whole domain of interest. Third, a very interesting phenomenon arises when the geometry of the interpolation points $\{x_0, \ldots, x_n\}$ is considered via a beautiful relationship with a potential theory. For that, let us define ℓ and comment on it.

Given a set of points $\{x_0, \ldots, x_n\}$, the function $\ell \in \mathcal{P}_{n+1}$ is called the *node polynomial*,

$$\ell(x) = \prod_{k=0}^{n} (x - x_k). \tag{3.10}$$

Let us see what happens with the integrand in Equation 3.9 when we fix f and x but let the set of points $\{x_i\}$ vary. Notice the variable t runs on the contour Γ, while x on the interval $[-1, 1]$. Clearly, $f(t)$ and $(t - x)$ are not affected by the geometry and size of $\{x_0, \ldots, x_n\}$. However, the term $\ell(x)/\ell(t)$ is. It should therefore not come as a surprise that different geometries potentially give very different errors of approximation $f(x) - p(x)$.

The term $\ell(t)$ is directly related to the *discrete potential function* of a set of points $\{x_0, \ldots, x_n\}$. The potential function is defined by

$$w_n(t) = \frac{1}{n+1} \sum_{i=0}^{n} \log(t - x_i). \tag{3.11}$$

Using Equations 3.10 and 3.11, and after some algebraic manipulation, one obtains the following important relationship:

$$\left| \frac{\ell(x)}{\ell(t)} \right| = e^{(n+1)[w_n(x) - w_n(t)]}. \tag{3.12}$$

This expression says that the error of approximation depends (exponentially) on the difference between the potential evaluated on points on the interval $[-1, 1]$ and the potential evaluated on the path Γ. Minimising this quantity minimises the error.

One can think of the set of points $\{x_0, \ldots, x_n\}$ as a set of charges on the real line and Equation 3.11 as the potential field generated by this system of point charges. In other words, similar to the Newtonian gravitational theory, where the force scales with r^{-2} and the potential with r^{-1}, in this context the force scales by r^{-1} and its potential by $\log(r)$.[5]

One of the crucial properties of Chebyshev points is that as n tends to infinity, the potential field defined is constant. This means the force goes to zero. One can think of it as the equilibrium configuration that attains minimal energy. These are precisely the type of systems that help minimise the difference $w_n(x) - w_n(t)$, which in turn minimises the approximation error.

For a more in-depth discussion of what has been presented so far, we recommend Chapters 11 and 12 of [72].

Other families of polynomials and grid points

The family of Chebyshev points is not the only one with an associated potential field that attains minimal energy. Other families of polynomials, such as Legendre, Jacobi and Gegenbauer, have associated grids that enjoy this condition. These are discussed in more detail in Appendix A.

In principle, interpolation on such points gives good convergence properties. However, from a computational point of view, especially in contexts where simplicity and practicality matter, there are differences.

In this chapter, we discuss why Chebyshev polynomials stand out amongst them. Namely, they offer the simplest expressions to work with, paramount for applications like the ones relevant to this book. In the spirit of Occam's razor, it is always better to keep the tools and methods used to solve problems as simple as possible.[6]

There are plenty of examples that illustrate the difference made to the convergence properties of the approximating scheme by changing the interpolation points. We already saw an example of a well-behaved function for which equidistant interpolation gave very bad results. This was the Runge function, which is analytic. The surprising thing is that while equidistant interpolation gives exponential divergence, Chebyshev completely corrects this behaviour and gives exponential convergence (see Figure 3.6).

---

[5]The variable r denotes the distance between two charges.
[6]Occam's razor is normally associated with the idea that "the simplest solution is most likely the right one".

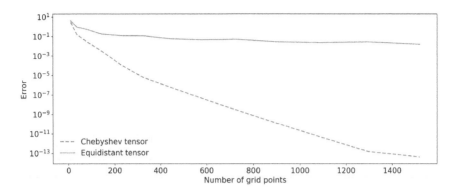

FIGURE 3.13 Comparison of errors obtained with equidistant tensors and CTs on a spot-volatility Black-Scholes surface.

Example 3.5.2 The following is another example but in a dimension greater than one, where changing the geometry of the points completely alters the rate at which we approximate a function. The function is the Black-Scholes formula, which is commonly used in finance. The domain variables considered were spot and volatility. Two families of tensors were built to approximate it. The first family consisted of tensors defined on equidistant points, the second of CTs. For each of these geometries of points, a varying number of points were considered.

Figure 3.13 shows the accuracy of each of these tensors. The x-axis denotes the number of grid points on the tensor, the y-axis the empirical error in logarithmic scale. The empirical error was obtained by defining a very fine grid of points on the domain and comparing the values of the Black-Scholes function with the corresponding values obtained by the tensor. The maximum of the absolute values of the point-wise differences was taken as the measure of error, that is, an estimate of the supremum norm.

As Figure 3.13 clearly shows, equidistant points define tensors or interpolants that converge toward the function very slowly as the size of the grid increases. The rate of convergence, however, completely changes when we switch to Chebyshev points. The error decay shown in Figure 3.13 is quasi-exponential, which is the rate at which CTs converge in dimension greater than one, as stated in Theorem 3.3.10.

3.6 EVALUATION OF CHEBYSHEV INTERPOLANTS

So far it has been established that Chebyshev interpolants have great convergence properties for smooth and analytic functions (Section 3.3.7). Also (and very important for our applications), expressions in terms of Chebyshev polynomials are easy to obtain. However, this section will show that we can do even better: Chebyshev interpolants can be evaluated efficiently and in a perfectly stable manner with just the values of the function on Chebyshev points. This endows Chebyshev interpolants with fantastic qualities when it comes to applications where computing cost, speed and accuracy of evaluation are paramount, such as the ones presented in Part IV.

One could naively think that evaluating a polynomial is always easy on a computer. Surprisingly, this is not necessarily the case. When carrying out computer calculations, it is important to work with robust and fast algorithms, especially in contexts where accuracy and speed are paramount, such as the ones that concern us. It is often missed that rounding errors on a computer can accumulate to the point that the values returned are completely different than what they should be in theory.

A good and pertinent example is one of the most popular algorithms for polynomial fitting and polynomial interpolation via the Vandermode linear system of equations, which is exponentially unstable (see Chapter 5 of [72]). Figure 3.15 shows this numerical instability on a function in which exponential convergence should be observed. This highlights how important it is to avoid methods such as the Vandermode one and instead use stable ones.

It is surprising that despite the numerical instability of the Vandermode method, it is widely used in standard software packages. For example, it figures as the *polyfit* command in MATLAB. It also appears in Python packages such as SciPy within methods such as *chebfit* and *polyfit*.

This section presents two ways of evaluating Chebyshev tensors and their corresponding interpolants in a fast and stable manner: the *Clenshaw algorithm* and the *barycentric interpolation formula*.

3.6.1 Clenshaw algorithm

In Section 3.3.4, we worked with the following expression for Chebyshev interpolants:

$$p_n(x) = \sum_{k=0}^{n} c_k T_k(x). \tag{3.13}$$

One major advantage of this expression is that the coefficients c_k are very easy to obtain. All that is needed is to evaluate the function f at Chebyshev points and then apply the Fast Fourier Transform. Another advantage is that it helps reveal, through the aliasing phenomenon presented in Theorem 3.3.6, some of the strong mathematical properties CTs and interpolators have, for example, the strong convergence properties of Theorem 3.3.8 and the error estimate capabilities presented in Section 3.4.

Another advatange of Equation 3.13 is that it can be evaluated in a fast and stable manner using the *Clenshaw algorithm*. The algorithm is defined in the following way.

Clenshaw algorithm

Set $v_{n+1} = 0, v_n = c_n$ and

$$v_k = 2xv_{k+1} - v_{k+2} + c_k, \qquad k = n-1, n-2, \ldots, 0. \tag{3.14}$$

Then $p(x) = \frac{1}{2}(c_0 + v_0 - v_2)$.
  Note the coefficients c_k are the ones in Equation 3.13.

There are three important aspects of this algorithm to highlight. The first is that it only uses the coefficients c_k. This means that the Clenshaw algorithm can be used once the function f has been evaluated on Chebyshev points and the Fast Fourier Transform has been applied on the resulting values, a process that only takes $\mathcal{O}(nlog(n))$, with respect to n, the degree of the interpolant. Second, it has linear complexity $\mathcal{O}(n)$. Third, it is numerically stable ([68]).

3.6.2 Barycentric interpolation formula

While the expression in Equation 3.13 offers many advantages, there is a more efficient way of evaluating Chebyshev interpolants (indeed interpolants in general), which bypasses the need to apply the Fast Fourier Transform while retaining all the advantages of the Clenshaw algorithm. This comes in the form of the *barycentric interpolation formula*, which is, as we will see, ideal for intensive computations.

The barycentric interpolation formula lies at the centre of the confusion about the effectiveness of polynomial interpolation presented in Section 3.3.2. Although Jacobi presented its most basic form back in 1825, the results by Faber ([24]) and Runge ([63]) at the beginning of the 20th century gave polynomial interpolation a bad name.

At this point, most of the work in numerical analysis was theoretical. Computers had not been invented and there was little interest in practical computations. This changed dramatically in the second half of the 20th century. From the 1940s onward, the tools that make polynomial interpolation effective were developed, with Dupuy developing the barycentric interpolation formula for general points in 1948 ([21]) and Salzer the specific case for Chebyshev points in 1972 ([66]). However, between 1950 and 2000, virtually all textbooks omit the barycentric interpolation formula (with a few exceptions) and (wrongly) say that polynomial interpolation is full of problems.

In the last few decades, numerical analysts have become aware of the relevance of the barycentric interpolation formula and its remarkable properties. One of the main proponents of the use of Chebyshev interpolants has been Professor Trefethen, who has made it his duty, alongside his collaborators, to raise awareness of its effectiveness.[7] There is no doubt that the applications presented in this book are an indirect consequence of his efforts.

The deduction of the barycentric interpolation formula starts with how easy it is to express polynomial interpolants in terms of Lagrange polynomials. For a set of points $\{x_0, \ldots, x_n\}$, the j-th *Lagrange polynomial* is defined as the unique polynomial that takes value 1 on x_j and value 0 on x_i, for $i \neq j$, where $0 \leq i \leq n$,

$$\ell_j(x_i) = \begin{cases} 1, & i = j, \\ 0, & i \neq j. \end{cases}$$

Its expression is given by

$$\ell_j(x) = \frac{\prod_{i \neq j}(x - x_i)}{\prod_{i \neq j}(x_j - x_i)}.$$

---

[7] Professor L.N. Trefethen RFS is a professor of numerical analysis at the University of Oxford.

When it comes to polynomial interpolation, the main advantage of working with Lagrange polynomials is that an expression for the interpolant is obtained with only the values of the function on the points of interpolation. That is, let the points of interpolation be $\{x_0, \ldots, x_n\}$ and the values of f on them $\{v_0, \ldots, v_n\}$. Then p_n, the unique polynomial interpolant to f of degree at most n, on the points $\{x_0, \ldots, x_n\}$, can be expressed as

$$p_n(x) = \sum_{i=0}^{n} v_i \ell_i(x). \tag{3.15}$$

This is the direct consequence of the way in which Lagrange polynomials are defined.

As it stands, Equation 3.15 has an evaluation cost of order $\mathcal{O}(n^2)$. However, by noting that some of the products present in $\prod_{i \neq j}(x - x_i)$ are repeated many times when evaluating Equation 3.15, Jacobi modified this expression (in his PhD thesis in 1825 [47]) to obtain one that has linear evaluation cost $\mathcal{O}(n)$:

$$p_n(x) = \ell(x) \sum_{j=0}^{n} \frac{\lambda_j}{x - x_j} v_j, \tag{3.16}$$

where $\ell(x)$ is the node polynomial defined in Equation 3.10 and λ_j is defined as

$$\lambda_j = \frac{1}{\prod_{i \neq j}(x_j - x_i)}.$$

Equation 3.16 is known as the *modified Lagrange formula* or *barycentric interpolation formula of type 1*. Note that it does not assume any particular geometry for the points $\{x_0, \ldots, x_n\}$. This formula was later altered by Dupuy ([21]) into what is today known as the *barycentric interpolation formula of type 2*:

$$p_n(x) = \sum_{j=0}^{n} \frac{\lambda_j v_j}{x - x_j} \Big/ \sum_{j=0}^{n} \frac{\lambda_j}{x - x_j}. \tag{3.17}$$

When the points of interpolation are Chebyshev points, Equation 3.17 simplifies further and we obtain the *barycentric interpolation formula on Chebyshev points*. This formula first appeared in [66] in 1972.

Barycentric interpolation formula on Chebyshev points

Theorem 3.6.1 (Barycentric interpolation formula on Chebyshev points). *Let $\{x_0, \ldots, x_n\}$ be the first $n + 1$ Chebyshev points and let $v_0, \ldots, v_n$ be the values of f on these points. Then the polynomial interpolant p_n to f on $\{x_0, \ldots, x_n\}$ is given by*

$$p_n(x) = \sum_{j=0}^{n}{}' \frac{(-1)^j v_j}{x - x_j} \Big/ \sum_{j=0}^{n}{}' \frac{(-1)^j}{x - x_j} \tag{3.18}$$

where $p_n(x) = v_j$ if $x = x_j$. Also note the symbol ' in Equation 3.18 means the summation is multiplied by 0.5, when $j = 0, n$.

There are several advantages to using Equation 3.18. The first is that only the values of the function f at Chebyshev points are needed to evaluate $p_n(x)$. This means that all that is needed to evaluate the interpolant is the tensor, hence no need for an intermediate FFT step to go from CT to Chebyshev interpolant. The second is that evaluating such formula requires linear effort $\mathcal{O}(n)$ with respect to the degree of the polynomial. Third, the formula may seem unstable, especially when x approaches the grid points x_i in the denominator, but this formula was proved to be stable in floating point arithmetic for all x within the domain of approximation in [39]. Moreover, it is scale-invariant, meaning that the formula does not change when we consider a general interval of the form $[a, b]$.

The combination of Theorem 3.3.8 and Theorem 3.6.1 yields a technique that approximates functions to a high degree of accuracy by calling it a small number of times, where the resulting proxy, a polynomial of low degree, can be evaluated in no time and in a numerically stable manner. Also note that the information that defines a tensor consists of just grid points and values on these points. If the dimension is not too high, the memory footprint of such object is very small. Moreover, CTs require, due to their exponential convergence, fewer grid points than most other tensors to approximate a function to a high degree of accuracy. This in turn makes them very light in terms of memory usage when implemented on a computer.

3.6.3 Evaluating high-dimensional tensors

There are a number of proposed approaches to evaluate multidimensional Chebyshev frameworks. These vary depending on how Chebyshev interpolants of dimension greater than one are defined. We refer the reader to some of the different examples found in the literature: [2], [33] and [27]. Next, we describe the one we consider optimal within practical settings and which has been implented within the MoCaX Library.

Without loss of generality, consider the point (x, y). To evaluate the two-dimensional Chebyshev interpolant $p_{n,m}$ on (x, y), consider the horizontal one-dimensional Chebyshev interpolants in Figure 3.14 and evaluate them at x. This gives values on the black circles of Figure 3.14. These black circles lie on the horizontal lines defined by the Chebyshev points on the y-axis. Hence, the black circles, along with the values on them obtained from the evaluation of the horizontal one-dimensional Chebyshev interpolants, define another one-dimensional Chebyshev interpolant (running vertically as a dashed line in Figure 3.14) that can be evaluated on y. The result of the latter evaluation is the value of $p_{n,m}$ at (x, y).

The evaluation just described can be extended in a straightforward manner to higher dimensions. If we start with a Chebyshev mesh of dimension n, we evaluate a collection of one-dimensional Chebyshev interpolants to reduce the problem from n dimensions down to $n - 1$ dimensions. Continuing this way, the problem is reduced to the dimension 1 case, where the evaluation of the resulting one-dimensional Chebyshev interpolant gives the result.

The barycentric interpolation formula presented in Equation 3.18 has been implemented within the MoCaX Library to evaluate CTs. Making use of this algorithm within the library is straightforward, as is shown in Section 24.2.1.

Note that the values used to define the one-dimensional CT running vertically in Figure 3.14 are obtained through the horizontal CTs. Therefore, these values are not

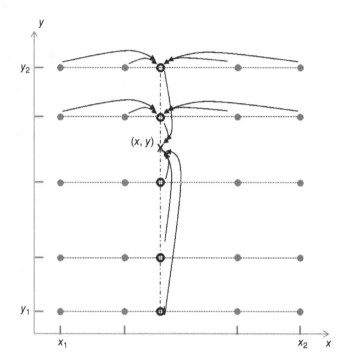

FIGURE 3.14 CT evaluation in dimension 2.

the function values, but an approximation of them. However, the lack of accuracy is controlled by the exponentially convergence of the one-dimensional CTs. Details of this can be found in Appendix B.

3.6.4   Example of numerical stability

The following example illustrates what happens when the wrong algorithm is used to evaluate an object that has all the right properties. Consider the function $\cos(30x)$ on the interval $[-1, 1]$. This function is not just analytic but entire, meaning that it can be extended, analytically, to the entire complex plane.

As we know, CTs and interpolants approximate these functions very well (Theorem 3.2.6). However, different evaluation algorithms can give very different results. This is shown in Figure 3.15, where the size of the tensor, on the x-axis, is plotted versus the tensor error, in logarithmic scale, on the y-axis.

The dashed line in 3.2.6 was obtained by evaluating the CTs with the barycentric interpolation formula. The decay of this curve is in line with what Theorem 3.3.8 predicts. In fact, it converges at a faster than exponential rate, which can happen with entire functions such as $\cos(30x)$.

The other curve was obtained using one of the most commonly used algorithms to evaluate polynomial interpolants. This is based on the use of Vandermode matrices to solve a system of linear equations. In essence, the system of linear equations is solved

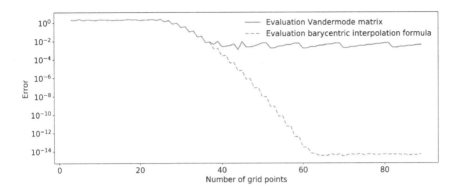

FIGURE 3.15 Dashed curve is error obtained when evaluating with barycentric interpolation formula. The other corresponds to the use of the Vandermode matrix.

to obtain an expression for the interpolant in terms of monomials, the canonical basis for the space of polynomials. The problem is that this algorithm is exponentially ill conditioned. This is a well-known fact that has made a lot of numerical analysts skeptical of the use of polynomial interpolants as approximators. What has been often missed is that using the right algorithm, such as the barycentric interpolation formula, corrects these numerical problems.

As mentioned before, even though the results for fast and stable polynomial interpolation have existed for quite some time, these have remained in the shadow of ill-conditioned algorithms such as the Vandermode one.

3.7 DERIVATIVE APPROXIMATION

Say we have a process or technique that yields a proxy or approximator $\tilde{f}$ for any given function f. It does not generally follow, regardless of the level of accuracy, that derivatives of $\tilde{f}$ give good proxies to the derivatives of f.

For example, in some cases, spline interpolation can approximate continuous functions f to a decent degree of accuracy, sometimes sufficient for the corresponding application. Yet the derivatives of these splines will often give very poor approximations to the derivatives of f. It is also well known that this is a problem that DNNs suffer from.

3.7.1 Convergence of Chebyshev derivatives

We already know that CTs and their corresponding interpolants converge exponentially to f when f is analytic. This section shows that Chebyshev interpolants carry their special approximation properties through to their derivatives. More specifically, Theorem 3.7.1 says that under the same conditions, the derivatives of these interpolants converge exponentially to the derivatives of f. Therefore, all that is needed to obtain a good proxy for the k-th derivative of f is the Chebyshev interpolant p_n corresponding to f and a way of obtaining the k-th derivative of p_n. This is concisely stated in the following theorem, which appears in [72].

Exponential convergence of derivatives

Theorem 3.7.1 *Let f be an analytic function on the interval $[-1, 1]$. Then for each $k \geq 0$, the Chebyshev interpolants p_n satisfy*

$$\|f^k - p_n^k \| = \mathcal{O}(\rho^{-n}) \tag{3.19}$$

as n tends to infinity, where f^k and p_n^k are the k-th derivative of f and p_n, respectively, and ρ is the radius of the open Bernstein ellipse E_ρ onto which f can be analytically extended.

3.7.2   Computation of Chebyshev derivatives

The natural subsequent question asks how easy it is to obtain expressions for these derivatives. Given that polynomials are well understood mathematical objects, expressions for such derivatives should be easy to obtain. Indeed, the generation and evaluation of derivatives of Chebyshev interpolants decompose rather beautifully into the multiplication of a matrix known as the *Chebyshev differentiation matrix* with the vector of values of f on Chebyshev points.

To understand how this happens, consider the k-th derivative p_n^k. Since p_n is a polynomial, then p_n^k is too. Moreover, the polynomial degree of p_n^k is less than the degree of p_n. This means that the unique polynomial that interpolants p_n^k on the interpolating points $\{x_0, \ldots, x_n\}$ is p_n^k itself. Therefore, if there is an effective way of computing $p_n^k(x_i)$, for all x_i in $\{x_0, \ldots, x_n\}$, which is all we need to compute the interpolant to p_n^k on $\{x_0, \ldots, x_n\}$, then we have an effective way of representing the derivatives p_n^k.

To find a way of computing $p_n^k(x_i)$, consider, as was done in Section 3.6, the interpolant p_n to f expressed in terms of Lagrange polynomials:

$$p_n(x) = \sum_{j=0}^{n} v_j \ell_j(x),$$

where $\{v_0, \ldots, v_n\}$ are the values of f on $\{x_0, \ldots, x_n\}$. Then, the derivative of p_n' at x_i is given by

$$p_n'(x_i) = \sum_{j=0}^{n} v_j \ell_j'(x_i).$$

Using the values of $\ell_j'(x_i)$, for all i, j, such that $0 \leq i, j \leq n$, the vector $\{p_n'(x_0), \ldots, p_n'(x_n)\}$ can be represented as the product of a matrix $\mathcal{D}_n$ by $\{v_0, \ldots, v_n\}$, where $(\mathcal{D}_n)_{i,j} = \ell_j'(x_i)$.

Note this matrix is completely determined by the points $\{x_0, \ldots, x_n\}$ and nothing else. This means that $\mathcal{D}_n$ can be computed with no reference to any particular function f, before any approximation calculation is done. The information of the function f being approximated comes in the form of its values $\{v_0, \ldots, v_n\}$ on $\{x_0, \ldots, x_n\}$. The latter is needed only when the values of p'_n on the grid points are needed to compute or generate an interpolant to it (in this case the interpolant being itself).

The question then reduces down to how simple it is to compute the interpolating grid $\{x_0, \ldots, x_n\}$ and the corresponding values $\ell'_j(x_i)$. In the case when $\{x_0, \ldots, x_n\}$ are Chebyshev points, the matrix $\mathcal{D}_n$ reduces down to a very simple expression, given in the following theorem that can be found in [74].

Theorem 3.7.2 (Chebyshev differentiation matrix). *For $n \geq 1$, the entries of the Chebyshev differentiation matrix $\mathcal{D}_n$ are given by*

$$(\mathcal{D}_n)_{00} = \frac{2n^2 + 1}{6}, \qquad\qquad (\mathcal{D}_n)_{nn} = \frac{2n^2 + 1}{6}$$

$$(\mathcal{D}_n)_{jj} = \frac{-x_j}{2(1 - x_j^2)}, \qquad\qquad l = 1, \ldots, n - 1.$$

$$(\mathcal{D}_n)_{ij} = \frac{c_i}{c_j} \frac{(-1)^{i+j}}{x_i - x_j}, \qquad\qquad i \neq j, \;\; i, j = 0, \ldots, n,$$

where

$$c_i = \begin{cases} 2, & i = 0 \text{ or } n, \\ 1, & \text{otherwise.} \end{cases}$$

Once the matrix $\mathcal{D}_n$ and vector $\mathcal{D}_n v$ have been computed, where $v = \{v_0, \ldots, v_n\}$, we have an expression for the derivative p'_n. If the grid of points are Chebyshev points, then p'_n is a good approximator to f', because of Theorem 3.7.1. Moreover, the barycentric interpolation formula gives us a very efficient and stable method of evaluating p'_n.

For derivatives of higher order, we iterate the process described. Obtaining the values $\{p^k(x_0), \ldots, p_n^k(x_n)\}$ reduces down to multiplying $\mathcal{D}_n^k$ with $\{v_0, \ldots, v_n\}$. Once again, the matrix $\mathcal{D}^k$ can be obtained before any function f is considered or computed with.

Note that obtaining an expression for p_n^k involves only linear algebra operations. Efficient implementations of these exist in many software packages. This means once a tensor or interpolant p_n is obtained for f, obtaining corresponding proxies p^k for f^k takes no time whatsoever.

3.7.3 Derivatives in high dimensions

The corresponding result to Theorem 3.7.1 in high dimensions can be found in [27]. This theorem says that the partial derivatives of the Chebyshev interpolants p_n to an analytic function f of dimension greater than one, converge polynomially to the partials of f.

Convergence of derivatives for CT in high dimensions

Theorem 3.7.3 *Let f be a d-dimensional analytic function defined on $A = [-1,1]^d$. Consider its analytic continuation to a generalised Bernstein ellipse E_p. Then for every $m \in \mathbb{N}$, there exists a constant $K(m)$ such that*

$$\|f - p_n\|_{C^l(A)} \leq K(m)n^{-m} \|f\|_{C^{2(l+1)+d+m}(A)}$$

where

$$\|f\|_{C^l(A)} = \max_{|\alpha| \leq l} \max_{x \in A} |\partial^\alpha f(x)|.$$

The details of Theorem 3.7.3 are beyond the scope of this book. For details on the notation used and its proof, we refer to [27].

The question now is how to obtain the tensors that represent the partial derivatives of p_n. Say the function f is of dimension greater than one, and T a CT that approximates f to a high degree of accuracy. Just as in Section 3.7, we want to compute the derivative of T, which by Theorem 3.7.1 is a good proxy for the derivative of f. As f has dimension greater than one, there are multiple derivatives to consider. Next we explain how to extend the differentiation of one-dimensional tensors to higher dimensional ones.

To illustrate how this is done, consider a simple case in dimension 2. The description easily extends to higher dimensions. A CT T of dimension 2 has two variables with respect to which partial derivatives can be computed. We describe how to compute partials with respect to each variable, T_x, T_y, along with how to compute the mixed partial T_{xy}.

Keeping Figure 3.14 in mind, as T is two-dimensional, every Chebyshev point along the y-axis defines a one-dimensional CT running in the x-axis. This axis has a Chebyshev differentiation matrix D_x that gives the derivatives of the one-dimensional tensors running along the x-axis. Similarly, every Chebyshev point along the x-axis defines a one-dimensional CT running in the y-axis. In the same way as before, there is a Chebyshev differentiation matrix D_y. Remember both D_x and D_y are very easy to compute and do not depend on the point to be evaluated. Therefore, these can be computed before any evaluation of the CT derivative takes place.

To obtain T_x, simply apply the Chebyshev differentiation matrix D_x to every one-dimensional CT running along x. The resulting tensor, T_x, can then be evaluated using the barycentric interpolation formula. To obtain T_y, apply D_y to every one-dimensional CT running along y. Once again, the resulting tensor can be evaluated by the barycentric interpolation formula.

To obtain T_{xy}, first apply D_x to the tensors running along x. This gives T_x. Then apply D_y to T_x to obtain T_{xy}. As before, the resulting tensor can be evaluated by the barycentric interpolation formula.

Notice there is one tensor per partial derivative. For our example, if we need derivatives up to and including order two, we end up with four tensors: T, T_x, T_y and T_{xy}. These can be obtained by applying D_x and D_y as described before any evaluation is needed. This amounts to little more than multiplications of matrices that can be performed in a very efficient way.

The methods described so far to compute the derivatives of a CT have been implemented in the MoCaX Library. Details of how to use this functionality can be found in Section 24.2.1.

3.8   CHEBYSHEV SPLINES

So far we have been considering functions f that are smooth. However, some of the functions of interest have discontinuities or points of inflection. In these cases, building a global CT or interpolant is problematic. The problem manifests itself as the *Gibbs phenomenon*.

3.8.1   Gibbs phenomenon

The Gibbs phenomenon appears when the function f or one of its derivatives has a jump discontinuity. When a polynomial interpolant, even a Chebyshev one, is built to approximate it, a series of oscillations around the discontinuity appear that cannot be resolved regardless of the size of the grid. That is, regardless of the degree of the polynomial, the Chebyshev interpolant will not be able to approximate the function f.

The problem is not just at the point of discontinuity. As can be seen from Figure 3.16, the oscillations propagate away from the discontinuity. More specifically, the oscillations for Chebyshev projections and interpolants decay algebraically. That is, if the function f has the discontinuity, then oscillations decay inverse linearly. If the discontinuity is on the derivative of the function, then the oscillations decay inverse quadratically (see [72] Chapter 9).

Understanding the intricacies of this phenomenon is of little consequence for practical approximation theory. This is left to theoretical approximation theory. As it will

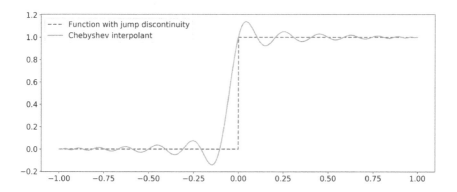

FIGURE 3.16   Oscillations from the Gibbs phenomenon around a jump discontinuity.

become clear, this is a problem with a straightforward solution for the cases that concern us. However, it serves as a warning of what happens if there are discontinuities or singularities and one tries to use global interpolants.

3.8.2 Splines

A type of mathematical object that is very good at dealing with bad local behaviour (such as jumps like the one in Figure 3.16) is splines. Splines are functions defined by polynomials in a piece-wise manner. This is made precise in the following definition.

Definition of a spline

Definition 3.8.1 *A function* $s : [a, b] \to \mathbb{R}$ *is a spline if there are points* $t_0, \ldots, t_n$, *called knots, and polynomials* p_i, *where* $0 \leq i \leq n - 1$, *such that*

$$a = t_0 \leq t_1 \leq \cdots \leq t_{k-1} \leq t_n = b$$
$$s(t) = p_i(t), \quad \text{for } t_i \leq t < t_{i+1},$$

for all i, such that $0 \leq i \leq n - 1$.

If the collection of polynomials p_i have at most degree n, then the spline is said to be of degree at most n.

The knots that define the spline help deal with discontinuities. As long as the discontinuities are part of the set of knots, the effects from the Gibbs phenomenon can be controlled. For splines, the oscillations decay exponentially. This means that the oscillations present in Figure 3.16 cannot be seen by the naked eye, which massively contrasts with the algebraic decay for Chebyshev interpolants, which manifests itself in the oscillations in Figure 3.16.

A lot of work was done with splines in the 1960*s* and 1970*s*. Their ability to deal with discontinuities and the misconceptions about polynomial interpolation at the time were such that it is common to find warnings in textbooks of the time against the use of polynomial interpolants as a reliable and accurate way to approximate functions, suggesting the use of splines instead.

Remark 3.8.2 It should be clear from what has been presented in previous sections that this is not true at all. Splines are of a fixed order and will never reach the levels of accuracy of global Chebyshev interpolants if the function is analytic or even smooth. When it comes to dealing with discontinuities, however, their behaviour with respect to the Gibbs phenomenon is optimal.

As a result, it makes sense to couple splines and CTs to benefit from the core strengths of each. This combination is the topic of the next sections.

3.8.3 Splines of Chebyshev

For most applications of concern in this book, the discontinuities or points of inflection are local. This means that they can always be isolated by a neighbourhood around the point. Moreover, we know where these points are in the vast majority of the cases. For example, some of the functions of interest are the pricing functions of financial derivatives. Their discontinuities or points of inflection come in the form of payment dates, strikes or barriers. These points are usually specified in the contracts that define the trade. Therefore, identifying these points within the domain of the pricing function is straightforward.

To solve the problem of discontinuities in cases such as the one described, simply specify a knot (see Definition 3.8.1) at each of the points of discontinuity. Given that there are only a finite collection of these points, a spline can be defined where the associated polynomials p_i are Chebyshev interpolants. By construction, each of these Chebyshev interpolants will be approximating a function that is discontinuity free. The same applies for points of inflection. Therefore, at each of the sub-domains defined by the knots, we will have all the good properties of CTs and interpolants as function approximators.

The ability to generate Chebyshev Splines has been incorporated in the MoCaX Library. To see how this is used, we refer to Section 24.2.1.

In Appendix C, we present a context where the use of Chebyshev Splines on functions with no singularity points can also bring tangible benefits.

3.8.4 Chebyshev Splines in high dimensions

The generalisation of Chebyshev Splines to dimensions greater than one is straightforward. To do so, knots need to be specified in each of the intervals that define the domain in high dimensions. When the Cartesian product of these intervals is done, the knots naturally break the domain in high dimensions into sub-domains. At each of these sub-domains, a CT is built.

The generation of Chebyshev Splines in high dimensions has been implemented in the MoCaX Library. To learn about this functionality, we refer the reader to Section 24.2.1.

3.9 ALGEBRAIC OPERATIONS WITH CHEBYSHEV TENSORS

This section defines basic operations for tensors, in particular, scaling and addition of tensors. Although CTs are the go-to tensors in this book, due to the properties that have been discussed in previous chapters, most things presented in this section apply to general tensors.

The definition of a tensor and the evaluation of its corresponding polynomial interpolant using the barycentric interpolation formula (Equation 3.18) make some algebraic operations for tensors straightforward to define. As mentioned in Definition 3.3.1, a tensor consists only of grid points in Euclidean space along with real values associated with them. The polynomial interpolant associated with it can be evaluated by the barycentric interpolation formula with only the information at the level of the tensor. For the case of scalar multiplication, this means that $c \cdot f$ can be defined by multiplying the values at the grid points by c, where c is a given scalar value.

To define the addition of tensors, consider the following simple case. Let T_1 and T_2 be two tensors that share the same domain. In particular, note that they have the same dimension. If T_1 and T_2 have the same grid points, then $T_1 + T_2$ can be defined by adding the corresponding real values associated with the grid points. If the grid points do not coincide, consider the following.

Notice that any point in the domain of a tensor can be evaluated using the barycentric interpolation formula.[8] Therefore, the values of the tensors at any distribution of points in its domain can be obtained, in particular, at the grid points of other tensors. To define the addition of tensors T_1 and T_2 whose grids do not coincide, define a grid common to both tensors, and evaluate T_1 and T_2 on the common grid. The common grid along with the resulting values define tensors $\tilde{T}_1$ and $\tilde{T}_2$ that can be added directly.

Notice that tensors are used in this book to approximate functions f. The greater the number of grid points, the greater the accuracy. Therefore, to lose the smallest amount of precision possible, a common grid for T_1 and T_2 should be one that refines the grids that defined the tensors.

In the case of CTs, we leverage from their exponential convergence to obtain tensors through addition that approximate functions to a high degree of accuracy. That is, if T_1 is a CT for f_1 and T_2 for f_2, then we want $f = f_1 + f_2$ to be approximated by $T + T_1 + T_2$. This stands a much higher chance of happening when working with CTs.

A more general situation arises when the domains of tensors T_1 and T_2 are not the same. Say the domain of T_1 is D_1 and the domain of T_2 is D_2. The idea of adding tensors makes sense when the domains overlap, that is, when $D = D_1 \cap D_2 \neq \emptyset$. In this case, D becomes the domain of $T = T_1 + T_2$. First a grid must be defined on D. For that, take the configuration of the finest of the grids between D_1 and D_2 and use it to define one on D. As D is a subset of both D_1 and D_2, T_1 and T_2 can be evaluated on the newly defined grid on D. This defines new tensors: tensor $\tilde{T}_1$ and tensor $\tilde{T}_2$, both of which share the same domain D and same grid. These tensors can be added as described before to define T.

Once scalar multiplication and addition of tensors have been defined, the subtraction of vectors follows immediately.

There are good reasons to define the scalar multiplication and addition of CTs. For example, in some of the applications presented in Part IV, thousands of tensors that share a common domain need to be evaluated at particular moments throughout the day in as little time as possible. The creation of these tensors, however, can take place on a different day, or in overnight batches, under more relaxed time constraints. To accelerate the evaluation step, tensors could be added during their creation. On the day the tensors need to be evaluated, instead of evaluating thousands, the addition is evaluated, saving time when it is most critical.

Both the scalar multiplication and addition of CTs is part of the implementation of the MoCaX Library. Section 24.2.1 shows how these operations are done using this library.

---

[8]This is certainly the case for CTs. However, it also applies to other tensors at the cost, in some cases, of losing a few of the properties presented in Section 3.6.2.

3.10   CHEBYSHEV TENSORS AND MACHINE LEARNING

The ML methods discussed in Chapter 1 were predominantly regression models. These consist of families of functions, normally parametrised by a set of weights w, which learn the patterns of data sets of the form $\mathcal{D} = \{X, Y\}$, where X consists of data points x, in $\mathbb{R}^k$, for some $k > 0$, and Y consists of data points usually assumed to be scalar values. Moreover, each data point $x \in X$ has a unique corresponding value $y \in Y$, and every $y \in Y$ a point in X.

Training a regression model to a given data set $\mathcal{D}$ consists of finding a set of weights w, such that for every point $x \in X$, the value returned by f_w, that is, $\hat{y} = f_w(x)$ is close to the value y that corresponds to x in $\mathcal{D}$. More important, we say the training performed on $\mathcal{D}$ generalises well if given (x, y), data points not on the training set $\mathcal{D}$, $\hat{y} = f_w(x)$ are close to y.

Given the applications of interest in this book (presented in Part IV), out of all the ways in which data sets $\mathcal{D}$ can be generated, we are interested in the ones obtained by sampling a function f, that is, X consisting of a set of points on the domain of f and Y the values of f on X. Within this context, training a regression model that generalises well consists of finding a function f_w that closely mimics or replicates the function f used to generate the data set $\mathcal{D}$. Moreover, the better we generalise, the closer f_w is to f.

The DNNs we discuss in Chapter 2, which we use and mention throughout this book, are an example of an ML algorithm of the type described. Within the contexts of interest, we use DNNs to approximate — learn, using ML terminology — a function f. To do so, we sample the function f on its domain — this is the experience the model is subjected to and from which it learns. The aim of training the model is for it to predict what the value of f is at any given point in its domain. Moreover, one of the characteristics of DNNs (indeed any ML model) is that the more we expose the DNN to values of the function f, the better we expect the DNN to perform on its predictive task — approximation in our case.

There is not a single definition for an ML model. However, a widely accepted one that we used in Chapter 1 is the following: "A computer program is said to learn from experience E with respect to some class of tasks T and performance measure P if its performance at tasks in T, as measured by P, improves with experience E" ([57]). Clearly, DNNs satisfy this definition.

Nowadays, there are plenty of computer programs that have implemented within them all the instructions needed to compute with DNNs, for example, Tensorflow and PyTorch. The experience E is represented by the samples fed to the algorithm. The task T is the prediction of values of f on any given point on its domain. The performance measure P is any of the given metrics used to train and test the model. Finally, by the Universal Approximation Theorem (Theorem 2.3), the more we sample the function, the better we are placed to improve the measure (accuracy) of our task (predicting value of f).

The question we now put forward is, given the definition of ML algorithm given, and the context we work in, can CTs be viewed as an ML method?

Keeping in mind what we have said so far about DNNs, we can easily trace the similarities they have with CTs. Just like in the case of DNNs, experience E for CTs comes in the form of sampling a function f. As we presented in this chapter, the sampling is done at specific points (Chebyshev points), but it is nonetheless sampling like the one done to train DNNs. The task T, as with DNNs, is to approximate a function f with the purpose of predicting to a high degree of accuracy what the value of f is at any given point on its domain — remember we use both DNNs and CTs with the same objective in mind. The performance of the predictive task T is measured essentially the same way it is done with DNNs, for example, using the mean squared error or maximum error over a sample set. Finally, by Theorem 3.3.10 we know that the more the function f is sampled at Chebshev points, the higher the accuracy of approximation on the whole of the domain of f. In summary, we know that the more the CTs learn from experience E, the higher the performance measure P at performing the task T. Therefore, one could argue that the approximation methods within the theory of Chebyshev constitute ML models.

Although many of the algorithms and methods in the theory of Chebyshev approximation were developed at a time when computers did not exist, these have gradually made their way into different software packages. Two good examples are Chebfun and MoCaX.[9] Indeed, in recent decades, the field of numerical analysis has begun to appreciate the numerical properties and computational power that Chebyshev approximation theory brings to many applied fields.[10]

3.11 SUMMARY OF CHAPTER

- **High accuracy**. When we deal with well-behaved functions, CT converge quasi-exponentially as the number of grid points in each dimension increases. If the function has an input domain of dimension 1, then convergence is exponential. In practical settings, this means very few grid points are needed to reach high levels of accuracy.
- **Efficient and stable evaluation**. Through the use of the barycentric interpolation formula, CT can be evaluated very efficiently while retaining numerical stability. For most applications, this means thousands of scenarios can be evaluated in a fraction of a second.
- **Ex ante error control**. By only using the values on the tensor and the Fast Fourier Transform, we can obtain an accurate proxy for the error of approximation. This means approximation error estimates can be efficiently obtained allowing for a dynamic adjustment of the approximation power of the tensor.
- **Efficient derivative approximation**. The derivative of a CT can be efficiently obtained through simple linear algebra operations. Moreover, the derivative of the CT is also a good proxy for the derivative of the function being approximated by the CT. This means that once a CT with high accuracy has been built for a function f, we automatically have accurate proxies for all the partial derivatives of f.

---

[9]Chebfun can be found at https://www.chebfun.org/. MoCaX can be found at https://www.mocaxintelligence.com/download-mocax-intelligence/.
[10]An example of this is embodied by the book [72], which presents the main aspects of Chebyshev approximation theory implemented within computer programs.

The toolkit – plugging in approximation methods

Introduction: why is a toolkit needed

P art I presented the two main approximation techniques that have the potential of alleviating the computational burden associated with a wide range of financial calculations. The first, based on CT, is built on sampling the function in a deterministic manner. The second, based on DNNs, usually samples the function on randomly selected points. However, for reasons that will become clear in the following sections, if we try to use them directly in the context of risk calculations, their applicability is somewhat limited.

This part of the book covers a number of techniques that when coupled with the approximation methods let the latter unleash their full potential. These techniques, or set of tools, will set the industry practitioner on a clear path to successfully apply the approximation techniques to a wide range of cases.

4.1 THE PRICING PROBLEM

One of the main areas where the approximation techniques presented in Part I can be applied is the area of risk metrics calculations. Risk calculations have become increasingly expensive over the years. For the vast majority of these calculations, the main computational bottleneck comes in the pricing of the risk factor scenarios involved. This pricing step is what we identify as the *pricing problem in risk calculations*.

Risk calculation flow

To better understand the pricing problem in risk calculations and how this can be alleviated with the approximating methods presented in Part I, let us take a look at Figure 4.1, which shows the typical flow of a risk calculation done in a risk engine.

First, a portfolio is chosen along with the set of risk factors that affect the price of the portfolio. In the vast majority of risk calculations — at least the ones of interest — a large collection of risk factor scenarios are generated. This is step 1 in Figure 4.1. How they are generated depends on the type of risk calculation and the methods employed. For the time being, the important point to note is that the number of scenarios is large — in fact, typically very large. In Figure 4.1 we have chosen 10,000 as an example. The number of scenarios can sometimes be lower (e.g. in the hundreds for market risk) or higher (e.g. in the millions for CVA).

Once the set of risk factor scenarios has been obtained, it is passed to the pricing engine for step 2 of the process in Figure 4.1. The pricing function of every trade in the portfolio is then called on every scenario. In doing so, a price distribution for every trade is obtained. By adding the price distributions of every trade, a price distribution of the portfolio is obtained in step 3. From this price distribution all sorts of risk metrics can be obtained in step 4, ranging from expectations to tail metrics like Expected Shortfall.

As mentioned, the pricing step in the vast majority of risk calculations presents a bottleneck, that is, the calling of all pricing functions in the portfolio on every risk factor scenario. In Figure 4.1 this corresponds to going from step 1 to step 3. The reason why this constitutes a bottleneck is that pricing functions can be computationally expensive to run. Add to that the thousands (sometimes millions) of scenarios that need to be priced and the thousands (sometimes millions) of trades that constitute the typical portfolio of financial institutions.

Pricing problem example

To give an example of the magnitude of the computational problem, consider the pricing function of an interest rate swap. This is by far the most common trade type encountered in fixed income portfolios; it is not rare to encounter hundreds of thousands of swaps within the portfolios of banks. Its pricing function is considered to be pretty fast to evaluate. The average time of evaluation depends on range of factors such as implementation, type of system and so on. But it is not rare to find swaps that evaluate a single price within the micro-second range, using a single CPU.

Consider a calculation that requires one million evaluations done for a portfolio with 100,000 swaps. This means the calculation takes hundreds if not thousands of seconds, with a single CPU. If the financial institution is able to run a farm with thousands of CPUs, this calculation becomes manageable.

The case described is a best-case scenario as the trade type involved is computationally cheap to run. However, it changes completely for trade types with slower pricing functions. Take the example of a Bermudan Swaption. This is a common trade type encountered all over fixed-income portfolios. Its pricing function no longer takes microseconds to evaluate, but milliseconds if not seconds. This completely changes the computational burden. Assuming the same type of calculation described, we end up

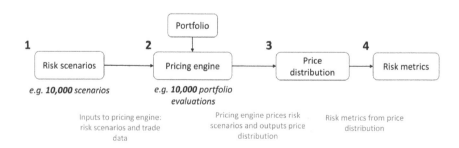

FIGURE 4.1   Main steps of a typical risk calculation.

with hundreds of thousands of hours of computational time on a single CPU. This is a computational burden that few CPU farms can handle.

This example considered only two typical trade types in portfolios, from a single asset class and a single risk calculation. Across asset classes one encounters trades with greater computational costs. Adding to all this the large number of risk calculations that need to be done on a regular basis, the task becomes monumental.

To make the challenge even more difficult, we must keep in mind that the goal of financial institutions is to produce these calculations in real time, as opposed to once a day or once a month. Any institution that wants to measure and control risk appropriately should aim at having a good idea of the incremental risk a new potential trade brings to the books. For OTC derivatives, this means the incremental risk calculations must be done in seconds or minutes at most.

The business of derivatives used to be based on creating the new exotic — the next new trade. However, since the 2008 financial crisis, banks have been forced by investors and regulators to manage their risk more closely, making the scope for new exotics much more constrained. Profit margins are decreasing, and the key source of profitability lies in portfolio optimisation. For example, a leading bank would need to run optimisation algorithms on its portfolios to find a pair of trades that, if allocated to the right counterparties, would decrease the overall risk, funding cost, capital amounts and so on. This can only be achieved if the underlying risk calculations can be run very fast and with a good level of precision.

4.2 RISK CALCULATION WITH PROXY PRICING

The question that naturally comes up is whether the approximation methods presented in Part I of this book can help alleviate the pricing problem.

To begin exploring this question, take a look at Figure 4.2.

Figure 4.2 shows how the flow of a typical risk calculation changes when a sampling approximation technique is used to replace the pricing functions normally used.

The set of risk factors is generated the same way as it was done in Figure 4.1. The goal is to build proxies for the pricing functions and use them to evaluate the set of risk scenarios.

In step 2a in Figure 4.2, a collection of grid points (sampling points) within the space spanned by the risk factor scenarios is determined. These are the points at which the pricing functions will be called to generate the proxy function. Remember that the techniques presented in this book rely on sampling the function at points of its domain. For example, in the case of CT, these grid points are Chebyshev points. In the case of a DNN, these can be, for example, randomly selected — although as we will see in Section 10, there are smarter ways of selecting them.

As presented in Figure 4.2, assume the number of grid points is 500. Once generated, they are passed to the pricing engine. The resulting values are used to generate the proxy function in step 2b. In the case of a CT, this is enough to generate it. In the case of a DNN, the weights or parameters of the DNN have to be tuned through training.

If the proxy function is built appropriately, the level of accuracy will be such that the price distribution obtained in step 2c in Figure 4.2 will be very close to the price

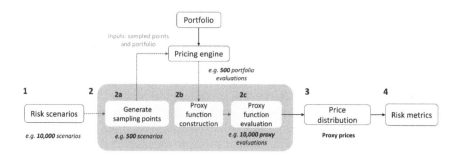

FIGURE 4.2 How the typical steps of a risk calculation are modified when using a smart sampling approximation technique such as CT.

distribution in step 3 in Figure 4.1. This in turn means the risk metrics from both figures are almost identical.

However, the advantage of using the proxy function is that one does not incur the overhead of calling the pricing functions the number of times they get called in Figure 4.1. Take the example in Figure 4.2. To build the proxy pricer, the pricing functions get called 500 times (step 2*b*). This is only 5% of the number of times they get called in Figure 4.1. Once the proxy pricer has been built, evaluating the set of risk factor scenarios takes only a fraction of a second. This means a computational gain has been obtained at the point of pricing, which is the biggest bottleneck of the calculation, of 95%, without a significant loss of accuracy at the level of the risk metrics computed.

There are a multitude of benefits obtained by setting up a system like the one shown in Figure 4.2. These will become clear in following chapters — specifically in the applications presented in Part IV. For the time being, it suffices to say that they come in the form of cost savings in infrastructure (for example, saving on hardware), fast what-if type of risk analysis, being able to do calculations so far deemed impossible (e.g. risk optimisation routines) and connecting disjoint systems within banks, to name a few.

The computational flow shown in Figure 4.2 is not new. For example, market risk VaR calculations use it with so-called partial revaluation grids, in the case of CVA, with Longstaff-Schwartz type regressions. Their use, however, has so far been limited because the levels of accuracy tend to be poor, and when the latter are improved, it usually comes at an increased number of samplings, which makes the techniques useless from the point of view of cost savings.

The advent of advanced approximation techniques like CT and Neural Networks has changed the *accuracy versus calibration effort* balance significantly. As a result, the spectrum of applicability has increased tremendously, as we will see in Part IV. Indeed, this is one of the core underlying motivations in this book.

4.3 THE CURSE OF DIMENSIONALITY

One of the main problems affecting the approximation methods presented in Part I within practical settings is the curse of dimensionality. This says that as the dimension of the input space of the function being approximated increases, the number of sampling points needed to generate the approximating function or proxy function increases substantially.

For example, in the case of CT, as the dimension of the tensor increases, the number of points on the grid grows exponentially. Namely, if d is the dimension and there are n points per dimension, then the number of points on the tensor is n^d.

DNNs are also affected, although not in the same drastic way. As the dimension of the DNN increases, the number of training points needed to obtain a good result increases as well. This is made precise in a result by Barron ([4]). It says that for a single-layered Neural Net, the error of approximation is given by

$$\mathcal{O}\left(\frac{C}{k}\right) + \mathcal{O}\left(\frac{kd}{n}\log(n)\right) \tag{4.1}$$

where C is a constant associated with the function being approximated, k is the number of neurons in the net and n the number of sample points. Notice there are two components. The first only involves the constant C and the number of neurons. To reduce it, we must increase the number of neurons. The second is the component that captures the effect of the dimension of the function being approximated. This component increases in size with the number of neurons and the dimension. The way to reduce it is by increasing the number of points sampled.

The question is why this is a problem for the applications we are interested in. The reason is very simple. Most financial functions of interest — for example, pricing functions — have an input domain with a large dimension. Consider an Interest Rate Swap. This is typically sensitive, within a risk calculation, to two yield curves. Each yield curve normally consists of tens of interest rates. This means the dimension of the domain of this pricing function is in the tens, possibly low hundreds.

Much more dramatic examples exist that are very common. A Bermudan Swaption depends on two yield curves, plus a whole plethora of implied volatilities the number of which can be in the hundreds. This makes the dimension of the input domain of the pricing function of a Bermudan Swaption in the hundreds.

The example just mentioned is not unique to the interest rate asset class. Similar examples exist in all asset classes, such as FX, equity, credit, commodities, and so on.

To give a sense of how problematic this is for tensors, consider a tensor with just 2 points per dimension (which is the minimum) and 100 dimensions. This gives a total of 1.27×10^{30} grid points. This figure is astronomical.

As already mentioned, DNNs suffer from this problem to a lesser extent. If the dimension of the domain increases, the sample points needed for training may increase to the point that the whole exercise becomes impractical.

Applying the approximation techniques described in Part I directly, without some adjustments, is suboptimal in the best cases, or impossible in the worst ones. Hence the need for a toolkit!

The techniques introduced in Part II of the book are the nuts and bolts needed to use the approximating techniques mentioned in Part I within the context of financial risk calculations.

4.4   THE TECHNIQUES IN THE TOOLKIT

The following chapters cover the techniques or tools that will potentiate the use of the approximation methods presented in Part I within the practical setting of financial risk calculations.

The first technique is the Composition Technique (Chapter 5). This technique is designed to take advantage of the models typically used in risk calculations done with Monte Carlo simulations. If the right conditions are present, and the technique is applied appropriately, the curse of dimensionality virtually disappears.

Chapter 6 discusses a set of algorithms that extends partial information on the tensor to the whole tensor. Specifically, with values on only a fraction of the grid points, these algorithms guess what the values on the whole grid should be. This means functions do not need to be evaluated on the whole grid, allowing practitioners to use tensors of a dimension that normally would be impossible. If a typical tensor can only be considered up to dimension 5 or 6 — due to the curse of dimensionality — these algorithms extend this limit significantly. In part, there are examples where the dimension is extended up to four times, but depending on the function being approximated it could be more.

The Sliding Technique is covered in Chapter 7. This technique approximates pricing functions in much the same way that the Taylor approximation does, but relying on more powerful approximating objects than just the sensitivities of the function. If properly applied — in some cases in tandem with dimensionality reduction techniques — it can decrease the burden imposed by the curse of dimensionality by orders of magnitude.

Well known dimensionality reduction techniques like PCA and Auto-Encoders will be presented in Chapter 5.2. Their main use will be to help the approximation techniques presented in Part I with the curse of dimensionality.

Finally, Chapter 8 will cover a clever technique particularly suited to the simulation of sensitivities, which makes use of the Composition Technique (Chapter 5) and the Jacobian transformation in risk factor diffusion models.

Composition techniques

As mentioned in Section 4.3, pricing functions — indeed many functions in finance — are high dimensional, meaning that if the input space of the function has n variables, then n is a large number. As the approximation techniques mentioned in Part I suffer from the curse of dimensionality, it is important to reduce, whenever possible, the dimension over which the approximation takes place.

This chapter presents — from the perspective of the applications given in Part IV — a very important way of reducing the dimension of the problem. In this chapter, we work with a function P — usually a pricing function that needs to be called many times within some process. The idea is to approximate it using one of the techniques in Part I. To do so effectively, we want to reduce that dimension from n to a much lower value k. Given that in most applications of concern in this book, the function P has to be evaluated on a given set of points X in $\mathbb{R}^n$, and one way of reducing the dimension of the problem is by parametrising X in terms of a set Y of dimension k. The following makes this situation precise.

Let P be a function with domain in $\mathbb{R}^n$. Assume there is a set X in $\mathbb{R}^n$ that needs to be evaluated by P. Suppose there is a parametrisation $g : Y \subset \mathbb{R}^k \to \tilde{X}$, where $\tilde{X}$ is either X itself or a set that closely approximates X, and $k < n$. Then, consider the following composition:

$$Y \subset \mathbb{R}^k \xrightarrow{\ g\ } \tilde{X} \subset \mathbb{R}^n \xrightarrow{\ P\ } \mathbb{R}. \tag{5.1}$$
$$\underbrace{}_{f}$$

The resulting function f has the following important properties. The first is that every point in $\tilde{X}$ has at least one in Y such that $g(y) = x$. This means that the value of the function P at $x \in \tilde{X}$, namely $P(x)$, is $f(y)$. The second, is that if k is sufficiently low, then the approximation methods presented in Part I willnot be affected by the curse of dimensionality when applied on f.

The last point is very important. The curse of dimensionality can be a limitation when using the approximation techniques presented in Part I. Sidestepping this sets us on our way to successfully extract all the benefits of these approximation techniques.

A context like the one just described gives rise to an instance of what we call the *Composition Technique*. The next few sections describe different situations where this type of technique can be taken advantage of.

5.1   LEVERAGING FROM EXISTING PARAMETRISATIONS

The parametrisation g from Equation 5.1 is sometimes already provided by the context — although in some cases somewhat hidden. An example is when the inputs to a given function P are generated by mathematical models of low dimension. In particular, we have in mind risk factor diffusion models that generate market risk factors to pricing functions.

This section describes how market risk factors diffusion models give rise to the Composition Technique. Later chapters, such as Chapter 15, describe how it can be used in particular risk calculations.

5.1.1   Risk factor generating models

The models typically used to generate risk factors are stochastic. These models — which we denote by $\mathcal{M}$ — consist of a set of stochastic differential equations expressed in terms of a set of parameters θ and a set of stochastic drivers $\mathcal{Z}$. Once the set θ has been specified, usually through calibration, the equations can be used to simulate what we call the *model risk factors* $\mathcal{R}$. The latter, in turn, usually generate the space of *market risk factors* through a smooth parametrisation expressed in terms of the parameters θ and the model risk factors $\mathcal{R}$.

Let us illustrate the previous notions through a simple example. Consider the class of market interest rates. This is one of the most important classes of risk factors in the market. The range of financial products affected by them is huge. The models typically used to simulate market rates (e.g. swap rates and their implied volatilities) do so in two steps. The first step generates the model risk factors $\mathcal{R}$. The second generates the market risk factors (market rates) $\mathcal{S}$, in terms of the model risk factors, usually through a smooth parametrisation.

Consider the popular Hull-White (HW) model for interest rates. The most basic is the one-factor model that is described by the following stochastic differential equation:

$$dr_t = a(b - r_t)dt + \sigma dW_t. \tag{5.2}$$

The parameter set θ consists of $\theta = (a, b, \sigma)$, while the stochastic drivers set $\mathcal{Z}$ of the Brownian motion W_t. The parameters θ may or may not have a time term structure, but they, or their term structures, are fixed before the simulation takes place and remain fixed throughout; in fact, the simulation cannot take place until this has been done. This is a key point in what follows.

We refer to the number of stochastic drivers in a model as the *degrees of freedom* of the model $\mathcal{M}$. As we will see, this number is crucial for the Composition Technique and determines, to some extent, its effectiveness. The HW one-factor model only has one stochastic driver W_t, which in turn simulates a single-model risk factor: the short rate r. Models such as this, which have only one degree of freedom, are often called "one factor models".

This model comes equipped with the following smooth parametrisation

$$g_{a,\sigma} : \mathbb{R} \longrightarrow \mathbb{R}^n,$$

given by the following expression

$$\left(S(t, T_1), \ldots, S(t, T_n)\right) = \left(A(t, T_1)e^{B(t,T_1)r(t)}, \ldots, A(t, T_n)e^{B(t,T_n)r(t)}\right) \qquad (5.3)$$

where $r(t)$ is the short rate generated in Equation 5.2, T_i a time point in the future ahead of t and

$$B(t, T_i) = \frac{1 - e^{a(T_i - t)}}{a}$$

$$\ln A(t, T_i) = \ln \frac{P(0, T_i)}{P(0, t)} + B(t, T_i)F(0, t) - \frac{1}{4a^3}\sigma^2(e^{-aT_i} - e^{-at})^2(e^{2at} - 1)$$

where

$$F(0, t) = -\partial \ln P(0, t)/\partial t.$$

This parametrisation expresses the market risk factors $\{S(t, T_i)\}_{i=1,\ldots,n}$ (for example, swap rates) in terms of the short rate, which is the only variable in the model risk factor space in this example.

Notice the function g depends on the model parameters θ and the short rate. As mentioned, model parameters are fixed at calibration, before any simulation takes place. Once fixed, the short rate can be simulated. The whole collection of swap rates $\left(S(t, T_1), \ldots, S(t, T_n)\right)$, which constitute the market risk factors, are generated through g. Notice the dimension of the market risk factor space, specified by n in this example, is independent of the model; one can specify as many tensors as desired independent of the single-model risk factor.

There are many models used to simulate interest rates in risk calculations, some of which are generalisations of the HW model (for example, Gaussian models, for which any number of factors may be specified). However, the vast majority have the properties exhibited by the HW model: a small number of stochastic variables (degrees of freedom) and a smoothing function g that parametrises a market risk factor space of high dimension in terms of a small number of model risk factors.

Pretty much the same applies to the models used to simulate implied volatilities of interest rates, as well as models that simulate market risk factors of all other asset classes.

5.1.2 Pricing functions and model risk factors

In the context described so far, the Composition Technique consists of using the parametrisation that expresses market risk factors in terms of model risk factors (such as g in Equation 5.1.1) to express a given pricing function P in terms of the model risk factors. This defines the function f in Equation 5.1, changing the problem from one of approximating a high-dimensional function P to one of approximating a low-dimensional function f.

Consider the following example of a pricing function P. Say we have a Bermudan Swaption. Its pricing function depends on a whole collection of risk factors. The ones of interest in most risk calculations are the market risk factors that the Bermudan Swaption is sensitive to — these tend to be the ones that vary across scenarios in a risk calculation. For Bermudan Swaptions, these are swap rates and implied volatilities. There can be tens of different swap rates and hundreds of different implied volatilities. For illustration pursposes, assume there are 50 swap rates and 300 implied volatilities. These constitute typical examples for the space of market risk factors of a Bermudan Swaption.

Suppose $\mathcal{M}_1$ is the risk factor model used to generate swap rates and $\mathcal{M}_2$ the model used for implied volatilities. The model $\mathcal{M}_1$ has a function g_1 that parametrises the market risk rates in terms of the model risk variables. Equivalently, $\mathcal{M}_2$ has g_2 doing the corresponding parametrisation for implied volatilities.

The key element to consider is that both model risk factor spaces tend to have low dimension. Typical examples would be 3 for interest rates, 2 for implied volatilities. Using these parametrisations, the pricing function P, which has a domain with 350 dimensions, can be modified by considering the following composition:

$$\mathbb{R}^5 \xrightarrow{g} \mathbb{R}^{350} \xrightarrow{P} \mathbb{R},$$

$$\underset{f}{\xrightarrow{\hspace{3cm}}}$$

where g is defined as $g = (g_1, g_2)$

$$\begin{array}{ccc} \textbf{Model Space} & & \textbf{Market Space} \\ \mathbb{R}^5 & \xrightarrow{g} & \mathbb{R}^{350} \end{array}. \tag{5.4}$$

This means that a given market risk scenario $s = (s_1, \ldots, s_{50}, v_1, \ldots, v_{300})$, which consists of 50 swap rates and 300 implied volatilities, is the image of $r = (a_1, a_2, a_3, b_1, b_2)$, an element in the space of model risk scenarios conformed by $\mathcal{M}_1$ and $\mathcal{M}_2$.

Note that f, the function obtained as a result of the composition in Equation 5.1.2, is a function with domain in the model risk factor space of $\mathcal{M}_1$ and $\mathcal{M}_2$, which is of only five dimensions.

5.1.3 The tool obtained

There are two crucial things to notice at this point. The first is that every market risk scenario in $\mathbb{R}^{350}$ comes from a model risk scenario in $\mathbb{R}^5$. That is, every market risk scenario in $\mathbb{R}^{350}$ is *fully determined* by at least one model risk scenario in $\mathbb{R}^5$. This means that the value of the pricing function P at a risk scenario s, namely $P(s)$, is the same as $f(r)$, where r is the model risk scenario that determines s under the parametrisation g.

The second is that building CT or DNNs for f is straightforward, as we are no longer affected by the curse of dimensionality. In the case of CT, the number of deterministic sample points for the pricing function is small due to the low dimension of f. In the case of DNNs, the number of sampling points to train on decreases substantially as we are no longer exploring a space of 350 dimensions.

5.2 CREATING A PARAMETRISATION

In Section 5.1, we presented a situation where a suitable parametrisation was given by the context itself. In particular, it comes with the way in which the set X is generated. This section deals with sets X that need to be evaluated by functions P, where we cannot assume X has been generated by models such as the ones presented in Section 5.1. We simply assume that X carries enough structure so that dimensionality reduction techniques can be used.

Essentially, we use dimensionality reduction techniques to parametrise sets $\tilde{X}$ — which under certain conditions closely resemble X — and take advantage of such parametrisations to come up with an instance of the Composition Technique.

5.2.1 Principal Component Analysis

PCA is a simple and fast technique that leverages from the correlation displayed by data to describe it in terms of variables that live in a space of lower dimension. Given that financial data often exhibits high degrees of correlation, PCA works very well with many financial data sets, such as families of interest rates and implied volatilities, and Credit Default Spreads, just to name a few.

How does PCA work

Given a data set X in $\mathbb{R}^n$ and a dimension $k \leq n$, the dimension of X is reduced by projecting X onto the hyper-plane H of dimension k, that minimises the average of the projection distances.

Let ψ denote such projection. As the image of X under ψ lies in a hyper-plane (by definition), a change of coordinates T reduces the dimension of the projected data; that is, it gives an expression for every point in X as a point in the lower dimensional space $\mathbb{R}^k$.

The change of coordinates T is an automorphism of $\mathbb{R}^n$, that is, a bijective linear map from $\mathbb{R}^n$ to itself. This means it has an inverse:

$$T^{-1} : \mathbb{R}^k \to \mathbb{R}^n. \tag{5.5}$$

Strictly speaking, T^{-1} is defined on $\mathbb{R}^n$, not in $\mathbb{R}^k$. However, as the image of H under T lies in $\mathbb{R}^k$, it defines a function from $\mathbb{R}^k$ to $\mathbb{R}^n$. Therefore, T^{-1} changes the low-dimensional expression of any point in $\mathbb{R}^k$ to a high-dimensional one in $\mathbb{R}^n$.

Notice that T^{-1} defines a parametrisation of the projected set $\psi(X)$ by $\mathbb{R}^k$. It is precisely this parametrisation that helps reduce the dimension of the financial functions we are interested in.

Advantages of PCA

PCA has several advantages over other dimensionality reduction techniques. First, it is widely known and easy to use. Second, the correlation displayed by financial market risk factors, such as interest rate term structures or implied volatility surfaces, is very high. This means that a relatively low number of factors need to be specified to describe the dynamics of the market risk factors with good precision. For example, yield curves tend to be very well described with 10 or fewer principal components.

Another advantage is that (using ML terminology) the only hyper-parameter that PCA has is the dimension of the hyper-plane onto which the data are projected. Other dimensionality reduction techniques in ML have many hyper-parameters. Although greater numbers of hyper-parameters usually give more flexibility to a model, potentially improving results, it introduces the often tricky issue of hyper-parameter optimisation, that is, finding the optimal hyper-parameter configuration for the model to work well. With PCA, one does not have to worry about this issue too much.

Moreover, PCA training has an analytic solution. This means the parameters that specify the hyper-plane H can be found through an equation for which there is an analytic solution. No numerical optimisations are needed to find these parameters. This is somewhat of a unique situation amongst ML techniques; most need optimisations to find their corresponding parameters, leading to delays and sometimes inaccuracies in the solutions.

PCA and the curse of dimensionality

The way that PCA serves as a tool to sidestep the curse of dimensionality is the following. As an example, consider a function P (for example, a pricing function) that takes its input from $\mathbb{R}^n$. Say there is a large collection of points X (for example, market risk scenarios) in $\mathbb{R}^n$ that need to be evaluated by P. As explained, if PCA is applied to X, then there is a parametrisation T^{-1}, shown in Equation 5.5, that can be composed with P to define the following function:

$$\mathbb{R}^k \xrightarrow{\ T^{-1}\ } \mathbb{R}^n \xrightarrow{\ P\ } \mathbb{R}.$$
$$\underbrace{\phantom{\mathbb{R}^k \xrightarrow{\ T^{-1}\ } \mathbb{R}^n \xrightarrow{\ P\ } \mathbb{R}}}_{f}$$

This defines a function f of dimension k, where $k < n$. Note that the strategy is the same as with the Composition Technique presented in Section 5.1. The function P is composed with a parametrisation to obtain a function of lower dimension f that is then approximated by one of the techniques presented in Part I.

There is a difference to highlight between the Composition Technique presented in Section 5.1, where risk factor diffusion models are used to parametrise the input space X, and the cases where a dimensionality reduction technique, such as PCA, is used. In the former case, there is no loss of information when the composition of P with g (Equation 5.1) is done. That is, the data set being parametrised is X itself. In the latter case, there is a loss of information that needs to be considered.

The original data set is X. However, the parametrised data set is $\tilde{X} = \psi(X)$. Therefore, the loss of information is given by the difference between X and $\tilde{X}$. Normally, the higher the k, the lower the information loss. At the same time, the higher the correlation exhibited by X, the closer X and $\tilde{X}$ will be for a fixed k. This means that this form of the Composition Technique will not work for our purposes unless the input data X exhibits relatively high degrees of correlation. Fortunately, this is the case for many families of risk factors in finance.

As it will be seen in Chapter 16, the value of k may change from application to application. In some cases $k = 3$ suffices and the application of the approximation methods presented in Part I is straightforward. In others, the dimension has to be higher, for example, $k = 30$. In these cases, the approximation methods from Part I need to be adapted (for example, using the Sliding Technique presented in Chapter 7) to obtain the desired results.

5.2.2 Autoencoders

Autoencoders are DNNs that have the general architecture depicted in Figure 5.1.

The layer presented in the middle in Figure 5.1 is the one with the smallest number of neurons. We refer to this layer as the bottleneck of the Autoencoder. The function defined by the layers between the input layer and the bottleneck, denoted by ψ, is called the *encoder*. As the name suggests, ψ encodes data in $\mathbb{R}^n$ as data in $\mathbb{R}^k$, where $k < n$. If X is a data set in $\mathbb{R}^n$, applying ψ to X gives a data set $Y = \psi(X)$ in $\mathbb{R}^k$. The function defined from the bottleneck to the output layer, denoted by φ, is called the *decoder*. As its name suggests, it decodes data in $\mathbb{R}^k$ and represents it as data in $\mathbb{R}^n$.

One of the key characteristics of an Autoencoder is that the dimension of the output is the same as the dimension of the input. The aim behind the training of an Autoencoder is to find the weights or parameters for the DNN that minimise the difference between X and $\tilde{X} = \varphi(Y)$ by forcing X through a space of lower dimension.

Like any other Neural Net, Autoencoders have activation functions in each neuron. These activation functions let the Autoencoder learn non-linear features on X. If the activation function chosen on all neurons is the identity function, then the encoder

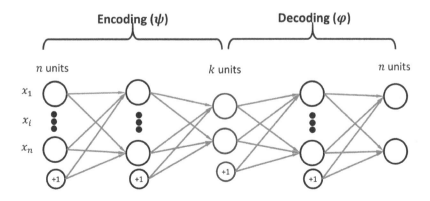

FIGURE 5.1 Autoencoder architecture.

and decoder would end up being the projection and parametrisation of PCA (see Section 5.2.1). In this sense, Autoencoders generalise PCA.

The possibility of learning non-linearities makes Autoencoders more powerful than PCA as data compressors. This means that for a fixed dimension k, the loss of information of an Autoencoder tends to be less than that for PCA. This, however, comes with a complexity cost. Autoencoders have a range of hyper-parameters that need to be specified before training, for example, the number of neurons in each layer, the type of activation function, the optimisation algorithm used for training, and so on. The tuning of these hyper-parameters, known as hyper-parameter optimisation, can be difficult in some cases.

In addition to this difficulty, there is the added problem of training time. PCA trains in no time whatsoever due to the analytic solution of the optimisation problem involved. Autoencoders, however, must resort to numerical opimisation routines that can often take a long time to run.

Autoencoders and the curse of dimensionality

Autoencoders are used in very much the same way as PCA when reducing the dimension of a function P. The key aspect is having access to a function that parametrises the original data set, or a modified version of the data set, in terms of just a few variables. In the case of the Autoencoder, this parametrisation comes in the form of the decoder φ.

Let P be a function defined on $\mathbb{R}^n$ (for example, a pricing function) that needs to evaluate a large collection of scenarios or points X. An Autoencoder can be trained on X to reduce its dimension from n down to k by encoding X, $Y = \psi(X)$. The encoded data Y can be decoded to obtain $\tilde{X} = \varphi(Y)$. If the training is done properly, the difference between X and $\tilde{X}$ is small. Then, the composition

$$\mathbb{R}^k \xrightarrow{\ \varphi\ } \mathbb{R}^n \xrightarrow{\ P\ } \mathbb{R}$$
$$\underbrace{\hspace{4cm}}_{f}$$

defines a function f such that by construction, its value on each scenario of Y is very close to the value of P on each scenario of X. The key difference is that k, the dimension of f, is much lower than n, the dimension of P. Hence one of the approximating techniques presented in Part I can be applied without the difficulties presented by high values of n.

5.3   SUMMARY OF CHAPTER

- **Dimensionality reduction.** The main purpose of the Composition Technique is to reduce the dimension of the input domain of a given function P through the appropriate choice of data parametrisations. For most applications presented in Part IV, the functions considered P are pricing function.

- **The importance of context**. The Composition Technique takes different forms depending on the characteristics of the calculation involved. Sometimes, the required parametrisations are obtained from the risk factor generating models present in the calculation. Other times, these parametrisations are the result of applying a dimensionality reduction technique on the input data, such as PCA or Autoencoders.
- **Benefit**. In some contexts, this technique can substantially reduce the dimension of the input space of a function that we want to replicate. In these cases, the problems of function replication are significantly reduced with this technique.

## CHAPTER 6

Tensors in TT format and Tensor Extension Algorithms

A s mentioned in Section 4.3, one of the main problems affecting tensors is the curse of dimensionality. This says that as the dimension of the tensor increases, the number of grid points increases exponentially. The issue is of a practical nature: beyond a certain dimension — that tends to be relatively low, for example five dimensions — evaluating the function f on every single grid point within the time constraints and storing the tensors in memory becomes problematic. The algorithms presented in this chapter offer a way to sidestep this problem for tensors of high dimensions.

The different sections in this chapter are based on the contents of [29] and references therein (such as [69] and [60]). The central idea is to approximate tensors $\mathcal{X}$ of high dimensions by tensors in $\mathcal{F}_r$ — the family of tensors of rank up to r when expressed in TT format. This set will be defined in Section 6.1. For the time being, it suffices to know that tensors $\mathcal{A} \in \mathcal{F}_r$ admit a representation in terms of matrices, which is memory efficient and can be operated with very efficiently.

Tensors in $\mathcal{F}_r$ are a gateway to working with tensors of dimension greater than 5. If one can approximate tensors $\mathcal{X}$ to a high degree of accuracy with tensors $\mathcal{A}$ in $\mathcal{F}_r$, then $\mathcal{A}$ can be used instead of $\mathcal{X}$.

In [29], tensors in TT format are used to approximate pricing functions. The results reported are remarkable. Examples of up to 25 dimensions are given (basket option with 25 underlyings), and the compression factor is a dramatic 3×10^7. Accuracy reaches fifth digit precision, obtaining an acceleration of about 4,000 times, with respect to the pricing function evaluation speed. As the reader will see, some of the results presented in Part IV give further proof of the extraordinary applicability of the methods presented in this Chapter. Although the examples in [29] and the ones presented in Part IV are all of dimensions less than 25, there is no reason why this technique should not work for higher dimensions — this will depend on the function being approximated.

The rest of the chapter is structured as follows. First, the tensors in TT format are discussed. Then we cover a collection of algorithms, called *Tensor Extension Algorithms*, that aim at finding a tensor $\mathcal{A}$ in $\mathcal{F}_r$ to approximate $\mathcal{X}$ (the tensor we want to work with) to a high degree of accuracy.

6.1 TENSORS IN TT FORMAT

We remind the reader that tensors are just a set of grid points in Euclidean space with real values at each of the grid points.

For the purposes of this section, the grid of points of a d dimensional tensor $\mathcal{X}$ is defined in the following way. Let X_i be a set of points of dimension 1, where $1 \leq i \leq d$. Then $M = X_1 \times \cdots \times X_d$, the Cartesian product of the one-dimensional grid points X_i, defines a mesh of points in $\mathbb{R}^d$. If X_i has n_i points, then the tensor $\mathcal{X}$ has a total of $n_1 \cdots n_d$ points. We denote the space of tensors on M by $\mathbb{R}^{n_1 \times \cdots \times n_d}$. All tensors considered from now on live in this space.

From now on, assume the distribution of the grid points X_i is fixed given a value n_i. Note that everything that is said about these tensors equally applies to any other distribution.

6.1.1 Motivating example

In order to ease the introduction of the concept of tensors in TT format, let us start with a simple example.

Consider a grid of points in two dimensions ($d = 2$), with three and four points in each dimension ($n_1 = 3$, $n_2 = 4$). The points can be distributed in any way; for example, they can be equidistant, they can be Chebyshev points or any other family of points. This grid has 12 points.

Now we define values at each grid point to obtain a two-dimensional tensor $\mathcal{A}$. To define these values, consider a vector U_1 in $\mathbb{R}^{n_1}$ and U_2 in $\mathbb{R}^{n_2}$. For example, we may have $U_1 = (7.2, 6.2, -2.3)$ and $U_2 = (0.5, -3.4, 6.1, 86.9)$. With these vectors, we can define the value of the tensor $\mathcal{A}$ at a given grid point as the multiplication of the corresponding values in the vectors U_1 and U_2. For example, $\mathcal{A}(2, 3) = U_1(2) \cdot U_2(3) = 6.2 \cdot 6.1 = 37.82$.

More generally, given a grid of points in d dimensions ($n_1, n_2, \ldots, n_d$), let U_i be a vector of real values with length n_i, where $1 \leq i \leq d$. Define a tensor $\mathcal{A}$, at the grid point $(j_1, \ldots, j_d)$, in the following way:

$$\mathcal{A}(j_1, \ldots, j_d) = U_1(j_1) \cdots U_d(j_d). \tag{6.1}$$

Notice that $\mathcal{A}$ has been defined in a very specific manner: via the vectors $\{U_1, U_2, \ldots, U_d\}$. By construction, the value of $\mathcal{A}$ on the grid point $(j_1, \ldots, j_d)$, is the product $U_1(j_1) \cdots U_d(j_d)$. Since not all tensors can be expressed this way, the family of tensors expressed as in Equation 6.1 constitute a proper sub-class of the larger class of general tensors.

An important advantage of tensors defined as in Equation 6.1 is that they require much less information compared to a general tensor. Normally, a tensor with dimension d and $n_1 \cdots n_d$ grid points requires storing $\mathcal{O}(n^d)$ elements, where $n = max\{n_1, \ldots, n_d\}$. A tensor such as $\mathcal{A}$, which is fully defined by the vectors U_i, requires only $\mathcal{O}(dn)$. Notice the following fundamental difference: exponential growth, which characterises the curse of dimensionality for tensors, has been changed for linear growth.

6.1.2 General case

Now let us generalise the example in Equation 6.1 in a manner that will be convenient later on.

The entries of the vectors U_i, that is, $U_i(j)$ in Equation 6.1, are real values. However, they can be thought of as matrices of size or rank 1. A natural way of generalising this is making the vectors $\{U_i\}_{i=1}^{i=d}$ — also known as the *cores* of $\mathcal{A}$ — vectors of two-dimensional matrices. A core U, then, has the property that $U(i)$ is a matrix of rank $r_1 \times r_2$, for some values r_1 and r_2. From this perspective, Equation 6.1 presents the simplest example of a tensor in TT format, as the ranks of the matrices used to define tensor $\mathcal{A}$ are 1, the lowest possible value.

Now that we are dealing with matrices, if we want to preserve the expression in Equation 6.1, we need to impose conditions on the ranks of the matrices so that they can be multiplied. This means that if the rank of the matrices in U_i is $r_{i-1} \times r_i$, for some r_{i-1}, r_i, then the rank of the matrices in U_{i+1} has to be $r_i \times r_{i+1}$, for some r_{i+1}. Finally, so that the product gives a real number, the first and last rank — r_0 and r_d — need to be 1.

Tensors in TT format

Definition 6.1.1 *A tensor $\mathcal{A}$ in $\mathbb{R}^{n_1 \times \cdots \times n_d}$ expressed in TT format with ranks $(r_0, \ldots, r_d)$, consists of the following,*

1. *A set of vectors of matrices U_i, where $1 \leq i \leq d$.*
2. *$U_i(j)$ is a matrix of rank $r_{i-1} \times r_i$, for $1 \leq j \leq n_i$ and*
3. *The first and last rank are one. That is $r_0 = r_d = 1$.*

This is sufficient information to recover the whole tensor in the following way

$$\mathcal{A}(j_1, \ldots, j_d) = U_1(j_1) \cdots U_d(j_d). \tag{6.2}$$

The information that defines a tensor in TT format (Definition 6.1.1) is often presented as a tensor network diagram. Figure 6.1 shows an example of such diagram, where the dimension of the tensor is 5. The core corresponding to the i-th dimension is represented by U_i. The core U_i is defined by n_i points and each matrix in the core has rank $r_{i-1} \times r_i$.

The main advantage of working with tensors in TT format is the huge reduction in storage cost. The cost of $\mathcal{O}(n^d)$ associated with ordinary tensor is reduced down to

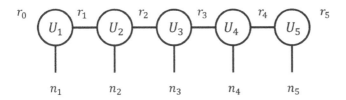

FIGURE 6.1 TT Tensor diagram.

$\mathcal{O}(dnr^2)$.[1] Clearly, if the rank r is low, then the reduction in cost as the dimension grows is considerable.

The second main advantage comes when operating with tensors. In Section 6.1.3 we present two of the most basic operations for tensors in TT format: addition and scalar multiplication. But most relevant to this book, as it directly affects the applications presented in Part IV, is the efficient evaluation of the interpolant defined by the tensor in TT format when the grid is given by Chebyshev points. Section 6.1.4 describes how this is done.

6.1.3 Basic operations

One of the main advantages of the TT format for tensors is that a significant number of linear algebra operations can be performed in an efficient manner. In this section, we cover two of them: addition of tensors and the multiplication of a tensor by a scalar value. These are important within the applications of interest in Part IV as tensors are often added and scaled to increase the efficiency of the calculation in question (e.g. if two tensors represent the pricing functions of two trades, adding them corresponds to creating the pricing function of a portfolio with both trades, and multiplying them by a scalar corresponds to changing the notional of the trade).

Other operations, such as the inner product of tensors and tensor by matrix multiplication, crucial for the evaluation of CTs in TT format, will be covered in Section 6.1.4. For other operations not mentioned in this chapter, we refer the reader to [60].

Scalar multiplication is straightforward with tensors in TT format. It suffices to multiply any of the cores by the scalar value in question. Therefore, if $\mathcal{A}$ is the tensor in TT format and α is a scalar, then

$$\alpha \mathcal{A}(j_1, \ldots, j_d) = \alpha U_1(j_1)U_2(j_2) \cdots U_d(j_d),$$

where, without loss of generality, the scalar α multiplies the matrices in the first core U_i.

Addition of tensors in TT format is performed as follows. Suppose we have $\mathcal{A}_1$ and $\mathcal{A}_2$, tensors in TT format. Denote the cores of $\mathcal{A}_1$ by $U_1, \ldots, U_d$ and the cores of $\mathcal{A}_2$ by $V_1, \ldots, V_d$. By definition, we have

$$\mathcal{A}_1(j_1, \ldots, j_d) = U_1(j_1) \cdots U_d(j_d),$$

$$\mathcal{A}_2(j_1, \ldots, j_d) = V_1(j_1) \cdots V_d(j_d).$$

Then the tensor $\mathcal{A} = \mathcal{A}_1 + \mathcal{A}_2$, has cores $W_1, \ldots, W_d$ defined as follows:

$$W_1(j_1) = \begin{pmatrix} U_1(j_1) & V_1(j_1) \end{pmatrix}, \quad W_d(j_d) = \begin{pmatrix} U_d(j_d) \\ V_d(j_d) \end{pmatrix} \tag{6.3}$$

---

[1]The value r is the maximum of all the ranks.

for the first and last cores, that is, when $k = 0, d$. For the remaining cores we have

$$W_k(j_k) = \begin{pmatrix} U_k(j_k) & 0 \\ 0 & V_k(j_k) \end{pmatrix}. \tag{6.4}$$

The verification that indeed Equations 6.3 and 6.4 define the sum of two tensors in TT format can be done by direct multiplication:

$$\mathcal{A}(j_1, \dots, j_d) = W_1(j_1) \cdots W_d(j_d)$$
$$= U_1(j_1) \cdots U_d(j_d) + V_1(j_1) \cdots V_d(j_d).$$

6.1.4 Evaluation of Chebyshev Tensors in TT format

In this section, we explain how a CT $\mathcal{A}$ in TT format can be evaluated on a point p that lies within its domain.

First notice that we start from the assumption that $\mathcal{A}$ is not a full CT (one that stores the values on every grid point). Therefore, we cannot apply the barycentric interpolation formula or the Clenshaw algorithm the way we do with full CTs (see Section 3.6). The authors of [29], however, present an efficient way of evaluating CTs in TT format, which we now describe.

For the time being, assume we are working with a full CT $\mathcal{T}$. We will first review a naive way of defining the evaluation of such tensor. Then we will see how this can be extended to CTs in TT format to define an efficient way of evaluating them.

In Section 3.3.7, we saw that the interpolant $I_{\mathcal{T}}$ defined by $\mathcal{T}$ can be expressed as

$$I_{\mathcal{T}} = \sum_{j \in J} c_j T_j.$$

The set J is given by $\{(j_1, \dots, j_d) \mid 0 \leq j_i \leq n_i\}$, where $n_i + 1$ corresponds to the number of Chebyshev points on dimension i ($1 \leq i \leq d$). The polynomials $T_j, j \in J$ are the Chebyshev polynomials of dimension d, given by

$$T_j(p_1, \dots, p_d) = \prod_{i=1}^{d} T_{j_i}(p_i), \tag{6.5}$$

where T_{j_i} is the one-dimensional Chebyshev polynomial of degree j_i. Finally, the coefficients c_j are the Chebyshev coefficients given by

$$c_j = \left(\prod_{i=1}^{d} \frac{2^{1(\{0 < j_i < n_i\})}}{n_i} \right) \sum_{k_1=0}^{n_1} {}' \cdots \sum_{k_d=0}^{n_d} {}' f_{(k_1, \dots, k_d)} \prod_{i=1}^{d} \cos \left(j_i \pi \frac{k_i}{n_i} \right), \tag{6.6}$$

where the symbol ' in Equation 6.6 means the summation is multiplied by 0.5, when $k_i = 0, n_i$.

Therefore, for a given point p within the domain covered by the interpolant $I_{\mathcal{T}}$, its value under the interpolant is

$$I_{\mathcal{T}}(p) = \sum_{j \in J} c_j T_j(p). \tag{6.7}$$

The evaluation presented in Equation 6.7 is certainly not the most efficient way of evaluating a tensor — the barycentric interpolation formula or the Clenshaw Algorithm offer much better alternatives when working with full CT (Section 3.6). However, in the case of CTs in TT format, the expression in Equation 6.7 can be used as a good starting point.

The authors of [29] noted the following crucial points: first, that Equation 6.7 can be recovered as the inner product of tensors; second, and most important, that the tensors involved in this inner product can be expressed in TT format. This is a very important point as the inner product of tensors in TT format can be performed very efficiently.

Let us define the inner product of tensors. Say we have two tensors $\mathcal{X}$ and $\mathcal{Y}$ of dimension d defined over the same grid. Then their inner product is defined as follows:

$$\langle \mathcal{X}, \mathcal{Y} \rangle(i_1, \ldots, i_d) = \sum_{i_1=0}^{n_1} \cdots \sum_{i_d=0}^{n_d} \mathcal{X}(i_1, \ldots, i_d) \mathcal{Y}(i_1, \ldots, i_d), \tag{6.8}$$

where $(i_1, \ldots, i_d)$ denotes a grid point on both $\mathcal{X}$ and $\mathcal{Y}$.

Evaluation efficiency for tensors in TT format

When $\mathcal{X}$ and $\mathcal{Y}$ are tensors in TT format, the complexity of the inner product relies directly, due to Equations 6.2 and 6.8, on the ranks of the cores that define $\mathcal{X}$ and $\mathcal{Y}$. Therefore, using tensors of low rank in TT format not only considerably reduces the storage costs of tensors but also increases the efficiency of the inner product.

As we see, the inner product defines the evaluation of CTs in TT format. Therefore, an efficient inner product computation translates into an efficient CT evaluation. As the reader will see in Part IV, this point is paramount in the applications of interest as we seek to use CT to efficiently evaluate large collections of points that financial functions (such as pricing functions) take a long time to evaluate.

Let us now see the two tensors in TT format that recover Equation 6.7 when their inner product is considered.

We denote the tensors we are after by $\mathcal{C}$ and $\mathcal{T}_p$. The tensor $\mathcal{C}$ represents the Chebyshev coefficients c_j in Equation 6.7, while $\mathcal{T}_p$ represents the terms $T_j(p)$.

The Chebyshev coefficients, as given in Equation 6.6, constitute a tensor $\mathcal{C}$ with $(n_1 + 1) \cdots (n_d + 1)$ grid points. However, we want $\mathcal{C}$ to be in TT format for two reasons. First, given the curse of dimensionality, if d is not small enough, then $\mathcal{C}$ is difficult to build and operate with. Second, if we are to recover the evaluation of the tensor $\mathcal{A}$ on p, through the inner product of tensors, then these tensors had better be in TT format so that the inner product operation can be performed efficiently. What the authors of [29] show is that the tensor $\mathcal{C}$ can be expressed as a tensor in TT format with the same rank as $\mathcal{A}$.

We will not give full details of how to obtain the tensor $\mathcal{C}$ in TT format. For that we refer to [29]. It suffices to note that the construction of $\mathcal{C}$ in TT format reduces down to the repeated application of the mode-μ multiplication between a tensor and a matrix — another operation that can be efficiently implemented with tensors in TT format. Also, this operation involves pre-computable matrices that depend only on the number of Chebyshev points in each dimension (that is, the values $n_1 + 1, \ldots, n_d + 1$) and the tensor $\mathcal{A}$. More importantly, the tensor $\mathcal{C}$ does not depend on the point p to be evaluated, which means it can be constructed once, before any evaluation takes place, irrespective of the number of points to evaluate.

For the second tensor $\mathcal{T}_p$, note that Equation 6.5 already gives an expression that defines a tensor in TT format. It suffices to note that $U_i(j_i) = T_{j_i}(p_i)$, which means we can define $\mathcal{T}_p$ as the tensor in TT format of rank 1 defined by Equation 6.5 at each grid point j.

Notice that this tensor depends on p and must be generated for every point p to be evaluated. However, the fact that it is of rank 1 and is obtained by evaluating Chebyshev polynomials makes it very efficient to compute.

In summary, using the expression to evaluate CTs in Equation 6.7, the definition of inner product in Equation 6.8, and the tensors $\mathcal{C}$ (of Chebyshev coefficients) and $\mathcal{T}_p$ in TT format, we obtain an efficient way of evaluating CTs in TT format.

6.2 TENSOR EXTENSION ALGORITHMS

General tensors $\mathcal{X}$ become increasingly difficult to work with — due to the curse of dimensionality — somewhere between dimensions 5 and 10. As we saw in Section 6.1, Tensors in TT format have a series of properties that allow us to work with tensors in higher dimensions. Therefore, if a given tensor $\mathcal{X}$ can be approximated by a TT format tensor $\mathcal{A}$ of low rank, then the dimension becomes a much smaller restriction as the cost of storing the latter is only $\mathcal{O}(dnr^2)$. Moreover, as we saw in Section 6.1.4, the evaluation of tensors in TT format (at least the ones defined over Chebyshev grids) can be evaluated in a very efficient manner.

However, working with tensors in TT format comes at a cost — we are restricting ourselves to a sub-class of tensors, one that might not have the tensors we are looking for. In this section, we are going to discuss how we can do so with a limited, if at all, negative impact, specifically in the context of the practical applications that we are interested in this book.

The goal of this section is to discuss different algorithms that we call *Tensor Extension Algorithms* to find the low-rank tensor $\mathcal{A}$ that is a good approximation to $\mathcal{X}$. We will present three of them: the *Completion Algorithm* — most fundamental and the basis for all the rest — the *Rank Adaptive Algorithm* and the *Sample Adaptive Algorithm*.

6.3 STEP 1 – OPTIMISING OVER TENSORS OF FIXED RANK

The aim of this section is to show how the space of tensors with fixed ranks can be explored to find one that approximates a given tensor $\mathcal{X}$. We will not justify every statement made; this is beyond the scope of the book. We aim to present and identify the main elements involved in the algorithm. We refer to [29], [69], and [60], along with references therein, for further details.

Denote the space of tensors in TT format with ranks $r = (r_0, r_1, \ldots, r_d)$ by $\mathcal{F}_r$.[2] The ranks r_i, where $0 \leq i \leq d$ can take any natural number greater than 0, with the obvious exception of the first and last (r_0 and r_d), which by definition must be equal to 1 (see Definition 6.1.1).

A very important property of $\mathcal{F}_r$ is that it is a Riemannian manifold. This means $\mathcal{F}_r$, as a subspace of the space of tensors $\mathbb{R}^{n_1 \times \cdots \times n_d}$, can be navigated without encountering edges or sharp points; everywhere, from within $\mathcal{F}_r$, looks smooth. This means algorithms that rely on the gradient of a function defined on this space can be used. This applies to the Riemannian Conjugate Gradient (CG) algorithm that navigates $\mathcal{F}_r$ in search of a tensor $\mathcal{A}$ that is close to a given tensor $\mathcal{X}$ in $\mathbb{R}^{n_1 \times \cdots \times n_d}$. This algorithm is the one used in [29] to find a tensor $\mathcal{A}$ of low rank that approximates $\mathcal{X}$ — a general tensor — which is used instead of the latter in a range of different calculations.

The search for a suitable tensor $\mathcal{A}$ in $\mathcal{F}_r$ to replace $\mathcal{X}$ takes the form of an optimisation problem. The aim is to minimise the error or difference between the tensor $\mathcal{X}$ and the space $\mathcal{F}_r$, that is, find $\mathcal{A}$ in $\mathcal{F}_r$, which gets as close as possible to $\mathcal{X}$.

Notice that the main problem of working with $\mathcal{X}$ is that we cannot evaluate and store its values at every grid point. Therefore, the difference between $\mathcal{A}$ and $\mathcal{X}$ is computed only on a subset $\mathcal{K}$ of the grid; indeed, if we could work with the values of $\mathcal{X}$ on all grid points, there would be no need to find a tensor of low rank $\mathcal{A}$.

The minimisation problem in the optimisation exercise has the following expression:

$$\min_{\mathcal{A} \in \mathcal{F}_r} \| \mathcal{X}_\mathcal{K} - \mathcal{A}_\mathcal{K} \|^2 \tag{6.9}$$

where $\mathcal{X}_\mathcal{K}$ means $\mathcal{X}$ restricted to a subset $\mathcal{K}$ of its grid points.

The formula in Equation 6.9 can be minimised using different optimisation algorithms. An example is the conjugate gradient algorithm used in [29]. However, irrespective of the algorithm, the aim is to obtain a tensor $\mathcal{A}$ in TT format that approximates the information we have of $\mathcal{X}$, that is, $\mathcal{X}$ restricted to $\mathcal{K}$. As the tensor $\mathcal{A}$ is fully defined on the whole grid, we use it as a proxy to $\mathcal{X}$ even when the approximation only takes place on the subgrid $\mathcal{K}$. Intuitively, it is via $\mathcal{A}$ that we extend the information of $\mathcal{X}$ from $\mathcal{K}$ to the whole grid.

A Note on Optimisation Algorithms

In general, the vast majority of optimisation algorithms work on a trial-and-error basis. At each iteration they make an educated guess, based on the previous result, of a good candidate $\mathcal{A}$ to approximate $\mathcal{X}$. This process is repeated, often thousands of times, with the intention of improving the result.

What normally distinguishes different optimisation algorithms is the method used to improve the tensor $\mathcal{A}$ from the previous iteration. Gradient-based algorithms use the gradient of so-called objective or cost functions, such as the one in Equation 6.9, to

---

[2]The family $\{\mathcal{F}_r\}_{r=1}^{\infty}$ is a filtration within the space of general tensors as shown in Equation 6.12. Notice we make the assumption that $r_0 = r_1 = \cdots = r_d = r$.

search for optimal tensors $\mathcal{A}$. This requires both the function and space over which it is defined to be smooth. Given that the objective function in 6.9 is smooth and $\mathcal{F}_r$ is a smooth Riemannian manifold, the conjugate gradient algorithm lends itself well to this problem. As mentioned before, this is the algorithm of choice in [29] and [69], on which a lot of the content of this chapter is based.

It is important to note, however, that there are many other algorithms that can be used to solve Equation 6.9. Just as there is a large number of gradient-based algorithms, there are others that do not make any assumptions about the smoothness of $\mathcal{F}_r$ or the objective function in Equation 6.9. These algorithms have gained quite a lot of popularity in recent years given their ability to deal with high dimensions, non-convex problems and non-smooth objective functions. Their main downside, however, is their speed. For a good review of a wide range of gradient-free optimisers, we refer to [61].

6.3.1 The Fundamental Completion Algorithm

This section describes the main steps followed by a generic Completion Algorithm, that is, an algorithm that extends the values of a tensor $\mathcal{X}$ on a subset of its grid, to the whole of it, by finding a solution to Equation 6.9.

Every iteration of the Completion Algorithm considers a tensor $\mathcal{A}$ of low rank that is a proxy to $\mathcal{X}$. How $\mathcal{A}$ is obtained depends on the particular algorithm used at line 5 in Algorithm 1. What is common to all is that at each iteration, the difference between $\mathcal{A}$ and $\mathcal{X}$, restricted to the subset $\mathcal{K}$, is measured — line 6. If a certain level of accuracy ε is reached, the algorithm stops. Given that there is no guarantee of reaching the level of accuracy, the iterations also stop if the accuracy no longer improves on consecutive iterations (measured through δ), or if the (predefined) maximum number of iterations N is reached. These conditions are checked in line 4 of Algorithm 1.

Algorithm 1 Completion Algorithm

1: **procedure** COMPLETION(r, N, ε, δ, $\mathcal{X}_{\mathcal{K}}$)
2:     $\mathcal{A}_{old} \leftarrow$ Random $\mathcal{A}$ in $\mathcal{F}_r$
3:     $\mathcal{A}_{new} \leftarrow \mathcal{A}_{old}$
4:     **while** $\varepsilon(\mathcal{A}_{new}) > \varepsilon$ & $\delta(\mathcal{A}_{new}) > \delta$ & iter $< N$ **do**
5:         $\mathcal{A}_{new} \leftarrow update(\mathcal{A}_{old})$
6:         $\varepsilon(\mathcal{A}_{new}) \leftarrow$ Error of approximation of $\mathcal{A}_{new}$ to $\mathcal{X}_{\mathcal{K}}$
7:         $\delta(\mathcal{A}_{new}) \leftarrow$ Error stagnation $|\varepsilon(\mathcal{A}_{new}) - \varepsilon(\mathcal{A}_{old})|/|\varepsilon(\mathcal{A}_{old})|$
8:         $iter \leftarrow iter + 1$
9:         $\mathcal{A}_{old} \leftarrow \mathcal{A}_{new}$
10:    **return** $\mathcal{A}_{new}$

Let us take a careful look at Algorithm 1.

Parameters

The following are the parameters that need to be specified in the Completion Algorithm. First, the ranks $r = (r_0, r_1, \ldots, r_d)$ must be specified and fixed. This specifies the space of tensors $\mathcal{F}_r$ over which the optimisation takes place. Second, a limit to the number of iterations is established. This is stored in N. If this many iterations have been reached, the algorithm stops and returns the currently held tensor $\mathcal{A}$. Third, a subset $\mathcal{K}$ of the grid points of $\mathcal{X}$ is chosen. In most cases, $\mathcal{K}$ is chosen randomly. These are points that contain all the information available about $\mathcal{X}$ and over which the optimisation is done. The aim is to infer the values of the rest of $\mathcal{X}$ using only the information over $\mathcal{K}$.

Remark 6.3.1   Note that the solution of Equation 6.9 gives no guarantee that $\mathcal{A}$ is a good proxy for the whole of $\mathcal{X}$. This depends on the characteristics of $\mathcal{X}$ and the subgrid $\mathcal{K}$ chosen. In all the applications presented in Part IV, the tensor $\mathcal{X}$ is associated with a function f. This means that the values of the tensor $\mathcal{X}$ on the subgrid $\mathcal{K}$ correspond to the values obtained by evaluating f on $\mathcal{K}$, where f is typically a pricing or sensitivity function. As we will see in Part IV, tensors $\mathcal{X}$ obtained this way tend to have the right characteristics to be approximated by tensors $\mathcal{A}$ in TT format with low rank. Further evidence of this is also presented in [29].

Convergence detection

There are two quantities that need to be measured carefully. The first is the accuracy of approximation. The second is the error stagnation. As in many optimisation exercises — such as the ones regularly used to train DNNs — there is the risk of optimising too much to the given data and underperforming with unseen data. To deal with this, it is common practice to keep some data on the side to be used for testing purposes only. In the same spirit, the elements in the subset $\mathcal{K}$ are divided into a training set $\mathcal{K}_{train}$ and a testing set $\mathcal{K}_{test}$.

   Two thresholds are chosen. The first, ε, is the desired level of approximation. If the error measured as in Equation 6.10 is less than ε, for both the training and the testing set, the algorithm stops and the tensor $\mathcal{A}$ returned. This tensor, restricted to the subset $\mathcal{K}$, has the degree of approximation looked for. This is one of the stopping criteria considered in line 4 of Algorithm 1.

   The second, δ, is the minimum level of error improvement desired. The error improvement stagnates if the difference between consecutive errors, as measured in Equation 6.11, falls below δ for both testing and training sets. In this case, the algorithm stops returning the tensor $\mathcal{A}$ of the iteration at which the algorithm stops.

   The error of approximation in each of the sets is measured using the following formulas:

$$\varepsilon_{\mathcal{K}_{train}}(\mathcal{A}) = \frac{\|\mathcal{X}_{\mathcal{K}_{train}} - \mathcal{A}_{\mathcal{K}_{train}}\|}{\|\mathcal{X}_{\mathcal{K}_{train}}\|}, \qquad \varepsilon_{\mathcal{K}_{test}}(\mathcal{A}) = \frac{\|\mathcal{X}_{\mathcal{K}_{test}} - \mathcal{A}_{\mathcal{K}_{test}}\|}{\|\mathcal{X}_{\mathcal{K}_{test}}\|}. \tag{6.10}$$

   The error stagnation is measured as the difference of consecutive errors normalised by their magnitude

$$\delta_{\mathcal{K}_{train}} = \frac{|\varepsilon_{\mathcal{K}_{train}}(\mathcal{A}_{k+1}) - \varepsilon_{\mathcal{K}_{train}}(\mathcal{A}_k)|}{|\varepsilon_{\mathcal{K}_{train}}(\mathcal{A}_k)|}, \qquad \delta_{\mathcal{K}_{test}} = \frac{|\varepsilon_{\mathcal{K}_{test}}(\mathcal{A}_{k+1}) - \varepsilon_{\mathcal{K}_{test}}(\mathcal{A}_k)|}{|\varepsilon_{\mathcal{K}_{test}}(\mathcal{A}_k)|}, \tag{6.11}$$

where $\mathcal{A}_k$ is the tensor in $\mathcal{F}_r$ corresponding to the k-th iteration of Algorithm 1.

6.4 STEP 2 – OPTIMISING OVER TENSORS OF VARYING RANK

The Completion Algorithm described in Section 6.3 is restricted to spaces of tensors in TT format with a specified rank $r = (r_0, r_1, \ldots, r_d)$. This has the limitation of working in a space that may not be capable of approximating a given tensor $\mathcal{X}$ to the desired degree of accuracy. The *Rank Adaptive* algorithm presented in this section is an enhancement of the Completion Algorithm and it aims at exploring spaces of tensors with varying ranks.

Recall the space $\mathcal{F}_r$ of tensors of rank up to r, introduced at the beginning of Chapter 6. These sets filter the space of tensors in TT format

$$\mathcal{F}_1 \subset \cdots \subset \mathcal{F}_r \subset \cdots . \tag{6.12}$$

This filtration offers a natural way of exploring bigger spaces of tensors. The higher up in the filtration, the bigger the space over which the optimisation takes place and the higher the chances to find a tensor $\mathcal{A}$ of low rank that approximates $\mathcal{X}$ to the required degree of accuracy.

The idea is to run the Completion Algorithm presented in Section 6.3.1 at each level of the filtration, gradually exploring bigger and bigger spaces in the hope of finding a tensor of low rank that is a good proxy for the tensor we want.

We want to stress the importance of finding tensors in TT format of the lowest rank possible. This is the direct result of the storage cost of tensors in TT format, which is of the order of $\mathcal{O}(dnr^2)$. The lower the rank r, the cheaper it is to build and store tensors with TT format. Also, the lower the ranks, the more efficient the inner product of tensors, and subsequently, the evaluation of CTs in TT format (Section 6.1.4).

The details of the Rank Adaptive Algorithm are given in Section 6.4.1. As the reader will find out, there is no guarantee that for a given tensor $\mathcal{X}$, there is a tensor $\mathcal{A}$ of low rank that approximates it to a high degree of accuracy. Whether there is or not partly depends on the structure of $\mathcal{X}$, essentially, whether or not $\mathcal{X}$ is close, in some sense, to having a low rank structure.

Relevance of Rank Adaptive Algorithm

The relevance of the Rank Adaptive Algorithm for this book comes from the fact that the applications we seek are for tensors $\mathcal{X}$ that approximate pricing functions P.

As we know, these functions — with a few exceptions that are discussed in other parts of the book — tend to have nice properties. Indeed, in most cases they do not change in convexity more than once (along any given dimension) and exhibit high degrees of smoothness such as being piece-wise analytic (see Section 13.1). Therefore, the tensors obtained from these functions — defined by evaluating P over a Chebyshev grid on its domain — inherit these properties. It is therefore, reasonable to think that these tensors can be approximated to a high degree of accuracy with tensors of low rank.

Part IV of this book gives empirical evidence that supports this hypothesis.

6.4.1 The Rank Adaptive Algorithm

In this section, we give some of the details behind the Rank Adaptive Algorithm. These are summarised in Algorithm 2 and further described in the following paragraphs. For more details, we refer to [29].

Algorithm 2 Rank Adaptive Algorithm

1: **procedure** RANKADAPTIVE(r_{max}, $\mathcal{X}_{\mathcal{K}}$)
2:     $\mathcal{A}_{current}$ ← Random $\mathcal{A}$ with $r = (1, \ldots, 1)$
3:     $\mathcal{A}_{current}$ ← Apply Completion Algorithm to $\mathcal{A}_{current}$
4:     *rejected* ← 0
5:     i ← 1
6:     **while** $max_i \ r_i < r_{max}$ & *rejected* $< d - 1$ **do**
7:        $\mathcal{A}_{new}$ ← Increase i-th rank of $\mathcal{A}_{current}$ by 1
8:        $\mathcal{A}_{new}$ ← Apply Completion Algorithm to $\mathcal{A}_{new}$
9:        **if** $\varepsilon(\mathcal{A}_{new}) > \varepsilon(\mathcal{A}_{current})$ **then**
10:          *rejected* ← 1 + *rejected*
11:        **else**
12:          *rejected* ← 0, $\mathcal{A}_{current}$ ← $\mathcal{A}_{new}$
13:        i ← $1 + (i \bmod d - 1)$
14:     **return** $\mathcal{A}_{current}$

The Rank Adaptive Algorithm consists of running the Completion Algorithm on spaces of tensors in TT format as their rank is increased. Therefore, the first parameter that needs to be specified is the maximum rank of the space to be explored. This is specified in the parameter r_{max}. If the space of tensors explored has at least one core with such rank, the algorithm stops, returning whichever tensor $\mathcal{A}_{current}$ was currently the proxy to $\mathcal{X}$ (see Algorithm 2).

The algorithm starts by considering the space of tensors in TT format of constant rank 1, that is, $r = (1, \ldots, 1)$. The Completion Algorithm is run and a tensor $\mathcal{A}_{current}$ obtained (line 3 in Algorithm 2). If $\mathcal{A}_{current}$ has the desired degree of accuracy, the process stops. Otherwise, the rank of the space over which the Completion Algorithm runs is increased in the following way.

The rank of the space so far considered is given by $(1, r_1 \ldots, r_{d-1}, 1)$, where $r_i = 1$, for $1 \leq i \leq d - 1$, and d is the dimension of the tensors. The space of tensors considered next is obtained by increasing the ranks from left to right. The first rank that can be changed is r_1. This is increased by 1. The rank of the space to which the Completion Algorithm is now applied is $(1, 2, 1, \ldots, 1)$. The tensor $\mathcal{A}_{current}$ obtained in the previous iteration is used as a starting point.

Once the Completion Algorithm finishes on the space of ranks $(1, 2, 1, \ldots, 1)$, there is a decision to be made. The tensor $\mathcal{A}_{new}$ returned, in line 8 of Algorithm 2, may or may not be one we want to keep. Whether we keep it or not is based on comparing $\varepsilon_{current}$, the error of approximation of $\mathcal{A}_{current}$, with the ε_{new}, the error of approximation of $\mathcal{A}_{new}$. If ε_{new} is an improvement over $\varepsilon_{current}$, then $\mathcal{A}_{new}$ becomes $\mathcal{A}_{current}$, and the next iteration of the Completion Algorithm run on ranks $(1, 2, 2, 1 \ldots, 1)$. In this case we reset the variable *rejected* to 0. If, however, $\varepsilon_{current}$ is better than ε_{new}, then $\mathcal{A}_{new}$ is discarded, and the next iteration of the Completion Algorithm run on ranks $(1, 1, 2, 1 \ldots, 1)$. In this case, we increase the value of *rejected* by 1.

The Rank Adaptive Algorithm continues increasing each rank by 1, from left to right, testing each time whether the resulting tensor $\mathcal{A}_{new}$ is an improvement over the previous one. The algorithm stops if any of the next three criteria are met:

1. The error of $\mathcal{A}_{current}$ is less than ε. In this case, the algorithm has found a tensor $\mathcal{A}$ which is a good proxy to $\mathcal{X}$.
2. All ranks have been increased and no improvement has been obtained. That is, the algorithm has gone through a cycle of all ranks, increasing them by 1, one at a time, and for none has a tensor $\mathcal{A}$ been found, which is better than the previous one.
3. The rank r_i reaches r_{max}, for some i, where $1 \le i \le d - 1$.

Out of these three stopping criteria, the only one that gives a positive result is the first. The other two simply say an optimal proxy $\mathcal{A}$ has not been obtained.

If a tensor $\mathcal{A}$ with the desired accuracy is not obtained, something must be modified. One possibility is to increase the rank of the space of tensors by more than 1. This however, comes at the detriment of the memory size needed to store tensors in TT format — $\mathcal{O}(dnr^2)$ — an important consideration to have in mind; this is why the Rank Adaptive Algorithm increases the rank in a very conservative manner.

Another possible modification is to change the set $\mathcal{K}$ over which the optimisation takes place. This is proposed in [29], where every time the Rank Adaptive algorithm finishes, if a good proxy $\mathcal{A}$ has not been obtained, the number of points in $\mathcal{K}$ is increased. The next section focuses on this adjustment.

6.5 STEP 3 — ADAPTING THE SAMPLING SET

The Sample Adaptive Algorithm is the third of the Tensor Extension Algorithms we present. This is proposed in [29] as a way of helping the Rank Adaptive Algorithm find a suitable proxy to a given tensor $\mathcal{X}$.

The rationale behind the Sample Adaptive Algorithm is the following. There is no rigorous way of knowing how many points $\mathcal{K}$ should have for the Rank Adaptive Algorithm to give good results. This partly depends on the tensor $\mathcal{X}$ to be approximated and partly on the randomly selected set of grid points $\mathcal{K}$. Moreover, we do not want to over-sample the tensor $\mathcal{X}$ as this costs; remember that reducing computational cost is at the core of all the applications covered in this book.[3] Therefore, a conservative approach is to sample a small subset of $\mathcal{X}$, run the Adaptive Algorithm, and if needed, expand the sample set over which the Adaptive Algorithm is run.

---

[3]Computational cost comes in two forms: evaluation cost and memory or storing cost. Each point in $\mathcal{K}$ requires the evaluation of the function f we want to approximate — most often a pricing function — which can be expensive to compute. Also, each point $\mathcal{K}$, along with its corresponding value under f, needs to be stored.

6.5.1 The Sample Adaptive Algorithm

This section presents the details of the Sample Adaptive Algorithm. For further details, we refer to [29].

Algorithm 3 Sample Adaptive Algorithm

1: **procedure** SAMPLEADAPTIVE($\mathcal{X}_{\mathcal{K}}$, p, ε)
2:     $\mathcal{K}_{current} \leftarrow \mathcal{K}$
3:     $\mathcal{A}_{new} \leftarrow$ Random $\mathcal{A}$ with $r = (1, \dots, 1)$
4:     $\mathcal{A}_{current} \leftarrow$ Apply Rank Adaptive Algorithm to $\mathcal{A}_{new}$ using $\mathcal{X}_{\mathcal{K}_{current}}$
5:     **while** $|\mathcal{K}|/size(\mathcal{X}) < p$ **do**
6:         $\mathcal{K}_{new} \leftarrow$ New set of grid points such that $\mathcal{K}_{new} \cap \mathcal{K}_{current} = \emptyset$
7:         $\mathcal{K}_{current} \leftarrow \mathcal{K}_{current} \cup \mathcal{K}_{new}$
8:         $\mathcal{A}_{new} \leftarrow$ rank $(1, \dots, 1)$ approximation to $\mathcal{A}_{current}$
9:         $\mathcal{A}_{current} \leftarrow$ Apply Rank Adaptive Algorithm to $\mathcal{A}_{new}$ using $\mathcal{X}_{\mathcal{K}_{current}}$
10:         **if** $\varepsilon(\mathcal{A}_{current}) < \varepsilon$ **then**
11:             break
12:     **return** $\mathcal{A}_{current}$

Each iteration of the Sample Adaptive Algorithm consists of running the Rank Adaptive Algorithm for a different set of grid points $\mathcal{K}$. If at the end of an iteration, the proxy $\mathcal{A}$, denoted by $\mathcal{A}_{current}$ in Algorithm 3, is not good enough, the size of $\mathcal{K}$ is increased.

One of the parameters that needs to be specified is p. This controls the maximum size of $\mathcal{K}$ we are willing to consider and is expressed as a proportion of the total number of grid points in $\mathcal{X}$. For example, p can be 1% of the total number of grid points in $\mathcal{X}$. This means that the total number of points used by the Sample Adaptive Algorithm is at most 1% of the number of points on the grid defining $\mathcal{X}$. If a good proxy $\mathcal{A}$ is obtained — as is the case in some of the applications in Part IV — then memory and computational savings of at least 99% would have been achieved, compared to building $\mathcal{X}$ by evaluating the function f on each grid point.

At the end of each iteration, two criteria are tested to decide whether to stop the algorithm or start a new iteration:

1. If $\varepsilon_{\mathcal{A}}$, the error of $\mathcal{A}$ as a proxy of $\mathcal{X}$ is less than ε.
2. If the proportion of points sampled exceeds p.

The first condition essentially says that the proxy $\mathcal{A}$ has reached the desired level of accuracy, at least restricted to the part of $\mathcal{X}$ we can see, which is given by the set $\mathcal{K}_{current}$. This is the optimal result.

The second condition says that if another iteration of the Rank Adaptive Algorithm is run, we will go over the number of sample points we set as an upper bound.

6.6   SUMMARY OF CHAPTER

- **Curse of dimensionality**. Tensors suffer from the curse of dimensionality. This says that the number of grid points explodes exponentially as the dimension increases. In practical settings, this means we can rarely define tensors to compute with for dimensions that are not low. As a rule of thumb, in many applications, tensors with dimensions greater than six can be impractical to work with.
- **Tensors in TT format**. Compared to ordinary tensors, tensors in TT format only require a small fraction of the information for their definition. This means we can work with tensors in TT format in dimensions as high as 30 or more — something that is impossible with ordinary tensors.
- **Basic operations**. The addition of tensors in TT format and multiplication by scalars are easily defined.
- **Evaluation of CTs in TT format**. If the tensor is defined over a Chebyshev grid, there is an efficient way to evaluate the tensor. This is very important in practical settings such as the ones presented in Part IV.
- **Tensor Extension Algorithms**. This family of algorithms builds accurate approximations to regular tensors using tensors in TT format. In practical settings, this allows us to build accurate replicas for ordinary tensors in dimensions for which it is impossible to build them directly. We only need to evaluate the function to be replicated on a small proportion of the full tensor grid.

## CHAPTER 7

Sliding Technique

This chapter presents the *Sliding Technique*, yet another technique to sidestep the curse of dimensionality that affects the function-approximating techniques presented in Part I.

As the reader will find out, it borrows ideas from the Taylor approximation to tackle high-dimensional functions for which the Composition Technique or the Tensor Extension Algorithms need extra help.

One of its strong points is that it is flexible enough to couple with other techniques presented in this part of the book — such as dimensionality-reduction techniques — as well as with the approximating techniques in Part I.

Later chapters, such as Chapter 16, show how this technique becomes a tool that alleviates, for example, the computational burden associated with market risk metrics such as VaR or Expected Shortfall, and subsequently the risk management metrics and capital calculations associated with them, for example, IMA-FRTB capital.

7.1 SLIDE

A *slide* is an approximating object built in such a way that several of these can be put together to form a larger approximating object. The approximating objects can be instances of CTs, DNNs or any proxy of choice. The key point is that they are built in such a way that they can be amalgamated to form a *slider*.

Let f be a function and let n be the dimension of its domain. That is,

$$f : A \longrightarrow \mathbb{R}, \tag{7.1}$$

for some hyper-rectangle A in $\mathbb{R}^n$. Pick a point $z = (z_1, \ldots, z_n)$ in A. We call z the *pivot point* for the slider. The function f can be restricted to a lower dimensional space by letting some variables vary and fixing the remaining with the values given by z. For example, let the first three dimensions vary and fix the rest using the values in the pivot point, that is, with $z_4, \ldots, z_n$. Formally, this is equivalent to defining a new three-dimensional function g_1, which is the result of composing the injection

$$i : B \hookrightarrow A, \tag{7.2}$$

with f, where $B = \{(x_1, x_2, x_3) \in \mathbb{R}^3 \mid (x_1, x_2, x_3, z_4, \ldots, z_n) \in A\}$, and i takes (x_1, x_2, x_3) to $(x_1, x_2, x_3, z_4, \ldots, z_n)$, yielding

$$g_1 : B \hookrightarrow A \longrightarrow \mathbb{R}. \tag{7.3}$$

An approximating object, such as a CT, can be built for g_1. Notice the dimension of g_1 could have been any between 1 and n. If the approximating objects suffer from the curse of dimensionality — such as it happens for CTs — choosing a dimension such as 3 (or less) makes the building of these approximating objects straightforward.

The approximating object built for g_1, in the way described, is called a *slide*. If the approximating object is a CT, we have a *Chebyshev slide*. If the approximating object is a DNN, we have a *DNN slide*.

7.2 SLIDER

For ease of presentation, we assume from now on that slides are Chebyshev slides. All arguments presented are valid for any other type of approximating object.

A *Chebyshev Slider* is a collection of slides built to approximate a function f with the following two conditions: the first is that each of the variables in the domain of f is part of the domain of one and only one slide, and the second is that all slides share the same pivot point z. If there are k slides built for f, say, $\{s_1, s_2, \ldots, s_k\}$, then the sum of the dimensions of the slides $dim(s_1) + \cdots + dim(s_k)$, is n, which is the dimension of the input domain of f.

As the Chebyshev Slider consists of a collection of slides — which are CTs — the building of the slider consists of the building of at least one CT (k in our example). If there are k slides and each has l_i Chebyshev points on which f is evaluated, the total number of evaluations required to build the slider is $l_1 + \ldots + l_k$. If the slides are typically of one, two or three dimensions — for which at most a few tens of points are needed — the total number of points in the slider is substantially smaller than for an n-dimensional mesh, thus sidestepping the curse of dimensionality.

There are a few choices that need to be made when building a slider. One such choice is the number of slides and their dimension. Closely associated with this — and very important in some cases — is how variables get assigned to slides. For example, one might have chosen the first slide to have dimension 2, but this slide may consist of the first and second variable of f or the first and third variable. Another important choice is the number of sampling points of each slide.

The choices mentioned determine the configuration of the slider. As we now describe, choosing the configuration plays an important role in the use of Sliders as approximating objects, especially within the contexts we are interested in.

On the one hand, increasing the number of slides brings a reduction on the number of evaluations required to build the slider. In some cases, this can have a huge building cost impact. For example, if the slides are built using CTs, the exponential growth Chebyshev grids experience as the dimension increases can be modified, in some cases, to linear growth — when, for example, the dimension of all slides is bounded by some value. On the other hand, increasing the number of slides can sometimes reduce the accuracy of the slider. The practical challenge then becomes one of reducing the number of points to evaluate, while keeping the highest possible accuracy, which is, as we know, what we are after when applying the approximation techniques presented in Part I to the calculations — mostly risk calculations — in Part IV.

One way of increasing the accuracy of the slider without increasing the number of evaluations relates to the choice of variables that define each slide. This was mentioned as a choice that needs to be made when building the slider. Whenever possible, we put together variables that carry the highest non-linear relationships under f. The following simple example illustrates this point.

Say we have the following three-dimensional function $f = x_1^3 x_2^2 + x_3$. There are non-linear relationships between x_1 and x_2, but x_3 is independent of the others. What we do is group x_1 and x_2 in a two-dimensional slide, build a one-dimensional slide for x_3 and constitute a slider with these two slides. By doing this we reduce the building effort because we do not call f on a three-dimensional mesh, but only along the two- and one-dimensional domains defined by the slides. This can be of great help in cases where f is a function that is expensive to evaluate — for example, many pricing functions. Moreover, by grouping x_1 and x_2 in a single slide, we are not missing out on the relationship under f of these two variables. This will become clearer when we define how to evaluate a slider in Section 7.3.

As a result, designing an optimal slider configuration becomes a bit of an art. Sometimes an element of know-how to define an optimal slider configuration is essential. This is not dissimilar, for example, to finding the optimal hyper-parameter configuration for a DNN.

7.3 EVALUATING A SLIDER

The evaluation of the slider is done in the following way. Let $x = (x_1, \ldots, x_n)$ be a point in the domain of f and let v be the value of f at the pivot point z, $v = f(z)$. For ease of presentation, assume without loss of generality that $dim(s_1) = 3$, $dim(s_2) = 2$, and $dim(s_i) = 1$, for $3 \leq i \leq k$.

Let S_i represent the difference between the slider s_i and v, the value of f at the pivot point. That is,

$$S_1(x_1, x_2, x_3) = s_1(x_1, x_2, x_3) - v$$

$$S_2(x_4, x_5) = s_2(x_4, x_5) - v$$

$$S_3(x_6) = s_3(x_6) - v \tag{7.4}$$

$$\ldots$$

$$S_k(x_n) = s_k(x_n) - v.$$

Then, we approximate the value of f at x by

$$v + S_1(x_1, x_2, x_3) + S_2(x_4, x_5) + S_3(x_6) + \cdots + S_k(x_n). \tag{7.5}$$

From now on, sliders will be represented by the k-tuple obtained from the dimensions of its constituent sliders. The example is represented by the k-tuple $\{dim(s_1), dim(s_2), \ldots, dim(s_k)\}$, where the slider consists of the slides $\{s_1, s_2, \ldots, s_k\}$. Notice this will be of relevance in future chapters where Chebyshev Sliders are used, such as Chapter 16.

7.3.1   Relation to Taylor approximation

Equation 7.5 should remind the reader of Taylor approximation. Indeed, CTs (or DNNs if used) are to the slider what partial derivatives are to the Taylor approximation. However, instead of having partial derivatives of order one, or at most two, which often fail to fully capture the function in the domain spanned by the variables concerned, the slides, $S_1, \ldots, S_k$, can approximate their corresponding restrictions of $f, g_1, \ldots, g_k$, to a very high degree of accuracy. Given that the evaluation of the Chebyshev Slider relies on the evaluation of the CTs that constitute it, it is numerically stable and extremely efficient.

For example, consider the case where f is a pricing function of dimension 5. In this case, Taylor approximation consists of approximating f using its greeks — the so-called delta, gamma and cross-gammas. Taylor expansion, in practice, is rarely expanded beyond second order — at least in the applications of concern in this book. Therefore, the information contained in the greeks of order higher than two is not captured.

Using a slider, one can capture part of the information missed by Taylor approximation. For example, one can group x_1, x_2, x_3 in a slide, and x_4, x_5 in another. By doing this, the first slide would capture, to a high degree of accuracy, the changes of the function determined by x_1, x_2, x_3 and the changes of the function driven by x_4, x_5, through the second slide, essentially capturing all the information in the greeks and cross-greeks of all orders for each group of variables.

The price that we pay for this improvement is that while in the classic Taylor approach the cross-gamma between all dimensions can be considered, in the case of the slider we lose some of them. For example, the relationship between (x_1, x_2, x_3) and (x_4, x_5) is lost in the example. This highlights the importance of the practitioner's know-how in order to create an optimal slider configuration, as the practitioner has to decide which cross-relationships to disregard and which level of accuracy (e.g. controlled by the number of points in each dimension, in the case of a CT) is needed in each dimension.

7.4   SUMMARY OF CHAPTER

- **Sliders to sidestep the curse of dimensionality**. A slide is a low-dimensional cross-section of a tensor. A slider is a collection of slides joined at a common point (pivot point). Sliders are designed for problems of high dimension. In practical settings, dimensions even in the many hundreds can be considered.
- **Approximation levels**. The approximation power depends on the slider configuration and the approximation power of the constituent slides. In most applications, slides are CTs, which enjoy high degrees of accuracy; therefore, sliders also enjoy high degrees of accuracy.
- **Evaluation efficiency**. Slides are evaluated by evaluating each individual slide and adding the resulting terms, in a similar way to how it is done in Taylor approximation. The evaluation of each slide is very efficient when these are CTs. Therefore, the evaluation of Chebyshev Sliders also inherits the efficiency and numerical stability of CTs.

## CHAPTER 8

The Jacobian projection technique

Part IV of this book deals with a range of financial calculations where a function P must be evaluated on a large distribution of input scenarios. From these calculations, the most relevant to this book are those for which the evaluation of P on the distribution of input scenarios is, computationally speaking, a very big challenge.

To solve the computational challenge presented in the calculations described in Part IV, we put forward a set of solutions. These solutions are presented in Part III. One of the most important components in some of these solutions is the Composition Technique — described in detail in Chapter 5. Its strength becomes apparent when it is appropriately combined with the fundamental methods presented in Part I. The result is a reduction of the computational burden associated with many calculations in finance, where the evaluation of a function P, on a large distribution of scenarios, is computationally very costly.

We will briefly remind the reader what the Composition Technique consists of, given that it will be used prominently throughout this chapter.

The Composition Technique is summarised by the following equation:

$$\mathbb{R}^k \xrightarrow{\ g\ } X \subset \mathbb{R}^n \xrightarrow{\ P\ } \mathbb{R}. \tag{8.1}$$
$$\underbrace{\phantom{\mathbb{R}^k \xrightarrow{\ g\ } X \subset \mathbb{R}^n}}_{f}$$

The function P is the function we need to evaluate on a large distribution of input values. Each input value is a market scenario. Denote the collection of market scenarios by X; this lies in $\mathbb{R}^n$, for some n. Assume that evaluating P on all these scenarios is (computationally) expensive. The Composition Technique consists of taking advantage of functions g — which have domain in $\mathbb{R}^k$, where $k < n$ — so that when g is composed with P, we obtain f, a function with a domain of dimension k. When k is suitably low, f can then be approximated with any of the fundamental approximating methods presented in Part I. The key thing to notice is that for $k < n$, it is easier (often, much easier) to replicate f in a computationally efficient manner than P.

The approximation methods in Part I are either CTs or DNNs. When used appropriately in combination with the Composition Technique, these are built cheaply (computationally speaking) and to a high degree of accuracy to be used instead of f in any calculation required.

There are some applications, however, that require the evaluation of the partial derivatives of a function P, on a whole distribution of input scenarios, rather than simply the value of P on these scenarios. This chapter explains a technique presented in [12], that makes use of the *Composition Technique*, the *chain rule* from calculus and *orthogonal projections*, to obtain estimates of these partial derivatives. We call it the *Jacobian Projection* technique.

8.1   SETTING THE BACKGROUND

Let P be a function that takes a collection of input variables. The types of input variables can be any in principle. However, for illustration purposes, we assume from now on that P is a pricing function and that its input variables are market risk factors or market quotes. For example, P can be a Bermudan Swaption that takes, as inputs, a set of interest rate values and a collection of implied volatilities.

In some applications that we discuss in Part IV of this book, pricing functions (such as P) need to be evaluated on a distribution of market scenarios. The instances of such applications, which are relevant to this chapter, are those where the distribution of such scenarios is generated by models that parametrise the market risk factors in terms of model parameters and model risk factors. For example, in the case of interest rates that constitute part of the input variables to the pricing function P of a Bermudan Swaption, these can be generated by models such as the one-factor HW model. This model parametrises whole collections of interest rates in terms of model parameters (denoted by a, b and σ in Equation 5.2) and the short rate, which in the case of the one-factor HW model is the only model risk factor. From now on, we will denote such a parametrisation — for example, the one that expresses interest rates in terms of the short rate for the one-factor HW model — by g.[1]

The reason this is important lies in the fact that the dimension of the space of model risk factors is typically much smaller than the space of market risk factors. Therefore, by composing the parametrisation g with the pricing function P, we obtain a function f that has an input domain with dimension much lower than the dimension of the input domain of P. An example of such composition is presented in Equation 8.1.

Note that f is able to recover all the prices that we need from P. That is, if we need the values of P at a set of market risk factors $s \in \mathbb{R}^n$ generated by the model, these can be recovered by considering the set of model risk factors $r \in \mathbb{R}^k$ that correspond to s under g, and evaluating f on r. By construction, f at r returns the value of P at s. What we effectively do when f is constructed is express prices in terms of model risk factors.

In summary, we have a function f with a much lower domain dimension than P that is at the same time able to recover the prices from P we need. The fundamental approximation techniques presented in Part I — CTs or DNNs — can then be used to build replica functions that return the prices from P we are after by accurately approximating f in a very efficient manner, due to the low dimension of the domain of f.

---

[1]The situation described is one that appears in different applications, such as the ones presented in Chapters 15 and 17.

By approximating f with either a CT or a DNN we obtain a replica function that can be used in a whole range of calculations where P — typically a slow function to compute — would normally be used. The key step described — which consists of taking advantage of the low dimension of the model risk factor space by composing P with g — is precisely what is embodied by the Composition Technique presented in Chapter 5.

The Composition Technique works very well in contexts where we need to evaluate P on a distribution of market risk factors. However, there are other applications where we are interested in computing the partial derivative of P with respect to market risk factor. We normally call partial derivatives *sensitivities*. An example of a calculation where the sensitivities of a pricing function are needed is the calculation of Initial Margin as defined by ISDA (see [43]), called the Standard Initial Margin Model (SIMM).[2]

The question that naturally arises is, if we can take advantage of the parametrisation g above to compute distribution of prices on collections of market risk scenarios, can we do the same to compute distributions of sensitivities with respect to market risk scenarios?

The first thing to note is the following. The Composition Technique gives us a pricing function f in terms of the model risk factors. Therefore, we can very easily obtain its sensitivities with respect to model risk factors once we approximate it with one of the fundamental approximation techniques. Note this is particularly true if we replicate f with CTs, as the derivatives of CTs also provide very good replicas for the derivatives of f. Therefore, computing the derivatives of f is an easy task once the CT for f has been built (see Section 3.7).

However, what we need in most applications are the sensitivities with respect to market risk factors. The question is, can we translate a sensitivity with respect to model parameters — which are easier to obtain in light of the Composition Technique and the ability that CTs have of approximating the partial derivatives of functions — to sensitivities with respect to a market risk factor?

Using the example of the pricing function of a Bermudan Swaption, the question becomes, can we obtain sensitivities with respect to a collection of interest rates (example of input market risk factors) using the sensitivity with respect to the HW short rate (for example)?

8.2 WHAT WE CAN RECOVER

As we mentioned in the previous section, we are interested in the situation where we need to compute the sensitivities of a pricing function P with respect to a set of market risk factors, where the collection of market risk factors has been generated using a risk factor generating model.

For illustration purposes we will continue to work with the following example. The trade in question is a Bermudan Swaption. Its pricing function is denoted by P. The input market risk factors are swap rates and implied volatilities. Without loss of generality, we assume P takes a single curve of swap rates with n tensors, where n is typically

---

[2]The high computational cost associated with the calculation of stochastic SIMM is addressed in Chapter 17.

greater than 10, say 20. In the case of implied volatilities, there could be hundreds of implied volatilities.

We assume the curve of swap rates is generated by the one-factor HW model. The parametrisation that generates the curve of swap rates in terms of the short rate and the HW model parameters is denoted by g. Moreover, we assume the HW model parameters are fixed throughout any calculation we perform.[3] From now on, we will only mention swap rates as the input risk factors of P. Whatever is said about them equally applies to the set of implied volatilities.

The example just given involves a curve of swap rates with 20 tensors and a model (HW) that has one single model risk factor. That is, the dimension of the market space is much greater than the dimension of the model space. Indeed, this is a common pattern in most cases where market risk factors are generated by models, and precisely the thing we take advantage of when we apply the Composition Technique.

In the example given, g goes from $\mathbb{R}^1$ to $\mathbb{R}^{20}$,

$$g : \mathbb{R}^1 \longrightarrow \mathbb{R}^{20}.$$

In the general case, g goes from $\mathbb{R}^k$ to $\mathbb{R}^n$, where $k < n$,

$$g : \mathbb{R}^k \longrightarrow \mathbb{R}^n.$$

8.2.1   Intuition behind *g* and its derivative *dg*

Intuitively, g describes how the model space navigates the market space. From now on, we will denote the model space by $\mathcal{R}$ and the market space by $\mathcal{S}$. In the case of the HW one-factor model, g defines a path of the short rate inside the space of swap rates. This is what Figure 8.1 represents, where we have assumed only two swap rates for simplicity.

The parametrisations g we work with are smooth. This is certainly the case for the one-factor HW model; see Equation 5.3. However, it is the case for the vast majority of risk factor evolution (RFE) models.

As g is smooth, we can take the derivative dg. This defines a linear transformation dg_r from $\mathbb{R}^k$ to $\mathbb{R}^n$ at every point $r \in \mathcal{R}$, the domain of g (Equation 8.2). This linear map is represented by a matrix called the *Jacobian* of g, which consists of the partial derivatives of g with respect to all its inputs. Given that the domain of g consists of the model space, then the Jacobian consists of the partials of g with respect to every model factor.

$$dg_r : \mathbb{R}^k \longrightarrow \mathbb{R}^n. \tag{8.2}$$

Moreover, g being smooth implies that the linear transformations (one for each $r \in \mathcal{R}$ as in Equation 8.2) are injective. That is, the image of dg_r always has the same dimension as the domain; that is k in the general case and 1 in our running example.[4]

---

[3]These parameters are normally determined by calibrating the model using historical or current market data.

[4]We would like to point out the difference between image and target space. The image of a function consists of the set of all possible function outputs. The target space of the function is the space where the image is contained. In the case of dg_r, the image is $\mathbb{R}^k$, which sits as a subspace of the target space $\mathbb{R}^n$.

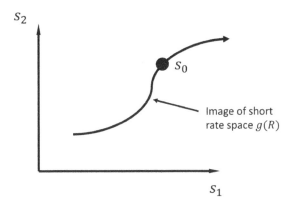

FIGURE 8.1 Path followed by the short rate within the space of swap rates. The path is given by the image of g. Only two swap rates s_1 and s_2 have been assumed for simplicity.

Let us gain some intuition as to what exactly we have with the derivative dg_r. Think of the domain of dg_r as a collection of *directions*, of which we have k, one per model risk factor. In the case of the HW one-factor model, we only have one direction, the one determined by the short rate. Likewise, the target space of dg_r consists of the space of swap rate directions, of which we have n, one per swap rate.

Let r_0 be a point in $\mathcal{R}$ and $s_0 = g(r_0)$. What the image of dg_{r_0} describes is the direction pointed to by the tangent at s_0 of the short rate path defined by $g(\mathcal{R})$, within the space of swap rate directions. This is what we have in our example where $k = 1$. In the more general case, the image of dg_{r_0} describes how the space of k directions at r_0 (one per model risk factor) sits inside the space of market risk factor directions in $\mathbb{R}^n$, at s_0.

Figure 8.2 shows an example of what was just described, where we assume only two market risk factors (s_1 and s_2) for simplicity. The image under g of the short rate passes through the point $s_0 = g(r_0)$. At s_0, the diagonal arrow represents the direction of the only model risk factor (short rate direction), sitting inside the space of market directions, at s_0, given by s_1 and s_2.

8.2.2 Using the derivative of f

We remind the reader we are working with a function P, a parametrisation g and its composition f, as presented in Equation 8.1.

One of the assumptions we are working with is that we can compute the partial derivative of f with respect to any model risk factor.[5] In our working example, it would be the partial of f with respect to the short rate, which is the only model risk factor available.

---

[5] In Section 3.7, we saw that if a CT is built for f, then the derivatives of the CT are very easy to obtain and are very good replicas of the derivatives of f. Moreover, the derivatives of the CT converge very fast to the derivatives of f as the number of Chebyshev points increases.

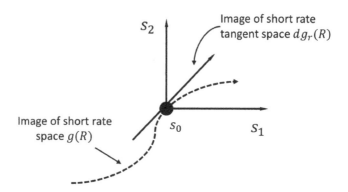

FIGURE 8.2   Short rate direction at s_0 inside the space of directions spanned by swap rates s_1 and s_2.

Another assumption is that the Jacobian of g is also available to us. Given that at each point $r \in \mathcal{R}$, the linear function dg_r is injective, we can define the inverse of dg_r restricted to its image

$$dg_r^{-1} : im(dg_r) \cong \mathbb{R}^k \longrightarrow \mathbb{R}^k, \qquad (8.3)$$

where the domain of dg_r^{-1}, denoted by $im(dg_r)$, is a copy of the space of model risk factor directions sitting inside the space market risk factor directions, as described in Section 8.2.1. Note that Equation 8.3 presents the general case where g has a domain with dimension k. In our running example, the domain of the inverse at s_0 has dimension 1 and is given by the space spanned by the tangent to the short rate path shown in Figure 8.2.

One thing we can do is take the composition of dg_r^{-1} with the partial derivative of f with respect to any model risk factor. In our example, we compose the function in Equation 8.3 with the only partial derivative available: the partial of f with respect to the short rate $\partial f / \partial r$,

$$\mathbb{R} \xleftarrow{\;dg_{r_0}^{-1}\;} \mathbb{R} \subset \mathbb{R}^n \xrightarrow{\;dP_{s_0}^{-1}\;} \mathbb{R}. \qquad (8.4)$$
$$\underbrace{\qquad\qquad\qquad}_{\partial f/\partial r_0}$$

Let us take a look at what is it that we get with the composition in Equation 8.4. Notice that the composition has the space of market risk factor directions as its domain. This domain is the same as the domain of the derivative of P. Therefore, we essentially recover the partial derivative of P in the direction determined by the image of dg_r. In our example, we recover the partial of P in the direction given by the tangent to the short rate path at s_0 in Figure 8.2. Given that our starting assumptions are that we can compute the derivative of f and the derivative of g, then what we have is the derivative of P in the directions given by the dg_r within the space of swap rate directions.[6]

---

[6]Hidden in these arguments is the use of the inverse function theorem and the chain rule. We prefer not to delve into the details of these results. We refer the reader to [15] for details on these.

The following observation is key. The set of partial derivatives of P with respect to the swap rates constitutes a basis for the space of directional derivatives of P. For example, in Figure 8.2, the space of directions centred at the point s_0 is spanned by the directions s_1 and s_2. Therefore, any directional derivative of P can be expressed as a linear combination of the partial derivatives given by the swap rates, in particular, the one determined by the image of dg_r in Figure 8.2, which is the direction given by the short rate within the space of swap rate directions.

However, what we cannot do is recover the partial derivatives with respect to all swap rates given just the directional derivative determined by the short rate. In Figure 8.2, this means we cannot recover the directions given by s_1 and s_2, centred at s_0, if we have the direction given by the image of the short rate tangent space $dg_r(\mathcal{R})$.

This is the problem we face. The assumption we have made along the way is that the only thing we have is the partial derivative of P along any direction within the image of dg_r.

8.2.3 When $k < n$ becomes a problem

In Section 8.2.2, we saw that starting from the assumption that we can compute the derivatives of f and g, we recover the partial derivatives of P in any of the directions determined by the image of dg_r. However, the reason why this does not recover all the partials of P is down to the assumption that $k < n$. Using our running example, the image of dg_r cannot cover the whole of the space of swap rate directions when $k < n$.

The observation just made is very important. For most applications of the Composition Technique we present in Part IV, we take advantage of the fact that k is much smaller than n. This is precisely what allows us to reduce the dimension of the pricing function P, producing a function f than can then be efficiently replicated with a CT or a DNN.

However, the fact that $k < n$ — for which the Composition Technique is vital — works against us in this case. The image of dg_r (Equation 8.2) cannot span the whole space of sensitivities with respect to market factors. That is, we cannot recover all market factor directions by just considering model factor directions.

The next section presents a way of *estimating* the partials of P with respect to every direction, using the partial derivatives of P with respect to the image of the Jacobian dg_r. Full details of such technique can be found in [12].

8.3 PARTIAL DERIVATIVES VIA PROJECTIONS ONTO THE JACOBIAN

The objective in this section is to obtain expressions for the partials of P with respect to every variable in its domain. If these variables are $(s_1, \ldots, s_n)$, then we want to compute $\partial P / \partial s_i$, for $1 \leq i \leq n$.

The function P is a function

$$P : \mathbb{R}^n \longrightarrow \mathbb{R}.$$

The partial derivatives of P constitute a vector known as the *gradient* or derivative of P

$$dP_s = \nabla P_s = \left(\partial P(s)/\partial s_1, \ldots, \partial P(s)/\partial s_n \right).$$

As explained in Section 8.1, we assume there is a smooth function $g : \mathbb{R}^k \to \mathbb{R}^n$, where $k < n$, which we compose with P to obtain f, as expressed in Equation 8.1.

Moreover, we assume that the derivatives of both f and g are available. That is, we have df_r and dg_r, for every r in $\mathbb{R}^k$.

The chain rule from calculus says that the derivative of a composition of functions is the composition of the derivatives of the functions that constitute the composition. In the case of $f = P \circ g$, this translates into

$$df_r = d(P \circ g)_r = dP_{g(r)} \circ dg_r. \tag{8.5}$$

Remark 8.3.1 Notice that dg_r is a linear transformation from $\mathbb{R}^k$ to $\mathbb{R}^n$. Also, if g is smooth, dg_r is injective. This means that the image of dg_r has dimension k. Hence, if w is an element in $im(dg_r)$, then there is a unique vector u in $\mathbb{R}^k$ such that $dg_r(u) = w$. Finally, given that we assumed from the beginning that we have an expression for the derivative of g with which we can compute, this means we can obtain u such that $dg_r(u) = w$.

Given that the derivative of a function is always a linear map, dP_s is linear, where $s \in \mathbb{R}^n$. This linear map is given by the gradient, which consists of the partials of P with respect to the variable s_i in $\mathbb{R}^n$. Therefore, we recover any partial derivative in the following way.

Consider the i-th entry and the vector v_i in $\mathbb{R}^n$ defined by $v_i = (0, \ldots, 0, 1, 0, \ldots, 0)$. That is, v_i is 0 in all its entries with the exception of the i-th entry where it is 1. Then

$$\partial P(g(r))/\partial s_i = \nabla P_{g(r)} \cdot v_i = dP_{g(r)}(v_i). \tag{8.6}$$

That is, that partial derivative of P with respect to the variable s_i, at $g(r)$, is given by the product (as matrices) of the gradient of P and the vector v_i.

Notice that v_i is a vector in $\mathbb{R}^n$, where $im(dg_r)$ is a subspace of dimension k. In principle, we do not know if v_i is an element of $im(dg_r)$. However, what we know is that v_i can be decomposed as the sum of its orthogonal projection onto $im(dg_r)$ and its orthogonal complement. That is

$$v_i = v_i^{||} + v_i^{\perp}, \tag{8.7}$$

where $v_i^{||}$ is the closest element to v_i in $im(dg_r)$, and $v_i^{\perp}$ is the unique element in $\mathbb{R}^n$ perpendicular to $im(dg_r)$, such that Equation 8.7 holds. In view of this decomposition and using Equation 8.6, we have

$$\partial P(g(r))/\partial s_i = dP_{g(r)}(v_i) = dP_{g(r)}(v_i^{||} + v_i^{\perp}) = dP_{g(r)}(v_i^{||}) + dP_{g(r)}(v_i^{\perp}). \tag{8.8}$$

What Equation 8.8 does is recover the partial of P we want as the sum of two components. The first of these components is $dP_{g(r)}(v_i^{||})$. Notice that as $v_i^{||} \in im(dg_r)$, then by Remark 8.3.1, there is a vector $u \in \mathbb{R}^k$, the domain of f, such that $dg_r(u) = v_i^{||}$. This means that

$$dP_{g(r)}(v_i^{||}) = dP_{g(r)}(dg_r(u)) = df_r(u),$$

where the last equality is down to the chain rule. Therefore, this component is accessible to us given that we assumed from the beginning that we can compute with the derivative of f.

The second component $dP_{g(r)}(v_i^{\perp})$ is more elusive. However, as is shown in [12], for some applications this component tends to be small and hence we can use $dP_{g(r)}(v_i^{||})$ as proxy for $\partial P(g(r))/\partial s_i$. That is

$$\partial P(g(r))/\partial s_i \approx dP_{g(r)}(v_i^{||}) = df_r(u), \tag{8.9}$$

where u is the orthogonal projection of v_i onto $im(dg_r)$.

In Appendix G, we present results of dynamic sensitivities and Initial Margin simulation obtained using the technique just described in this chapter.

Hybrid solutions – approximation methods and the toolkit

## CHAPTER 9

Introduction

This chapter highlights how the approximation techniques presented in Part I and the toolkit from Part II can be combined to constitute what we call *hybrid solutions*. The reasons for these hybrid methods have already been touched upon throughout Part II. To make this part self-contained and for ease of reading, we present them once more in a cohesive manner.

9.1 THE DIMENSIONALITY PROBLEM REVISITED

There are two approximation techniques presented in Part I that constitute the main theoretical approximation tools used to tackle the applications presented in Part IV: DNNs and CTs. The effectiveness of both techniques, however, can be hindered by the characteristics of the application in question, for example, when the dimension of the domain of the function being approximated is too large or when the curvature of the function is too great or changes aggressively. The toolkit in Part II has been carefully chosen with the purpose of alleviating these issues when correctly combined with the approximation techniques, taking advantage of the characteristics of the application where the computational solution is needed. The details of how this is done in each application are presented in Part IV.

When designing the solution for a computational problem, taking into consideration the context is very important. If a given risk calculation has a bottleneck at a given step, and we try to solve the problem with a solution that is too generic, the computational improvement obtained may be suboptimal. However, if we study the context where the bottleneck exists and incorporate some of the intrinsic characteristics of the risk calculations into the solution, the computational performance obtained is often better — in some cases substantially better.

Chapter 2 presented the properties that make DNNs good function approximators. Specifically, the Universal Approximation Theorem (Theorem 2.3.1 in Section 2.3) says that as long as the function f to be approximated is continuous, it can be approximated to any degree of accuracy by DNNs, where the DNN with the appropriate accuracy can be found by increasing the number of neurons. This is irrespective of the dimension of f.

In addition to the power they have as approximating objects, their evaluation is very efficient, as it boils down to simple linear algebra operations. Also, storing them is usually not a problem as the information needed is all concentrated on a — possibly large — set of weights or parameters that usually amount to little computer memory.

However, the number of data points needed to effectively train a DNN increases as the dimension of f increases. As Equation 4.1 shows, at least for single layered Neural Nets, the effect of the dimension on the number of training points is linear. As the number of layers increases, DNNs gain in approximation power but become harder to train, usually requiring more points. This means that in high dimensions, the number of sample points needed to obtain well-trained DNNs can be huge. Given that in all applications presented in Part IV the main aim is to reduce the number of calls to pricing functions — since that is where the computational bottleneck tends to be — we should always think of ways of doing so. The toolkit presented in Part II helps in this respect as Section 10 explains.

Chapter 3 presented the properties that make CTs great function approximators. They have the rare property of approximating functions exponentially as the number of grid points increases (Theorem 3.3.10). This means that very few values of the function are needed to approximate it to a high level of accuracy. Moreover, these tensors are simple objects with a small memory footprint, which can be evaluated using only the values of the function at Chebyshev points in a numerically stable manner (Theorem 3.6.1).

CTs — like any other tensor — suffer from the curse of dimensionality. This says that the number of grid points increases exponentially as the dimension of the tensor increases. This is a problem for two reasons. First, a dimension is quickly reached at which storing the tensor in memory becomes problematic. Second, even if a tensor can be stored in memory, evaluating the function to be approximated on all the grid points may take more time than what is available in a given situation.

To give an intuitive idea of the scale of the problem, consider the number of atoms in the universe. This is quantified by the Eddington number estimated at 10^{80}. If we consider a tensor with six points per dimension, we only need 103 dimensions to have a grid that exceeds the Eddington number. The same characteristic that describes the convergence power of CTs (*exponential* convergence with size of mesh) is its Achilles heel (*exponential* growth in size with dimension).

The functions to be approximated within the applications of interest (presented in Part IV) are for the most part high dimensional. This hinders the power of DNNs and CTs when directly applied to these functions. This is where the tools presented in Part II come to the rescue. In the following sections, we show how the tools can be coupled with DNNs and CTs in different ways. These will constitute part of the solutions to the range of problems addressed in Part IV.

9.2   EXPLOITING THE COMPOSITION TECHNIQUE

The main characteristics that define the Composition Technique were presented in Chapter 5. The central idea is that data on which a costly function (e.g. a pricing function) need to be evaluated can in some cases be described or represented in a space of lower dimension through a smooth parametrisation.

In Chapter 5, two possibilities were considered. The first is when the context of the problem itself provides the low-dimensional representation of the data, for example, when the data are generated via risk factor diffusion models of low dimension

(Section 5.1). The second is when the parametrisation is generated by applying a dimensionality reduction technique such as PCA or Autoencoders (Section 5.2).

Composition Technique

Either way, the aim of a Composition Technique is to take advantage of this low-dimensional description of the data to obtain a function of low dimension on which the approximation techniques presented in Part I can be applied. The following equation describes the idea.

$$Y \subset \mathbb{R}^k \xrightarrow{\ g\ } \tilde{X} \subset \mathbb{R}^n \xrightarrow{\ P\ } \mathbb{R}. \tag{9.1}$$

$$\underbrace{\qquad\qquad\qquad}_{f}$$

The function P is the original function for which we want a fast proxy. The data X to be evaluated by P is a subset of $\mathbb{R}^n$. The parametrisation g models $\tilde{X}$ — a set that either is equal to X or closely approximates it, expressed in terms of Y, and is a subset of $\mathbb{R}^k$, where $k < n$. The composition of g with P defines a function f that has dimension k. In the context of interest, k is much lower than n, as will be shown in IV, thus potentiating the use of DNNs and CTs.

In summary, the challenge is to find or generate a function g that parametrises $\tilde{X}$ where $\tilde{X} \sim X$ or, even better, $\tilde{X} = X$, with k being as small as possible.

As mentioned before, some contexts already provide such g. For example, when X is generated in a risk engine, then g is a parametrisation that comes with the models used to generate X. We can view this case as *endogenous* because g is part of the risk calculation. This is the case, for example, with XVA engines. On the flip side, sometimes X is not generated by the risk engine, for example, scenarios in a Market Risk VaR engine. In this case, one must take advantage of the characteristics of X to generate a parametrisation g that we can take advantage of.

## CHAPTER 10

The Toolkit and Deep Neural Nets

One of the main advantages of DNNs is that they can handle high dimensions with relative ease. Therefore, the option of building a DNN directly on P without using the parametrisation g can be considered. However, if such a g exists, not using it tends to be suboptimal and limits the use of the DNN.

If a DNN is trained without a function g, it involves sampling the domain of the function P — usually randomly — from where training, validating and testing sets are obtained. As n tends to be high in the contexts of interest, the number of sample points may be significant, making the sampling computationally expensive and the training slow.

In contexts such as the one described by Equation 9.1, the parametrisation g can be used to improve training times and convergence of DNNs. There are two ways a DNN can be applied in this type of situation. The first involves building a DNN on P but using valuable information from g, specifically, using g to identify the regions where the training, validating and testing sets should be sampled from. The second consists of build a DNN on f.

10.1 BUILDING ON *P* USING THE IMAGE OF *G*

The interest in the function P stems from the fact that in the applications of interest (Part IV), sets such as X need to be evaluated by P. For example, X can be a set of market risk factor scenarios in a risk calculation.

When a situation like the one described in Equation 9.1 is present, X can be described by a set Y of lower dimension through the parametristion g (e.g. the first 10 principal components in the data after PCA has been applied).

Given that g is typically smooth, its image $\tilde{X}$ — which is X itself or closely approximates it — lies inside of $\mathbb{R}^n$ as an object of lower dimension, specifically of dimension k. Exploring the whole of $\mathbb{R}^n$ is a huge waste of effort as P only needs to evaluate X. Therefore, it makes sense to sample around a neigbourhood of X for training purposes. Given that $\tilde{X}$ is of dimension k — which is typically much smaller than n — the sampling needed to train a DNN on P becomes much more efficient compared to when the exploration is done randomly across a regular region (say a ball or hyper-rectangle) in $\mathbb{R}^n$.

Figure 10.1 shows a simple but clear example of this situation. For simplicity we have chosen $n = 2$ and g parametrises a set X in $\mathbb{R}^2$ in terms of a single variable, that is, $k = 1$. In this example, the function P has domain in $\mathbb{R}^2$. Instead of exploring a rectangular domain of P, one can restrict the exploration to the region given by the image of g, essentially the set X and neighbouring areas. As sampling this region is cheaper

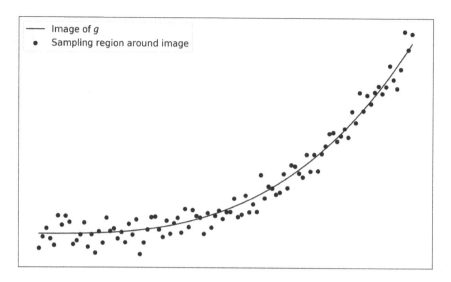

FIGURE 10.1 Image of parametrisation g. The image has dimension 1 but sits inside the space of market risk factors that have dimension 2.

than exploring a rectangular domain for P, obtaining a training set for the DNN is much cheaper and training can be done more efficiently. This example is trivial; just two dimensions being reduced down to one. However, in the applications presented in Part IV, the reductions can be much more dramatic, going from hundreds of dimensions down to a handful. For the latter cases, the benefits are significant.

10.2   BUILDING ON *F*

Building a DNN as described is particularly effective when — for reasons of the applications in question — the input values available to the practitioner are the ones in $\mathbb{R}^n$ and not the ones in $\mathbb{R}^k$. However, if the input values in $\mathbb{R}^k$ are readily available, one may build a DNN on f, which, as denoted by Equation 9.1, is the composition of g with P.

Even when DNNs are good at dealing with high dimensions, if the dimension of the function to be approximated can be reduced, this should be considered, as there is little to no benefit in training the DNN in regions of $\mathbb{R}^n$ that are irrelevant to where evaluations need to be performed. Given that f has domain in $\mathbb{R}^k$, where $k < n$, a random exploration of the domain of f is much more efficient than a random exploration for P. This reduces the number of times the function needs to be called, which is always a goal in the applications presented in Part IV. Moreover, it allows for shorter training times.

## CHAPTER 11

The Toolkit and Chebyshev Tensors

Consider once again the situation described in Equation 9.1, where the dimension of a function P that needs to be approximated has been reduced by composing it with a parametrisation g. Once the function f has been obtained, a CT can be built for it. Three different ways to build a CT are described in what follows, each appropriate for a different dimensionality range of f.

11.1 FULL CHEBYSHEV TENSOR

The first way is to build a CT by evaluating every grid point in the Chebyshev grid. This is what we call a *full* CT. Conceptually, this is the most straightforward method of the three. All that it takes is the identification of a domain or range of approximation, the definition of Chebyshev points on this domain and finally the evaluation of f on the Chebyshev points.

There is an important point to make regarding the definition of the domain over which a CT is built. The final goal is to obtain the values of P on a data set X. However, as explained in Section 9.2, the appropriate use of the Composition Technique allows us to use the values of f on Y to represent $P(X)$. Therefore, the CT built for f does not need to be defined outside the smallest hyper-rectangle that contains Y. The way to obtain the boundary of this hyper-rectangle is to compute the minimum and maximum values of Y for each dimension. This gives all the information needed to define Chebyshev points as given in Definition 3.3.4.

Due to the curse of dimensionality, the number of grid points increases exponentially as the dimension increases. This means — at least for the applications of interest (see Part IV) — that the naive approach just described applies to functions f of low dimension.

It must be stressed that the dimension limit for full CTs depends on the function to be approximated. There are cases for which a tensor of dimension greater than 5 will be very difficult to build. Other cases exist where building tensors of dimension greater than 5 is a genuine possibility. However, for the vast majority of cases, dimension 10 will certainly be an upper bound. In fact, beyond dimension 5, the number of times f needs to be called is typically such that computational savings decrease significantly, especially in the context of risk calculations.

11.2   TT-FORMAT CHEBYSHEV TENSOR

The second method involves building a CT for f using the Tensor Extension Algorithms described in Chapter 6. What these algorithms do is build CTs by evaluating f on a small fraction of the whole Chebyshev mesh. The fraction of the mesh used by the algorithm depends on the case in question. But from the reports found in the literature and the results presented in Part IV, the fraction ranges from 10% to a minuscule 1×10^{-15}% of the total mesh.

There are two situations where it is convenient to use TT-format CTs. The first is when the dimension of f is too great and, as a result, the number of grid points on the mesh is larger than the number of times the function P needs to be evaluated to do the risk calculation in a brute-force manner (i.e. using only the function P). In the applications we are interested in, this usually happens when the dimension is greater than 5 or 6. In these cases, the number of grid points is such that evaluating every single one of them comes at the expense of little if any computational savings. It therefore becomes imperative to reduce the number of calls to the function f.

The second situation is when, regardless of dimension, there is a need to reduce the calls to f due to the time this takes: for example, when P is the pricing function of a highly exotic derivative and we need the incremental CVA of the netting set it belongs to in a matter of minutes to gain an edge over competitors. The CT to build may even be of a dimension one would normally expect to build a full tensor for, say dimension 3 or 4. In fact, it may be the case that building such a tensor in full yields high computational gains when compared to the brute-force approach. However, given the business context, building a full CT may mean losing the bid with a competitor because building it takes too long. In this case, obtaining a CT in TT format can increase substantially the computational gains with limited loss of accuracy. In contexts like the one described, the computational edge provided by the Tensor Extension Algorithms may mean the difference between winning or losing a bid.

From the results presented in Part IV of this book, CTs in TT format can be used successfully in the context of risk calculations for dimensions up to 25. However, depending on the characteristics of the pricing function in question, this dimension may be much higher.

11.3   CHEBYSHEV SLIDER

When the domain of f surpasses about 20 dimensions, one should consider using the Sliding Technique presented in Chapter 7. As mentioned in Chapter 7, sliders consist of a collection of proxy objects joined at a pivot point. The proxy objects built can either be a DNN or a CT. However, the slides tend to be of dimensions where CTs excel due to their exponential convergence. We therefore assume CTs are used as proxy objects every time the sliders are considered.

One of the main properties of sliders is that they can be built for functions of very high dimensions. Therefore, in cases where the value of the k — the dimension of the input space of f — is greater than, for example 20, one should consider building a Chebyshev Slider for f. This, of course, does not mean that for lower values of k one cannot build one. However, for these values, there are at least two other techniques to choose from, which typically perform, from an accuracy perspective, better than the Chebyshev Slider.

A particular case of interest is when Chebyshev Sliders are combined with parametrisations g coming from the orthogonal transformations defined by PCA. As the reader will see in Chapter 16, this hybrid — which we call the *Orthogonal Chebyshev Slider* — gives very good results within the context of Market Risk calculations, and more in particular in the context of IMA-FRTB, where an accurate full portfolio revaluation is needed in order to pass the regulatory proxy-pricing thresholds.

11.4 A FINAL NOTE

It should be noted that all three methods mentioned in this chapter — building full CTs, TT-format CTs and Chebyshev Sliders — were all put in the context of the Composition Technique. This does not mean they cannot be applied directly on the function P. However, for many of the applications of interest presented in Part IV, it is the combination of approximation methods in Part I and tools in Part II that creates stable risk calculation systems.

In fact, realising the power that blending certain techniques has on risk calculations is what motivated us to write this book. As discussed with the real examples presented in Part IV, a careful mix of these techniques can unleash the power of the methods presented in Part I for function approximation and optimal computational settings in risk calculations.

## CHAPTER 12

Hybrid Deep Neural Nets and Chebyshev Tensors Frameworks

C hapters 2 and 3 review the fundamentals of DNNs and CTs as function approximators. Both have very strong capabilities, but also some limitations that are to a large
extent complementary.

On the one hand, DNNs are excellent at solving problems that require a lot of flexibility. However, they tend to explore the domain of the function to replicate somewhat
inefficiently — quite often done by randomly choosing points on the domain of the
function. When it comes to adjusting the flexibility of DNNs, the practitioner mostly
relies on heuristic techniques to scan the hyper-parameter space (see Section 1.4.3).

On the other hand, CTs are extremely efficient at extracting information from the
input domain of the function to replicate. The exploration of the function at Chebyshev
points ensures that the function is replicated throughout its domain quasi-exponentially
as the number of Chebyshev points increases. This, however, imposes a rigidity that has
as its downside the curse of dimensionality. The Tensor Extension Algorithms discussed
in Chapter 6 help substantially with the curse of dimensionality, but do not solve the
problem completely.

A couple of years ago the authors of this book sat down and wondered if it were
possible to build an ML framework that takes advantages of the strengths of both DNNs
and CTs so that each covers the other one in their respective weaknesses. The results of
the research project, obtained so far, are outlined in this chapter.

This chapter will establish the fundamentals of a hybrid DNN+CT framework.
Some illustrative examples will be discussed, as well as future research avenues. We
call this type of ML architecture a *hybrid Neural Network* (hNN).

It must be noted that, by the time of this book going to press, we had not had the
time to extend the results to the functions that are most relevant to the applications in
this book. However, since the results so far are relevant and encouraging, we did not
want to let the opportunity of sharing these ideas go by.

12.1 THE FUNDAMENTAL IDEA

Let us illustrate the intuition that has been guiding us with an example. Assume we
want to train an ML method to recognise images of cats with a DNN. Training this DNN
consists of finding the weights that best predict images of cats by showing it labeled

images of cats and non-cats in a supervised learning manner. Once trained, the DNN outputs the probability that the image has a cat. Then, an appropriate probability threshold is chosen to determine whether the DNN architecture outputs a positive or negative result to the question of whether the image represents a cat or not.

Let us say the images have 640×480 pixels. Each pixel has a degree of intensity in three possible colour channels, hence, an image is defined by $640 \cdot 480 \cdot 3 = 921{,}600 \sim 10^6$ features. A possible DNN architecture for this problem could have 10^6 neurons in the first layer.[1] Then, the number of neurons is gradually decreased in subsequent layers. The last few layers will typically have only a few neurons, ending up with an output layer of a single neuron, which outputs the probability we are seeking. This is illustrated in Figure 12.1.

Intuitively, what the DNN is doing is putting together pixels into increasingly larger concepts. That is, it starts with a super granular view (10^6 features) that decreases in granularity as it gradually moves through the layers, getting to the point in which the last few layers may represent things like legs, eyes, tails, and so on. The DNN's neurons in the last few layers may represent other features that are non-obvious to the human brain but that the DNN learns as representative of a cat. The main point is that the DNN *funnels* the information from a "micro" view of the image to a "macro" perspective.

This same idea can happen when a DNN is used for function approximation. We may start with a vast number of dimensions in the input domain, and the DNN finds a way to reduce all these dimensions to a few relevant ones. Then, the dependency

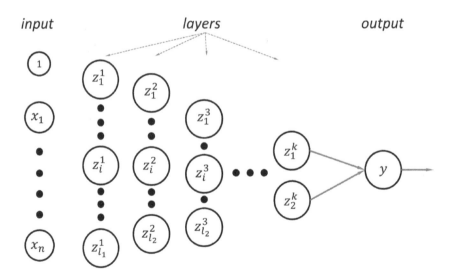

FIGURE 12.1   Illustration of how a DNN funnels information in a forward pass.

---

[1]It is known that for these types of problems, Convolutional Neural Networks can be more efficient than the suggested architecture. However, this example is given for illustrative purposes of the funnel effect.

between the relevant ones is further trained to come up with the DNN output that is an approximation to the original function.

Seen like this, we can think of a DNN as having two parts. The first part produces an effective dimensionality reduction from the input feature space to a *main features* space. A second part finds the non-linear rules between those main features that result in the final function value.

The other architecture that is central to this book, CTs, has no rival at generalising non-linear rules in functions from very few sampling points. This is the result of its strong mathematical convergence properties. However, it has the problem that the dimensionality of the input space cannot be too large.

So, what if we set a DNN to find the main features of a given function and set a CT to find the non-linear rules between those main features? If we manage to make it work, we will benefit from the strengths of each framework. That is, each framework will focus on a task it is suited for, while covering the weaknesses of the other.

This makes sense, at least in principle. This hybrid ML architecture should be a good candidate to improve classical DNNs and CTs. The very high efficiency of the CTs at generalising non-linear rules means that the new hybrid architecture should be able to find a more accurate solution from a smaller training set compared to its pure DNN equivalent. Also, the training process may need fewer iterations. Moreover, the evaluation of the hybrid architecture may be faster than its classical DNN equivalent, as CTs are ultra fast to evaluate.[2]

This is the fundamental idea that set the authors up for the piece of research presented in this chapter.

12.1.1 Factorable Functions

This type of framework should work well for functions that are factorable. For example, consider the function

$$f(x_1, x_2) = x_1^4 + x_2^4 + 2x_1^2x_2^2 - x_1^2 - x_2^2 + 1. \tag{12.1}$$

This function can be expressed as the composition of the following functions:

$$f_1(x_1, x_2) = \sqrt{x_1^2 + x_2^2}$$
$$f_2(a) = a^4 + a^2 + 1 \tag{12.2}$$
$$f(x_1, x_2) = (f_2 \circ f_1)(x_1, x_2).$$

Notice f is a two-dimensional function as given by Equation 12.1. However, its values can be recovered by a one-dimensional function as expressed in Equation 12.2. a is the feature that determines the value of f at any point (x_1, x_2). This is because f is perfectly factorable.

---

[2]Having said that, this benefit may be only marginal, as DNNs tend to be fast when evaluating, too.

If f is instead

$$f(x_1, x_2) = x_1^4 + x_2^4 + 2x_1^2 x_2^2 - x_1^2 - x_2^2 + 1 + \varepsilon(x) \qquad (12.3)$$

where ε represents a small perturbation, then we can say that the factorisation expressed in Equation 12.2 is an approximation to f.

When a function is factorable, there are hyper-surfaces on which f attains a constant value. For example, in the case of f as in Equation 12.1, these hyper-surfaces are concentric circles centred at the origin. Each of these surfaces are called an *isosurfaces*. This property will be relevant later in the chapter.

Factorable functions in finance

Factorable functions are indeed common in finance. Practitioners know that, quite often, the vast majority of the risk that drives changes in prices is dominated by a handful of features, for example, parallel shifts or rotations in yield curves and not the changes of every individual element in the yield curve. Indeed, this type of property is exploited in the applications relevant to this book, presented in Part IV.

12.2 DNN+CT WITH STATIC TRAINING SET

Let $\mathcal{D} = \{X, Y\} = \{x_i, y_i\}_{i=1}^m$ be a training set with m samples. The feature vector x is n_0-dimensional, while target variable y is a scalar variable. We assume that there is a function $\hat{f}$ that connects inputs with target values, $y_i = \hat{f}(x_i)$. Our goal is to replicate such function with an hNN architecture, represented by f.

Given the input value x, $\tilde{y}_i = f(x_i)$ represents the output through such architecture. This hNN is composed of two parts.

The first consists of a DNN with l layers. The number of neurons in the last layer is $n_l > 1$. This first part is represented by a function $a = f_1(x)$, where a is a n_l-dimensional vector. The second part consists of an interpolation framework, denoted by $\tilde{y} = f_2(a)$. We have decomposed f into the composition of two functions $f = f_2 \circ f_1$. Figure 12.2 shows a visual representation of this architecture.

Denote the input domain of f by $\mathcal{X} \subset \mathbb{R}^{n_0}$ and the image of f by $\mathcal{Y} \subset \mathbb{R}$. Also, let $\mathcal{A} \subset \mathbb{R}^{n_l}$ be the image of f_1, which is also the input domain of f_2.

The function f_1 transforms each sample in the training set to a point $a_i = f_1(x_i)$. This is illustrated for the case of $n_0 = 2$ and $n_l = 1$ in Figure 12.3. Each dot in the top left pane represents a sample $x_i \in \mathcal{X}$, each cross in the top right pane represents a transformation of a sample in the training set onto a point $a_i \in \mathcal{A}$, and each circle in that top right pane represents the target value y_i associated with each a_i value.

The function f_2 is an interpolation framework from $\mathcal{A}$ onto $\mathcal{Y}$. Interpolation frameworks are rooted in a number of interpolating anchor points $\{a_j^*\}_{j=1}^{n_I} \in \mathcal{A}$. These points are represented by squares in Figure 12.3 for the case of $n_I = 4$. The value of f_2 on the anchor points is denoted by triangles in that Figure 12.3. We will soon discuss how to obtain them; let us say for now that we have them.

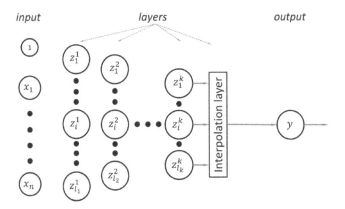

FIGURE 12.2 Hybrid DNN and interpolation architecture.

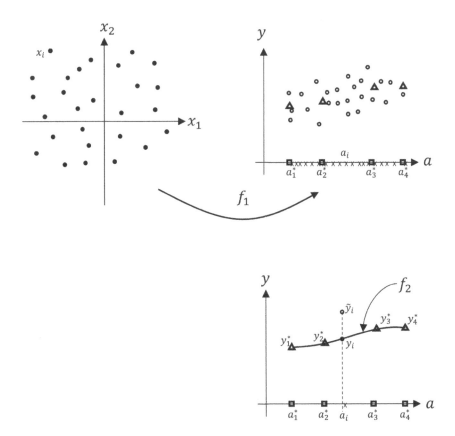

FIGURE 12.3 Illustration of static data key features.

We have now all the ingredients to build the interpolation framework $y = f_2(a)$ and, subsequently, a way to compute $y = f(x)$. Hence we can now compute the hNN's output for every sample of the training set, $\tilde{y}_i = f(x_i)$. One of these $\tilde{y}_i$ values is represented by a dot in the bottom right pane, Figure 12.3; its corresponding target value y_i is represented by a circle.

Calibration of f_2

The output of f_2 depends on the interpolating framework. Interpolating frameworks are defined by the interpolating points, the values of the function on these points, and the algorithm used to evaluate the interpolant. Consider these choices hyper-parameters of the hNN.

Given the strong mathematical properties of CTs, this will be our choice of interpolating framework used for f_2.

Once we have the interpolating points (in our case Chebyshev points), we need to obtain values for f_2 at the Chebyshev points, that is, the triangles in Figure 12.3, top right pane. The only thing missing to determine the interpolation framework, which is the algorithm to evaluate the resulting interpolant, is given by the barycentric interpolation formula (see Section 3.6).

There are a number of ways in which values for f_2 at the Chebyshev points can be estimated. For example, given a Chebyshev point a_i^*, we can take the N closest values of the image of the training samples under f_1 and average them out to obtain a candidate for $f_2(a_i^*)$. The number N must not be too small nor too big, for example, $N = 10$. An alternative method could be to define a ball for each a_i^*, and take $f_2(a_i^*)$ as the average of those values in the ball, perhaps weighted by the distance to a_i^*. As the reader can see, there are a number of ways to define $f_2(a_i^*)$.

Training the hNN

Our goal is to make y_i as close as possible to $\tilde{y}_i$. This means we want the learning process to align the y_i values along the interpolant $f_2(a)$. This is illustrated in Figure 12.4. As a result, the learning process consists of updating, at each learning iteration, the weights of the DNN f_1 to make $\tilde{y}_i$ increasingly closer to y_i. When this happens, we know that the function f has been factorised into two functions, and the output space of the first function, which is the input of the second, has dimension n_l.

We can use any typical cost function to train this hNN. For example,

$$\phi(w; X, Y) = \frac{1}{m} \sum_{i=1}^{m} (f_w(x_i) - y_i)^2 \tag{12.4}$$

where w are the DNN weights or parameters.

The training process will be practically the same as in a standard DNN. The DNN weights are initialised and a forward pass followed by backward propagation every time the weights of the DNN are updated, as per Equation 2.19. This is done iteratively until the cost function reaches a stable value.

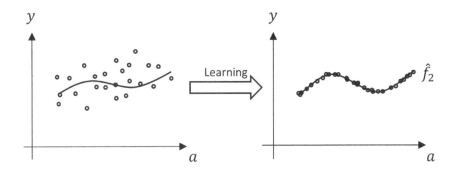

FIGURE 12.4 Illustration of learning process with static training set.

The only difference with a standard DNN is that, now, the last layer is an interpolation function; therefore, it needs to be treated somewhat differently. The forward pass of the interpolation layer is trivial. All that needs to be done is evaluate the interpolator. Regarding the backward pass, the gradient descent algorithm requires the computation of

$$\frac{\partial f_w}{\partial w} = \sum_{j=1}^{n_l} \frac{\partial f_2}{\partial a_j} \frac{\partial a_j}{\partial w}. \tag{12.5}$$

The computation of $\frac{\partial a_j}{\partial w}$ is done as with any other DNN, given that a_j is the j-th output of f_1. For the computation of $\frac{\partial f_2}{\partial a_j}$, we take advantage of the fact that the partial derivatives of CTs converge exponentially to the corresponding partial derivative of the function it approximates (Section 3.7.1). We also take advantage of the fact that evaluating the partial derivatives of CTs is very efficient once we have the value of the function at the interpolating points (Section 3.7.2).

We have now all the ingredients needed to calibrate an hNN. We should expect this hNN to be more efficient at dealing with factorable functions than a traditional DNN. By more efficient we mean it should reach a higher level of accuracy with the same training set, or reach the same level of accuracy as a given DNN but with a smaller training set.

12.3   DNN+CT WITH DYNAMIC TRAINING SET

The previous discussion for an hNN architecture assumes that the training set $\mathcal{D}$ is static. This means that the data $\{X, Y\} = \{x_i, y_i\}_{i=1}^m$ used for training cannot be changed. The second version of the hNN that we review now assumes that we have a way to compute new training samples as needed, in a dynamic way. One possible benefit of this new version of the hNN is that it may need a smaller training set compared to its static counterpart. This could be beneficial if obtaining sample points for the training set is computationally expensive.

To build the CT for f_2, we need only the value of f_2 at Chebyshev points on $\mathcal{A}$. Moreover, very few of them are needed to obtain a high degree of accuracy, due to the convergence properties of CTs (see Chapter 3). As a result, we only need few but very specific points to construct the hNN.

The question is, thus, how can we propagate backwards the Chebyshev points from $\mathcal{A}$ to $\mathcal{X}$, when we do not know the weights w in f_1?

This can be done in an iterative process, in which we take advantage of the fact that factorable functions define isosurfaces — that is, sets of points on which f outputs the same value, regardless of which point of the isosurface is selected. As a result, finding the value of the function f that corresponds to a Chebyshev point in $\mathcal{A}$ is equivalent to finding the isosurface that corresponds to that Chebyshev point.

Let us say that we have a training set $\{x_i, y_i\}_{i=1}^m$. Given the initial values of the DNN parameters, each element of the training set outputs a value a_i, for which we have its corresponding y_i value. Using these values, we can create a candidate for f_2 similarly to the way it was done in Section 12.2. All this together yields a candidate for f. So far, we have done nothing different with respect to the case when the training set was static.

Backwards propagation will, however, be done slightly differently. In the static training data set case, the gradient descent algorithm says how to update the weights of the DNN f_1. Now, in addition to that, we are going to update the training set with the idea of moving the x points toward the isosurfaces that correspond to Chebyshev points. Once this is done and the learning is completed, the training set should align all points along these isosurfaces, and all their corresponding a values should coincide with the Chebyshev points a_i. This process is depicted in Figure 12.5.

The training set can be moved in each iteration according to a gradient decent algorithm. However, to do so, we consider the derivatives with respect to x instead of the derivatives with respect to w.

$$x_{k+1} = x_k - \eta_k \nabla_x \phi(w_k; X_k, Y_k). \tag{12.6}$$

Note that we now have a new hyper-parameter, the learning rate of the training set η. Also, the training set $\{X, Y\}$ is different at each iteration k.

The potential benefit of the dynamic version of the hNN compared to its static one is that, to calibrate f, we only need information from a few training samples per Chebyshev point, perhaps as low as one data point per Chebyshev point. This can be an upside when the evaluation of the original function is computationally expensive and we want to minimise the number of times we call it.

12.4   NUMERICAL TESTS

In order to test these algorithms, we implemented both a static and dynamic version of the DNN+CT hybrid architectures for fairly simple functions. If it does not work for simple functions, there is no hope it will work on more complex ones.

12.4.1   Cost Function Minimisation

Test 1

Consider the function

$$f(x_1, x_2) = (x_1 + x_2)^2. \tag{12.7}$$

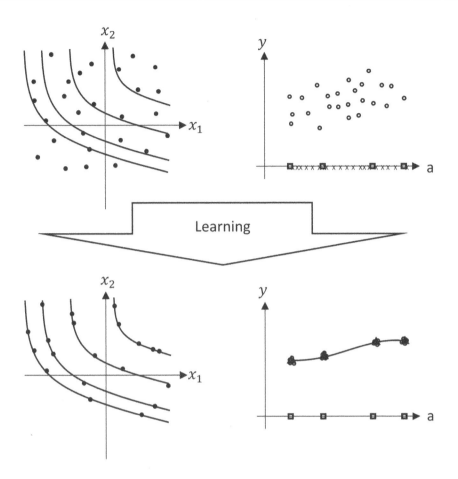

FIGURE 12.5 Illustration of learning process with dynamic training set.

We trained a simple DNN with two layers and two neurons per layers and compared the results to the ones obtained by training an hNN with one layer and two neurons in f_1 and a CT for f_2. The results are shown in Figures 12.6 and 12.7.

The graphs speak for themselves. The hNN clearly attains lower cost values both on training and testing sets for the function in Equation 12.7.

Test 2

For the second test, we chose a more complex function:

$$f(x_1, x_2) = \cos^3(x_1 + x_2). \tag{12.8}$$

Again we compared results between a simple DNN with two layers and two neurons per layers with those of an hNN with one layer and two neurons in f_1 and a CT for f_2. The results are shown in Figures 12.8 and 12.9.

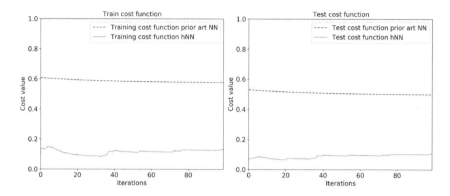

FIGURE 12.6   The *x*-axis represents the number of learning iterations. The *y*-axis represents the cost value at each iteration for static training in Test 1.

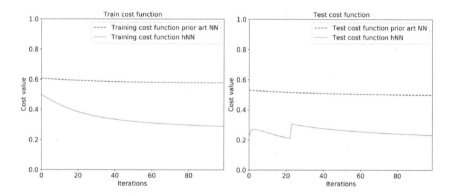

FIGURE 12.7   The *x*-axis represents the number of learning iterations. The *y*-axis represents the cost value at each iteration for dynamic training in Test 1.

The results also speak for themselves. The hNN attains lower cost values on both training and testing data with fewer iterations than the DNN.

12.4.2   Maximum Error

We also computed the maximum error for each hNN as a replica of the original function. The results are shown in Table 12.1. The hNN was better than the DNN in all cases.

12.5   ENHANCED DNN+CT ARCHITECTURES AND FURTHER RESEARCH

So far we have seen how a DNN can be combined with a CT to create a potentially stronger ML architecture, which we call a hybrid Neural Network, or hNN. Tests indicate that this hNN is more efficient at replicating factorable functions than DNNs.

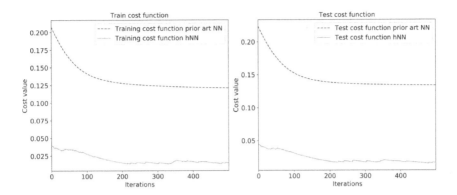

FIGURE 12.8   Cost function versus number of learning iterations static training in Test 2.

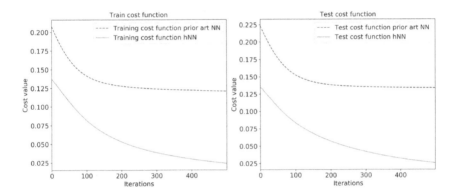

FIGURE 12.9   Cost function versus number of learning iterations dynamic training in Test 2.

TABLE 12.1   Maximum error of each hNN architecture.

	DNN	hNN static training set	hNN dynamic training set
Test 1	3.47	0.49	0.00000014
Test 2	0.59	0.18	0.16

However, a limitation that the hNN has, as explained so far, is the number of features that it can deal with, because that number is limited by the dimensionality of the input domain in the interpolation framework f_2, which suffers from the curse of dimensionality.

In order to overcome this limitation, we could use dimensionality extension techniques such as the Tensor Extension Algorithms from Chapter 6 or the Sliding Technique from Chapter 7. These techniques, which are applied with success in some of the applications in Part IV, enable an increase in the number of input dimensions a CT can deal with, and hence the number of features that the hNN can manage.

The problem that we face when using the dimensionality extension techniques mentioned is that the calibration of the hNN requires the computation of the gradient of the interpolation layer. The direct CTs are ideal for that, as the derivative of the CT is easy to obtain and approximates the derivative of the function it replicates very well. However, this may not be the case with these dimensionality extension techniques, as computing their gradient is not a trivial calculation.

To circumvent this problem, we could try a similar idea to the one developed so far in a slightly different way. The training of the hNN can be done in two stages. First, we can use an auto-encoder architecture to investigate the features that drive f. Once it has been calibrated, we can use the encoder part as f_1. Then, in order to calibrate f_2, we need the value of f_2 at the Chebyshev points. Now this can be done because f_1 has already been calibrated, and so we can invert its evaluation and, given a Chebyshev point a_i, we can compute its corresponding x_i by evaluating f_1 backwards. Then, we can evaluate the original function in x_i; this value is the needed $f_2(a_i)$.

Now, we have all the components needed to replicate the original function via an hNN, despite the high number of features, and f_2 could be based on any dimensionality extension techniques so that the curse of dimensionality in the interpolation framework can be sidestepped.

The results so far are, in our view, positive and encouraging. Further research could focus on the enhanced hNN just explained, as well as testing these techniques with derivative pricing functions or other functions relevant to the applications presented in Part IV of this book.

Applications

The aim

Part I of this book presented the fundamental approximation methods. In Part II, we explained a set of techniques — which constitute what we call the "toolkit" — that are combined with the approximation techniques to produce the solutions that are the focus of Part III. In this part, we describe how to apply these solutions to a range of real-life computational challenges within finance with the aim of alleviating some of the computational bottlenecks present in these applications.

The main goal of this book is to discuss the solutions to the real-life computational problems presented in this part. In this sense, all chapters covered so far set the scene for this part of the book.

The chapters that constitute this part describe the different applications in detail. They start with a description of the problem, then describe the computational challenges involved, how the different techniques or solutions presented throughout this book can be applied along with — most of the time — numerical calculations that support the effectiveness of the techniques.

The solution to every application presented consists of generating both accurate and fast-to-compute proxies to functions. The methods employed are the hybrid methods presented in Part III, which rely on a mix of either DNNs or CTs, adapted, depending on the application, with the tools presented in Part II. These methods provide objects that if properly used within each context can provide high degrees of accuracy with relatively small evaluation times of the function being approximated, solving the main computational bottleneck in each application. Given the importance of the calculations presented herein, the benefits are profound.

We cannot stress enough the importance of the calculations presented in this part of the book for financial institutions. Some of these calculations lie at the core of the systems designed to track, identify and adjust some of the most important risks financial institutions face on a regular basis.

It is important to note that there are other contexts where the techniques and methods presented next can be applied with great success. Indeed, the reader may have already identified such applications by now. We leave these for future projects.

13.1 SUITABILITY OF THE APPROXIMATION METHODS

The hybrid solutions presented in Part III use the fundamental approximation methods presented in Part I. Since the applications presented in the coming chapters rely on approximating financial functions — mostly pricing functions — it is important that these functions satisfy the hypothesis of the theorems that constitute the mathematical framework of each of the approximating methods. The following justifies the use of these approximating methods on the functions that we build proxies for in each of the applications we present in coming chapters.

Pricing functions, outside isolated points, are differentiable and often analytic.[1] Not only is there growing evidence of this (for example [27]), but for the most part, practitioners assume so, at least implicitly; the use of Taylor expansions to locally approximate pricing functions is an acknowledgement of this.

This means that for the most part, the hypotheses of the theorems that constitute the mathematical framework of the approximation methods we use are satisfied. In the case of CTs, we need functions to be analytic to obtain the strongest result: quasi-exponential convergence. Weaker conditions also guarantee convergence, such as smoothness and even Lipschitz continuity. In any case, for the most part, the functions we want to approximate in the applications presented in coming chapters are analytic. In the case of DNNs, the assumption made by the Universal Approximation Theorem (Theorem 2.3.1) is just continuity, which is much weaker and hence satisfied, too.

We said that pricing functions (and other financial functions we are interested in) satisfy the conditions we need for the approximating theorems to hold, outside isolated points. These isolated points usually come in the form of payment dates, barriers, strikes, and so on. An important thing to note about these points is that it is possible to locate them within the domain of the function; often, they are defined by the trade itself. To prevent these points from affecting the convergence properties of the fundamental approximation methods, one splits the domain of approximation along these points. By doing so, one is left with a collection of sub-domains free of singularities.

Singular points can also be the result of structured payoffs. For example, taking the maximum between continuation and exercise value in an American option introduces a singularity. However, the continuation function is free of this type of singularity and carries nearly all the computational cost. Hence, we build proxies for this function, obtaining the expected benefits.

In relation to CTs, it is important to note that convergence rates are determined by the smoothness of the function (see Section 3.3). How non-linear the trade is does not affect its smoothness. Linear products will likely need fewer Chebyshev points than non-linear ones, but the type of convergence does not change.

Another case to consider is that of pricing functions that rely on numerical simulations for their evaluation. For these, the values are themselves approximations of the true value. What the authors have observed empirically is that both DNNs and CTs approximate the function up to the level of accuracy provided by the implementation of the pricing function. For example, if prices are obtained through Monte Carlo simulations and the simulations come with a noise of $1e^{-3}$, then the approximating objects will reach this level of accuracy exponentially, but will remain within this noise regardless of any further sampling.

---

[1] See Definition 3.2.1 of an analytic function.

13.2 UNDERSTANDING THE VARIABLES AT PLAY

Another very important aspect we must address to thoroughly understand the solutions presented in this book is the type of parameters affecting the functions we apply the hybrid solutions (Part III) to. Identifying them will play a key role in each of the applications we discuss.

Denote a generic pricing function by P. There are four families of parameters affecting P that need to be identified.

Model parameters

As a function, P gives the price of some financial derivative $\mathcal{D}$. By definition, financial derivatives are contracts between two parties under which payments related to an underlying asset S are agreed to be made at future times; therefore, the modelling of the dynamics of S is key to P. We denote any model used to describe the dynamics of S by $\mathcal{M}$ and the space where the parameters of $\mathcal{M}$ can take values by Θ. This set constitutes the first set of parameters that pricing functions P depend on.

For example, consider an option defined over a stock S. There are many different models used to simulate the movement of S. For the sake of illustration, take the Heston model. This model consists of the following stochastic process:

$$
\begin{aligned}
dS_t &= \mu S_t + \sqrt{v_t} S_t dW_t \\
dv_t &= a(b - v_t)dt + \sigma \sqrt{v_t} dZ_t.
\end{aligned}
\tag{13.1}
$$

The behaviour of S can be simulated using Equation 13.1. To do so, the parameters $\theta = (a, b, \sigma, \rho)$ in Θ must be specified. Usually, Θ does not have many variables, ranging from a couple to, in the worst case, a few tens of variables. A common exercise — done daily within financial institutions — is the specification (calibration) of such parameters based on observable market quotes. The computational issues arising from such an exercise, along with suggested solutions, will be covered in detail in Chapter 18.

Market risk factors

The second set of parameters is denoted by $\mathcal{S}$. This set consists of market risk factors that affect the value of P. Examples of these parameters are stock values, interest rates, implied volatilities, commodities, and so on. The number of market quotes that can affect a function like P can be in the tens, hundreds and in some cases thousands, for example, options that depend on several families of quotes defined over a range of tensors and strikes.

Model risk factors

There is another set of parameters closely linked to market risk factors that we must bear in mind. These are the *model risk factors*. They will not feature in every application, but for some, they are crucial.

We first mentioned model risk factors in Section 5.1 when discussing the Composition Technique. Indeed, one of the most important instances of the Composition Technique is the one that takes advantage of the parametrisations provided by the models that simulate market risk factors. In Section 5.1, we explained that if $\mathcal{M}$ is such a model, then it first simulates a set of model risk factors $\mathcal{R}$. The space generated by these variables, which we call model risk factors, has the useful property of smoothly parametrising the market risk factors.

A good yet simple example of this situation was provided in detail in Section 5.1. The aim of the HW one-factor model is to generate interest rates. These could be zero rate curves, discount curves, swap curves, and so on. All of these live in the market risk space. However, to generate these curves, the model first generates a single stochastic variable r known as the short rate. The short rate then parametrises any of the curves the model can generate in the market risk space.

As explained in Section 5.1, one of the main forms of the Composition Technique is obtained by taking the composition of the parametrisation g provided by the model with the pricing function P to obtain a function we denoted by f. This composition changes the question of pricing with P within the space of market risk factors to that of pricing with f on the space of model risk factors.

Notice that it is general practice to define P so that it never takes model risk factors as inputs but market risk factors. Also, not all applications in this book involve market risk factors that have been generated by model $\mathcal{M}$. Therefore, model risk factors will only feature in some applications, such as the ones covered in Chapters 15 and 17. For these types of situations, the question of identifying the parameters that affect P changes to the question of identifying the parameters that affect f — viewing the problem in this way makes the risk computations involved substantially easier.

Trade parameters

The final set of parameters is $\mathcal{T}$. This consists of the parameters specified by the derivative contract $\mathcal{D}$. If $\mathcal{D}$ is an option over some underlying S, the strike and maturity are examples of parameters in $\mathcal{T}$.

There is a subtle but noteworthy point to highlight. The strike and maturity are defined within the contract of $\mathcal{D}$. However, we consider P to be a function that depends on both strike and maturity. In this sense, P is not the pricing function of $\mathcal{D}$, but of a family of derivative contracts, all of which share the same underlying S. If a strike and maturity are fixed, this defines a contract $\mathcal{D}$ and $\mathcal{P}$, restricted to this strike and maturity, gives the price of $\mathcal{D}$.

Choosing carefully

Identifying the previous types of parameters for the function $\mathcal{P}$ and the role each play within each application is part of the solution itself. Depending on the problem, some parameters will be kept constant while some vary. Which are kept constant and which are allowed to vary partly depends on the context and the choices made by the practitioner. Let us illustrate this point with an example.

Consider a CVA calculation. For simplicity and without loss of generality, assume there is only one derivative transaction $\mathcal{D}$ in the netting set, with pricing function P. The calculation consists of simulating, at different time points in the future, the market risk factors $\mathcal{S}$ that affect the price given by P. This means model parameters in $\mathcal{M}$ remain fixed throughout the simulation. Equally, given that the strike is a defining feature of $\mathcal{D}$, it remains constant.

One possible strategy is to define the input domain of the proxy function with only the market factors, ignoring model parameters and trade-specific parameters. By doing this we reduce the number of variables in the input domain, making the problem less complex. At the same time, as the risk is driven by $\mathcal{S}$, the market parameters, and nothing more, we capture all the risk in the calculation. In this case example, we build a proxy function for the specific trade instance.

An alternative strategy would include the strike as a variable in the proxy function. This approach gives a more flexible solution, as the proxy can work for a range of options with different strikes. This, of course, is at the cost of increasing the computational building cost of the proxies.

A central driver of a successful proxy building strategy for a risk calculation is a good understanding of the advantages and disadvantages of including or leaving out a variable from the input domain of the proxy function. The more variables used to define the input domain, the more complex the building process. However, the more variables we include in the input domain, the more flexible the solution, if the variables have been smartly chosen.

Let us stress that, as long as we capture all or most of the risk we are trying to measure, there is no right or wrong solution when it comes to choosing the variables for the input domain of the proxy functions. It all depends on the context and on what we are trying to achieve. However, in our experience, the cleaner and simpler the solution, the better it performs. These tend to give more control over the proxy function; its error and demand lower computational loads when building. If one treats all parameters that affect P equally, the approximation exercise can easily explode in complexity and the solutions obtained are either suboptimal, difficult to work with or even unworkable in a real-world setting.

As subsequent chapters show, the solutions to the pricing problem in the different contexts involve carefully deciding which fundamental method of approximation to use — whether DNNs or CTs — deciding how to adapt it to the particular application — which tool from Part II to combine it with — while deciding which parameters to discard and which to consider in the building of the proxy so that the computation in question is optimised for the particular use in which it lives. When we present a solution, we do not claim it is the best. Our goal is to share our experience and illustrate different ways to solve the problem so the reader can design the best solution for the problem at hand.

## CHAPTER 14

When to use Chebyshev Tensors and when to use Deep Neural Nets

The aim of this chapter is to make a comparison between CTs and DNNs as function approximation objects. We highlight their strengths and weaknesses bearing in mind the applications presented in this book. The discussion will focus on three points. The first is the convergence and evaluation of the approximation methods. The second is how the methods deal with the curse of dimensionality. The third is with respect to partial derivatives and error estimation.

14.1 SPEED AND CONVERGENCE

Both CTs and DNNs are function approximation objects. The type of function f we are interested in approximating has its domain in $\mathbb{R}^n$ and takes values in $\mathbb{R}$. That is,

$$f : \mathbb{R}^n \to \mathbb{R}.$$

The way in which CTs and DNNs approximate functions such as f is by evaluating the domain of f. That is, both CTs and DNNs are examples of sampling approximation techniques. CTs do the sampling deterministically on prespecified points called Chebyshev points, while DNNs are not restricted to any particular geometry.

After f has been evaluated on the sampling points, proxy objects must be built. For CTs, this is a trivial exercise when the dimension of the input space of f is restively low (roughly dimension 5 and less). The building of the proxy object simply consists of storing the values of the function f on Chebyshev points. No other parameter needs be computed. The proxy object is ready to be evaluated at this point. If the dimension of the input space for f is large (above 5, in most applications), then the Tensor Extension Algorithms, as described in Chapter 6, must be run to obtain the proxy object ready to be evaluated. In the case of DNNs, once the sampling has been done, we need to run a learning or calibration routine that determines a set of parameters or weights needed to evaluate the proxy object (see Section 2.4).[1]

---

[1]Note that at different points in the book we refer to the calibration of CTs. Unless the Tensor Extension Algorithms are used, the calibration of CTs simply consists of storing together Chebyshev points and the values of f on Chebyshev points, nothing else.

14.1.1 Speed of evaluation

A central characteristic of both approximation methods is their speed of evaluation. In the case of CTs, the barycentric interpolation formula and the Clenshaw algorithm guarantee efficient and numerically stable evaluation (see Section 3.6.2). In the case of DNNs, evaluation reduces down to a series of matrix multiplications and activation functions evaluations, for which there are highly optimised and stable libraries. However, the authors know of some applications where the number of layers and neurons needed for the DNN was such that evaluation speed was an issue as a result of the large number of neurons. Despite this, in general, the speed of evaluation tends to be orders of magnitude faster than the speed of evaluation of the functions, which we want to approximate using CTs and DNNs. Using these approximation methods would otherwise be pointless, as this is a key property to obtain the computational gains we are after.

14.1.2 Convergence

Another central aspect of both CTs and DNNs is the collection of theorems that guarantee their convergence to functions f with reasonable properties. In the case of CTs, if the function f is Lipschitz continuous, convergence is guaranteed. Moreover, the smoother the function, the faster the convergence. When the function f is smooth, convergence is polynomial; when f is analytic, convergence is quasi-exponential for dimension greater than 1 and exponential when the dimension is 1 (see Section 3.3 for convergence results and Definition 3.2.1 for what it means to be analytic). In the case of DNNs, the Universal Approximation Theorems guarantee the convergence for continuous functions (see Section 2.3).

However, it is important to note a difference between the convergence theorems for CTs and DNNs. The theorems that concern CTs say that for a given function f with certain properties (for example Lipschitz continous), convergence is guaranteed by simply increasing the number of sampled points — which is equivalent to increasing the granularity of the Chebyshev mesh. By contrast, the convergence theorems for DNNs (Universal Approximation Theorems; see Section 2.3) guarantee convergence as long as we adjust the depth or width of the DNN. Notice, however, that the Universal Approximation Theorems say that there is *a* configuration of the DNN that increases the accuracy of the approximation; what they do *not* say is how to obtain the right configuration. To add a degree of difficulty, different numbers of sampled points are needed for different configurations. This contrasts with CTs, where there is no ambiguity as to what needs to be done to increase accuracy: simply increase the granularity of the Chebyshev mesh.

In terms of the applications presented in coming chapters, the important thing to note is that all functions that we want to approximate enjoy high degrees of smoothness over their domains. Occasionally, these functions have singularity points (e.g. a barrier level in a barrier option). However, we can easily deal with these points by using Chebyshev Splines (Section 3.8), splitting the domain of approximation along these points, leaving sub-domains where the functions are smooth. This is what we do in some of the applications presented in this book, such as the one in Chapter 15. Therefore, what we have are approximating objects that converge with the functions of interest as the number of sample points increases.

We have said that both CT and DNN approximation methods guarantee convergence for the functions that come up in the applications presented in subsequent chapters. This is a good starting point. However, given the nature of the applications of interest, the faster the convergence, the higher the benefits obtained. The reason is down to the following.

14.1.3 Convergence Rate in Real-Life Contexts

Most of the applications of interest involve alleviating a computational bottleneck within a numerical calculation, for example, the calculation of a risk metric. The bottlenecks we focus on are the result of evaluating functions — for example, pricing functions — thousands or even millions of times within the calculation. Denote an instance of such function by f. The idea is to significantly reduce the computational cost associated with the evaluation of f within the calculation by using a proxy function. This is done by building a *sufficiently accurate* proxy to f — where what we mean by sufficient accuracy depends on the application at hand. If the approximation has a sufficient degree of accuracy, then the approximating object can be used instead of f to run the computation in question. Given the speed at which CTs and DNNs can be evaluated, the calculation can be done in a fraction of the time of what it would take using f.

To assess the magnitude of the computational cost reduction obtained when using one of the approximating objects, we must remember that these proxies are obtained by evaluating the function f, and in some cases, running a training algorithm after f has been evaluated. We should also remember that, in many cases, the approximating objects built are evaluated orders of magnitude faster than f. Therefore, the size of the computational gain can be estimated by comparing the time it takes to evaluate f during the numerical calculation (when no approximating object is used) with the time it takes to build the approximating object (time it takes to sample f and run any needed training exercise) if the latter is used in the numerical calculation instead of f. Therefore, the number of times we sample the function to build the proxy gives us an estimate of the computational gain we obtain when using a proxy function. This is why the convergence rate of the approximating objects can be crucial; the smaller the number of times we need to evaluate f to build the proxy, the higher the computational gains.

For example, say we need to evaluate a pricing function f within a risk calculation 1,000,000 times (e.g. a CCR calculation, such as the ones in Chapter 15). Moreover, assume, as it happens in many real-life calculations, that performing these 1,000,000 evaluations with f exceeds the time or economic cost that makes the CCR number useful. To alleviate this computational cost, we can approximate f with either a CT or a DNN. To do this, we must sample f. As we mentioned, the less we sample f, the greater the computational gains. This is one of the aspects where CTs excel over DNNs — in fact, over pretty much any other approximation technique. The quasi-exponential convergence they display over analytic functions means that compared to DNNs, they need far fewer evaluations to reach a specific level of accuracy. Moreover, nothing other than the number of mesh points needs to be adjusted. This contrasts with all the hyper-parameters that may need to be adjusted in a DNN to increase its accuracy, where it is not always known whether a particular change in the values of the hyper-parameters will yield the desired results.

A similar situation arises when we consider other well-known and often used approximation methods in finance. For example, linear interpolation frameworks are sometimes used to build proxy pricing functions.[2] One of their advantages is their fast evaluation time, just like CTs and DNNs. However, their convergence rates in terms of sampled points is very slow. As computational gains are directly driven by the number of times the function f is sampled, we want the number of evaluations to be as small as possible. Slow convergence rates means f needs to be sampled many times to achieve a specified degree of accuracy.

Figure 14.1 illustrates this point. The pricing function f used to generate it was the Black-Scholes pricing function. A total of five different variables were taken into consideration for the approximation: spot, strike, volatility, interest rate and time to maturity. The fact that it is the Black-Scholes function is immaterial for our purposes; the only thing we need is a function that satisfies the hypothesis of the theorems that guarantee the convergence of both CTs and DNNs.

We built CTs and DNNs to approximate f as we increased the number of points sampled. CTs were built both as full tensors (that is, evaluating every single grid point) and through the use of the Tensor Extension Algorithms (evaluating a subgrid of the total grid and training a CT in TT format; see Chapter 6). Once built, we computed their empirical approximation error by comparing the proxies with f on a fine grid over the domain of f. The plot in Figure 14.1 shows how the approximation error of both proxies decreases.

In the case of the full CTs, only the size of the grid was increased — the grid, in this case, determines the points on which the pricing function is evaluated. For CTs in TT format, it is the subgrid (and not the full grid) that determines the points on which the pricing function is evaluated.[3]

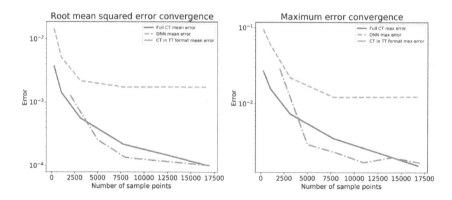

FIGURE 14.1 Comparison of how errors of approximation (logarithmic scale), on the Black-Scholes option pricing function with dimension 5, decrease for CTs (both full and in TT format) and DNNs as the number of sampled points increases. The plot on the left compares the decay of the root mean squared error. The plot on the right, the decay of the maximum error.

---

[2]For example, VaR calculations in some banks.
[3]When the CTs used were calibrated in TT format in this experiment, the full grid was fixed and the size of the subgrids used to build the tensor was increased.

For DNNs, the situation is more complex. On the one hand, we know that a single layer for a DNN is enough to guarantee convergence (Universal Approximation Theorem). However, as the error estimate of single-layered DNNs shows (see Section 4.3)

$$\mathcal{O}\left(\frac{C}{k}\right) + \mathcal{O}\left(\frac{kd}{n}log(n)\right),$$

we need to increase both the total number of neurons k and the number of sampled points n if we want to decrease the overall error. This is exactly what we did in the implementation of the numerical calculations used to obtain Figure 14.1.

What is very clear from Figure 14.1 is how the error for CTs decreases quasi-exponentially as the number of sampled points increases, whereas the error of the DNNs is far from it.[4]

The behaviour of the error that is seen in Figure 14.1 is quite typical. Over the past few years — a period during which we have worked on this topic extensively — we have consistently seen that as the number of sampled points increases, Chebyshev methods converge very fast (quasi-exponentially), while the error decay flattens out for most other approximation methods. For example, Figures 16.12 and 16.13 show, in a different way, the same behaviour, this time in the context of market risk and approximation grids. Also, Chapter 18 shows how, in the context of model calibration, the same accuracy can be achieved with CTs compared to DNNs with about 10 to 100 times fewer sample points.[5]

Going back to Figure 14.1, let us take, for example, 15,000 sample points in the experiment. The DNN displays an approximation error of almost 1×10^{-2}. However, both CTs (full CT and in TT format) have an error of around 1×10^{-3}. The difference is a whole order of magnitude, which translates into much more precise risk metrics for the given computational load required to build the proxies. If we want to increase the accuracy with the DNN, we need to test, via trial and error, different hyper-parameter configurations, possibly having to adjust the number of samplings for each. In the case of CTs, all we need to do is increase the number of points in the mesh and the quasi-exponential convergence guarantees a substantial improvement.

Regardless, if we are happy with, say, an average error of 5×10^{-2}, the DNN needs about 8,000 samples to get close to this level of accuracy (maximum error in Figure 14.1), while the building cost of the CT for the same level of accuracy is at about 1,000 samples. This constitutes a building cost reduction of about eight times. This, in some cases, may be the difference between running the risk calculation within the time constraints and not.

We insist that the behaviour displayed by Figure 14.1, as our experience indicates, has important practical considerations. If we want to increase the accuracy of the proxy built out of CTs, we *know* that it can be done with a relatively low number of extra sampled points. However, if we want to do so pretty much with any other approximation method, we need to increase the number of sampled points substantially. With

---

[4]Note that the dimension d of the function f is fixed and that C, a constant that depends on f, is also constant.

[5]Figures 16.12 and 16.13 compare CTs to linear interpolation. Cubic splines tend to display a similar behaviour.

these methods, the accuracy improvement stagnates. That is, even though *in theory* the error may converge to zero as the number of sample points goes to infinity, the rate of convergence is so slow that we cannot improve the quality of the proxy in reality. This contrasts significantly with the dramatic error decay exhibited by the quasi-exponential convergence of CTs.

There is another important element to highlight here. As we just mentioned, in order to decrease the error of approximation of the DNN, it is not enough to simply sample the function more times. The error is decreased through the right combination of architecture with an adequate number of points sampled. This makes the use of DNNs, for many of the applications of interest in this book, more complicated than that of CTs. This is particularly relevant if the calculations at hand are key to the organisation and, hence, are highly audited and/or regulated. Imagine a scenario where the proxy functions used in a strategically key calculation stop working in the middle of a market turmoil. If the calculation was done using CTs, all we have to do is increase (by a relatively low number) the sampled points; if they were obtained via DNNs, we could potentially face a situation where a new DNN architecture that fits the requirements has to be found, along with a new set of points sampled — the last thing you want in the middle of a market turmoil.

14.2   THE QUESTION OF DIMENSION

Another very important aspect to consider when deciding what approximation method to use is the dimension of the input domain of the function f we want to approximate. One of the main challenges when using CTs (indeed any tensor) is the curse of dimensionality. This says that for a fixed number of Chebyshev points per dimension, the size of the Chebyshev grid grows exponentially as the dimension of the tensor increases.

This presents a challenge for all the applications of interest that we discuss in coming sections — the greater the number of grid points for the CT, the greater the computational effort required to build the proxy. DNNs also suffer from the curse of dimensionality, but to a notably lesser extent.

Full Chebyshev Tensors

Consider once again a numerical calculation that computes a risk metric for which we need to price f, a pricing function, 1,000,000 times. Assume we want to replace f with a full CT to run the numerical calculation. Given that the size of the Chebyshev grid grows exponentially with the dimension of f, it makes a big difference whether f has a domain of dimension 2 or of dimension 7.

Table 14.1 shows how the size of the Chebyshev grid grows with dimension and how, as this happens, the computational gain rapidly decreases. In terms of computational gains, the curse of dimensionality means the dimension of the function f does not need to be very high for computational gains to significantly decrease. We go from a formidable 99.9% in dimension 3 to a Chebyshev grid, which has 40,000,000 points in dimension 9 — a grid that is 40 times greater than the (assumed in this example) total

TABLE 14.1 This table shows how the number of Chebyshev points increases with dimension and how the computational gain decreases as a result. We assume seven Chebyshev points per dimension and a calculation that requires evaluating a function f a total of 1,000,000 times.

Dimension	3	5	7	9	11
Grid size	343	16,807	823,543	40,353,607	1,977,326,743
Computational gain	99.9%	98.3%	17.6%	0%	0%

number of times f needs to be evaluated in the calculation when no proxy is used. Note we assume seven Chebyshev points per dimension (a reasonable assumption given the quasi-exponential convergence of CTs) and no further training after sampling, that is, no Tensor Extension Algorithm run is required.

Chebyshev Tensors in TT format

Chapter 6 explains how we can use the Tensor Extension Algorithms to calibrate CTs in TT format and with them substantially reduce the curse of dimensionality that tensors suffer from. This is done by sampling the function f to be approximated on a subgrid (often a very small subgrid) of the full CT, using this information to train a set of matrices that let one recover values over any point of the domain of approximation — similar to how DNNs use grids to find a set of weights with which one can do the same.

Unfortunately, it is not clear what is the maximum number of dimensions that TT-format CTs can handle, as it depends strongly on the characteristics of the function being approximated. From the tests performed for this book and the results in the literature (for example, [29]), the technique works for a few tens of dimensions. However, we expect it to work well for some pricing functions of even higher dimensions.

These techniques improve the curse of dimensionality that full CTs suffer from, but only up to a limit.

Deep Neural Nets

DNNs are also not immune to the effect of the dimension of the input domain of f. In Section 4.3, we said that as the dimension of f increases, the number of points that need to be sampled to achieve a specific level of accuracy also grows. In particular, from Equation 4.1, the approximation error grows linearly with the dimension d if the number of neurons and the number of sample points n remain constant. Equation 4.1 also says that increasing the number of sample points n helps counteract the error introduced by the increase in dimension. Specifically, given dimension d, we need n sample points so that $log(n)/n$ is approximately d to keep a certain level of accuracy. Clearly, DNNs generally have the capability to deal better with functions f that have a large number of inputs, compared to CTs.

We expand on these important points in the next sections.

14.2.1   Taking into account the application

So far in this section we have discussed the effect that the dimension has on the two fundamental approximation methods: CTs and DNNs. However, for the applications we are interested in — which constitute most chapters in this part of the book — we should always consider the context within which we want to use the approximation methods. Doing so is what allows us to push the limit of the dimension for which these techniques normally apply well beyond the obvious.

The techniques or tools presented in Part II are what allow us to take advantage of the context presented by each application and make the most out of CTs and DNNs. The multiple ways in which these tools and the approximation methods can be combined is what constitute the solutions (called *hybrid solutions* in Part III) we use within the applications presented in coming chapters. Next, we briefly describe them.

DNNs or CTs with the Composition Technique

In many of the applications that we are going to discuss, the function f we want to approximate appears, at first glance, to have a high-dimensional input domain. However, when the context where these functions are used is considered — type of calculation and models used, amongst other things — we see that the dimension of the input space of f can be reduced, sometimes significantly. This is done by defining a low-dimension parametrisation g of the input domain of f and composing g with f.

The result of this composition is a function φ with an input domain of a much lower dimension, which can be approximated much more easily by either a CT or a DNN. One of the characteristics of the parametrisations g — obtained in each of the applications — is that the composition φ returns values identical or very similar to those of f. That is, there is virtually no information loss by working with either f or φ. Examples of this situation are presented in Chapters 15 and 17.

It must be noted that, in principle, we could think of training DNNs without taking advantage of the dimensionality reduction offered by the Composition Technique, that is, building the DNN directly on the input space of the pricing function. In principle, the Universal Approximation Theorem ensures the existence of a DNN that approximates the pricing function for a given level of accuracy. However, we find this approach, as a general strategy, suboptimal for the reasons explained in this chapter.

Let us illustrate this point with a trivial example. Assume we want to approximate a pricing function that depends on a yield curve. Suppose the range of rates we choose to sample from goes from −1% to 5%. Without any further considerations, we will probably sample interest rate curves that never occur in practice, for example, curves where all tensors are close to −0.5% except, say, the 10-year rate, which is about 4%. Given that this scenario never occurs, there is no point in sampling these types of scenarios, wasting precious computational power.

What the Composition Technique effectively does is force us to sample regions where the evaluation of the pricing function is needed for the overall calculation in question. As we know from Chapter 5, there is more than one way of obtaining the parametrisation used in the Composition Technique. However, it makes sense to always use the parametrisation offered by the context, the one given by the calculation itself, for example, in CCR calculations (Chapter 15), using the function g (Eq. 15.1) that comes with the diffusion models used in the CCR engine.

CTs and Extension Algorithms

In Chapter 6, we saw how a set of learning algorithms, called Tensor Extenstion Algorithms, can help us build CTs with input domains of a dimension well beyond that of a typical tensor.

Table 14.1 shows how a normal CT requires a substantial number of evaluations once it goes past dimension 5. The example shown in Table 14.1 goes from a manageable 16,807 for dimension 5 to a well beyond problematic 40,353,607 for dimension 9. Table 14.2 shows an example when the CT is built using one of the Tensor Extension Algorithms.

As Table 14.2 shows, CTs of much higher dimensions can be built with a small number of Chebyshev point evaluations. It is important to note that the number of evaluations reported in Table 14.2 were obtained from simulations run and only represent examples of what is possible. The number of evaluations needed varies from case to case. The size of the subgrid does not just depend on the dimension of the tensor but also on the function being approximated. In the different applications covered in subsequent chapters, we will see how the size of the subgrid used varies even between tensors of the same dimension. However, Table 14.2 faithfully represents the fact that only a fraction of the Chebyshev grid needs to be evaluated, especially in higher dimensions; in some cases, this fraction is minuscule. This means that the computational gains do not deplete the same way as in Table 14.1. In some cases, we would also expect high computational gains beyond dimension 20.

The question of the size of the subgrid to use in the Tensor Extension Algorithm is an important one. After all, computational gains — one of our main goals — are directly related to the number of times the function to be replicated is sampled.

There is no way of knowing what is the size of the subgrid needed to achieve a specific degree of accuracy. As is the case with most hyper-parameters in ML models, a certain degree of user knowledge is needed. However, when it comes to choosing the size of the subgrid for the Tensor Extension Algorithms, there are a few considerations that can help.

TABLE 14.2 This table shows how the number of Chebyshev point evaluations needed to run the Tensor Extension Algorithms increase with dimension. Also computational gains are estimated compared to a calculation where a function f needs to be evaluated 1,000,000 times. We assume seven Chebyshev points per dimension.

Dimension	4	8	12	16	20
Full grid size	2,401	5,764,801	1.4×10^{10}	3.3×10^{13}	8.0×10^{16}
Evaluations needed	500	3,000	10,000	20,000	50,000
Fraction of grid evaluated	21%	0.05%	$7.1 \times 10^{-5}\%$	$6.1 \times 10^{-8}\%$	$6.3 \times 10^{-11}\%$
Computational gain	99.9%	99.7%	99.0%	98.0%	95%

An effective way of finding a subgrid that gives the required degrees of accuracy is through the use of the Sampling Adaptive Algorithm (see Section 6.5.1). This algorithm starts with a small subgrid and tries to find a suitable CT in TT format. If such CT is found, the algorithm stops; otherwise, the function is sampled further and a new subgrid is obtained.

Although very useful in some cases, the Sampling Adaptive Algorithm relies on repeatedly sampling the function and running the Rank Adaptive Algorithm. The problem with this dynamic is that, in some financial institutions, pricing engines and risk systems have limited connectivity — the result of being in different departments, for example. Limited connectivity can in some cases make an algorithm such as this difficult to use.

Another element that can be used to decide the size of the subgrid relates to computational gains. We know that computational gains are achieved only if the size of the subgrid is at most the total number of samplings needed to run the benchmark (i.e. the calculation via full revaluation, without any acceleration). This is because the subgrid needs to be evaluated by the function being replicated. Therefore, the total number of samplings required by the benchmark constitutes an upper bound for the size of the subgrid.

Moreover, given that the computational load associated with the use of CTs is concentrated on the sampling of the function needed to build the CT, a good estimate for the computational gains is obtained by comparing the number of samplings needed to run the benchmark with the number of samplings needed to build the CT. Therefore, if, for example, one is after a 90% computational gain, one can estimate the size of the subgrid one does not want to exceed (e.g. 10% of the number of function calls when run via full revaluation). Notice there is no guarantee the accuracy of the CT in TT format will be the one needed, but at least it gives us an idea of the size of the grid we are after. If the subgrid is not adequate, one can think of alternative ways in which the function to replicate may be modified so that a subgrid of the size required for specific computational gains works; in fact, these types of techniques are central to many of the use case applications shown in this book.

Finally, there are empirical estimates on the size of the subgrid needed to reach a particular level of accuracy given in terms of the dimension of the tensor. An example of these estimates is shown in [29], where for the cases tested, the size of the subgrid needed to reach levels of accuracy between 1×10^{-2} and 1×10^{-3} is proportional to the square of the dimension. This can be used as a good starting point in some cases. However, the reader should be aware this is only a guideline for which there are many exceptions.

It is worth highlighting that there is an error incurred when Tensor Extension Algorithms are used. This means a full or normal CT will normally be more accurate than a CT build with these algorithms. However, as we will see in many applications in coming chapters, the level of accuracy is well within what we need.

CTs with Sliding

Sometimes the characteristics of the function f and its input data are such that the approximation of f, possibly a function of very high dimension (in some cases more than

1,000 dimensions), can be reduced down to the creation and aggregation of a collection of low-dimensional CTs. If applied correctly in the proper context, the building of such proxies requires very few evaluations of f, giving as a result very high computational gains, while maintaining high levels of accuracy.

This solution is used, for example, in Chapter 16 in the case of IMA-FRTB capital calculations. The calculations involved in this case are run on very few scenarios, sometimes as few as 250. Therefore, we need to reduce the number of samplings as much as possible in order to achieve computational gains. Simultaneously, the proxy built this way must be accurate enough so that it passes the regulatory proxy-pricing thresholds — the so-called P&L attribution tests. The combination of sliders and CTs has a good balance between low computational building costs and sufficient accuracy for calculations such as the ones in Chapter 16.

DNNs

When the dimensionality of the problem is very high, and when the characteristics of the function f to be replicated do not lend themselves to any of the techniques with CTs, then we are left with DNNs. Their strength is their high degree of flexibility and that we know, via the Universal Approximation Theorems, that they can approximate any reasonable function to any desired level of accuracy. Their weakness comes, however, from that same flexibility, as little more than trial and error and a few heuristic rules exist for a practitioner to find the DNN architecture that yields the desired results.

14.3 PARTIAL DERIVATIVES AND EX ANTE ERROR ESTIMATION

There are another two properties worth mentioning that CTs have, which make them unique as function approximators, especially when considering the applications of interest. The first relates to the approximations of the partial derivatives of a given function f. The second relates to the control over the error of approximation.

Partial Derivatives

Say we have a function f to approximate with a given approximation technique. That is, the technique lets us build a proxy p for f. Regardless of the accuracy of p as an approximator for f and regardless of how efficiently we can build it, we cannot guarantee that the derivative p' will be a good approximator for the derivative f'.

This is not true for CTs. A strong point that CTs have is that not only can its partial derivatives be obtained in a very efficient way (remember, after all, that CTs are represented by polynomials), but the partial derivatives of the CT are very good approximators of the partial derivatives of f; in fact, their convergence rates are also remarkable. The details of these two facts can be found in Section 3.7.

The derivative properties just mentioned are unique and interesting in themselves, but they are also very useful in some applications that concern this book, such as the one presented in Chapter 17.

Error Control

The other relevant characteristic we ought to highlight is the ability that CTs have of estimating the error of approximation without the need to directly compare the approximating function with the function being approximated. Moreover, this error estimation can be done very efficiently. We call this the ex ante error estimation.

Normally, if we want to assess the level of approximation of a proxy p for a function f, we evaluate both on a fine grid over their domain and compute metrics using the values of p and f on the grid. For example, we can compute the maximum of the absolute value of the differences; this constitutes a very common way in which the error of approximation is measured empirically. This, however, involves evaluating f on the grid selected. If the evaluation of f is anything other than cheap (computationally speaking), evaluating f on the whole grid can be an expensive exercise, one for which we do not always have the necessary resources in real-life applications — in fact, the reason why we need to build a fast proxy for f in the applications presented is precisely because f is expensive to run. Therefore, the ability to estimate the empirical error ex ante — that is, without having to evaluate the function f on any grid other than the one used to build the approximating function — becomes a very valuable asset.

The details of how CTs estimate this error can be found in Section 3.4. The important thing to highlight is that in some applications we want to reach a specified level of accuracy. Instead of building several proxies and empirically estimating the error of approximation of each, we can gradually build a nested set of Chebyshev grids (for example, Chebyshev grids with size 2^{k+1} are nested as k increases), estimate the error of approximation ex ante at each stage and stop whenever we deem the level of accuracy to be adequate. Not only does this save the practitioner the time that it would take to estimate the error of approximation empirically but also it gives her the ability to stop from increasing the size of the Chebyshev grid, once an adequate level of accuracy has been reached.

A direct application of this for risk calculations is the following. Say we have a risk calculation where f needs to be called thousands of times. Moreover, assume — as we often do in this book — that in order to run it within the time constraints of the business, we need to build a fast proxy for f. Once built, proxies to f have a fixed degree of accuracy. To change their accuracy, we need to rebuild the object. Moreover, to estimate their new accuracy we typically need to measure it empirically, which as we said requires computationally expensive runs.

One of the problems with this situation is that we cannot react quickly to sudden market changes, especially aggressive ones. Say, for example, that the market goes into turmoil. In these situations, we run the risk that the proxy stops delivering accurate results. The problem becomes particularly acute because it is during periods of market turmoil when we most need reliable calculations.

If we have implemented the algorithm to compute the accuracy of the CT ex ante, the calibration of the CT will dynamically adapt to the new market conditions and will sample the function the required number of times so that a given degree of accuracy is reached. This minimises the chances that key calculations for the financial institution do not comply with audit/regulatory requirements. We do not know of any other approximation technique that can do this.

14.4 SUMMARY OF CHAPTER

This chapter mostly discussed the advantages and disadvantages of the two fundamental function approximation methods covered in this book: CTs and DNNs. Both have strong properties, which is why they are our approximation methods of choice. However, which is best depends not only on the characteristics of the function being approximated but also the characteristics of the context within which the function needs to be repeatedly evaluated. As has been explained at different points in the book, making use of the context where the function to approximate lives can significantly ease the approximation problem.

In general, when the dimension of the input domain of the function to be approximated f can be reduced down to a few variables, say, less than six, then as a rule of thumb we choose a full CT to approximate it, as this takes advantage of the strong mathematical properties of CTs. If the dimension is of a few tens of dimensions, approximately, then CTs in conjunction with the Tensor Extension Algorithms tend to constitute an ideal choice — they cover a good dimension range and we still take advantage of the mathematical properties of CTs. In some cases, the space over which we wish to evaluate f can be slit into orthogonal spaces over which the approximation can take place. In these case, we can produce Sliders of CTs to create proxy functions that require a very small number of samplings for calibration and proxy function creation — this, even in cases when the function f has a very high number of dimensions in the input domain. Finally, if the problem requires a high degree of flexibility, then DNNs are the optimal choice. This is summarised in Figure 14.2.

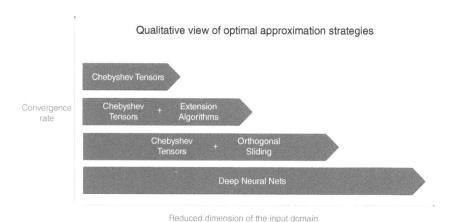

FIGURE 14.2 Which hybrid solution to use depending on the dimension of the problem.

For reasons that we hope are by now clear to the reader, techniques that reduce the dimensionality of the input domain of the approximation problem without affecting the accuracy of the overall risk calculation, combined with the fundamental approximation methods, CTs or DNNs, are computationally optimal.

It should be noted that our philosophy is cemented in the belief that the most effective approach at proxy object building in the contexts we are interested in involves building objects as cheaply as possible, even if these objects have to be built on a regular basis — be it daily, weekly or monthly. In fact, from this viewpoint, building objects regularly allows us to adapt to the given market conditions. In this case, the important thing is that we reduce the building cost as much as possible.

## CHAPTER 15

Counterparty credit risk

CCR is the area of risk analysis that quantifies the impact on a financial institution of a counterparty defaulting. There is a wide range of metrics that quantify this risk, some of the most relevant being CVA and DVA price adjustments (and its sisters in the XVA world), tail risk metrics like potential future exposure (PFE) profiles and IMM capital amounts.

Although the specifics of the calculations leading to these metrics vary from case to case, they all share a lot in common. First, they are all computed at the netting set and/or portfolio level. Second, a large number of risk factor paths affecting the netting set are diffused into the future at a number of time points — usually within a Monte Carlo simulation. Third, the trades in the netting set are priced at each node of the simulation (a node being the intersection of a path with a time point). Finally, once the distribution of prices is obtained, each CCR metric is obtained by processing the distribution of prices in a specific manner.

If there were no computational power limitations, we would use Monte Carlo simulations with millions of paths and a time point per day, covering the maturity of each trade in the calculation. This would significantly reduce the limitations derived from present Monte Carlo simulations, for example, spurious profile spikes. However, in practice there are computational power limitations that force practitioners to bound the number of paths to within a few thousands and the number of time points to a few tens. These restrictions limit the quality of the metrics, something practitioners have learnt to live with. This situation is clearly suboptimal and should be avoided if possible.

In particular, from the steps described, the pricing step is the one we focus on because it often carries most of the computational demand (see Section 4.1).

In this chapter, we explain how the solutions presented in Part III can be applied within CCR calculations to significantly reduce the computational cost associated with the pricing step. There are papers in the literature that use similar approaches to the ones presented in this chapter, for example, [29] and [32]. These ideas have direct business benefits, which range from being able to compute CVA prices quickly and accurately, reducing economic costs associated with running CCR calculations, to computing seemingly impossible calculations such as CCR portfolio optimisations.

We first cover the steps within a CCR calculation that precede the pricing step, drilling into the parts of the process that are relevant to the solutions presented in this chapter. Then we discuss the techniques from Part III that can help alleviate the computational pricing problem, giving details of how to use them. Then we present numerical results obtained when applying these techniques in a range of cases, highlighting the flexibility of the methods. Finally, we close with a section where we summarise the results obtained and make concluding remarks.

15.1   MONTE CARLO SIMULATIONS FOR CCR

Most CCR calculations are done at the level of netting set using Monte Carlo simulations. Some are done at portfolio level (e.g. FVA, KVA on market risk capital), but for ease of explanation we assume, without loss of generality, CCR calculations at netting set level.

As discussed, first the distribution of market risk factors that affect the netting set is generated. A typical simulation generates 10,000 paths of market risk factors into the future at about 100 time points. Under these assumptions, there are 1,000,000 nodes generated in a CCR calculation. In this chapter, unless otherwise stated, we use MC simulations of this size as reference.

Then comes the pricing step. Each trade in the netting set must be priced at each node generated. This means that each trade is priced $\mathcal{O}(10^6)$ times. Given that netting sets can contain thousands of trades, and that a bank may have hundreds or thousands of netting sets, the computational load associated with the pricing step is humongous. This is one instance of what we refer to as the *pricing problem* in risk calculations. It constitutes the main computational bottleneck of these calculations — typically more than 90% of the computational load, sometimes in excess of 99%, most often being the main impediment to computing such risk metrics.

15.1.1   Scenario diffusion

An *optimal* design of a solution to the pricing problem in CCR calculations should leverage from a careful understanding of the generation of market risk factors within Monte Carlo simulations. Without such understanding, potential solutions can easily become unnecessarily complicated, computationally costly to run and inaccurate.

In CCR calculations, market risk factors are typically diffused using diffusion models. As Section 5.1 explained, these models $\mathcal{M}$ are stochastic. To simulate market risk factors, a set of model parameters θ need to be specified, which are typically calculated via market-implied or historical methods.[1] Once the model has been calibrated, the model risk factors are diffused — for example, the short rate in the HW one-factor model presented in Equation 5.2. Model risk factors in turn parametrise market risk factors — for example, a whole yield curve through the parametrisation in Equation 5.1.1. As a result, a distribution of market risk factors is obtained at each node of the Monte Carlo simulation.

15.1.2   Pricing step — computational bottleneck

Each trade in the netting needs to be priced at each simulated node. This generates a distribution of prices that are then aggregated to obtain the price of the netting set at the node in question. All CCR metrics covered in this chapter require the aforementioned aggregated netting set price per node. From this point onward, the calculations

---

[1] The exercise of calibration can also be, computationally speaking, very expensive. This is the focus of Chapter 18.

vary depending on the metric computed. However, it must be stressed that although conceptually not straightforward at times, all calculations, from price per node to final metric, are computationally speaking not very costly.

Examples of metrics computed include XVA values such as CVA on uncollateralised portfolios, which require computing EPE and ENE profiles (the netting set's price average, where prices have been floored to zero when negative). For CVA on collateralised portfolios, the change in price of the netting set over a prescribed time horizon (e.g. 10 days) is used. This means each node of the simulation involves the computation of two prices: the first at the node in question, the second 10 days after. If the Monte Carlo simulation consists of 10,000 nodes per time point, then one must compute 20,000 prices per time point. Other risk metrics like PFE profiles or IMM capital require similar computations.

As we have seen, the computational bottleneck resides in producing the price of the netting set at each node of the simulation. These prices should be obtained by calling the pricing functions of the trades in the netting set on the market risk factors simulated at each node. Ideally, the officially approved pricing functions should be used. These are often called the "front-office pricers" in banks.[2]

15.2 SOLUTION

The risk calculations described in Sections 15.1 are, computationally speaking, very expensive, mainly due to the pricing step. If computational power is not an issue, the front-office pricing functions — the gold standard in these calculations — should be used. This constitutes the benchmark against which any other approach should be measured. Unfortunately, using these pricing functions, even with large CPU and GPU farms, can pose big computational challenges, making it virtually impossible to use in a real-life setting.

15.2.1 Popular solutions

As computational demand has increased over the years, the industry has resorted to increasing the power of hardware farms, some being reported in the tens of thousands of CPUs or GPUs. However, we are at a point where economies of scale do not favour these types of hardware-based solutions any more. It is estimated that farms such as the ones mentioned have a multimillion annual cost in capital and operational expenditures of buying, running and upgrading computing farms.

Cloud computing (i.e. outsourced farms) seems to be the way forward when it comes to the question of hardware. However, although often cheaper than in-house farms, they can still be expensive. Therefore, practitioners have resorted to algorithmic alternatives, which in combination with hardware farms (either in-house or outsourced), optimise the cost/benefit ratio.

---

[2]This point sometimes creates a discussion about simulation coherence and arbitrage, which is far beyond the scope of this book.

As the main bottleneck is the pricing step, most methods for computing CCR metrics look for ways to produce the netting set prices at each node of the Monte Carlo simulation, calling the pricing functions as little as possible, if at all. One such example is American Monte Carlo. First introduced by Longstaff and Schwartz in [52], it relies on regressions built from the payoff of trades to produce price distributions along the Monte Carlo simulation. Although efficient to run, they tend to lack precision, particularly on the tails of the price distributions. Also, it is difficult to control the precision they offer — that is, it is not always clear what should be done in order to increase accuracy when needed. This is particularly a problem for highly regulated calculations like IMM capital and PFE. In the attempt to make them more precise, practitioners have come up with all sorts of modifications and adjustments that make them difficult to use; therefore practitioners tend to have difficulties obtaining good results. At times, tuning them appropriately seems to be more of a "black art" than a science.

Another alternative that has been gaining attention in recent years is Differential Machine Learning ([42]). Differential Machine Learning essentially trains ML models — such as DNNs — not only on inputs (market risk factors) and outputs (prices) but also on the differentials of the outputs with respect to the inputs. Although, reportedly, models seem to train fast and give good accuracy along with important computational reductions, the implementation of such a technique requires a working Adjoint Algorithmic Differentiation (AAD) framework, the implementation of which is known to be very complicated in some cases.

In fact, successful implementations of AAD often require developing CCR engines from scratch; incorporating AAD to existing engines tends to be virtually impossible. Even when the engine is built from scratch, the implementation of AAD often comes with considerable practical challenges related to project management, budget approval and delivery of results in reasonable time frames.

Indeed, in our experience, despite not being intellectually stimulating, problems of a practical nature such as budgeting, approvals and deliveries are of paramount importance. In our view, practitioners should carefully consider these types of problems, too, as otherwise projects will likely fail. In particular, we find that financial institutions see solutions that enhance existing CCR engines favourably over those that require a systems overhaul.

Next, we present in detail how the techniques in Part III can be applied, yielding solutions for the pricing problem in CCR calculations.

15.2.2 The hybrid solution

The solution proposed in this chapter removes the pricing bottleneck by applying the methods presented in Part III to the pricing functions used to price portfolios in a CCR Monte Carlo simulation. Specifically, the Composition Technique as presented in Section 9.2 is central because it significantly reduces the computational burden associated with the creation of proxy functions without loss of precision. In Section 15.2.7, we explore the situation where the technique presented in this section cannot be implemented as a result of the existing computational infrastructure.

For simplicity and without loss of generality, consider a netting set with a single trade $\mathcal{D}$, which has pricing function P. The Monte Carlo simulation generates a distribution of market risk factors scenarios to be priced. The distribution of market risk factors is generated using risk factor diffusion models. These models first need to be calibrated. The parameters obtained at calibration are kept constant throughout the Monte Carlo simulation.

Take a yield curve as an example of a set of market risk factors. The vast majority of risk factor diffusion models used to generate yield curves first diffuse model risk factors — for example, if the model is the HW one-factor model, the model risk factor is the short rate. The key element is that the market risk factors are parametrised in terms of the model risk factors diffused and the fixed parameters obtained at calibration. In our example, the whole yield curve, regardless of number of tensor points, is parametrised by the short rate and the fixed HW parameters.

The crucial point about the Composition Technique (as explained in Section 5.1) is that it takes advantage of this parametrisation; it identifies a line that starts with model risk factors and ends with prices. In the example used, this line starts with the short rate that generates a corresponding yield curve, which in turn is evaluated to return a price. Moreover, there is no loss of precision in this process compared to the one that starts at the market risk factor (yield curve) and ends with the price. Therefore, the pricing step can be recast, as explained in Section 9.2; instead of using P, where the inputs are the market factors, one can compose g followed by P, from Equation 15.1, to obtain f, which uses model factors as inputs. The dimension of the domain of f will typically be much lower than that of P; instead of building a proxy for P, we build a proxy for f.

Expressed mathematically, the key thing to notice is that if x corresponds to y under the parametrisation g (that is $y = g(x)$), then $f(x) = P(y)$. This means no information is lost. Moreover, the dimension of the problem has been transformed from n, which is typically high — possibly in the hundreds — to k, which is typically low — often between 1 and 5, sometimes up to 10, as we see in Section 15.3.

$$\mathbb{R}^k \xrightarrow{\;g\;} \mathbb{R}^n \xrightarrow{\;P\;} \mathbb{R}, \qquad (15.1)$$
$$\underbrace{\phantom{\mathbb{R}^k \xrightarrow{\;g\;} \mathbb{R}^n \xrightarrow{\;P\;}}}_{f}$$

15.2.3 Variables at play

The hybrid solution presented changes the focus of the pricing problem from P to f as shown in Equation 15.1. However, the question of exactly which parameters constitute the variable inputs to f has not been explained in detail. This is key to the proper use of the technique.

The number of input variables of f determines the dimension of the function to be approximated. As was explained in Chapter 9, the question of dimension is very important when applying the hybrid methods from Part III. To a great extent, it drives the difficulty of the problem. The practitioner must always identify the different variables or parameters involved and decide, after careful scrutiny, which ones to discard and which to keep when defining the composition in Equation 15.1.

Section 13.2 presented a collection of parameters or variables that affect a pricing function P. We should always bear these in mind when faced with an application. The first type is given by the parameters Θ from the diffusion models $\mathcal{M}$ that simulate the market risk factors, for example, μ, a, b and σ in Equation 13.1. The second are the market risk factors $\mathcal{S}$ that affect P, such as underlying spots, interest rates, volatilities and other market quotes, for example, S and ν in Equation 13.1. Another important set of variables are the model risk factors, which are closely related to market risk factors. As we said in Chapter 13.2, model risk factors are relevant in some applications but not in others. For the application that concerns us at present (CCR), they play a vital role. The third type of parameter or variable is $\mathcal{T}$, the parameters specific to the trade, for example, strike and maturity.

Next, we discuss each of them in more detail, analysing which are vital in the definition of f and which can be ignored, depending on the context. The practitioner should do this type of assessment when applying the Composition Technique to define f, every single time. Smart choices will yield optimal results.

Model parameters

All the elements in Θ — the space of parameters of the risk factor diffusion model $\mathcal{M}$ — are fixed at calibration. Calibration takes place at time t_0, which represents the time point when the simulation is run. At every time point in the future t_i, the values of the parameters in Θ are the same as at t_0. These parameters can therefore be ignored when defining the domain of f, most of the time.

Next we clarify what we mean by leaving out parameters from the domain of f. The discussion will also lead us to model and market risk factors and how we deal with them when defining the domain of f.

Model and market risk factors

Let us illustrate with an example how to determine if a parameter can be left out of the domain of f. Suppose we want to compute the EPE profile of a netting set that consists of a single option. Assume the option underlying is diffused stochastically via Geometric Brownian Motion (GBM) with local volatility, and the interest rates are diffused using a one-factor HW model.

In this example, the model parameters for the GBM are drift and volatility skew; for the HW model the parameters are mean reversion level, mean reversion speed and volatility. The market risk factors (market snapshot consisting of underlying spot, implied volatility surface and yield curve, perhaps hundreds of values) at a Monte Carlo node is *fully* defined by the value of the underlying spot and HW the short rate at that node. Even when g — the parametrisation in Equation 15.1 — requires the parameters in Θ (such as mean reversion level) to produce the market snapshot, these parameters do not change across nodes in the Monte Carlo simulation; they are fixed at time t_0 and remain so for the rest of the simulation. Therefore, they do not constitute a variable within the simulation and hence can be left out of the domain of f when defining it.

In other words, the risk we are trying to measure from the EPE profile is all driven by the underlying spot (market risk factor) and the HW short rate (model risk factor). Any other parameters needed, such as those in Θ, can therefore be ignored.

Trade parameters

Trade-specific parameters in $\mathcal{T}$ also require particular attention. For example, the variable defined by time to maturity of the trade — of which there typically are about 100 in a CCR simulation — changes across Monte Carlo time steps,

There are two courses of action here. On the one hand, given that at each time point the maturity of the trade does not change, a function f that does not consider time to maturity as a variable within its domain may be defined. This is akin to not including model parameters within the domain of f given that they are fixed. However, an alternative in the case of time to maturity is define f across time points, making time to maturity part of the input of f, as shown in Figure 15.1.

When there is a choice to be made, practitioners must consider pros and cons. For example, considering time to maturity as a variable increases the dimension of f and hence the building effort of the proxy — for example, a CT, the advantage being, however, that only one proxy is built instead of one per time point. If the proxy was built including time to maturity as a variable, one would be able to compute CCR metrics using daily time steps with hardly any incremental computational cost at the pricing step. This is a functionality that any XVA trader or IMM/PFE risk manager would significantly benefit from.

There are other trade parameters, such as strikes and barriers, that remain fixed throughout the simulation — these are defining features of the trade. As such, they remain constant throughout the Monte Carlo simulation. Therefore, they can be discarded in the definition of the domain of f.

This, however, does not mean they *must* be discarded. Adding these parameters as variables creates functions f that do not just represent an instance of a trade type, but a collection of instances. For example, not adding strike as a variable defines a function f for a specific trade, say, an American option $\mathcal{D}$ with strike 100. Adding the strike as a

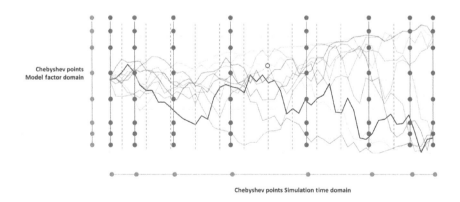

FIGURE 15.1 Monte Carlo simulation showing time points in the future and model risk factors diffused across time dimension. A Chebyshev grid is obtained for the whole MC simulation, taking the product of a grid along the time dimension (horizontal) and a grid along the model risk factor dimension (vertical).

variable in the range [50,150] defines f, which covers American options like $\mathcal{D}$, which can have any strike as long as it falls within the range [50,150].

Special variables

There are some variables that fall into one of the categories already mentioned, but that have special characteristics that are worth highlighting. This section mentions them and explains how to deal with them.

Variables with singular points

These are variables over which the function f has singular points — that is, non-smooth points. These could be, for example, points of inflexion or discontinuities. There are many examples of such variables, for example, the underlying of a barrier option or the time to maturity of a swap. In the first example, the barrier constitutes a point at which the pricing function of the option has a point of inflexion or a discontinuity — depending on the type of barrier option. In the second example, the payment dates of the swap are points at which the pricing function of the swap has discontinuities along the time to maturity variable, caused by cash-flows.

The reason why these variables can be problematic is that the convergence of both CTs and DNNs can be affected by singularities. In particular, the convergence theorems for CTs presented in Section 3.3 are valid for functions with no singularities. The presence of the latter significantly slows down convergence rates.

This, however, can be easily remedied. The important thing to notice is that singular points in all the functions considered in the applications of interest are isolated points in the domain of f. This means we can split the domain along the singular points, yielding subdomains free of such points. The result is that the function f defined over each subdomain has no singluar points and hence can be easily approximated.

There is another situation where it may be convenient to split the domain the way we do it with singular points, even in the absence of the latter. Say we have an option that is close to expiry. Assume there are no singularities along the spot dimension. In principle, the function f is analytic along this dimension and CTs converge quasi-exponentially.[3] However, as the option approaches maturity, the function f gets closer and closer to its payoff. If the payoff has a singularity at the strike — as is often the case — then this singularity could affect the speed at which convergence takes place. The rate will still be quasi-exponential, but convergence will be slower than when the singular point is far removed. Therefore, in some cases — such as when expiry is about to happen — it may be convenient to split the domain of approximation to reduce the building cost of the proxy. This is a technique that is taken advantage of in Chapter 19, where the implied volatility function is approximated using Chebyshev points in a very efficient way, despite not having singular points on the domain of approximation.

---

[3]The mathematical definition of an analytic function is given in Definition 3.2.1. Also, read Section 13.1 for a discussion on pricing functions and the property of being analytic.

Memory variables

These are, for example, typical in Asian options. Think of the arithmetic or geometric averages of the underlying of an option. These are not, strictly speaking, market risk factors. However, they are obtained directly from market risk factors and constitute variables that directly affect the transformed pricing function f. These variables should be considered as any other risk-carrying variable, so they must be considered when defining the domain of f.

15.2.4   Optimal setup

Practitioners should always have in mind that the more variables considered, the greater the effect of the curse of dimensionality and, hence, the more difficult the approximation problem. However, the more variables considered, the more generic f is, and, hence, the proxy built for it can be used more broadly.

For example, let us assume an MC simulation with 100 time steps for which calibration — of the risk factor diffusion model parameters — is done daily. A possible strategy is to create one proxy pricing function for each individual trade and time step in an overnight batch. These proxies can be serialised and loaded the next day to run simulations. Under these assumption, our simulation engine will have 100 proxy functions — one per time step and existing trade — that can be used as many times as needed for intra-day calculations without the need to re-create the proxies.

An alternative is to include time to maturity as a variable in the domain of the proxy function. In this case, the engine will have one single proxy function per individual trade for the whole simulation. Once again, this can be serialised and loaded for use as often as needed during the day. As we mentioned before, this setup would allow MC simulations with as many time steps as needed without incurring any extra computational cost, a very valuable feature in some cases.

Another alternative would be to include the strike in the input domain of f. In this case, the proxy function can be used for a whole family of individual trades.

The previous examples should make the following message clear: the greater the number of variables in the domain of f, the more versatile the proxy built for it is. However, this comes at the cost of (often substantially) greater training effort for the proxy and/or lower precision in the approximation. The ideal setup depends totally on the existing infrastructure and computing goals.

In Section 15.3, we present a range of results that show the flexibility of the Composition Technique. Sometimes the approach is aggressive, aiming to work with the lowest dimension possible for f. Sometimes more variables are incorporated, defining more generic functions f.

15.2.5   Possible proxies

Once the Composition Technique has been applied and a function f obtained, the practitioner has to make a decision on how to approximate it.

There is the option of building a DNN or a CT; each has advantages and disadvantages. In Chapter 14, we discussed how CTs and DNNs compare to one another, bearing in mind the applications that constitute the main body of this part of the book. Here we briefly discuss them once more, with particular attention to CCR calculations.

Once the Composition Technique has been applied, the dimension of the input domain of f, in the vast majority of cases, will be one that a DNN can handle without problems. If the proxy of choice is a CT, the way it is built depends on the dimension of f. If the dimension is less than 5, a full CT can be built. If the dimension is greater than 5, the Tensor Extension Algorithms of Chapter 6 should be considered. In CCR calculations — such as the ones presented in Section 15.3 — we find that after applying the Composition Technique as explained in previous sections, the dimension of f is rarely greater than 10.

As we saw in Chapter 14, in the cases we are interested in (where the function f has low dimension), the computational building effort tends to favour CTs over DNNs. Remember, both proxies rely on evaluating the function f over a grid of points. Given that CTs converge quasi-exponentially as the number of sample points increases while DNNs do not, CTs need a smaller number of sample points to reach a specific level of accuracy. This translates into lower building costs and greater computational gains. Moreover, unless we use the Tensor Extension Algorithm to build CTs, these are fully built and ready to be used once the grid points have been sampled by f.

However, DNNs always require training after the grid has been sampled. Although in some cases the training of DNNs can take place in a short period of time, it can sometimes take significant time, making the building of such proxy less attractive. This is particularly the case if a series of hyper-parameters must be explored in order to increase the accuracy of the DNN. Remember that it is not enough to simply increase the number of sample points to increase the accuracy of the DNN. Sometimes we need to increase the number of sample points and adjust the architecture of the DNN simultaneously to achieve this, something that translates into longer training times. Overall, for a given dimension for which a CT can be built (say less than 10), the computational cost of building a CT is more attractive than that of building a DNN.

Another point that favours CTs over DNNs is the strength and tractability of its mathematical framework. First, for the vast majority of the functions we are interested in, we have guaranteed quasi-exponential convergence as the number of sample points increases (Section 3.3). Second, there is an algorithm that is able to estimate the empirical error of the CT without having to evaluate f on any points other than the Chebyshev points used to build the CT (Section 3.4). Third, CTs are efficiently differentiated and the partial derivatives obtained constitute a good proxy to the partial derivatives of f — this is done with barely any computational cost, and the CTs obtained after differentiation can be evaluated with the same efficiency of the original CT (Section 3.7).

By contrast, although the Universal Approximation Theorems (Section 2.3) give DNNs a solid foundation as function approximators, DNNs are often perceived as "black boxes" over which we have little control of when and why they work; this can be problematic in some applications. Just as there are cases where the size of the DNN needed to approximate a pricing function is not large (a few layers and a handful of neurons per layer), we have come across instances where the number of layers and neurons needed to achieve a reasonable level of accuracy is huge. The problem this can create is that the evaluation of the DNN is no longer negligible compared to the evaluation time of the original pricing function.

In our experience, different practitioners place different weights on the advantages and disadvantages we have mentioned of each approximation method. We tend to favour CTs whenever possible as these give the practitioner more control over the building/calibration process, be it because they can be built more efficiently, because they offer more control over the error of approximation, or any of the other properties we have mentioned. However, whether we can use CTs or not is principally driven by the dimension of the function f we end up with after applying the Composition Technique.

The rule of thumb is the following. If the dimension of the domain of f is less than 5, full CTs are an obvious choice. If the dimension is greater than 5 or 6, approximately, then we opt for CTs in TT format, built using the Tensor Extension Algorithms. The crucial point to note here is that the dimension we end up with after applying the Composition Technique within CCR calculations is usually within the grasp of such algorithms. For the remaining cases (usually not many), we choose a DNN.[4]

15.2.6 Portfolio calculations

The description presented so far covers a single trade $\mathcal{D}$. It is important to highlight that the approach relies on characteristics shared by all trade types. Therefore, it can be applied to any given trade type and hence any netting set or portfolio. Once a proxy is created for each trade (and serialised if needed), the price of a netting set, or other type of portfolio, is computationally cheap to calculate, regardless of the combination of trades that constitute the netting set or portfolio.

When the trades in a netting set or portfolio share the same risk factors, one may consider the following alternative. Instead of creating the proxy function for each single trade, one can create it for the whole netting set (or portfolio). Essentially, the function f being approximated is that of the whole netting set. In this case, one ends up with a single proxy. Hence, obtaining the distribution of prices for the whole netting set is much faster regardless of the number of trades. However, when done this way, the granular information per trade is lost.

An interesting combination of the previous two approaches consists of creating a proxy pricer for each trade, which are then aggregated into one single proxy function before the netting set evaluation. This can be done in certain situations, for example, when the trades in the netting set share the same risk factors. If the proxy functions built are CTs, the addition of these tensors essentially boils down to the addition of the values of each tensor at each of the Chebyshev points, as explained in Section 3.9.

15.2.7 If the model space is not available

There are instances when a unit or department in a financial institution wants to improve the computational performance of the pricing step in a CCR Monte Carlo calculation, but the unit only has access to the market risk factors and not the model risk factors. For example, the FX desk in the front office of a bank is given the market

---

[4]The potential use of Chebyshev Sliders will be discussed later in the chapter.

scenarios on 10,000 paths and 100 time points in the future generated by a CCR Monte Carlo simulation. They are asked to price the trades of a portfolio at each of these market snapshots — one million market snapshots in total.

To apply the Composition Technique, the FX desk needs to have access to the model space, which is the domain of the function f obtained through the Composition Technique. In our example, the FX desk needs to know the ranges of FX rates and, for example, HW short rates diffused (assuming HW one-factor model is used to diffuse interest rates) that generated the 1,000,000 market snapshots. Assuming, for illustrative purposes, that the desk intends to use CTs to approximate the pricing function, they need to compute the Chebyshev points in the model space — say, 1,000 points — generate the market risk factors associated with the Chebyshev points (market Chebyshev scenarios) and finally price the financial instruments at each of these scenarios.

Ideally, the FX desk should have access to the functions g (for example, 15.1). This would let them generate the market Chebyshev scenarios themselves. If that is not the case, it should provide the unit that controls the function g the values in the model space that correspond to the Chebyshev points. Whoever controls g can return the market Chebyshev scenarios, which can then be used by the FX desk to obtain the needed prices to finalise the building of the CTs.

At this point, the desk has all the needed information to construct the approximating object (for example, the CT). Once built, the barycentric interpolation formula (Sections 3.6.2 and 3.6.3) is used to evaluate the 1,000,000 scenarios on the model space and obtain a price at each of the nodes of the MC simulation. In this example, only 1,000 Chebyshev points were used, which translates into 1,000 evaluations of the original pricing function, hence, computational savings of about 99%.[5]

So, what can the FX desk do if, for some reason, they do not have access to the model space and its values at each node of the MC simulation, but only have access to the market risk factors at each node? In this case, we need to find a way to generate a substitute for the function g to apply the Composition Technique.

This is a very similar situation to the one presented in Chapter 16, where a given portfolio needs to be priced on a set of market scenarios that are generated using historical simulations. In this case, there is no obvious function g.

We will only give a summary of the method here. For full details, we refer to Chapter 16. To generate the parametrisation g, methods such as PCA or Auto-Encoders are used. These dimensionality reduction techniques are trained using the market scenarios generated by the MC simulation. The parametrisation g (inverse to the function that reduces the dimension of the market scenarios) is then used to generate a function f through the Composition Technique. If the dimension of the domain of f is low enough, full CTs can be used. If the dimension is too high for full CTs to work effectively, the Tensor Extension Algorithm, the Sliding Technique or DNNs can be used to approximate f.

---

[5]The evaluation of the barycentric interpolation formula is very efficient. Therefore, the computational savings are mainly determined by comparing the number of evaluations needed to build the CT with the number of pricing function evaluations needed to run the MC simulation with no proxies.

It is important to note that the created parametrisation function *g* is only an approximation of the parametrisation we would ideally use — the one that comes with the risk factor diffusion model. When we generate parametrisations using techniques such as PCA, the error of the proxy built for *f* is driven by the error introduced by both the proxy itself and the technique that generates *g*.[6]

The PCA technique just mentioned has been tested by the authors with a Tier-1 global bank in their IMM calculation on a portfolio of swaps. The results obtained were remarkable.

An alternative method to generate the parametrisation *g* is provided in Appendix F. The parametrisation described there is defined within the context of sensitivities simulations. However, it also applies when we are interested in simulating prices.

15.3   TESTS

In this section, we show the results of numerical tests obtained by applying the techniques presented in Section 15.2 to the computation of CCR metrics. The aim is to show the large computational gains and small, if at all, losses of accuracy obtained.

As mentioned in Section 15.1, optimal CCR calculations are usually done using MC simulations. As a benchmark reference, we consider about 1,000,000 nodes in an MC simulation. A typical simulation run within risk systems of financial institutions would have thousands of paths (say 10,000) with several tens or a few hundred (say 100) time points in the future.

We have pointed out before that with unlimited computational power, MC simulations would be much bigger. Any XVA trader or risk manager would benefit substantially from daily time steps and about 1,000,000 paths — that is, about $5,000 \times 1,000,000 = 5,000,000,000$ nodes. This would reduce the numerical noise from the MC simulation and virtually eliminate all the manipulations and adjustments regularly done on the results due to the lack of granularity. The only reason why MC simulations in CCR have about no more than 1,000,000 nodes is down to the computational challenge we have discussed throughout this chapter.

The computation of risk metrics requires a price at each node of the simulation. It is this step — going from risk scenario to prices — that constitutes the main computational bottleneck when pricing functions such as the ones in risk systems are used. This is particularly the case when the engine uses the official so-called front office pricing functions; these are usually built for precision and with enough flexibility so that they can encompass every type of trade within each family of derivatives, but not for computational speed.

Indeed, given that these pricing functions represent the "official" pricing functions in the institution, it would be ideal to use them to run CCR calculations, for accuracy of

---

[6]Some consider PCA to be a poor tool when reducing the dimension of data. This normally stems from the fact that very few principal components are used and a significant amount of the information in the data is lost. However, the approximating techniques that make use of PCA suggested in this book allow for 10, 20 and even 50 components (in some cases more), virtually eliminating the information loss that comes from the dimensionality reduction.

calculation, compliance and so on. However, the computational demand often prevents banks (and financial institutions in general) from using them to obtain the metrics in a timely manner. If used, CCR computations are very slow to run. Nonetheless, their accuracy means we take them as benchmarks with respect to which we measure alternative techniques, such as the ones in Section 15.2.

The techniques presented in this chapter consist of replacing pricing functions at the pricing step in the MC simulations with proxies. The challenge is to build proxies that are highly accurate, easy to build and fast to evaluate.

Generally, these proxies will be fast to evaluate and so most of the computational burden associated with running CCR calculations with proxies is down to the building cost of such proxies at the required level of precision. Since the proxies we use are CTs and DNNs, both of which are techniques that require sampling the pricing function, the less we sample the function, the higher the computational gains.

For the tests presented next, a range of different trades were chosen to show how the techniques in Section 15.2 can be applied in different ways. Moreover, the trades were chosen to cover a range of dimensions representative of typical examples across portfolios that arise with the use of the Composition Technique.

All the MC simulations used in our tests had 10,000 paths. The number of time points in the future, however, varied between the tests, mainly due to the computational demand imposed by the benchmark computation (brute force). That is, in some cases the computation of the brute-force benchmark CCR simulation was prohibitively large. In these cases, we decreased the number of time points in the simulation so that the relative gain can be assessed; full computational savings should easily be extrapolated from the ones obtained in the tests.

In each of the tests performed, a price at each node of the MC simulation is obtained. With the distribution of prices we compute the Expected Profile Exposure (EPE) and the Potential Future Exposure at 95th percentile. Along with the profiles just mentioned, we also compute CVA values. These metrics are computed using both the benchmark approach — using only pricing functions — and with at least one of the hybrid solutions presented in Section 15.2.

All tests were performed on a standard laptop with i7 cores. Calculations were parallelised whenever possible, in particular for the benchmark calculations, given their high computational cost.

Regarding the pricing functions used, some calculations were done in C++ using the pricing functions in the QuantLib library, the open source software framework for quantitative finance.[7] Other calculations were done using the pricing functions found in MATLAB's financial toolbox.

15.3.1   Trade types, risk factors and proxies

The trade types used to run numerical tests, results of which we present in this section, were interest rate swaps, barrier options, cross-currency swaps, Bermudan Swaptions

---

[7]https://www.quantlib.org/.

and American options. These cover a range of risk factor diffusion models, a range of asset classes and a range of dimensions both at the market risk factor and model risk factor spaces when using the Composition Technique (Section 15.2).

For the trades chosen, interest rates, exchange rates and equity spots have to be diffused along with (in some cases) their volatilities. There is also a range of payoffs present in these trades, some of which include singular points. Cross-currency swaps have a vanilla payoff, while the American options a structured one. Finally — and very importantly — these trades were chosen to cover a wide range of dimensions both at the market factor and model factor space, which is representative of typical examples across portfolios in financial institutions.

Another important aspect illustrated by the trades chosen is the question of which variables to include in the definition of the function f (Equation 15.1). In Section 15.2, we mentioned that variables fall into the following categories: model parameters, model risk factors, market risk factors and trade-specific parameters. Which ones are considered in the definition of f depends on the context.

Once the Composition Technique has been applied and a function f obtained, an approximation method must be chosen to approximate it. Throughout this book we consider two approximating methods: CTs and DNNs. As mentioned in Chapter 14, each has strengths and weaknesses. In Section 15.2.5, we highlighted the characteristics of each approximation method that play a role in deciding which one to use for CCR calculations.

The following sections illustrate different strategies that can be pursued to find computational solutions for each of the trade types encountered in financial institutions. The goal is to notably enhance the computational performance of the calculation in a seamless manner, the latter possible, especially with CTs, due to their powerful convergent properties and effective error control at a low computational cost.

Having established the theoretical framework that we will use, the goal for the remainder of the chapter is to illustrate, with examples, how these techniques can be used, in which contexts and under what conditions. We will start with fairly simple examples, steadily increasing the complexity of the solution from that point on. In this chapter, we report the key metrics regarding the performance of the techniques being tested, while granular details are shown in the Appendix D.

15.3.2 Proxy at each time point

We start our tests with a very simple case. Complexity will be subsequently increased.

CCR Monte Carlo simulations have a number of known simulation time points. We can create a proxy for each individual trade at each simulation time point.

To achieve this, the Composition Technique (Section 15.2) is applied at each MC time point. We can take an aggressive approach when deciding which parameters to include as variables within the domain of the function f from Equation 15.1. By *aggressive* we mean that we define the function f so that it has the lowest domain dimension possible, as this will lead to the least number of sampling points in order to construct the proxy functions. The trades chosen for illustration are an interest rate swap, a barrier option and a cross-currency swap.

Interest Rate Swap

The first example is the simplest case we can think of: an interest rate swap. The trade was at-the-money and had 15 years to maturity The pricing routine used relies on an analytic formula and is the one implemented in QuantLib (C++ version). The trade depends on two yield curves: one for forwarding and one for discounting. Each yield curve had 20 tensors, which gives a total of 40 market risk factors that are simulated at each scenario of the MC simulation.

The MC simulation used consisted of 10,000 paths and 15 time points. The model used to diffuse the yield curves was the HW one-factor model. We kept it very simple to clearly illustrate the main points involved when the techniques presented in Section 15.2 are applied; more sophisticated examples will follow. One single HW diffusion governed the diffusion of both curves, hence only one variable — the short rate from the HW model — parametrised both yield curve.

The reader may be familiar by now with the importance of choosing the variables that determine the domain of the function f to be approximated obtained through the Composition Technique. This is a key driver of the computational effort required to build the proxy pricing function. As a quick reminder, f is the composition of the functions g and P, as per Equation 15.1. This composition lets us focus on the variables that affect the risk of the trade, disregarding the rest of the variables. In this way, we optimise the construction of the proxy pricing function.

For the test in question, we opted for an aggressive approach and reduced the dimension of the domain of f as much as possible. The risk of the one-factor simulation used is fully determined by the HW short rate. Therefore, this was the only input variable considered for f, no risk information is lost and we end up with a domain of dimension 1. All other variables or parameters such as the fixed rate, maturity and HW calibration parameters (such as the mean reversion speed and volatility) were kept constant. This means that a function f with only one input variable was defined per time point and per trade.

The function f with domain of dimension 1 can be replicated very well with a one-dimensional CT. To build a CT at each time point of the CCR Monte Carlo simulation for each trade, we do the following:

1. Take the 10,000 scenarios at the given time point and select the minimum and maximum value of the HW short rate. This defines the range over which we build the CT.

2. Compute n Chebyshev points within the range determined in the previous step. In our experience, between 5 and 10 Chebyshev points are more than enough to achieve a high level of accuracy (e.g. 10^{-5}) in an example such as this one.

3. Obtain a swap price at each of the n Chebyshev points. Note that first, we need to apply the function g on the Chebyshev points — which are short rates. This gives market scenarios that we call Chebyshev market scenarios, as they correspond to actual Chebyshev points under g. Then, we evaluate the pricing function P on the Chebyshev market scenarios. These are the swap prices needed to finish the building of the CT.

4. Optionally, we can apply the ex ante error estimation algorithm (see Section 3.4) that automatically determines the number of Chebyshev points needed to reach a desired level of accuracy. The algorithm first estimates the accuracy of the CT built

with n points. If the accuracy is the desired one, we have our CT ready. Otherwise, it samples more points and estimates error once again. This step is repeated until we reach the desired level of accuracy. The process is run in very little time as the algorithm that estimates the error is very efficient and we increase the number of Chebyshev points at each iteration in a nested way, reducing the number of points on which we call the pricing function.[8] Note that, as a result of the exponential convergence of CTs as n increases, a relatively low number of iterations should quickly deliver the desired level of accuracy.

To be noted, this optional step may be important when the trades in the portfolio are non-linear. For this example, the trade is linear so we know by experience that n between 5 and 10 will suffice.

5. Once all the prices on Chebyshev points have been obtained, we have all the information needed for the CT. The barycentric interpolation formula can be used to evaluate the price of the IR swap in each scenario.

6. Evaluate the CT on all 10,000 scenarios, taking as input the HW short rate of each scenario.

In our test, the number of Chebyshev points used in the building of the CTs was 6. The evaluation of 10,000 scenarios took an average of 1 second with the IR swap pricing function from QuantLib, in C++ — that is, 0.1 millisecond per evaluation. The same number of evaluations took an average of 0.0006 seconds with CTs in C++ — that is, 60 nanoseconds per evaluation. This means the CT is between 1,000 and 2,000 times faster than one of the fastest pricing functions in finance. This is a clear example of how efficient the barycentric interpolation formula (Section 3.6) is compared to even the fastest pricing functions in finance.

In terms of accuracy, the maximum error of the CTs compared to the IR swap pricing function was 1×10^{-4} across all 10,000 scenarios. In practice, this is considered perfect pricing.

The bulk of the computational costs associated with the use of the proxy technique is taken by the evaluations of the pricing function needed to build the CT, which in this particular test were 6 per time point (for a single trade). The speed of evaluation of the CTs is such that it hardly affects the computational gains — only by 0.06%. Table 15.1 shows a total computational gain of 99.88%.

Figure 15.2 shows PV profiles at expectation and at the 95th percentile for the MC simulation run, obtained both through the benchmark (full revaluation) approach and with the one-dimensional CTs. Table 15.2 gives numerical estimates of the errors for both profiles and CVA value computed.

As can be seen in both Figure 15.2 and Table 15.2, the levels of accuracy obtained are very high. In all three categories, we were always within a relative error of 1×10^{-4} from the benchmark.

The results are encouraging. This technique allows us to do effectively the same calculation as when the pricing function is used (brute force), but almost 1,000 times faster.

---

[8]If at each iteration k we consider $2^k + 1$ Chebyshev points, we end up with a nested set of Chebyshev points.

TABLE 15.1 Computational gain of running the CCR calculation for an IR swap with a CT as a proxy. Note that the compute time of the CT (extra comp cost) is negligible compared to the IR swap evaluation. The computational gain essentially comes from the difference between total evaluations via brute force (full revaluation) and the number of samples needed to calibrate the CT.

Brute-force (benchmark) evaluations	Sampling evaluations	Reduction of calls to function	Extra comp cost	Comp savings
10,000	6	99.94%	0.06%	99.88%

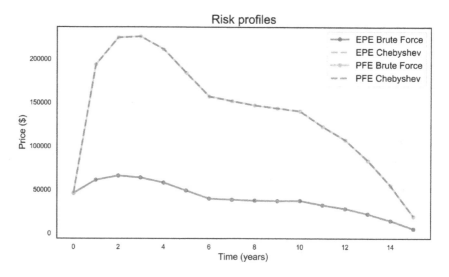

FIGURE 15.2 PV profiles — at expectation and 95th percentiles — for an IR swap obtained with the benchmark and with a one-dimensional CT.

TABLE 15.2 Mean and maximum relative errors for PV profiles at expectation and 95th percentiles, for an IR swap obtained with the benchmark and with a one-dimensional CT. Also CVA maximum relative error is presented.

	EPE mean error	EPE max error	PFE mean error	PFE max error	CVA error
IR Swap	0.00008%	0.00029%	0.00003%	0.00012%	0.00010%

It must be noted that the IR swap pricer is usually fast to compute, so the incentive to run the calculation with CTs is limited. However, financial institutions tend to have a very large number of IR swaps, so the computational savings obtained when we consider the full volume of swaps will not be negligible.

Barrier option

We established the fundamentals of the technique with a very straightforward example. Now we increase the difficulty. We will increase the dimension of the domain of f, consider a non-linear pricing function, a payoff with a singularity point, and a pricing that relies on Monte Carlo simulations.

The trade that satisfies the conditions just mentioned is an up-and-out put barrier option. The trade used had one year to expiry; this means the curvature of the pricing function, which is the result of being close to maturity, should be present and challenge the technique for a good part of the MC simulation. The pricing function used was taken from QuantLib, in C++. This pricing function is MC based, which means that a whole MC simulation is run to obtain every price. The number of paths used inside the pricing function were set to 9,000. This gave a noise of 3.1% at the 95th percentile.

The resulting MC simulation used to obtain risk profiles is therefore a nested-type of MC simulation. This type of MC simulation would be the standard in risk engines for some trade types, were it not for the huge computational challenge it poses. The outer MC simulation is the one that generates the distribution of prices needed to produce risk profiles like EPE or PFE; the inner simulations are the ones that produce a price at each node of the outer simulation.

One of the reasons why a barrier option was chosen to run these tests is that its pricing function has a singularity along its most important risk factor — the underlying spot. The combination of non-linearity displayed by this function — especially when it's close to maturity — along with the presence of a singularity make it an interesting example to test the techniques presented in Section 15.2. As mentioned in Section 15.2.3, variables with singular points require the use of Chebyshev Splines; if considered and applied appropriately, the strong convergence properties that characterise CTs apply.

The market risk factors affecting barrier options are its underlying spot, implied volatility and interest rates. Both the spot and the interest rate curve were diffused stochastically. The spot was diffused using a Geometric Brownian Motion (GBM) model (which has one stochastic factor), while the interest rates were diffused with a one-factor HW model.

A note on volatility

There is a point regarding the diffusion of volatility that is worth making. In a typical risk system, spot and zero rates are usually diffused stochastically. Volatility, however, is not always diffused. Volatility is either constant throughout the simulation — where a single value or a non-stochastic term structure is used — diffused locally stochastically (that is, via a local volatility model) or it is fully stochastically diffused.

If the volatility is constant and has a single value throughout the simulation, there is no need to include it as a variable in the definition of the domain of f — it basically has no effect on the function f.

If a constant term structure volatility model is used, the volatility changes from time point to time point, but is constant at each time point. Given that our approach

(continued)

(continued)

for the barrier option consists of applying the Composition Technique time point per time point, volatility once again can be discarded as a variable in the domain of f.

If a local volatility model is used, the implied volatility changes from scenario to scenario within the same time point. However, the dependency of such volatility is fully determined by the value of the spot. Such dependency tends to be smooth, which means that it is part of the function g in Equation 15.1. Therefore, it can be neglected as an input of the function f.

The only case when volatility needs to be considered as a variable for f is when it is diffused stochastically all the way throughout the MC simulation. In this case, the drivers or model risk factors of the stochastic volatility model should be incorporated as variables in the domain of f.

In our experience, CCR risk systems do not tend to use stochastic volatility models. Therefore, the assumption made for the barrier option example, of taking volatility constant throughout the MC, is a realistic one.

We will include examples where the volatility is diffused stochastically in later section.

When it came to the dimension of the domain of f, we opted for an aggressive approach and kept it as low as possible. Only two market risk factors — diffused stochastically — were kept: underlying spot and interest rates. As a result, no trade-specific parameters (such as strike) or risk factor diffusion model parameters (such as HW mean reversion speed) were included in the domain of f. This means that a function f was defined per time point. Moreover, if this was done in the context of a portfolio of barrier options, we would have defined an f per trade. As the spot and interest rate curve were diffused with a one-factor model each, the function f has a domain of dimension 2.

This is a dimension that can easily be handled by a full CT, which for this case is a perfect choice of approximator. Remember that the pricing function P has a singular point along the spot dimension; therefore, we must consider Chebyshev Splines.

The Chebyshev Spline consisted of two CTs joined at the line defined by the singular point along the spot dimension. Given that the pricing function is more sensitive to the spot than the interest rates, we used more Chebyshev points for the spot dimension (16 in total) than for the short rate one (6). This gave a CT spline with a total of 96 Chebyshev points. Once the function f has been sampled in those 96 points, there is no further training to be done; the Chebyshev Spline is ready to be evaluated with just this information.

The computational gains or savings are shown in Table 15.3. All estimates can be obtained at any given time point of the simulation as the number of scenarios in each is the same and the hybrid solution is applied time point per time point. There are 10,000 scenarios to evaluate per time point, but only 96 Chebyshev scenarios to evaluate to generate the Chebyshev Spline; there is no training time involved — all that is needed to build the CT are the Chebyshev points and the values of the pricing function on them. Moreover, the evaluation time of the CT splines on the 10,000 scenarios (extra

TABLE 15.3 Computational gain of running the CCR calculation for a barrier option with a CT as a proxy. Note that most of the computational gain comes from the reduction to the number of calls to the function. The extra computational cost comes from the evaluation of the CT.

Brute-force (benchmark) evaluations	Sampling evaluations	Reduction of calls to function	Extra comp cost	Comp savings
10,000	96	99.04%	1.11×10^{-4}%	99.04%

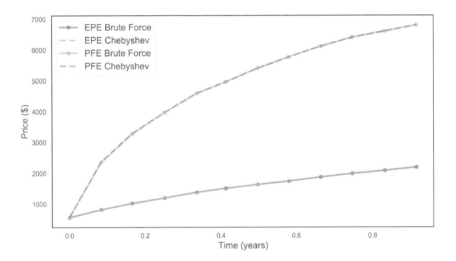

FIGURE 15.3 PV profiles — at expectation and 95th percentiles — for a barrier option obtained with the benchmark and with a full Chebyshev Spline.

TABLE 15.4 Mean and maximum relative errors for PV profiles at expectation and 95th percentiles for a barrier option obtained with the benchmark and with a full Chebyshev Spline. Also CVA maximum relative error is presented.

	EPE mean error	EPE max error	PFE mean error	PFE max error	CVA error
Barrier option	0.27%	2.14%	0.18%	0.65%	0.02%

comp cost) is negligible compared to the 96 evaluations of the MC pricer needed to build the proxy object. Therefore, computational gains come to 99.04%, as can be seen in Table 15.3. More granular details related to computational savings can be found in Appendix D.1.

Figure 15.3 shows PV profiles at expectation and at the 95th percentile for the MC simulation run, obtained both through the benchmark approach and with the full Chebyshev Spline. Table 15.4 gives numerical estimates of the errors for both profiles and CVA value computed.

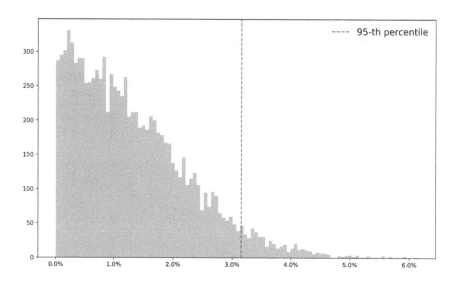

FIGURE 15.4 Noise distribution of the Monte Carlo type (i.e. original pricing, not the proxy) of pricing function for the barrier option. The mean and the 95th percentiles are marked with vertical lines.

As can be seen in Table 15.4, the levels of accuracy obtained are very high. In fact, they are within the noise of the pricing function shown in Figure 15.4, which stands at 3.1% at its 95th percentile. In practice, this is considered perfect pricing.

The level of accuracy is not surprising as the function f being approximated only had dimension 2 in its input domain, and we were using full CTs — very few points are needed to reach levels of accuracy within the noise of the MC pricing function.

Cross-currency swap

In this example, we introduce two elements that increase the difficulty of the problem. First, we introduce discontinuities along the time dimension. Second, we increase the dimension of the function f that results from the application of the Composition Technique.

Cross-currency swap pricing functions have discontinuities along the time dimension as a result of payment days. As the MC simulation covers the full maturity of the trade, these discontinuities will affect the time to maturity variable. By applying the Composition Technique at each time point, one excludes the time variable from the domain of f, yielding pricing functions free of discontinuities.

The cross-currency swap used in tests was at-the-money and had five years to maturity. The pricing routine used was the one implemented in the swapbyzero function in MATLAB, which is analytic. The trade depends on two currencies. For each currency, there are two yield curves (one for discounting and one for forwarding) each with 25 tensors. In addition to yield curves, there is one exchange rate. This gives a total of 101 market risk factors that need to be simulated at each scenario of the Monte Carlo simulation.

To simulate the market risk factors just mentioned, a two-factor Gaussian model was used for each yield curve and a one-factor Geometric Brownian Motion model for the exchange rate. This gives a total of nine model risk factors diffused.

As in the previous example, the model and trade-specific parameters (e.g. strike) have been fixed, hence, the function f defined through the Composition Technique depends only on the model risk factors. Therefore, the input domain to each function f has dimension 9.

The proxy built on each f was a CT. With nine dimensions it is virtually impossible to build a *full* tensor. Therefore, we opt for the Tensor Extension Algorithms (Section 6.2) to build a Chebyshev Tensor in TT format that we can work with. In particular, the Sample Adaptive Algorithm was used, the implementation of which was in MATLAB.

The pricing function being approximated is analytic and the trade fairly linear.[9] Therefore, we put a limit of 700 pricing function evaluations for the Sample Adaptive Algorithm. Not only does it makes sense to try a low bound given the properties of the pricing function mentioned but also the lower the number of evaluations to the pricing function, the higher the computational gains.

The hybrid technique is applied the same way across time points; therefore, computational gains can be estimated by looking at just one of them. There are 10,000 nodes per time point that need to be evaluated through the brute-force approach. The Sample Adaptive Algorithm needed between 300 and 700 evaluations to build the CT in TT format. This already represents a 95% reduction in calls to the pricing function (assuming 500 evaluations).

Given that we are working with CTs in TT format, there is a training routine that needs to be accounted for, as well as the evaluation of the CT on the 10,000 scenarios. The extra computational cost that results from this constitutes 8.25% of the brute-force approach, giving 91.75% for the total computational savings. These results are summarised in Table 15.5. More granular details related to computational savings can be found in Appendix D.2.

Figure 15.5 shows PV profiles at expectation and at the 95th percentile for the MC simulation run, obtained both through the brute force approach (the benchmark) and with the TT-format CTs. Table 15.6 gives numerical estimates of the errors for both profiles and CVA value computed.

TABLE 15.5 Computational costs and savings obtained by using TT-format CTs to compute PV profiles — at expectation and 95th percentiles — and CVA, for a cross-currency swap.

Brute-force (benchmark) evaluations	Sampling evaluations	Reduction of calls to function	Extra comp cost	Comp savings
10,000	300 ~ 700	95%	8.25%	91.75%

---

[9] By analytic we mean that the pricing routine is given by an analytic formula, hence does not rely on Monte Carlo simulations, trees or any other approximation technique to the real price.

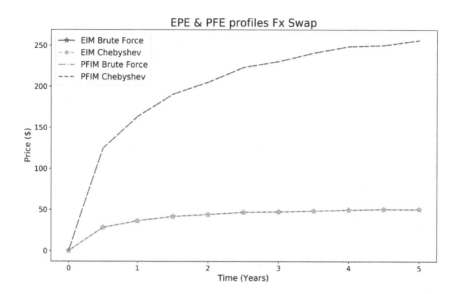

FIGURE 15.5 PV profiles — at expectation and 95th percentiles — for a cross-currency swap obtained with the benchmark and with TT-format CTs.

TABLE 15.6 Mean and maximum relative errors for PV profiles at expectation and 95th percentiles, for a cross-currency swap obtained with the benchmark and with TT-format CTs. Also CVA maximum relative error is presented.

	EPE mean error	EPE max error	PFE mean error	PFE max error	CVA error
FX Swap	0.13%	0.36%	0.05%	0.14%	0.07%

As can be seen in Table 15.6, the levels of accuracy obtained are very high. This is also reflected in the computational saving obtained. Despite dealing with a pricing function of dimension 9, the number of grid points considered in the Tensor Extension Algorithm were enough to give TT tensors that approximated the pricing function to a high degree of accuracy. In fact, the 700 pricing function evaluations put in place as an upper bound for the algorithm, which represents only 0.036% of the total grid, was not reached every time and was enough, in most cases, to reach the error threshold of 1×10^{-3} on the sampled grid.

Remark 15.3.1 Notice that in all trade examples so far, CTs were used as a proxy for the functions f constructed. This is not to say that DNNs cannot be considered. However, remember that computational gains are directly proportional to the number of times the function f is evaluated to produce its proxy. Given that CTs converge quasi-exponentially to f while DNNs do not, CTs tend to deliver higher computational gains. However, situations where it makes more sense to consider a DNN are those where dimensions are higher and hence become problematic for CTs. Examples where DNNs are built as proxies to the functions f are shown in sections that follow.

15.3.3 Proxy for all time points

So far the strategy has been to create a proxy pricing function for each of the MC simulation time points. This time we add a degree of difficulty and consider the case when time to maturity is added as a variable of the domain of the function f obtained through the Composition Technique. We also use — apart from CTs — a DNN to approximate the function f.

The aim of including time to maturity as a variable is to increase computational gains. Note that doing so increases the dimension of f by 1. This means the size of the Chebyshev grid increases by, approximately, a whole order of magnitude; the case of DNNs will be dealt with in later sections. However, given that there are typically 100 time points (i.e. two orders of magnitude) in a CCR MC simulation, these two orders of magnitude outweigh the extra building cost of incorporating time to maturity as a variable. This is especially the case when there are no singularity points or discontinuities to consider along the time dimension.

Another advantage of including time to maturity within the domain of f is that we can compute CCR profiles with daily time steps, up to maturity, quite easily. The reason is that the evaluation speed of the proxy object is very high, hence we can add as many time points to the MC simulation as desired without any sizeable increase in computational effort.

The trade type chosen for illustration purposes is a Bermudan Swaption. The pricing function used to price this trade is tree based and was taken from QuantLib, in C++. To achieve high degrees of accuracy with the pricing function, one must use a considerable number of time steps. However, a large number of time steps equates to high computational costs. As a consequence, a CCR metric calculation for a portfolio with a few hundred Bermudan Swaptions can be very difficult to run from a computational standpoint. Unfortunately, this is a common occurrence in risk systems of financial institutions.

The MC simulation used for testing consisted of 10,000 paths and 20 time points in the future. An MC simulation would typically have about 100 time points. However, due to the cost of running the benchmark (brute-force use of pricing functions) calculation, only 20 were used. In any case, the computational gains obtained can easily be extrapolated to MC simulations with a greater number of time points.

The Bermudan Swaption considered was at-the-money and had five years to maturity with possible exercise dates every year. The market risk factors that serve as inputs to the pricing function are two yield curves, one for forwarding and one for discounting, and a whole surface of volatility values. Each yield curve was modelled with 25 tensors, while the volatility surface consisted of 88 points. The combination of these market parameters gives a pricing function P with a domain of 138 dimensions.

In principle there is no limit to the number of tensor points and strikes used to model yield curves and volatility surfaces. In some cases, these can reach several hundred points, giving pricing functions with a domain of several hundred dimensions. It is to be noted that nothing that is being done in these tests would be done differently if the pricing function had a domain with hundreds of dimensions. Remember that the key point of the input risk factors is the dimension of the risk factor diffusion models used; this is what drives the dimension of f and hence the difficulty of approximation.

In the tests run, each yield curve was diffused using a two-factor Gaussian model. The implied volatility surfaces were diffused using a one-factor SABR model. After applying the Composition Technique, the dimension of the domain of the pricing function is reduced down to 5. By adding time to maturity to the definition of f, we end up with a function of dimension 6.

Just as in previous examples, we keep trade-specific and model diffusion parameters — such as strikes and volatility of volatility — constant, hence not within the domain of f. As a result, we create an approximating function or object per trade. If we had a portfolio with, say, 500 Bermudan Swaptions, we would build 500 proxy functions.

Significant dimension reduction

Bermudan Swaptions are an example where the Composition Technique massively reduces the dimension of the problem. We started with more than 100 dimensions and reduced it down to six. Handling six dimensions is a much easier task than the hundreds we started off with. Notice we would also end up with a pricing function f with a domain of dimension 6 regardless of the number of tensors used to model the yield curves and the volatility surfaces. What matters is the dimension of the model risk factor spaces and not the number of tensors. This is the sum of the number of stochastic drivers in the risk factor diffusion models — plus time to maturity in this example — that determine unequivocally the state of each simulated scenario.

Once the dimension of the problem has been reduced, we can build a full CTs, TT-format CTs or a DNN to approximate the function f. Following we show results obtained using each type of fundamental approximation techniques.

Full Chebyshev Tensors

Linear products, such as cross-currency swaps previously considered, can be approximated by CTs with a small number of grid points in each dimension. However, non-linear products like Bermudan Swaptions need more points. Here is where the quasi-exponential convergence of CTs helps keeping building cost low and, hence, computational gains high. Despite the non-linearity of Bermudan Swaptions, only a few more points per dimension give us good degrees of accuracy as shown next.

A total of seven points were chosen for the dimensions that correspond to the interest rates. These are the dimensions (first four) that correspond to the two-factor Gaussian models used to generate the forwarding and discounting interest rate curves. For the remaining two dimensions (stochastic factor used in the SABR model and time to maturity), six Chebyshev points were used.

The reason for the number of Chebyshev points mentioned is drawn partly from experience and partly from desired computational cost savings. Experience tells us that most of the risk in a Bermudan Swaption is concentrated in the interest rate curves. Therefore, we need more Chebyshev points in the dimensions that correspond to interest rates to make sure we capture the risk properly. At the same time, the greater the number of Chebyshev points, the smaller the computational cost savings. Therefore, we should not freely increase the number of Chebyshev points, and whenever possible, we should reduce them. A number between 5 and 10 points per dimension is usually a good starting points.

For the MC simulation run, with 10,000 paths and *only 20 time points*, the computational savings stand at 57%. In an MC simulation with, say, 100 time points, which more accurately reflects an MC used in risk systems, there are 1,000,000 evaluations through the brute-force approach. The total number of Chebyshev points in the CT built is 86,436. This gives a reduction in the number of calls of 91.34%. There is no training cost associated with full CTs. The only other computational overhead comes from the evaluation of the CT. In our tests, this corresponded to 0.14% of the brute-force approach, giving a total computational gain of 91.21%, as can be seen in Table 15.7. More granular results can be found in Appendix D.3.1.

It is important to note that since the CT has been built with the time dimension as a variable in its input domain, lots of time points can be added to the MC simulation resulting in hardly any extra computational cost. For example, the computational gain of an MC with 1,000 time points would be of 97.74%, relative to its brute-force computation.

Figure 15.6 shows PV profiles at expectation and at the 95th percentile. The results through the brute-force approach (the benchmark) and with full CTs are shown. Table 15.8 gives numerical estimates of the errors for both profiles and CVA value computed.

TT-format Chebyshev Tensors

The grid size used for the CT in TT format was more granular than the one for the full tensor just described. One of the advantages of using the Tensor Extension Algorithms is that one only needs to evaluate the function on a subgrid of the full grid. This means that one can afford a more granular grid — hence benefiting from the higher accuracy it provides — without incurring significant computational overheads.

In the case of the Bermudan Swaption, a grid with 14 points per dimension was chosen. This gives a total of 7,529,536 grid points. The Tensor Extension Algorithm used

TABLE 15.7 Computational gain of running the CCR calculation for a Bermudan Swaption with a full CT as a proxy. Note that the time it takes to evaluate the CT is negligible compared to the Bermudan Swaption evaluation. The computational gain essentially comes from the difference between total evaluations via brute force and number of samples needed to calibrate the CT.

Brute-force (benchmark) evaluations	Sampling evaluations	Reduction of calls to function	Extra comp cost	Comp savings
1,000,000	86,436	91.34%	0.14%	91.21%

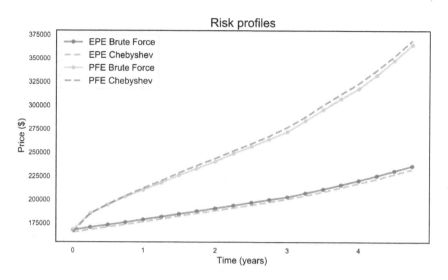

FIGURE 15.6 PV profiles — at expectation and 95th percentiles — for a Bermudan Swaption obtained with the benchmark and with a full CT.

TABLE 15.8 Mean and maximum relative errors for PV profiles at expectation and 95th percentiles for a Bermudan Swaption obtained with the benchmark and with a full CT. Also CVA maximum relative error is presented.

	EPE mean error	EPE max error	PFE mean error	PFE max error	CVA error
Bermudan Swaption	1.41%	1.53%	1.25%	1.83%	1.38%

to build the TT-format tensor was the Sample Adaptive Algorithm. A total of 5,000 grid points were randomly sampled and evaluated with the pricing function. Notice this represents 0.07% of the memory cost of full tensor.

The MC simulation considered only had 20 time points. A more faithful representation of such a calculation in a bank's setting would have about 100 time points. Given that time to maturity was included as one of the variables within the domain of the proxy built, the number of time points does not affect the way the technique is applied — the CT is built the same way independently of the number of time points.

Assuming 100 time points, the brute-force approach involves 1,000,000 evaluations. The number of samplings needed to build the CT in TT format was 5,000. This gives a reduction in the number of calls of 99.50%. The overhead costs coming from running the Sample Adaptive Algorithm and evaluating the CT on all 1,000,000 nodes of the MC simulation amount to 0.53% of the brute-force approach. This brings the total computational gains to 98.97%, as can be seen in Table 15.9. For more details on the simulations run and associated computational gains, we refer to Appendix D.3.2.

TABLE 15.9 Computational gain of running the CCR calculation for a Bermudan Swaption with a CT in TT format as a proxy. Note that the training and compute time of the CT is negligible compared to the Bermudan Swaption evaluation. The computational gain essentially comes from the difference between total evaluations via brute force and the evaluations needed to build the CT in TT format.

Brute-force (benchmark) evaluations	Sampling evaluations	Reduction of calls to function	Extra comp cost	Comp savings
1,000,000	5,000	99.50%	0.53%	98.97%

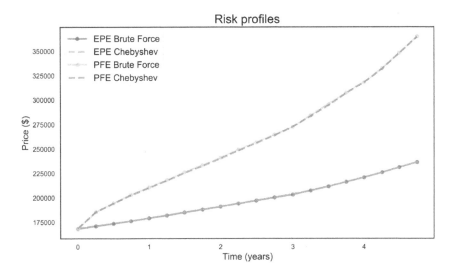

FIGURE 15.7 PV profiles — at expectation and 95th percentiles — for a Bermudan Swaption obtained with the benchmark and with a TT-format CT.

TABLE 15.10 Mean and maximum relative errors for PV profiles at expectation and 95th percentiles for a Bermudan Swaption obtained with the benchmark and with a TT-format CT. Also CVA maximum relative error is presented.

	EPE mean error	EPE max error	PFE mean error	PFE max error	CVA error
Bermudan Swaption	0.13%	0.34%	0.27%	0.46%	0.11%

Figure 15.7 shows PV profiles at expectation and at the 95th percentile. The results through the brute-force approach and with the CT in TT format are shown. Table 15.10 gives numerical estimates of the errors (mean and max error) for both profiles and CVA value computed. All errors are below 0.46%.

Deep Neural Nets

This section presents the results obtained when a DNN is used to approximate the function f that results from applying the Composition Technique to the pricing function of the Bermudan Swaption.

The DNN consisted of three hidden layers, each with 30 neurons and one output layer with a single neuron. The activation function used was the rectified linear unit (ReLU; see Section 2.2), and the gradient descent algorithm used to train the DNN was the Adam optimiser (see 2.4.5).

The hyper-parameters just mentioned were chosen based on results found in the literature that deal with similar problems, for example, [25] and [41].

A total of 5,000 values of the pricing function were used to train the DNN. These were obtained by randomly sampling the pricing function of the Bermudan Swaption within the ranges determined by the MC simulation — that is, in the case of the market risk factors, the ranges determined by their diffusion, and the maturity of the trade in the case of the time to maturity variable.

Assuming an MC simulation with 100 time points, we have 1,000,000 evaluations of the pricing function with the brute-force approach and only 5,000 evaluations to build the DNN. This represents a reduction of 99.50% in pricing function evaluations. There is an extra computational cost that comes from training the DNN and evaluating it on the 1,000,000 MC nodes, which amounts to 0.33% of the brute-force effort. When all components are considered, we get computational savings of 99.17% as shown in Table 15.11.

Figure 15.8 shows PV profiles at expectation and at the 95th percentile for both the brute-force approach (using the pricing function) and the DNN. The plots show the high levels of accuracy achieved by using the DNN. Table 15.12 presents the numerical errors of approximation for both profiles and CVA value. All are less than 0.64%.

15.3.4 Adding non-risk-driving variables

In most examples presented so far, the approach has been aggressive when deciding which parameters to include as part of the defining variables of f — that is, we have tried to reduce the dimension of the input domain of f as much as possible. Section 15.3.3 showed an example where we relaxed this approach and included time to maturity as a variable within the domain of f. Although this comes at the cost of increasing the dimension of f and hence the building effort for the proxy chosen (CT or DNN), we

TABLE 15.11 Computational gain of running the CCR calculation for a Bermudan Swaption with a DNN. Note that the time for training and evaluation of the DNN is negligible compared to the Bermudan Swaption evaluation. The computational gain essentially comes from the difference between total evaluations via brute force and the combination of sampling and training needed to build the DNN.

Brute-force (benchmark) evaluations	Sampling evaluations	Reduction of calls to function	Extra comp cost	Comp savings
1,000,000	5,000	99.50%	0.33%	99.17%

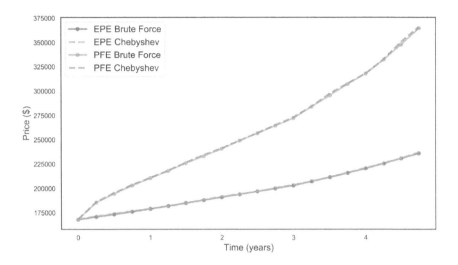

FIGURE 15.8 PV profiles — at expectation and 95th percentiles — for a Bermudan Swaption obtained with the benchmark and with a DNN.

TABLE 15.12 Mean and maximum relative errors for PV profiles at expectation and 95th percentiles for a Bermudan Swaption obtained with the benchmark and with a DNN. Also CVA maximum relative error is presented.

	EPE mean error	EPE max error	PFE mean error	PFE max error	CVA error
Bermudan Swaption	0.26%	0.53%	0.31%	0.82%	0.22%

showed by using a Bermudan Swaption that the computational gains obtained were worth the trouble.

This can be taken a step further by including trade-specific parameters within the defining variables for f. The result is a function f generic enough to represent a collection of trade instances as opposed to a function f that represents a specific trade, as has been the case of the examples presented so far.

We use an American option to illustrate this approach. This is an exotic trade present in most bank's portfolios. We opted for an MC simulation-based pricing function. Therefore, once again, the computation of CCR metrics involves a nested MC simulation. The pricing function routine was taken from QuantLib, implemented and run in C++. The number of paths used inside the pricing function was set to 9,000. This gives a nice balance between a pricing noise of 2.35% (at the 95th percentile, see Figure 15.10), while still allowing for brute-force calculations to benchmark within a local setup.

All the American options considered had less than a year to expire and a range of strikes. The market risk factors diffused stochastically in the MC simulation were the underlying spot, its volatility and a curve of interest rates. The spot and its volatility were diffused using the Heston model, while the curve of interest rates was diffused using a one-factor HW model. The rest of the market factors affecting the trade were kept constant.

There are three dimensions in the domain of f coming from the risk factor diffusion models used to diffuse the market risk factors: the spot, the spot volatility and the interest rates factors. Including time to maturity increases the dimension by one. If the strike is included too — the trade-specific parameter considered in this approach — there is an extra dimension to consider. This gives a total of five dimensions.

Adding trade-specific parameters

When the strike is not included as a variable, the function f defined through the Composition Technique gives the price of an American option with a specific strike, the strike being the value at which the strike was fixed. The advantage of including the strike as a variable is that f now returns the price of an American option with any strike, as long as the strike is within the chosen range.

Including a trade-specific parameter such as the strike is an important consideration in some cases. Increasing the dimension of f increases the building time of any proxy for f, regardless of whether it's a CT or a DNN. However, once built, this proxy can be used to generate the distribution of PVs for a whole portfolio of American options within a CCR MC simulation, without the need to build any other proxy. In some cases, this translates — as we show next — into substantial computational gains.

Once the function f has been defined through the Composition Technique, either a TT-format CT or a DNN is built as a proxy to it.

The numerical result presented in the next two sections were obtained on a portfolio with three American options. One was at-the-money, the second out-of-the-money and the third in-the-money. The reason for such a small portfolio is down to the significant computational cost associated with the brute-force approach (benchmark) in the CCR calculations run.

TT-format Chebyshev Tensors

The Chebyshev grid chosen to approximate the function f, defined after applying the Composition Technique, consisted of 20 points per dimension. Linear products, such as the cross-currency swap tested before, can be approximated by CTs with much smaller grids. However, non-linear products, such as American options, especially when they are close to maturity, require more points to reach the noise level present in the MC pricing routine. Given the dimension of the grid, this defines a grid with 3,200,000 points.

Fine-tuning the Chebyshev grid

It must be noted that 20 points per dimension is in some instances quite conservative. Perhaps 20 points are needed along the dimension that carries most of the non-linearity, for example, the spot dimension in the case of an American Option. Dimensions along which the pricing function is more linear — such as the one that corresponds to the interest rates — may well be resolved with fewer than 10 points. If we want to reduce the size of the Chebyshev grid as much as possible, we need to specify different numbers of points for different variable inputs, for example, 20 for spot and 5 for rates. We do not implement this fine-tuning in this example for ease of illustration.

We used the Sample Adaptive Algorithm to generate the tensors in TT format to approximate f. To run it, we sampled a random subgrid consisting of 90,000 points. Notice this represents 3% of the original Chebyshev grid.

The portfolio tested consisted of three options. However, given that the strike was included in the domain of the CT built, we can increase the number of options without incurring any extra computational building cost related to the proxy technique. Therefore, we can easily extrapolate computational gains for a portfolio with 100 American options.

In a portfolio with 100 options, the brute-force approach requires 100,000,000 pricing function evaluations, if we assume an MC simulation with 100 time points and 10,000 paths. The CT in TT format built is the same as the one built for just three trades. Building such a CT required 90,000 evaluations. This represents a reduction in the number of calls to the pricing function of 99.91%.

The computational overhead determined by the running of the Sample Adaptive Algorithm and the evaluation of the CT on the 1,000,000 nodes 100 times (once per option) accounted for only 0.10% of the brute-force computational cost. Therefore, the computational gain obtained through the use of CTs is 99.81%, as can be seen in Table 15.13. Further details related to the computational cost of this simulation can be found in Appendix D.4.

TABLE 15.13 Computational gain of running the CCR calculation with a CT in TT format as a proxy on a portfolio with 100 American option trades and 100 time points. Note that the training and evaluation of the CT is negligible compared to the American option evaluation. The computational gain essentially comes from the difference between total evaluations via brute force (benchmark) and the evaluations needed to build the CT in TT format.

Brute-force (benchmark) evaluations	Sampling evaluations	Reduction of calls to function	Extra comp cost	Comp savings
100,000,000	90,000	99.91%	0.10%	99.81%

Figure 15.9 shows PV profiles at expectation and at the 95th percentile for the MC simulation run, obtained both through the brute-force approach (the benchmark) and with the TT-format CTs, on the portfolio with three American options.

Table 15.14 gives numerical estimates of the errors for both profiles and CVA value computed. As can be seen in Table 15.14, the levels of accuracy obtained are within the noise of the pricing function shown in Figure 15.10, which stands at 2.35% at its 95th percentile. If accuracy levels need to be increased, first the noise coming from the MC pricing function must be reduced.

Deep Neural Nets

This section presents the results when a DNN was used on a portfolio of three American options. Just like in the previous tests, the DNN is built on the function f that results from applying the Composition Technique.

The DNN had three hidden layers with 30 neurons each and one output layer with a single neuron. The activation function used in all neurons was the rectified linear unit (ReLU, see Section 2.2). The Adam optimiser (2.4.5) was the stochastic gradient descent algorithm of choice.

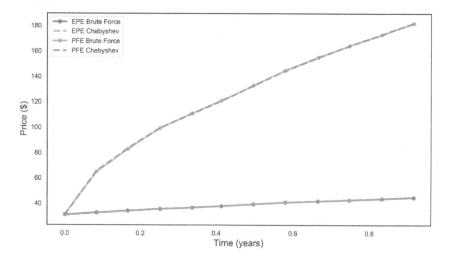

FIGURE 15.9   PV profiles — at expectation and 95th percentiles — for a portfolio of three American options obtained with the benchmark (brute force) and with a single TT-format CT.

TABLE 15.14   Mean and maximum relative errors for PV profiles at expectation and 95th percentiles for a portfolio with three American options obtained with the benchmark (brute force) and with a TT-format CT. Also CVA maximum relative error is presented.

	EPE mean error	EPE max error	PFE mean error	PFE max error	CVA error
American options	0.22%	0.67%	0.3%	1.25%	0.12%

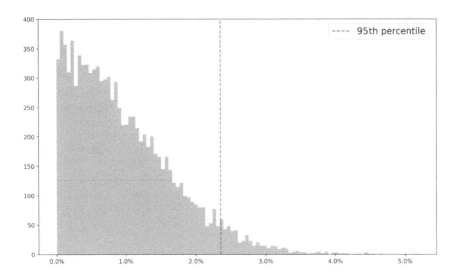

FIGURE 15.10 Noise distribution of the Monte Carlo type of pricing function for the American options. The mean and the 95th percentiles are marked with vertical lines.

The hyper-parameters chosen are partly based on our experience and on results obtained on similar applications found in the literature, for example, [25] and [41].

A total of 100,000 values of the pricing function were used to train the DNN. These were obtained by randomly sampling the pricing function of an American option where the strike was considered an input factor, along with spot, the volatility of spot, the short rate and time to maturity.

Assuming a portfolio with 100 trades and an MC simulation with 100 time points, the brute-force approach to the calculation involves 100,000,000 evaluations to the pricing routine. For this portfolio and MC simulation, the DNN would be built exactly the way it was done for the MC simulation ran (11 time points) and the portfolio with three trades. Given that the DNN used 100,000 evaluations of the pricing routine, the reduction in the number of calls stands at 99.90%. The computational overhead that comes from training and evaluating the DNN on all 1,000,000 MC nodes, once per trade (that is, 100 times), amounts to only 0.18% of the brute-force computational cost. The total computational gains therefore stand at 99.72%, as can be seen in Table 15.15. For more details on the computational savings of this simulation, we refer to Appendix D.4.2.

Figure 15.11 shows PV profiles at expectation and at the 95th percentile for both the brute-force approach (using the pricing function) and the DNN. The plots show the high levels of accuracy achieved by using the DNN. Table 15.16 presents the numerical errors of approximation for both profiles and CVA value. All are less than 1.53%.

Note on proxy choice

As can be seen in Table 15.17, computational gains and accuracy of approximation are good across the board regardless of the type of proxy object chosen. Note, however, that in the cases where both CTs and DNNs were tested, we do observe a slight advantage

TABLE 15.15 Computational gain of running the CCR calculation with a DNN on a portfolio with 100 American option trades and 100 time points. Note that the compute time of the DNN is negligible compared to the training and evaluation time of the portfolio of American options. The computational gain essentially comes from the difference between total evaluations via brute force (benchmark) and the sampling needed for training.

Brute-force (benchmark) evaluations	Sampling evaluations	Reduction of calls to function	Extra comp cost	Comp savings
100,000,000	100,000	99.90%	0.18%	99.72%

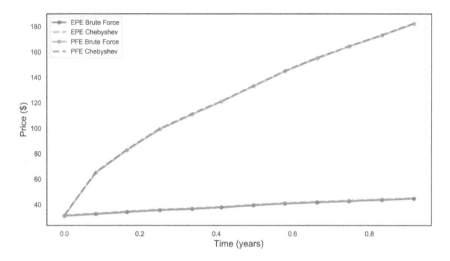

FIGURE 15.11 PV profiles — at expectation and 95th percentiles — for a Bermudan Swaption obtained with the benchmark and with a DNN.

TABLE 15.16 Mean and maximum relative errors for PV profiles at expectation and 95th percentiles for the porftolio of three American options obtained with the benchmark and with a DNN. Also CVA maximum relative error is presented.

	EPE mean error	EPE max error	PFE mean error	PFE max error	CVA error
American options	1.22%	1.53%	0.35%	0.96%	1.20%

of CTs compared to DNNs. In particular, in the case of American options, for compared computational gains — 99.81% for CTs compared to 99.72% of DNNs — the error made by CTs when computing CVA was 0.12%, compared to 1.2% by DNNs. This, of course, should not be a surprise due to the quasi-exponential convergence of CTs, which DNNs do not have.

TABLE 15.17 Comparison of computational gains and CVA errors of approximation among the different proxy objects — full CTs, TT-format CTs and DNNs — on all trade types tested.

	Full CTs		TT-format CTs		DNNs	
	Comp gain	CVA error	Comp gain	CVA error	Comp gain	CVA error
IRS	99.88%	0.00%	NA	NA	NA	NA
Barrier	99.04%	0.02%	NA	NA	NA	NA
CCS	NA	NA	91.75%	0.07%	NA	NA
Bermudan	91.21%	1.30%	98.97%	0.11%	99.17%	0.22%
American	NA	NA	99.81%	0.12%	99.72%	1.20%

Although the results obtained with DNNs are satisfactory in all tests run in this chapter, when presented with the option between CTs and DNNs, we tend to favour CTs in TT format in the context of CCR calculations because they converge notably faster and, if we need to increase precision, we simply increase the granularity of the grid and take advantage of their exponential convergence, while with DNNs the situation is not as straightforward and heuristics based on trial and error are needed. This is clearly illustrated in Figure 14.1, where we compare the rate at which CTs converge (full CTs and TT-format CTs), compared to DNNs as we increase the number of sampled points. All our tests indicate that CTs require a smaller number of sample points to obtain a desired level of accuracy, compared to DNNs.

15.3.5 High-dimensional problems

We started the examples with cases in which the approximation problem can be reduced to very low dimensions. In those cases, full CTs are ideal. The dimensionality of the problem was then increased and the strategy via TT-format tensors was explored. Alongside CTs in TT format, the solution via DNNs was considered. For the cases presented, we saw that CTs achieve greater accuracies and need fewer function samplings.

We know from Section 4.3 and Chapter 14 that the curse of dimensionality affects DNNs in a weaker manner than CTs. Therefore, for very high dimensions, DNNs seem a natural choice of approximator. We therefore pose the following questions: what is the dimensionality frontier beyond which it is better to use DNNs instead of TT-format CTs?

Unfortunately, there is no general answer to that as the frontier depends on the type of functions we are dealing with. Based on the tests performed for this book, dimensions of few tens generally work. However, in some cases dimensions may be much higher.

When the dimension is too high for the Tensor Extension Algorithms to work, the best option is to work with DNNs. In this case we exploit the main strength of DNNs, which is their flexibility, at the expense of its weaknesses, namely, having to sample the function in a potentially high number of points, uncertainty as to the right architecture of the DNN and limited control of the level of accuracy.

Another technique that can be used for high-dimensional cases is based on Chebyshev Sliders (Chapter 7). This was used with good success in the context of IMA-FRTB — results that are presented in Chapter 16. We will not give the details of how this technique could be applied for CCR calculations as it is explained in detail in that chapter. However, we do know of quants who have used it for CCR calculations reporting good results. A complete set of tests using the Sliding Technique within the context of CCR is left for future research. If results, in terms of accuracy, are as good as the ones presented in this chapter, this would be a huge tool for these types of calculations as the main strength of the Sliding Technique is the aggressive reduction of the number of sampling points, which is where computational gains come from.

An example of a trade type that is worth mentioning is that of a basket option. This trade type constitutes a high-dimensional problem (in most cases) where the underlyings are typically not as highly correlated as the tensors of interest rate curves or volatility surfaces are. Therefore, this trade type presents a challenge. However, we must bear in mind that both the Tensor Extension Algorithms and the Sliding Technique allow us to build proxies on a domain constituted by many principal components, for example, 10, 15 or 20. Such numbers of principal components should capture the information of the underlyings to a high degree of accuracy. The proxy techniques built with either the Tensor Extension Algorithms or with sliders should then have sufficient levels of accuracy. This has not been tested at the time of this book going to press, but from our experience we believe this approach should work. Such tests will be performed in the near future.

Our philosophy when solving the computational problem of risk calculations is grounded in looking for approximating frameworks that offer low computational cost and control over the performance achieved, the latter understood not only as accuracy but also as having reliable straightforward ways of increasing the accuracy when needed.

It is for these reasons that we tend to favour CTs over DNNs when possible. However, for cases where the dimension is too high for any of the CT techniques to work, we see no other option other than a DNN to produce a proxy function, because DNNs offer a high degree of flexibility at the cost of a more complex calibration exercise.

15.4   RESULTS ANALYSIS AND CONCLUSIONS

The results in Section 15.3 show the important benefits obtained when the techniques in Section 15.2 are applied in the right way.

Computational cost

As the numerical results from the tests show, computational gains are consistently at least 90%, reaching levels of more than 99% in some cases. From a practitioner's point of view, this means that the calculations currently done within a risk engine can be done with only 1%–10% of the computational load, or that one can increase the number of calculations done by about 10–100 times.

The results reported in Section 15.3 assume the computational cost incurred when building the proxy objects (either DNNs or CTs) is done every time the calculations are run. However, the proxy objects built can be serialised and stored without much difficulty due to their low memory impact. These objects constitute a replica of the pricing functions given the conditions of the day they were built. If these conditions change only a little, these proxy objects will still be good replicas of the pricing functions. This means one can potentially use them for a few days or even weeks in some cases, hence amortising the building effort of the proxy pricers during several days or weeks.

Take, for example, the case of the Bermudan Swaption used for the tests in Section 15.3.3. The proxies built for the pricing function after the Composition Technique has been applied did not include model parameters. This means that the replica of the function obtained corresponds to a fixed set of model parameter values. Model parameters can change day by day. As they change, they define different pricing functions. However, it is known that the variation of these parameters day in, day out is small, meaning the pricing functions they define are very similar. Therefore, the replica built for the pricing function of the Bermudan Swaption on a given day is likely to be a good replica in the coming days. In practice, this means that the computational load for the computation of CCR metrics, once the proxy has been built (day 1 of the exercise), amounts to the evaluation of the proxy pricers, which we know is very small (see, for example, Table 15.7).

Memory impact

There is another important application that results from the efficiency with which the proxy pricers presented in Section 15.2 can be serialised and loaded. When it comes to the subject of how to store results, there are two approaches in CCR. Let us briefly present the context.

Typically, there is an end-of-day (EoD) calculation when all the CCR calculations are performed. During the following day a series of intra-day calculations are usually performed. For example, for any potential incoming trade, one may want to compute the impact of such trade on various CCR metrics such as CVA, PFE and capital — an exercise commonly referred to as incremental CVA (PFE, capital). As computing the incremental impact of the incoming trade requires the distribution of prices obtained in the EoD MC simulation of the previous day, one option is to store in memory drives the collection of price distributions in every EoD calculation. These can then be loaded back into the MC engine during the day whenever needed. Of course, if we want to store simulated trade prices, every day, for portfolios with lots of trades, this approach uses a significant amount of disk memory. If these data are to be shared between different sites of the financial institution, some of which may be in different parts of the world, ample communication bandwidth is required. All this results in high economic costs. The second approach consists of generating the price distributions from the EoD calculation when the intra-day calculations are needed — a task that does not have the memory cost associated just described but, as we know, can be computationally expensive.

One big advantage of working with the proxy pricers presented in this chapter is that since they are light in memory, they can be serialised when the EoD calculations are done, then loaded during the day to quickly obtain the price distributions needed for the intra-day calculations. This strategy removes the memory limitations just described from the IT systems.

Pricing accuracy

It is very important to highlight the pivotal role that the accuracy of the techniques presented in Section 15.2 plays in the computation of CCR metrics. Sometimes it is assumed that one can afford to have approximation errors at the level of pricing — quite a common occurrence with some techniques — but there is a price to pay for it.

This belief is partly due to the fact that the dependence of XVA values on the prices is only through the average of the prices.[10] This means accuracy at each node of the simulation may be seen as not absolutely critical, since errors tend to decrease under averages. This will, however, limit the efficiency and usability of the CCR engine, for the following reasons.

Any technique based on proxies needs to have a sufficiently high level of accuracy to pass model validation and auditing tests, regardless of the type of calculation. In particular, for IMM capital and PFE calculations — normally performed in different departments of the financial institution than where XVA calculations are done — price accuracy at simulation node level is critical. This is because one must prove that pricing at each scenario is accurate or conservative, where the latter means consistently showing correct or higher exposures, but never lower. If proxy pricing is used, regulators tend to require proof of this at every node of the MC simulation. However, achieving consistent higher exposures is not a simple task; a proxy that gives conservative results for a long position typically underestimates the exposure for the corresponding short position. Therefore, in the case of pricing function replicas, one should aim for those that consistently give high degrees of accuracy.

Another reason why price accuracy is needed at the level of MC simulation node is related to pricing coherence in bank-wide governance, a recent trend in regulation. Different pricing calculations are performed in different areas within financial institutions, often in risk engines with different characteristics and levels of accuracy. In recent years, regulators have pushed for the prices obtained in different risk engines across financial institutions to be the same or as close as possible — for example, the P&L attribution test in the IMA-FRTB framework. This means that the level of accuracy across risk engines in an organisation should have the level of accuracy demanded by the calculations that require the highest levels of accuracy. For example, XVA values, which typically require lower levels of accuracy at the pricing level compared to those used for IMM capital and PFE calculations, may need to increase in the near future under this trend.

All these potential problems and limitations can be avoided if the pricing step in any CCR engine is done with demonstrable good levels of accuracy. The ideal approach would be full revaluation, but the computational burden it carries provides the case for high-quality proxy pricing.

---

[10]Strictly speaking, XVA values tend to rely on the average of prices that have been floored to zero if they are negative.

Balance between computational cost and accuracy

Most of the numerical results shown in Section 15.3 were obtained using CTs and not DNNs. Our approach when solving the computational problems presented in this book is based on identifying the combination of tools and techniques, such that, given a particular calculation or process, we obtain essentially the same accuracy as with the benchmark approach (which typically relies on using sophisticated but slow financial functions), at a fraction of the cost, while having as much control as possible over the speed and accuracy of the process.

In Chapter 14 and Section 15.2.5, we highlighted two properties of CTs over DNNs that make them particularly suited for the calculations and processes we are interested in: CTs need a smaller number of samples to reach a given level of accuracy (due to their quasi-exponential convergence); with CTs we have more control over the level of accuracy and ability to improve than with DNNs. Therefore, given our approach when solving the problems of interest, the type of calculations we are dealing with — where the input domain of f (Equation 15.1) is usually lower than 10 — and the properties of CTs and DNNs just mentioned, our choice is normally for CTs. However, if the dimension of the input domain is much larger, then DNNs should be the technique of choice, as they are better suited at dealing with high-dimensional replication problems.

Our aim

All in all, the goal of this chapter was to explain the basis of how techniques to approximate functions, namely CTs and DNNs, can be used to improve the computational load of CCR calculations. Most important, our goal is always to design algorithms that are implementable with a reasonable workload on an already existing CCR engine. We hope to have helped the quantitative and IT community on that front. The proposed ideas in this chapter follow the same philosophy as the ones put forward in [29] and [32].

15.5 SUMMARY OF CHAPTER

- **The computational problem in CCR calculations**. CCR calculations are Monte Carlo based. They rely on thousands of scenarios and hundreds of time steps, creating a grid of many simulation nodes. The price of every single trade needs to be evaluated in each of these nodes. Pricing functions tend to be slow to compute. Portfolios of financial institutions tend to have from thousands to a few million trades. Hence, the computation load is humongous.
- **Solution**. CCR calculations require pricing future market scenarios generated with risk factor diffusion models. The parametrisations from these models can be used to apply the Composition Technique. The resulting low-dimensional functions can be replicated with either CTs or DNNs. The CTs may be built directly (evaluating every tensor grid point) or with the use of the Tensor Extension Algorithms.
- **Proxy building**. The building of the proxy pricer can be done in an offline stage, often involving a small number of calls to the original pricing function.

- **Proxy evaluation**. Once the proxy pricer has been built, it can be evaluated in all the Monte Carlo nodes in no time.
- **Accuracy**. The error of the proxy pricer, and hence the exposure profiles, was low across all examples tested. When the pricing function was Monte Carlo based, the error of approximation was within the Monte Carlo noise.
- **Computational gains**. Computational gains in all cases tested stand at more than 90% when compared to the benchmark (using original pricing functions). In some cases, computational gains exceeded 99%.
- **Implementation effort**. The effort involved in implementing these is low for the vast majority of existing CCR engines.

## CHAPTER 16

Market Risk

M arket risk is the area of risk analysis that studies portfolio losses as a result of adverse movements in the market. The type of market risk calculations that will be the focus of this chapter estimate extreme cases of how much a portfolio might lose in a short period of time, for example, 10 days. Examples of these metrics are value-at-risk (VaR) and expected shortfalls (ES). Typically, these are used by financial institutions to understand the level of short-term risk a portfolio of derivatives carries and estimates the amount of assets needed to cover potential losses.

The pricing step in a VaR calculation poses a computational challenge. This is the result of the number of prices that are needed to estimate VaR and the computational cost of obtaining each price when highly tuned but slow pricing functions in risk engines are used. To reduce this computational cost, practitioners have resorted to different approximation methods. A common one relies on the Taylor expansion (also called sensitivity-based approach) of the pricing function on the day the calculation is performed. Another approach relies on so-called valuation grids, which relies on evaluating the derivative (or portfolio) on a number of grid points, typically in one- or two-dimensional space (for example, the spot and volatility for options). Once these values have been obtained, the values of the positions on the VaR scenarios are obtained using linear or spline interpolation frameworks.

Further on, the computational needs imposed by the capital calculation as specified in the Internal Model Approach (IMA) of the Fundamental Review of the Trading Book (FRTB) regulation has increased the challenge substantially, as the pricing methods used for it need to pass demanding accuracy tests.

In this chapter, we first describe the nature of a typical market risk calculation. Then we explain a simple way in which the existing revaluation grids typically used for VaR calculations can be improved using the approximation methods in Chapter 3. Then we present the nature of the computational challenge involved in IMA-FRTB and show how a blend of the approximation methods in Part I with the toolkit in Part II can be used to massively reduce the computational burden associated with such calculation. Finally, we present numerical results obtained within the systems of a tier-one bank for IMA-FRTB.[1]

---

[1]We would like to thank the bank for allowing us to use the data from the tests done within their systems.

16.1   VaR-LIKE CALCULATIONS

The most common metrics used in market risk calculations are the VaR and the ES values of a portfolio. Traditionally, VaR has been the common metric to compute. More recently, it has been replaced with ES in various regulatory calculations. In what follows, we describe the steps needed to compute either of the metrics, which, from now on, we refer to as VaR-like metrics.

In short, a VaR-like metric consists of the following three steps: first, a distribution of market risk factor scenarios is generated; then, the portfolio in question is priced at each scenario of the distribution; finally, a quantile-type value is computed on the distribution of prices obtained in the previous step.

These calculations are done at portfolio level, where the portfolios can be defined in many ways, ranging from the totality of the bank's derivative portfolio, to individual trading desks, legal entities, countries, asset classes and so on. To price the portfolio at each market risk factor scenario, each derivative product must first be priced at each scenario. The results are then aggregated to obtain prices at portfolio level, from where the VaR-like metric is computed. Needless to say, the market risk scenarios generated must be the ones that the portfolio is sensitive to. For example, if it is an interest rate portfolio with interest rate swaps and swaptions (and other interest rate products), then the market risk factors are interest rates, market-implied volatilities and other corresponding risk factors.

Market risk factors are generally obtained from historical data. The historical data accumulated over time are used to produce market shocks that correspond to market movements in a short period of time, typically between 1 and 10 days. These market shocks can then be applied to the market levels of the day to obtain a distribution of market scenarios.

The number of scenarios varies depending on the specifics of the calculation, normally in the hundreds. A typical VaR-like calculation involves between 250 and 500 scenarios, which correspond to one or two years of historical shocks. It is not strange, however, to encounter several hundreds and sometimes thousands of scenarios.

The portfolio in question is then priced on the set of scenarios generated in the previous step. The most accurate metrics are obtained using pricing functions — either the ones in the front office or in sophisticated risk engines. We refer to this approach as *full revaluation*. Calculations done this way constitute the benchmark in terms of accuracy. However, doing so comes at a substantial computational cost: portfolios can have up to a few million trades and each must be priced on hundreds if not thousands of scenarios. This step is precisely the *pricing problem in market risk calculations*. This becomes particularly acute in the case of IMA-FRTB, where a Taylor-based approach usually does not satisfy the accuracy constraints imposed by the regulation. A solution to this computational challenge is what we present in Sections 16.3.2 and 16.4.

Once the whole portfolio has been evaluated on the distribution of market risk factors, a quantile of the profit-and-loss distribution is calculated. For most calculations, the quantile q tends to be low. For VaR, q is typically 1% — normally called 99% VaR. This represents the simulated value of the portfolio below which the worst 1% of the losses are found. In the case of ES, the average of the losses below the quantile q

is computed. Other market risk measures — such as capital charges — compute similar values or values derived from these ones. However, they all have in common the evaluation of a portfolio on a collection of historically generated market risk factors.

For all these metrics, the pricing step constitutes the computational bottleneck. The process before and after pricing are typically computationally cheap.

16.1.1 Common techniques in the computation of VaR

Given the substantial computational demand associated with the calculations described under a full-revaluation approach, practitioners have developed methods to generate VaR-like metrics efficiently. Most of these rely on computing proxy prices in an efficient manner.

Taylor approximation — sensitivity-based approach

One of the most widely used methods to produce price distributions for VaR-like calculations is based on Taylor approximation. Taylor expansions are used to approximate the values of a function around a point using the derivatives of the function. In the context of pricing functions, the derivatives (greeks) of the pricing function need to be computed with respect to its risk factors.

The advantages of this method are the following. First, VaR tends to be calculated over a short time horizon, typically 10 days, and so Taylor approximations have been traditionally seen as good enough from a pricing accuracy standpoint. Financial institutions compute the sensitivities for hedging purposes every day, so it makes sense to use them in a Taylor-based proxy pricing for VaR. Finally, and very importantly, pricing with them is computationally very efficient.

However, it has some sizeable downsides. The first is that Taylor expansion as an approximation method has slow convergence rates. To achieve high degrees of accuracy, derivatives of high orders must be computed. The problem is that the number of relevant risk factors affecting each trade is easily in the hundreds. Also, analytical expressions for the derivatives are normally not available, forcing the practitioner to estimate them via finite difference methods. These two things mean that computing sensitivities is in itself computationally expensive. Therefore, for practical reasons, practitioners are forced to compute only first- or second-order derivatives, giving pricing approximations with an accuracy that is suboptimal for many relevant purposes.

Revaluation grids

Another method often used is based on revaluation grids. Given a trade and its set of risk factors, a grid of points is defined over the space of risk factors affecting the trade. The grid points are then evaluated by the pricing function of the trade and the resulting values interpolated, typically with splines (often linear). The interpolator is then used to evaluate prices at all the scenarios needed to compute VaR.

The advantage of revaluation grids comes from the following. Say the VaR calculation has 500 prices and that Taylor expansion is seen as not accurate enough. An alternative would be to reprice the portfolio 500 times via full revaluation, once in each VaR scenario. This is computationally very costly. Alternatively, if a revaluation grid is defined with fewer than 500 grid points, this means a reduction in the computational load associated with the VaR calculation, given that revaluation grids are very efficient at being evaluated.

Note one key aspect involved in the use of revaluation grids: their use may only make sense if the number of grid points is smaller than the VaR scenarios to evaluate. If more grid points are used, then we end up calling pricing functions a greater number of times (just in the creation of the revaluation grids) than if we did the VaR calculation with full revaluation.[2]

Standard revaluation grids have a couple of important downsides. The first is that the geometry of the grid is typically defined by equidistant points or perhaps in some cases with some concentration around areas where the function curvature is greatest (for example, around the strike). We know from Chapter 3 that these types of point distributions have poor convergence properties. In particular, to increase the accuracy of approximation of a traditional revaluation grid, we need to increase the number of grid points substantially (see Figure 16.1). In Figure 16.1, we see how the error convergence curve of traditional grids flattens out as the number of points is increased; hence, they arc ill-suited for accurate pricing approximation.[3] In practice, this means that traditional revaluation grids have low levels of accuracy even when we have as many grid points as VaR scenarios needed.

Second, revaluation grids suffer from the curse of dimensionality — that is, the number of grid points increases exponentially with the dimension of the grid. This forces practitioners to consider one, two or (maximum) three dimensions, being forced to ignore the effect some risk factors have on the VaR value — a phenomenon known in the industry as risks-not-in-VaR (RNIV).

For example, if the trade type in question for which we want to compute VaR is an equity option, one would normally build an equidistant grid on the two main risk factors, which are spot and volatility. The pricing function is then evaluated on the grid points from which we can build an interpolator — say a spline. The spline is then used to evaluate the VaR scenarios in a very short period of time.

Notice that, since we consider equidistant grids, the accuracy will probably be poor even when restricted to the two-dimensional spot-volatility domain. Second, by only considering two dimensions we leave out important risk drivers such as interest rates, an example of a market risk driver unaccounted for in this calculation.[4]

In the next section, we are going to see how some of the important limitations of traditional revaluation grids can be easily overcome.

---

[2]Revaluation grids with more than 500 points (following the example) may make sense if they are reused for several VaR calculations or other repricing needs.

[3]Figure 16.1 illustrates the point for equidistant points, but the same can be said about revaluation grids that are not based on Chebyshev, Legendre, Jacobi, Gegenbauer points. See Section 3.5.

[4]RNIV can be accounted for to some extent via Taylor, but this approach has its limitations, too.

16.2   ENHANCED REVALUATION GRIDS

With only a minor change, the performance of traditional revaluation grids can be improved significantly. The change consists of replacing the distribution of the traditional grids for Chebyshev grids and interpolating the values on the latter with polynomials. The resulting Chebyshev revaluation grids offer accuracy levels that are orders of magnitude greater than those of traditional ones at a fraction of the building cost. This is the result of the mathematical properties that CTs enjoy, discussed in detail in Chapter 3.

Using the language used in Chapter 3, revaluation grids are just another example of a tensor. We know from Chapter 3 that the convergence properties of tensors change a lot depending on how tensor points are distributed. As said before, revaluation grids are typically defined over equidistant points; other geometries are sometimes used, but to our knowledge, distributions that guarantee quasi-exponential rates of convergence as the size of the grid increases — as it happens with Chebyshev grids — are not commonly used. What has been ignored by many is that such a simple change can have drastic consequences.

Figure 16.1 illustrates this point. Two-dimensional revaluation grids were built on the spot-volatility domain of a European option. Two types of revaluation grids were considered: equidistant and Chebyshev grids. The error of approximation was measured for each revaluation grid as the *maximum* error over the whole range of interpolation.[5] The *x*-axis in Figure 16.1 represents the number of grid points on the revaluation grid, the *y*-axis the error of approximation *in logarithmic scale*. Notice the difference in decay rates between equidistant and Chebyshev grids. Take for example, 250 grid points. Equidistant grids have an error of approximation of 0.1 while Chebyshev grids 0.00005, between four and five orders of magnitude greater. Also, the error of approximation reached by equidistant grids with 250 points would have been reached with only 45 by Chebyshev points.

The results shown in Figure 16.1 translate into substantial computational gains. If we choose an equidistant revaluation grid with 250 points to compute VaR based on 500 scenarios, we would have, using the revaluation grids to produce Figure 16.1, an accuracy of 0.1. For this degree of accuracy, we can alternatively use a Chebyshev revaluation grid with only 45 points, which represents a computational gain over the standard grid of 82%.

Changing the distribution of the grid points can have big effects as Figure 16.1 shows, and it should be remarkably easy to implement in a market risk infrastructure that already uses revaluation grids: all that needs to be changed is the points of interpolation and the interpolator itself (i.e. from the current distribution of points to Chebyshev points and from the current interpolation scheme to polynomial interpolation via the barycentric interpolation formula [Section 3.6]).

---

[5]The error was measured as the maximum of the absolute value of the difference between the full-revaluation option price and the interpolated value, evaluated over a very fine grid of testing points.

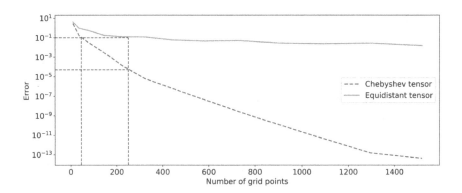

FIGURE 16.1 Comparison of convergence rates between revaluation grids on equidistant points and revaluation grids on Chebyshev points, applied to the pricing function of a European option over a spot-volatility domain.

An important added value that Chebyshev grids deliver is having control over the error of the grid. Section 3.4 explains how we can gauge the maximum error that a Chebyshev grids has, with respect to full revaluation, from only the values of the function on the Chebyshev points; this is a remarkable property that standard interpolation frameworks do not have. Suppose we want to make sure that the revaluation grids in the VaR engine always have an error lower than a given threshold, ε. The error of the Chebyshev grids can be explored with the methods described in Section 3.4 fairly easily so that if the error that the grid gives is greater than ε, appropriate action can be taken (e.g. take the trade with the error out of the VaR calculation, apply a conservative buffer, regenerate the grid with more interpolating points, etc.). This is, in our view, a highly valuable feature that Chebyshev grids provide in the context of highly regulated environments, like banks have.

As said before, revaluation grids suffer from the course of dimensionality (this applies all grids alike), which leads to the RNIV problem. If standard grids are substituted by Chebyshev grids, the computational savings achieved could be dedicated to incorporating an additional dimension to the grid, hence improving the RNIV problem.

One way of incorporating all risk factors into the VaR calculation can be through the use of sliders (Chapter 7) or the Tensor Extension Algorithms (Chapter 6). In fact, the combination of sliders and dimensionality reduction techniques with Chebyshev grids is at the core of the solution we propose for the computational revaluation problem in IMA-FRTB, calculation for which we show results in Section 16.4.

16.3 FUNDAMENTAL REVIEW OF THE TRADING BOOK

Before the FRTB regulation, Basel II, set in 2004, stipulated that market risk should be measured and managed based on a 99% 10-day VaR calibrated historically. The upgrade to the regulation that came after the 2008 crisis, the Basel II.5 framework, added a stress-VaR component, also at 99% confidence level and a 10-day time horizon.

These regulatory required calculations for market risk are to be replaced by the FRTB framework.

As a regulation, FRTB is one of the widest reaching and complex in recent times. It changes the way financial institutions manage and source data, the way capital risk is calculated, the borderline between the trading and banking book, the way to comply with regulations and many other aspects.

With regard to market risk capital, financial institutions for which FRTB applies will have to calculate and report that capital under the standarised approach (SA). Institutions can also opt for the internal model approach (IMA), a more challenging route for the calculations and the regulatory scrutiny involved. The main advantage, however, is that IMA is more risk sensitive than SA and hence better at reflecting the economic risk carried by the balance sheet. Also important, capital values should be generally significantly reduced with the IMA approach compared to SA, giving an economic advantage to those who implement it successfully.

16.3.1 Challenges

FRTB will present financial institutions with many challenges. The level of monitoring and governance will be enhanced, the volume of data to handle and share across the organisation will increase substantially, non-modellable risk factors (NMRFs) require special treatment under IMA, systems will have to be aligned significantly, amongst many other things. In particular, the IMA risk and capital calculations will involve a significant computational cost. This is because the accuracy of the pricing routines used need to pass a pretty demanding accuracy test. A full-revaluation approach, using the front office official pricing functions, solves this problem, but at a high computational cost — optimising this problem will be the focus for the remainder of this chapter.

The calculation of capital under IMA is based on a computation, which must be performed daily, of ES, with different liquidity horizons, for each of the portfolios under the IMA scope. The calculation of ESs requires the pricing of these portfolios on hundreds if not thousands of scenarios. This means each trade needs to be priced, depending on its different liquidity horizons, between 250 and a few thousand scenarios. On top of this calculation, there is a period of stress that must be estimated at least quarterly, which involves the valuation, of each trade, of about 3,000 scenarios (about 10 years of historical data). Although the latter must be done quarterly according to the latest regulations, there seems to be, at the time of writing this book, heavy pressure from a number of regulators to do it monthly at least.

To gain regulatory approval within the IMA approach, the financial institution must pass a backtesting and profit and loss (P&L) attribution (PLA) test, where the latter compares daily risk-theoretical P&L with the daily hypothetical P&L for each trading desk. This means financial institutions will need strict price alignment between market risk systems and the official pricing systems — the so-called front office pricing functions. In practice, organisations will be forced to either use front office pricing systems or come up with very accurate proxies of them.

In terms of satisfying the PLA test, using front office pricing systems would be ideal. However, doing so would be very slow and expensive. Not only can making pricing models available to risk analysts outside of front office be a big operational challenge in itself in some houses but also running them on all the scenarios specified by the regulation constitutes a more than sizeable computational cost.

If, however, there is a way of creating accurate proxies to front office pricing models, fast FRTB computations would be accessible, and compliance and regulatory approval would be achieved, all at a substantial reduction of the otherwise ongoing high computational costs.

The remainder of this chapter presents a way of coming up with such proxies. Section 16.3.2 will explain which technique from Part III to use and how. Section 16.4 will present numerical results obtained within the risk systems of a tier-one bank, where the solution in Section 16.3.2 was applied to an interest rate portfolio.

16.3.2 Solution

This section presents a solution, based on the approximations techniques in Part III, to the computational burden associated with the capital calculation under the IMA approach for the FRTB regulation. As was mentioned in Section 16.3, the capital calculation under the IMA approach relies on the frequent calculation of ES, with different liquidity horizons, for each of the chosen portfolios. This involves the pricing of these portfolios on hundreds if not thousands of different market scenarios. This constitutes a substantial computational challenge and another example of the pricing problem in risk calculations.

Due to regulatory requirements, the prices used in the computation of ES must be as close as possible to front office prices; any proxy to the pricing function must pass the mentioned PLA test. The aim of the solution presented in this section is to approximate the official front office pricing routines to a high degree of accuracy with proxies that are both very efficient to build and fast to evaluate. The high degrees of accuracy will enable regulatory approval and with it the benefits of the IMA approach. The speed of evaluation means the risk calculations in the IMA approach can be done in a timely manner with little computational cost. Also, it opens the possibility of doing pretrade analysis, conducting IMA-FRTB portfolio optimisation runs, comprehensive IMA-FRTB stress testing, and so on.

As described in Section 16.1, computing ES on a portfolio relies on collecting a set of market risk factor scenarios, pricing the portfolio on these scenarios, estimating a specified quantile of the price distribution, and calculating the average of all those prices that lie below the quantile. In the case of IMA-FRTB, there are 250 scenarios and the quantile used is 2.5%. The objective will be to approximate the pricing functions in the portfolio with one of the techniques in Part III and use the objects generated to evaluate the 250 scenarios of each ES value needed for the capital calculation.

There are guidelines on how market risk factor scenarios are generated for the IMA approach. The details of such conditions are irrelevant to the solution. The only important thing to note is that we assume that these scenarios are obtained via historical simulation — an assumption based on the fact that the vast majority of market risk engines in banks are based on historical simulations. These constitute the input values to the pricing functions of the trades in the portfolios considered.

The hybrid method

As we know, pricing functions — which we denote by P — are functions that have input domains of high dimension. The number of input variables is often in the tens or hundreds. For example, a European Swaption — an example of relevance to us as we present results using this type of trade — takes a collection of interest rates and implied volatilities. The total combined number is in the hundreds. The idea will be to apply the Composition Technique to the pricing functions P in combination with other relevant techniques, such as the Sliding Technique (Chapter 7), to enable an efficient and accurate approximation of P.

To apply the Composition Technique, we need a parametrisation g that when composed with P gives a function f with domain of lower dimension than the one of P. Reducing the dimension of the domains is important; however, another paramount aim is to lose as little information as possible through the composition. This means using the notation in Equation 16.1 that if y corresponds to x under g, then $P(x)$ is as close as possible to $f(y)$.

To generate the parametrisation g, we take advantage of the fact that market risk factors often display high degrees of correlation, for example, the points in a yield curve or the points on a volatility surface. This makes dimension reduction techniques, such as PCA, very effective at creating the parametrisations needed to apply a form of the Composition Technique (see Section 5.2).

To obtain the parametrisation through PCA, one must specify the number of principal components we want to keep. The number of principal components is the same as the dimension onto which we project the data we want to reduce in dimension, for example, the yield curves or the implied volatility surfaces. With PCA, the higher the dimension, the less information we lose. This translates into $P(x)$ being close to $f(y)$ for every y that corresponds to x under g. As mentioned before, this accuracy is one of the things we are after.

The other main aim of the Composition Technique is the reduction of dimension. Due to the curse of dimensionality, which affects the fundamental approximation methods (DNNs and CTs), we want to reduce the number of components as much as possible — that is, reduce the dimension of the domain of f as much as possible. The higher the dimension, the more points that f needs to sample. The more points sampled with f, the lower the computational gains. Therefore, it is paramount that we work with the lowest dimension possible.

Let us illustrate the effect this has with a concrete example. If we want to compute ES for two liquidity horizons (to be discussed in detail later in this section), we must evaluate the pricing function 500 times. This means we must obtain our proxy function with no more than, say, 250 points, if we want to achieve a ×2 computational gain, 166 points for a ×3 computational gain, and so on.

Unfortunately, PCA applied on real market data often requires a high number of principal components to achieve high levels of accuracy, for example, 20 principal components for implied volatility surfaces. When we apply the Composition Technique with this number of principal components, we obtain a function f with dimension 20. This is where the Sliding Technique comes to our rescue, as it enables the building of proxies in high dimensions without a significant number of sample points. Although the use of the Sliding Technique may sometimes come with a reduction in accuracy, for the application in question, we obtain high levels of accuracy, as presented in Section 16.4.

In summary, the solution consists of applying PCA to the market risk factors that constitute the inputs to a pricing function P. The transformation obtained after applying PCA is the function g used in the Composition Technique to obtain f, as shown in Equation 16.1. Finally, a proxy based on the Sliding Technique is built to approximate f.

$$Y \subset \mathbb{R}^k \xrightarrow{\ g\ } \tilde{X} \subset \mathbb{R}^n \xrightarrow{\ P\ } \mathbb{R}. \tag{16.1}$$

$$f$$

Possible proxies

Once the function f has been specified, there are several options that can be explored to approximate it.

In principle, a DNN could be trained to approximate f. However, we find DNNs to be suboptimal in this context. The number of pricing function evaluations needed in each ES calculation is very low, in some cases as low as 250 pricing calls. Therefore, we need an approximation method that is very efficient, one that can approximate the function f from Equation 16.1 with less than 250 samplings. This is an example of an application where we benefit from the high convergence rates of CTs versus the slower convergence rates of DNNs, as explained in Chapter 14.

Different CTs can be built for f. If the dimension of f is low enough — say, below 5 — a single CT is built on the domain of f. If the dimension is greater than 5, a Tensor Extension Algorithm may be considered with the objective of building a single high-dimensional tensor. If the dimension is too great for the Tensor Extension Algorithms, a Chebyshev Slider can be built.

Another important aspect to consider when choosing the proxy is the tractability and stability of approximation method. DNNs are perceived as black boxes; "they work because they work", as we were told once by a head of model validation. We have learnt that market risk quants and model validation units tend to feel uneasy with this lack of tractability as "the last moment we want these methods to break is in the middle of a financial crisis". This contrasts with CTs, where a more robust and well-understood theory exists, which ensures a strong degree of tractability and stability.

Variables at play

To apply the Composition Technique successfully, one must identify which of the parameters that affect the pricing function P play a role in the approximation. As is mentioned in Section 13.2, pricing functions are affected by the following families of parameters: model parameters, market risk factors or market quotes, and parameters built into the specification of the trade.[6]

---

[6]Note that in this application, RFE are not used to generate market factors. Therefore, model risk factors, which are vital for the solution presented in Chapter 15, do not play in the current application.

Let the day of the calculation be given by t_0. The pricing model of P is calibrated at t_0. This fixes the model parameters for the duration of the calculation. Therefore, these parameters do not need to be considered for the approximation scheme of P. Market quotes vary across the different risk factor scenarios used for the ES calculation. Which of these risk factors vary and how they vary is specified by the regulation and the specifics of the calculation. Therefore, if a market risk factor affects the pricing function P, it should, in principle, be considered in the application of the Composition Technique. Finally, with regard to parameters coming from the specifics of the trade, it is important to note, as specified by FRTB, that all scenarios on which P must be priced and correspond to a specific time point in the future ahead of t_0. This means the time to maturity of the pricing function P remains constant throughout the calculation. Clearly the strike and other specifics also remain constant. Therefore, the entire set of parameters of this type can be ignored.

The following point is worth highlighting. The Composition Technique is applied at the level of the pricing function. When we take the composition of g with P (as shown in Equation 16.1), we reduce only the dimension of the market risk factors that affect P. This means the variables that constitute the domain of f, and hence the domain of approximation, are only those that affect the trade and not any other type of risk factor. This is a subtle but important point. Take, for example, a GBPUSD cross-currency swap. When applying the Composition Technique, we consider only GPB and USD risk factors. Risk factors corresponding that are normally associated or grouped alongside GBP and USD, such as EUR, CHF and so on can be ignored.

Dealing with different liquidity horizons

Under IMA-FRTB, each trade is assigned a number of liquidity horizons. For each liquidity horizon, an ES value must be computed. Each ES value needed is obtained by shocking some input variables while keeping others fixed; which vary and which are fixed is determined by the liquidity horizon.

Liquidity horizons are very relevant from a computational standpoint. Each ES calculation involves the pricing of trades on 250 scenarios. The more liquidity horizons, the heavier the computation. For example, if a trade is affected by three liquidity horizons, it will have to price three sets of 250 scenarios, all consisting of the same type of risk factors, only differing by which ones vary and which are fixed.

The solution presented in Section 16.3.2 consists of applying the Composition Technique where the data X (which are the market risk factor scenarios) are first projected onto a lower dimensional space using PCA. Given that multiple liquidity horizons give rise to multiple data sets X, one would in principle apply different instances of the Composition Technique to each liquidity horizon. This would mean the building of a CT — be it a single tensor or slider — for each liquidity horizon along with its building cost. However, as we now describe, the Composition Technique can be applied in such a way to avoid this overhead: the Composition Technique is applied once, and the object built from it, used in the ES calculation of every liquidity horizon.

Let us use a particular example to illustrate how this is done. In fact, we use one of the trade types considered in the proof of concept (PoC) described in Section 16.4. The trade type is a Vanilla Swaption. In the case tested, Vanilla Swaptions were exposed to two families of market risk factors: interest rates and implied volatilities. This trade type is affected by two liquidity horizons: the 10-day one where all risk factors are shocked and the 60-day one where the volatilities are shocked while rates remain constant. The aim is to build a proxy $\tilde{f}$ to the function f in Equation 16.1 for the 10-day liquidity horizon case and use it in both the 10-day and 60-day liquidity horizon ES calculations.

The key idea is to use multiple PCA transformations. More specifically, risk factors with different liquidity horizons were transformed by different PCA models. In the swaption example, a PCA function, denoted by p_1, was trained on the shocked interest rates, and a second one, independent of the first, denoted by p_2, trained on the shocked implied volatilities. Using the parametrisations g_1 and g_2, coming from each PCA object, a parametrisation g is conformed by putting together the domains of g_1 and g_2. The compositon of g with the pricing function of the Swaption P gives rise to f, for which an approximator $\tilde{f}$ — a CT — is built.

For the 60-day liquidity horizon ES calculation, the volatility shocks are the same ones p_2 trained on (i.e. shocked implied volatilities), while the rates are fixed to today's shock.[7] To use the proxy $\tilde{f}$ built for the 10-day liquidity horizon in the computation of the 60-day liquidity horizon, the 60-day liquidity horizon shocks need to be projected, using the PCA models trained for the 10-day case, within the domain of $\tilde{f}$. Moreover, for this approach to be of any use, the error introduced by this projection should be immaterial. This is indeed the case since volatilities are projected through p_2 while today's shock is projected under p_1. The former is the same as what had been done in the 10-day liquidity horizon case. For the latter, as today's shock belongs to the collection of shocks p_1 got trained with, the error of projecting today's shock under p_1 will not be great and the projection will be within the domain of $\tilde{f}$. This ensures the proxy $\tilde{f}$ built for the 10-day liquidity horizon case can be used once again for the 60-day liquidity one.

Notice this approach works regardless of the number of liquidity horizons. The key is to use at least as many PCA models as collections of risk factors with individual liquidity horizons and train them on the shocks that correspond to the 10-day liquidity horizon. The key consequence is that the only proxy $\tilde{f}$ that needs to be built is the one that corresponds to the 10-day liquidity horizon; all others will be evaluated without any overhead.

16.3.3 The intuition behind Chebyshev Sliders

As discussed, we are going to approximate the pricing functions used in the IMA-FRTB calculations with sliders of CTs on principal components; these are what we call *Orthogonal Chebyshev Sliders*. In this section we review what they do from an intuitive standpoint.

One-dimensional Chebyshev Tensors

Approximation frameworks based on CTs work well for a relatively wide range of inputs values. This contrasts with the approximation framework typically used in market risk,

---

[7]Usually the zero shock.

Taylor expansions, also called sensitivity-based pricing. Taylor expansions work well in small neighbourhoods around the point where the expansion is done. However, CTs work well on the whole of their domain, as a result of the remarkable exponential convergence discussed in detail in Section 3.2.

Figure 16.2 illustrates the point just mentioned. It shows the behaviour of both a Taylor expansion and a CT as approximants to a function. Taylor expansions are good close to the point x_0, located at the centre of the interval defined by x_{min} and x_{max}. However, CTs achieve high degrees of accuracy on the whole interval. This level of accuracy is mathematically guaranteed to hold throughout the whole domain under certain conditions (see Theorem 3.2.6). The pricing functions ordinarily found in financial institutions are analytic or piece-wise analytic, which means Theorem 3.2.6 applies to them.[8]

Intuitively speaking, we could say that if we use N Chebyshev points for the CTs, the Chebyshev interpolant approximates the function well throughout the whole domain up to the $N-1$ derivative.[9]

Chebyshev Sliders

Chebyshev Sliders are collections of CTs joined at a pivot point (see Section 7.22 for more details). When we use them to replicate a slow-to-compute function, we sometimes lose some information compared to when we use a full CT, but we gain in computational performance. For example, if we have a function that depends on 10 variables, we can build a very accurate replica with a full CT by considering a Chebyshev grid with

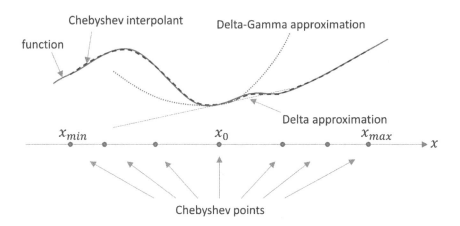

FIGURE 16.2 Illustration of function approximation via CT or via Taylor expansion (Delta and Delta-Gamma).

---

[8]See Definition 3.2.1 for what it means to be analytic and Section 13.1 for a discussion on pricing functions and the property of being analytic.

[9]Important to note that this is not a theorem; it is an intuitive rule we have obtained through experience.

seven points per dimension. However, this means we need the value of the function in $7^{10} = 282{,}475{,}249$ points. If instead we use 10 one-dimensional slides, we only need the value of the function in $10 \cdot 7 = 70$ points, a remarkable improvement.

However, by using the slider, we may not capture the cross-information between the variables in each slide. To visualise this, let us use Taylor expansions around the origin for a function that has an input of dimension 2.

$$f(x, y) \sim f(0, 0) +$$

$$a_{1,0} \left[\frac{\partial f}{\partial x} \right]_0 x + a_{0,1} \left[\frac{\partial f}{\partial y} \right]_0 y +$$

$$a_{2,0} \left[\frac{\partial^2 f}{\partial x^2} \right]_0 x^2 + a_{0,2} \left[\frac{\partial^2 f}{\partial y^2} \right]_0 y^2 + a_{1,1} \left[\frac{\partial^2 f}{\partial x \partial y} \right]_0 xy + \qquad (16.2)$$

$$a_{3,0} \left[\frac{\partial^3 f}{\partial x^3} \right]_0 x^3 + a_{0,3} \left[\frac{\partial^3 f}{\partial y^3} \right]_0 y^3 + a_{2,1} \left[\frac{\partial^3 f}{\partial x^2 \partial y} \right]_0 x^2 y + a_{1,2} \left[\frac{\partial^3 f}{\partial x \partial y^2} \right]_0 xy^2 +$$

$$\cdots$$

In terms of Equation 16.2, we can think of full CTs capturing the information in both the derivatives with respect to each variable and the cross derivatives. However, a slider (one slide per variable) disregards all the cross-terms in the expansion. This is equivalent to saying that

$$\frac{\partial^n f}{\partial x^m \partial y^{n-m}} \sim 0. \qquad (16.3)$$

Notice that sliders are not always constituted of one-dimensional slides. If, for example, we want to capture the cross-terms between the first and second variables, but we are happy to disregard the rest, then we build a two-dimensional CT for the slide that covers those two variables and one-dimensional CT for all other variables.

In market risk language, using sliders means we disregard the cross-gamma terms between variables in different slides in Equation 16.2. However, when we use sliders, we capture all partial derivatives (including cross-gamma of the variables in the slide) of the variables within the same slide very well.

Orthogonal Components

We have mentioned that CTs, in terms of the expansion in Equation 16.2, capture the information present in the partial derivatives of the function, including cross-partial derivatives, to very high orders. However, sliders disregard the cross terms in this expansion for those variables in different slides. However, they bring the benefit of decreasing the computational effort of building the approximation function most substantially compared to full CTs.

In order to minimise the potential loss of information that slides introduce, we want to choose an optimal set of variables on which they are defined. In other words, if we have a function f expressed in terms of a set of variables $x_1, x_2, \cdots, x_n$, where these x variables are, for example, tensor points in a yield curve, we want to express f in terms of other variables $PC_1, PC_2, \cdots, PC_n$ where

$$\frac{\partial^n f}{\partial PC^m \partial PC^{n-m}} \sim 0. \tag{16.4}$$

When this is the case, the function f, expressed in terms of the variables $PC_1, PC_2, \cdots, PC_n$, can be replicated by sliders of dimension 1, meaning, we only need to evaluate the function a very small number of times in order to generate the replicating function.

As the reader may have guessed by now, a clear candidate for these PC variables is the principal components from PCA. This is because we expect the sensitivity of pricing functions with respect to cross-changes between, say, the fifth and eighth principal components, to be very small. Moreover, when pricing functions are sensitive to cross-changes, it tends to be with respect to the first few principal components, but considerably less so to cross-changes between the remaining principal components. Indeed, what we have found through experience (for example, the results in Section 16.4) is that they tend to be hardly sensitive to changes even between the first and second components.

Now that we have discussed the theory and intuition behind the approximation framework used to conduct the tests, let us present in detail the PoC conducted, along with its results.

16.4 PROOF OF CONCEPT

This section describes a PoC, done within the systems of a tier-one bank, in which the solution to the pricing problem described in Section 16.3.2 was applied to the calculation of the different ES values needed for the capital calculation in IMA-FRTB. First, we describe the specific characteristics of the test. Then we present the numerical results obtained.[10]

16.4.1 Proof of concept specifics

This section describes the specifics of the tests carried out. The setting was the computation of ES values for two portfolios within the IMA-FRTB framework. The first portfolio consisted of 635 interest rate swaps, the second of 425 Vanilla Swaptions, both dependent on a single currency. The testing portfolio was constituted by actual trades from the bank's portfolio. These were randomly selected to create a realistic portfolio.

The market data that serves as input to the pricing functions of the trades consisted of two yield curves, one for projecting and one for discounting, each with 27 points, and a volatility surface with 371 points.

It was agreed that the portfolio of swaps would be priced on 3,131 historic shocks and the portfolio of swaptions on 3,108. In both cases, the number of shocks

---

[10]We would like to thank the bank for allowing us to use the data in public domains.

corresponds to the available data for a 10-year period, which includes a period of stress. In the case of swaptions, shocks were priced twice because they are affected by two liquidity horizons. The first is the 10-day liquidity horizon, which corresponds to all risk factors being shocked, the second for the 60-day liquidity horizon, which corresponds to rates being constant and volatilities shocked. This gives a total of three price distributions: one from swaps — as they are only affected by the 10-day liquidity horizon — and two from the swaptions. From each price distribution a P&L was obtained and from each P&L distribution an ES value computed.

It was decided that front office pricing functions would be approximated using a combination of PCA and a Chebyshev Slider, giving rise to an *Orthogonal Chebyshev Slider*. This hybrid technique is an instance of the Composition Technique as described in Section 11: PCA provides the parametrisation g — in this case an orthogonal transformation — that when composed with the front office pricing function P gives f, a function that is then approximated by a Chebyshev Slider.

The portfolios were constructed so that, overall, they were broadly hedged in order to reproduce difficult but realistic situations. It is known that the portfolio sensitivity to the first few principal components of PCA are broadly cancelled out in hedged portfolios, so in order to capture the risk correctly, one needs to use a high number of principal components that, as discussed before, increases the number of sample points needed to obtain an accurate-enough proxy pricer. The aim of this was to stress test the technique itself.

Training time window

As described, it was agreed for the PoC to use about 10 years' worth of data. This roughly equates to 3,000 data points. However, to perform the ES calculations needed for IMA-FRTB one can either train on 10 years' worth of data or only on 1 year's worth. In both cases, we obtain the ES values that need to be computed daily under IMA-FRTB rules. However, if 10 years' worth of data are used, we can also do the period of stress calculation that needs to be done quarterly.[11] Given the size of this data set, one can also perform other rolling calculations that are deemed beneficial, for example, stress testing and historic rolling risk metrics, such as VaR and capital.

However, the advantage of only using 1 year's worth of data is that PCA needs lower dimensions to obtain higher levels of accuracy. Lower dimensions translate into a smaller number of Chebyshev points, which in turn translates into lower building costs.

Technique configurations

In the interest of understanding the effects that changing the parameters of the PCA and Chebyshev Slider have on the accuracy and speed of the technique, several different parameters configurations were tested. This is crucial to understanding the stability of the methodology, as ideally one would want to change these parameters as little as possible from day to day. The results of these are presented in Section 16.4.2.

---

[11]The period of stress calculation, which is part of the IMA-FRTB regulation, was not included as part of the scope of the PoC.

Accuracy measurement

The accuracy of the hybrid technique used was ultimately measured on the ES values obtained. However, the accuracy of the P&L distributions obtained were also tested. This was done in two ways: first, by computing the Spearman correlation of the P&L obtained via full revaluation with the P&L obtained with the hybrid technique, and second, by running the Kolmogorov-Smirnov statistical test on these same two P&Ls. These are the metrics used in the PLA test, designed to detect differences between the benchmark distribution and the one obtained with the Orthogonal Chebyshev Slider.

As per the FRTB regulation, the results of the PLA test classify the trading desk being tested into one of the three possible zones. There is a green, an amber and a red zone. If the results correspond to the red zone, the desk in question cannot use the IMA to determine market risk capital requirements and must use the standardised approach. If the results correspond to the amber zone, the desk is subject to a capital surcharge. When in the green zone, the capital is the one computed from the ES calculations and there is no additional surcharge.

The green zone is assigned if the correlation metric is above 0.8 and the KS p-value is above 0.264. The red zone is determined when the correlation metric is less than 0.7 and the KS p-value is less than 0.055. Anything in between corresponds to the amber zone.

16.4.2   Test specifics

As explained in Section 16.3.2, Orthogonal Chebyshev Sliders are used to solve the pricing problem. Orthogonal Chebyshev Sliders are a combination of PCA and Chebyshev sliders and require the specification of parameters. Changing the parameters changes the accuracy and training effort. In the coming two sections, we explain which parameters were chosen for each and why.

PCA configurations

The main function of PCA within the Orthogonal Chebyshev Slider technique is to provide the parametrisation g in Equation 16.1. To do so, a dimension k must be specified — the number of principal components. This is the dimension onto which original data set X is projected. Such a projection gives rise to $\tilde{X}$ and the parametrisation g, which in turn gives rise to f.

The PCA projection introduces an error with respect to the benchmark of evaluating X using P. This error is reduced the closer $\tilde{X}$ is to X. This happens when the dimension k is increased. Given that k is the dimension of f, which is then approximated by a Chebyshev Slider, we emphasise the need to strike the following balance: on the one hand we need k to be low so the building of the Chebyshev Slider is as cheap as possible; on the other hand we need k to be as high as possible to reduce the error introduced in the PCA projection.

To test the effect introduced by varying the PCA dimension, a range of these was considered in the tests. The way in which such range was chosen is the following. The swaps considered depended on two zero rate curves. The values of zero rate curves exhibit high correlation. It is well known that only a few PCA components capture a good degree of the variance; therefore, the range of PCA dimensions chosen was 3, 5, 10 and 20. Note that the PCA was done on both curves together, that is, on $2 \times 27 = 54$ data points.

The swaptions used depended on the same zero rate curves as swaps plus a surface of implied volatilities. As explained in Section 16.3.2, two PCA transformations were used with swaptions so that the Orthogonal Chebyshev Slider built for the 10-day liquidity horizon movements could be reused for the 60-day liquidity horizon. Therefore, the dimensionality reduction is the sum of the dimensionality reduction for zero rates and the dimensionality reduction for volatilities. For simplicity the same dimension was chosen for zero rates and for volatilities. The dimensions considered were 10, 20, 30 and 50.

It should be noted, however, that the range of PCA dimensions for which good results are obtained depends on the quality of the data. Part of the exercise within the PoC was to identify this range and see how sensitive the accuracy of the methodology is to a change in the PCA dimension. This sensitivity is presented in Figure 16.4 for swaps, and Figures 16.7 and 16.10 for swaptions.

Slider configurations

Chebyshev Sliders have a few parameters to specify. First, the number of slides (or CTs) needs to be specified. Along with the number of slides, the dimension of each slide is also needed. Finally, the number of Chebyshev points in each slide must be specified. These parameters fully determine a collection of slides $\{s_1, s_2, \ldots, s_l\}$.

As explained in Section 7.2, if f is the function to be approximated with such slider, each of the variables in the domain of f will be part of the domain of one and only one slide. Moreover, the sum of the dimensions of the slides $dim(s_1) + \cdots + dim(s_l)$ is k, where k is the dimension of the domain of f and, equivalently, the number of principal components chosen when PCA is applied.

The choices made were the simplest possible. We started with the most basic slider and the one that gives the least number of interpolation points, that is, the slider with configuration $\{1, 1, \ldots, 1\}$. If we have k principal components, this slider works the k variables independently of one another: a one-dimensional CT is built per variable. The output of the k one-dimensional CTs is then added to obtain the final result. Therefore, if each CT uses, say, n points, the slider built captures pricing function sensitivities to each principal component up to order $n - 1$ (remember n points define a polynomial of degree $n - 1$), but does not capture pricing sensitivity across principal components.

Note that there are similarities between the way Chebyshev Sliders work and Taylor approximation. The slider described, with one-dimensional slides and n Chebyshev points per principal component, can be compared to a Taylor expansion done on the first k principal components of PCA, of order $n - 1$ along the components, but with no cross-gammas considered. One of the limitations of Taylor approximation is that they only work well within a vicinity of the point around which the expansion is done. CTs, however, guarantee exponential convergence for the whole domain of approximation, in this case, along each of the first k principal components.

To capture more complex movements of the function, one must define sliders composed of individual slides that have dimensions greater than one. Given that PCA components capture the directions of greater variance in the data, it was decided to group the most important components together and build a single slide for them. Therefore, apart from the configuration $\{1, 1, \ldots, 1\}$, two others were considered: $\{2, 1, \ldots, 1\}$ and $\{3, 1, \ldots, 1\}$. Relative to the first $\{1, 1, \ldots, 1\}$, these two new sliders now capture the pricing function sensitivity to cross-principal component shocks for the first two and first three principal components, respectively.

In this case, it is important to consider the balance between information lost (sliders with slides of low dimension incur greater information lost, as cross-principal component price sensitivities are lost) and computational gain (sliders with slides of low dimension are easier to build and, hence, provide greater computational gains).

For simplicity, the number of Chebyshev points per dimension in any of the slides was kept constant at 5. For linear products, such as swaps, this gives high degrees of accuracy for the portions approximated by each slide. In the case of swaptions, or any other product with curvature, only a couple of points more are needed, if at all, due to the exponential convergence of CTs (Theorem 3.3.10). Any more points will only incur greater building times when no greater accuracy is needed.

Type of Results

There are two sources of error when using the Orthogonal Chebyshev Slider technique. The first is due to the PCA projection — measured as the difference between prices on X and on $\tilde{X}$. The second comes from the approximation error of the Chebyshev Slider on f. In the attempt to identify each error component, results are presented as in Figures 16.3, for example.

Each figure consists of four plots, one for each number of principal components. Each plot has four subplots. The first three subplots are scatterplots; the fourth is a bar plot.

The first scatterplot (top left pane) is a comparison between the P&Ls obtained via full revaluation on the original data set X (horizontal axis) and the P&Ls obtained by full revaluation on the projected data set $\tilde{X}$; the idea is to give visual evidence of the error at the level of P&Ls that comes from the PCA dimensionality reduction. The second scatterplot (top right pane) makes a comparison of the P&Ls obtained by full revaluation on projected data set $\tilde{X}$ (horizontal axis) and the P&Ls obtained using the Chebyshev Slider (y-axis); this gives visual evidence of the error incurred by the Orthogonal Chebyshev Slider alone regardless of the PCA. The third (bottom left pane) is a comparison of the P&Ls obtained through full revaluation on X and the ones obtained with the Orthogonal Chebyshev Slider technique; this shows the resulting accuracy when we combine PCA with Chebyshev Sliders. The last plot in each figure is a bar plot. This shows the ES value obtained via full revaluation (bar plot) compared to the value of the ES obtained via the Orthogonal Chebyshev Slider (dot). A 10% error bar has also been added around the ES obtained through full revaluation as reference.

The idea behind plotting all three scatterplots is to identify where errors are coming from. If there is significant error between the P&Ls obtained from the Orthogonal Chebyshev Slider and the full revaluation P&Ls, we want to see whether the error is due to the Chebyshev Slider or the PCA projection. This can give an indication, for example, that perhaps the dimension of the PCA should be increased.

Each figure (like the one described), comes with a table that contains the following numerical values: the ES relative error, percentage of computational savings, P&L correlations and p-values for the Kolmogorov-Smirnov tests. The P&L correlations and p-values from the Kolmogorov-Smirnov tests were added to assess the overall quality of the P&L approximations obtained from the Orthogonal Chebyshev Sliders. In particular, the Kolmogorov-Smirnov test measures whether there is evidence that the two P&L distributions being compared (full revaluation versus Orthogonal Chebyshev Slider) are not the same.[12]

16.4.3   Results for swap

In this section, we present results for the IR swaps portfolio, using a slider configuration $\{1, 1, \ldots, 1\}$, and $n = 5$ Chebyshev points per slide.

Figure 16.3 shows that even for drastic reductions of dimensionality, results are very good. Its corresponding Table 16.1 shows that with PCA dimension 3 the ES relative error is already as low as 2.20%. As the PCA dimension increases, there is an improvement in the ES error. Meanwhile, at no point does the KS p-value show any evidence that the P&L distributions are different — indeed, the Spearman correlation coefficients and p-values of the KS test place the portfolio in the green zone under the PLA test. In fact, the Spearman correlation shows perfect monotonicity between the distribution of PnLs obtained by brute force and the distribution of PnLs obtained with the Orthogonal Chebyshev Sliders.

However, as expected, an increase in dimension comes with a detriment in computational savings. In any case, both the worse accuracy, which is 2.20%, and the worse computational gain, which is 96.77%, are very positive.

As can be seen from Figure 16.4, changing the configuration to $\{2, 1, \ldots, 1\}$ and $\{3, 1, \ldots, 1\}$ does not affect the quality of the results. The largest reduction in ES error is obtained as the PCA dimension increases and not when the configuration of the slider is changed. This indicates that the portfolio of swaps is hardly sensitive to cross-principal-component factors. Clearly, in the case of swaps, the best option is to keep the simplest and least expensive configuration, which is $\{1, 1, \ldots, 1\}$.

The results presented so far were obtained for 3,131 scenarios. Using the same Orthogonal Chebyshev Slider built for these many scenarios, but evaluated on the most recent 250, gives the results shown in Figure 16.5. The slider chosen to compute the last 250 scenarios has dimension 10 and configuration $\{1, \ldots, 1\}$. We would expect any of the four sliders to yield similar results, but dimension 10 already gives accuracy values of less than 1%; there is no need to increase the dimension.

Based on the number of times the pricing function was called to build such a slider, the computational gain stands at 80% if we only consider 250 scenarios to evaluate. However, this slider was built for 3,131 scenarios. If only 250 scenarios need to be evaluated (as opposed to also 3,131) a lower PCA dimension — higher computational savings — can be used with equally accurate results as for dimension 10. A lower PCA

---

[12]Low p-values — for example, lower than 0.05 — give an indication that the two distributions being compared are not the same.

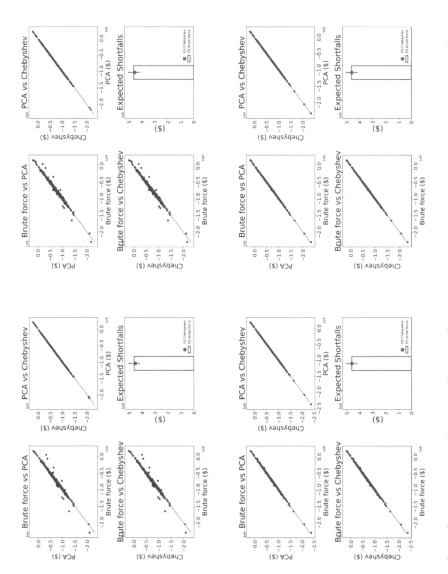

FIGURE 16.3 Portfolio of Swaps, slider configuration {1, 1, …, 1}. Top left: PCA dim. 3. Top right: PCA dim. 5. Bottom left: PCA dim. 10. Bottom right: PCA dim. 20.

TABLE 16.1   Portfolio of swaps, slider configuration {1, 1, ..., 1}.

Slider {1, ..., 1}	PCA dim. 3	PCA dim. 5	PCA dim. 10	PCA dim. 20
ES relative error	2.20%	1.26%	0.24%	0.02%
Computational savings	99.49%	99.17%	98.37%	96.77%
Spearman Correlation	1.00	1.00	1.00	1.00
KS p-value	0.89	0.94	1.00	1.00

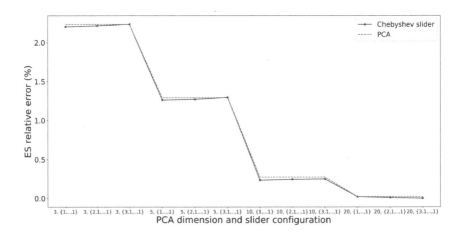

FIGURE 16.4   This figure shows how the Orthogonal Chebyshev Slider relative ES error changes as dimensionality and slider configuration change for portfolio of swaps.

dimension translates into fewer Chebyshev points, fewer pricing function evaluations and, as a consequence, higher computational gains.

16.4.4   Results for swaptions 10-day liquidity horizon

For simplicity, the Chebyshev Slider used for swaptions was the same as for swaps. The number of risk factors affecting swaptions, however, is far greater than that affecting swaps: 425 for swaptions compared to 54 for swaps. Therefore, the number of PCA dimensions used for swaptions was greater than for swaps. As explained in Section 16.3.2, two PCA transformations were used: one to transform the interest rates, the other to transform the implied volatilities. The dimensions chosen for each transformation were 5, 10, 15 and 25. This means the range of total dimensionality reduction used was 10, 20, 30 and 50.

Figure 16.6 and Table 16.2 show the results for the {1, ..., 1} configuration. As can be seen from the top left-hand plot in Figure 16.6, dimension 10 does a poor job. Moreover, the plots show that the source of error is at the level of PCA transformation, not the slider. As soon as the dimension is increased to 20, results improve considerably. With dimension 20, regardless of the configuration, the ES error is less than 4%. At dimension 30 and above, the ES error drops below 1%. Once again, the monotonocity of the PnL

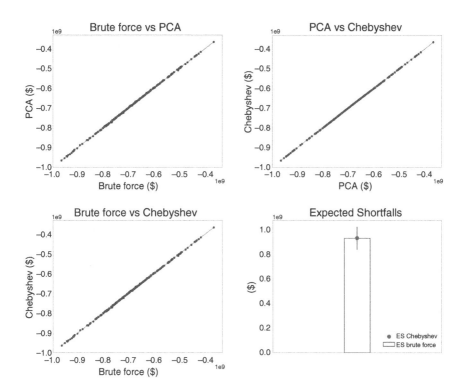

FIGURE 16.5 Portfolio of swaps, slider configuration {1, 1, . . . , 1}, PCA dimension 10, evaluated on the most recent 250 scenarios.

distributions measured by the Spearman correlation metric is perfect and in all but the dimension 10 case, the KS p-value gives a green zone result for the PLA test.

Computational savings are once again significant for the case tested. Even in the extreme case of 50 dimensions — highest computational building cost — the savings are 91.9% for the slider {1, . . . , 1}. Given that ES accuracy is well under 1% for dimension 30, one could choose this dimension, obtaining a computational gain of 95.14%. If the accuracy appetite is within the range 1%–5%, a lower dimension, such as 20, can be chosen, increasing the computational gain to 96.75%.

Just as with swaps, for every fixed PCA dimension, the Orthogonal Chebyshev Slider configuration did not make any material difference to the accuracy of the ES. Figure 16.7 shows how there is a big increase in accuracy going from dimension 10 to 20, which continues decreasing thereafter. However, as the configuration changes within the same dimension, the accuracy is pretty much unaffected.

As said, another lesson learnt from Figure 16.6 is that the error induced by the slider is minimal, despite dealing with a non-linear portfolio. Here we see the strength of the exponential convergence of the Chebyshev slides. The results show that the non-linearity of the function being approximated is well approximated by the slides.

The results presented so far for swaptions in the 10-day liquidity horizon were obtained for 3,108 scenarios. If the 20 dimensional slider with configuration {1, . . . , 1}

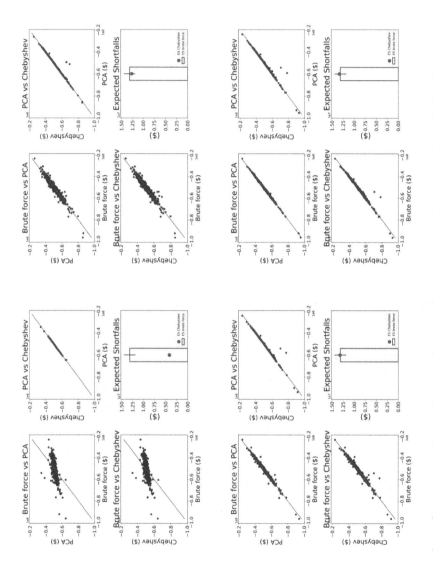

FIGURE 16.6 Portfolio of swaptions, slider configuration {1, 1, ..., 1}, on 10-day liquidity horizon. Top left: PCA dim. 10. Top right: PCA dim. 20. Bottom left: PCA dim. 30. Bottom right: PCA dim. 50.

TABLE 16.2 Portfolio of swaptions, slider configuration $\{1, 1, \ldots, 1\}$ on 10-day liquidity horizon.

Slider $\{1, \ldots, 1\}$	PCA dim. 10	PCA dim. 20	PCA dim. 30	PCA dim. 50
ES relative error	68.47%	3.75%	0.36%	1.41%
Computational savings	98.36%	96.75%	95.14%	91.92%
Spearman Correlation	1.00	1.00	1.00	1.00
KS p-value	0.00	0.93	0.83	1.00

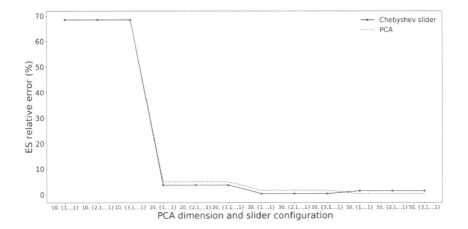

FIGURE 16.7 This figure shows how the Orthogonal Chebyshev Slider relative ES error changes as dimensionality and slider configuration change for portfolio of swaptions, 10-day liquidity horizon.

were used on the last 250 scenarios, for the computation of daily ES within the IMA-FRTB framework, one obtains the results shown in Figure 16.8. The ES relative error is 0.33%, the correlation 1.00, and Kolmogorov-Smirnov p-values 0.93, all excellent results. However, if the slider had been built on the 250 scenarios in question, a much lower dimension could have been used, reducing the building time considerably (see Box 16.4.6).

16.4.5 Results for swaptions 60-day liquidity horizon

As explained in Section 16.3.2, the Orthogonal Chebyshev Sliders built for the 10-day liquidity horizon were used for the 60-day liquidity horizon. This was possible because different PCA transformations were used for interest rates and volatilities, as discussed in Section 16.3.2 where we explain how to deal with different liquidity horizons.

Given that swaptions are more sensitive to rates than volatilities, and that in the 60-day liquidity horizon only volatilities are shocked, the accuracy results are better. This can be clearly seen in Figure 16.9, Figure 16.10 and Table 16.3. Note that

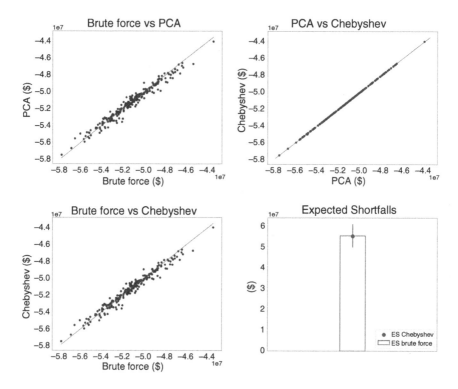

FIGURE 16.8 Portfolio of swaptions, slider configuration $\{1, 1, \ldots, 1\}$, PCA dimension 20, evaluated on the most recent 250 scenarios, for 10-day liquidity horizon.

computational savings in Table 16.3 have been put at 100%. The reason is that there is no overhead building cost involved for the 60-day liquidity horizon calculations; the objects used are the ones built for the 10-day liquidity horizon. Hence, the only cost involved in these calculations comes from the evaluation of the Orthogonal Chebyshev Sliders, which, given the properties presented in Chapter 7, can be evaluated in no time compared to the rest of the calculation. In terms of the metrics used for the PLA test, all sliders with the exception of the 10-dimensional one place the portfolio in the green zone.

Just as was done in other cases, the Orthogonal Chebyshev Sliders were also evaluated on the last 250 scenarios. The results for the 60-day liquidity horizon are shown in Figure 16.11. These correspond to the 20-dimensional slider with configuration $\{1, \ldots, 1\}$, the same one used in the 10-day liquidity horizon. This time, the ES relative error is 0.22%, the correlation 1 and Kolmogorov-Smirnov p-value 0.99; again, excellent results. The computational gain, however, focusing only on the 250 scenarios, is 80%. As has been mentioned, this value would be greatly improved if the Orthogonal Chebyshev Slider was instead built on only the last 250 scenarios, as a lower dimension for PCA can be used. We remind the reader that a lower dimension for PCA translates into fewer Chebyshev points and hence fewer pricing function evaluations (see Box 16.4.6).

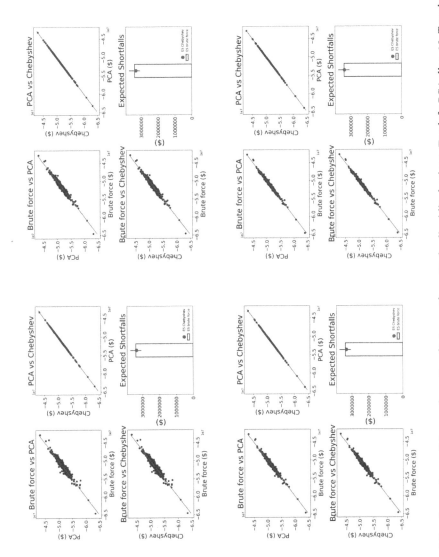

FIGURE 16.9 Portfolio of swaptions, slider configuration {1, 1, . . . , 1}, on 60-day liquidity horizon. Top left: PCA dim. 10. Top right: PCA dim. 20. Bottom left: PCA dim. 30. Bottom right: PCA dim. 50.

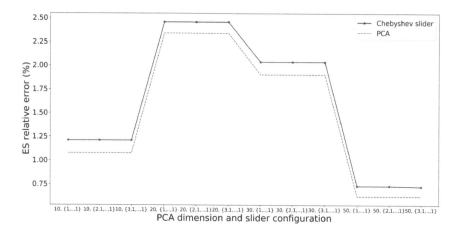

FIGURE 16.10 This figure shows how the Orthogonal Chebyshev Slider relative ES error changes as dimensionality and slider configuration change for swaptions portfolio, 60-day liquidity horizon.

TABLE 16.3 Portfolio of swaptions, slider configuration $\{1, 1, \ldots, 1\}$ on 60-day liquidity horizon.

Slider $\{1, \ldots, 1\}$	PCA dim. 10	PCA dim. 20	PCA dim. 30	PCA dim. 50
ES relative error	1.21%	2.46%	2.04%	0.73%
Computational savings	100%	100%	100%	100%
Spearman Correlation	1.00	1.00	1.00	1.00
KS p-value	0.11	1.00	1.00	0.99

16.4.6 Daily computation and reusability

Daily computation

It must be noted that the daily computation of ES for IMA-FRTB requires a smaller number of evaluations than the ones tested in the PoC. That has the following implications.

For swaps, only one ES value is needed, which means 250 prices suffice. For swaptions, two ES values need to be computed, meaning 500 prices. The Orthogonal Chebyshev Slider built in this PoC was constructed on 10 years' worth of data (about 3,000 days). This was done because the bank wanted to test the technique in the worst-case scenario — namely, when the historical time series contained periods of stress that were not present in the last year of historical data. This has a direct impact on PCA, as capturing the dynamics of the risk factors on 3,000 data points that include periods of stress is much more difficult compared to only 250 data points.

When the technique was calibrated to 3,000 scenarios, we obtained computational savings of 94% for swaps on the last 250 scenarios. This is the result of considering three principal components and five Chebyshev points per component, which gives a total of 15 calls to the pricing function compared to the 250 needed for ES. In the case of swaptions, computational savings stand at 80% when the technique was calibrated on 3,000 scenarios and evaluated only on the last 250 scenarios. The latter was obtained by considering 20 principal components and 5 Chebyshev points per component, which gives a total of 100 calls to the pricing function compared to the 500 needed to compute two ES values.

These computational savings would increase if the Orthogonal Chebyshev Sliders were built on only the last 250 scenarios. This is because a smaller number of principal components is needed to achieve the same level of accuracy, which translates into a smaller number of portfolio revaluations needed to create the Chebyshev Sliders.

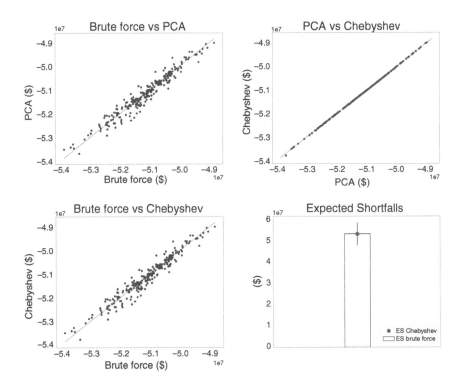

FIGURE 16.11 Portfolio of swaptions, slider configuration $\{1, 1, \ldots, 1\}$, PCA dimension 20, evaluated on the most recent 250 scenarios for 60-day liquidity horizon.

In addition, the question of reusability of Orthogonal Chebyshev Sliders must be seriously considered. The first obvious case — clear from the results presented — is when an Orthogonal Chebyshev Slider is built on 10 years' worth of data and used both for the identification of the period of stress and for the capital calculation of the day in question.

A second case concerns the use of an Orthogonal Chebyshev Slider built on a specific day and used for a whole period of time ahead. The scenarios used to obtain the P&L distribution needed for ES calculations change by only *one* single shock on a day-to-day basis. This means that the PCA built for an Orthogonal Chebyshev Slider on day one will work very well on subsequent days, unless there is a big movement in the market. Also, the Orthogonal Chebyshev Slider, essentially a snapshot of the trade on the day it is built, will be approximating a trade, on the following day, which will have changed very little: only a day closer to maturity. These two things can be monitored and, if carefully done, one should be able to reuse the Orthogonal Chebyshev Sliders for several days, making the computational savings obtained from using this technique much greater than expressed up to now. For example, a 20-dimensional Orthogonal Chebyshev Slider with configuration $\{1, \ldots, 1\}$ can be created every weekend and used for a whole week (5 days); one can then expect computational reductions of about 98% in the case of swaptions.

Another way of reducing the frequency with which Orthogonal Chebyshev Sliders are built is the following. So far all Chebyshev Sliders were built considering time to maturity as a fixed variable. However, the time to maturity of a trade can be included within the input domain of the function f in Equation 16.1. That is, we add time to maturity alongside the principal components obtained from the application of PCA to a set of market shocks. Doing so increases the dimension of the domain space of f. However, as the slider is designed to minimise the number of sampling points needed to build a tensor, increasing the dimension of the slider by one has a very small impact on the building cost of such slider.

For example, if a single slide is built for time to maturity, then the building cost increases only by the number of sampling points used for that slide. Assuming five points per dimension (as we have for the tests run in the PoC; see Section 16.4.2), the extra building cost of incorporating time to maturity in the slider corresponds to only five calls to the pricing function. If we think that time to maturity ought to be paired with another variable in the input domain of f (with the intention of capturing the combined effect of such variable with time to maturity under f), then the slide would need 25 sampling points compared to the 5 it had before time to maturity was incorporated; only 20 extra calls to the pricing function.

However, building a slider that includes time to maturity for a specific period of time (say, 12 weeks) means we would not incur the building cost of the slider for this period of time, considerably increasing computational savings. For example, in the case of the swaptions considered in the PoC, where 100 calls to the pricing function were used to build the object, we would need 105 calls to build the new object that incorporates time to maturity (assuming time to maturity has its own slide), which would be used for the coming 12 weeks. Assuming two ES calculations done five times per week, this translates into 99.7% computational savings compared to brute force.

There are two things to consider if the approach just mentioned is used. The first is that Chebyshev Sliders are built using PCA objects. These PCA objects are constructed using a set of shocks selected on the day the sliders are built. If, at some point in the future, the shocks that need to be evaluated by the slider for the ES calculations are very different from the ones the PCA objects were built with, there is potentially a source of error we need to consider. Therefore, one should monitor how much shocks change to reduce the error introduced by the PCA object obtained when it was first built. Having said that, one should note that if the period used to obtain the historical shocks includes a period of stress, then PCA tends to be quite stable over time.

Also, we need to be aware of possible singularity points along the time dimension of the pricing function of the trade we are building sliders for. If there are singularity points (the result, for example, of payments in the case of interest rate swaps), we would have to consider splines of Chebyshev Sliders. Otherwise, time to maturity is treated just as other variables have been treated throughout this chapter.

It must be noted that the memory footprint of the sliders is very small. This makes them easy to store and reuse once built in situations like the one described. In the PoC described here, the sliders had a memory footprint of about 3 kilobytes per trade.

16.4.7 Beyond regulatory minimum calculations

The point made in the previous Section 16.4.6 opens the door to create an infrastructure that supports the business well beyond the minimum requirements. Once the sliders have been calibrated, their evaluation can be run in a very efficient manner. Therefore, calculations such as what-if type of analysis, pre-trade capital impact, stress capital, intra-day capital calculations and others become computationally easy to do.

For example, let us say that a desk wants to understand the impact of a range of possible incoming trades on the IMA-FRTB capital. Without the solutions discussed in this chapter, the desk must compute the price distributions of the whole range of possible incoming trades. This can be computationally expensive.

With the solutions presented in this chapter, the computation of the price distributions needed takes only a fraction of the time, allowing for what-if type of analysis even within the time constraints of the business. In some cases, this type of analysis may be further accelerated. Indeed, one possibility would be to prebuild the sliders of a range of typical trade types that are frequently dealt. In this way, when the pretrade analysis is done, there is no need to build the sliders and the exercise takes a very short period of time.

Another example is stress testing. If we want to compute an ES under a new set of stressed scenarios, we can use the already existing sliders to do such a computation in no time.

In general, once the sliders of a book of trades have been built for IMA-FRTB, a number of calculations that may seem impossible to do via full revaluation becomes a reality. For more details on these types of calculations in the different applications presented in this book, we refer to Chapter 20.

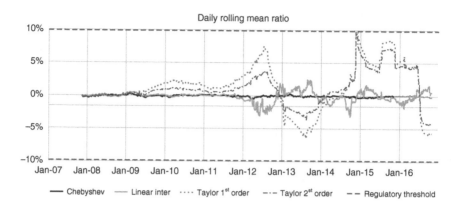

FIGURE 16.12 Daily rolling mean ratio over a period of 10 years for CT, linear interpolation and Taylor approximation to first and second order.

16.5 STABILITY OF TECHNIQUE

The following results show the stability of Orthogonal Chebyshev Sliders in turbulent markets. The test was done in 2016 on a portfolio consisting of a variety of swaps, Bermudan Swaptions, barrier options and American Options. The exercise consisted of an out-of-sample backtesting P&L attribution test, on 10 years of historical data.[13]

The hypothetical P&L was computed using the pricing functions of the trades in the portfolio. The risk theoretical P&L with one of the following methods: Orthogonal CTs, tensors on equidistant grids, Taylor expansion (first and second order). Given that four different approximation techniques were used, four different mean ratios and variance ratios time series were obtained. Figure 16.12 shows the results of all four techniques for the mean ratio test. Figure 16.13 shows the corresponding time series for the variance ratio tests.

In the first few years, the portfolio was out-of-the-money and its linear behaviour dominated. As a result, all approximation techniques do a good job. In 2012 (at the peak of the European Sovereign crisis), markets moved substantially and the non-linearities of the portfolio crystallised. As the figures show, the only technique that was able to price the portfolio with high accuracy, due to the robust mathematical framework it is based on, was the Orthogonal Chebyshev Slider.

16.6 RESULTS BEYOND VANILLA PORTFOLIOS – FURTHER RESEARCH

Here, we have described the results obtained at a tier-one bank for a portfolio of swaps and Vanilla Swaptions. The natural question is, how does this technique perform on other trade types and asset classes?

---

[13]P&L attribution test as per ([7]).

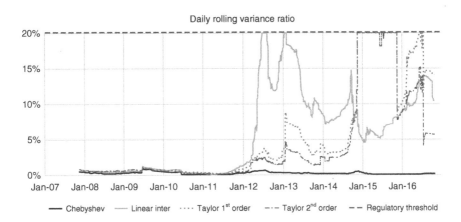

FIGURE 16.13 Daily rolling variance ratio over a period of 10 years for CT, linear interpolation and Taylor approximation to first and second order.

We extended the tests in another bank to Bermudan Swaptions, with similar results. In this case, we had to increase the PCA dimensionality slightly but the results were broadly similar. In general, we see no reason why these techniques should not work beyond these trade types, perhaps not in absolutely all, but we think they should work for the vast majority of trades in a bank's portfolio.

The central element is whether we can find a reasonable dimensionality reduction technique (e.g. PCA) that can transform the input domain of a pricing function to be approximated to a space of a lower dimension. Interest rate, FX, credit and commodity products take as inputs term structures that are highly correlated, hence these asset classes lend themselves naturally to the types of techniques presented in this chapter. In the case of equities, these techniques can be used to handle term structures such as borrow or dividend curves.

We have encountered a number of clients for whom the computational performance of basket options within IMA-FRTB is of great concern. For basket options, the correlation between the defining underlyings is not as great as the correlation within yield curves and volatility surfaces. Nevertheless, from experience we expect 20 or 30 principal components to capture enough of the information within the underlyings. Such dimensions are suitable for both the Tensor Extension Algorithms and the Sliding Technique. Therefore, the techniques presented in this chapter should also work with basket options. This idea has not been tested at the time of this book going to press, but we believe it has the potential to give good results.

16.7 SUMMARY OF CHAPTER

- **Computational load in market risk calculations**. The IMA-FRTB capital calculation requires a high degree of accuracy in the portfolio revaluation for the expected shortfall calculations. The thresholds that determine the required degrees of accuracy are specified in the PLA tests. Traditional techniques based on

Taylor expansions tend to fail such tests. Therefore, more sophisticated techniques are needed as an alternative to portfolio full revaluation with the aim of reducing the computational costs while computing expected shortfall values in a very efficient and accurate manner. In turn, this enables calculations beyond the basic regulatory requirement, such as intra-day what-if type of analysis, portfolio capital optimisation and so on.

- **Hybrid solution used**. The solution presented in this chapter relies on building proxies to the pricing functions used in expected shortfall calculations. The Composition Technique is first applied using the parametrisation obtained through PCA. The resulting function is then replicated with Chebyshev Sliders. The resulting objects (combination of PCA and Chebyshev Sliders) are called Orthogonal Chebyshev Sliders.

- **Accuracy**. The expected shortfall values obtained with Orthogonal Chebyshev Sliders had an error of about 1% when compared to the benchmark, the latter obtained using original pricing functions. Moreover, all PLA tests were passed with no major issues and were stable over time.

- **Computational gains**. When the test was performed on 10 years' worth of data, computational gains were generally greater than 95%. If applied to only the last year (250 scenarios), computational gains stand at about 90%. This assumes daily calibration of the Orthogonal Chebyshev Sliders, which is the worst-case scenario. However, if these are calibrated once and used for days or weeks, computational gains exceed 99%.

- **Revaluation grids**. Revaluation grids, often used by banks in the context of VaR calculations, can be enhanced substantially by simply moving the grid points to Chebyshev points.

## CHAPTER 17

Dynamic sensitivities

T his chapter presents another application of the techniques presented in Part III. This time, the focus is the computation of dynamic sensitivities, that is, the sensitivities of a given portfolio within a Monte Carlo (MC) simulation, in a stochastic fashion.

Sensitivities of portfolios are typically computed every day within banks. They are used on a vast range of calculations including daily P&L risk management and hedging, VaR calculations and the associated regulatory capital, stress testing, spot initial margins (IM) and so on. They are so ubiquitous and broadly used that sometimes the word *risk* is used as a substitute for *sensitivities*.

It is common practice for banks to compute forward portfolio valuations inside MC simulations (e.g. XVA and IMM capital simulations). Indeed, Chapter 15 is dedicated to solving the computational bottleneck for these types of calculations. However, to the our knowledge, very few financial institutions (if any) compute forward sensitivities.

Computing forward sensitivities would bring many advantages, for example, better understanding of expected and tail-event hedging needs, VaR and SA-FRTB capital simulations, better management of future IM funding costs, accurate margin value adjustment (MVA) values and so on.

If enough computational power is available, one would want to compute these sensitivities using the official pricing functions already found in the bank's pricing libraries. As a result, this constitutes the benchmark — in terms of accuracy — against which we measure any other method for computing dynamic sensitivities.

In this chapter, we will show how one of the hybrid techniques in Part III can be used to massively accelerate the computation of dynamic sensitivities within an MC simulation. In particular, we show through numerical calculations presented in Section 17.4 how dynamic sensitivities can be obtained with substantial computational reductions (up to 97.5%) compared to the benchmark approach — using pricing functions — while keeping very high levels of accuracy both at an averaged and tail-event level.

The chapter is structured as follows. First, we discuss how sensitivities are simulated using MC simulations and the computational bottleneck associated with these simulations. We then explain how to alleviate the computational bottleneck associated with the computation of dynamic sensitivities; this uses the techniques presented in Part III. Then we introduce one of the main uses of dynamic sensitivities: the computation of dynamic initial margin (DIM), where we take the definition of IM put forward by ISDA — and now a standard in the industry — which is based on sensitivities. Finally, we present the results of numerical tests done on two trade types — an FX Swap and a spread option — as examples, and discuss how the presented techniques can be extended to other trade types.

17.1   SIMULATING SENSITIVITIES

Dynamic sensitivities are a desired feature of MC simulations. For illustration purposes throughout this chapter, we focus on the computation of dynamic sensitivities for a single trade. Most calculations are done at portfolio or netting set level. Therefore, the computation of dynamic sensitivities for a given set of trades is done by computing the dynamic sensitivities of each trade in the set and then aggregating their individual contributions.

17.1.1   Scenario diffusion

To compute the dynamic sensitivities of a trade, we first have to simulate the market risk factors that affect the trade. Just as described in Chapter 15, market risk factors are simulated using risk factor diffusion models. These are stochastic models for which a set of model parameters need to first be specified at calibration. Once these are calibrated, model risk factors are diffused. Once again, for simplicity of illustration we use the HW one-factor model as an example. Once its parameters (such as mean reversion speed) have been specified at calibration, the model generates a value for the short rate at each node of the simulation, where a node is the intersection of a simulated path with a time point. The stochastic equation that models the behaviour of the short rate is given by Equation 5.2. Then, for each value of the short rate, a whole yield curve (with as many tensors as needed) is generated. This yield curve is expressed in terms of the parameters (fixed at calibration) and the short rate. Therefore, at each MC node, the whole yield curve is fully defined in terms of a single variable: the short rate.

The process just described determines a whole yield curve at every node of the MC simulation. If the trade in question, for which we want to compute sensitivities, depends on risk factors other than the ones in the yield curve just mentioned, then we generate them using a corresponding risk factor diffusion model, for example, an FX model, an equity model and so on.

17.1.2   Computing sensitivities

Once all the risk factors (for example, the HW short rate) affecting the trade in question have been generated for each node of the MC simulation, we compute the sensitivities of the trade with respect to its market risk factors at each node.

There is not a single way of obtaining sensitivities. However, the canonical and the one we use as benchmark is via finite differences using officially approved pricing functions, often called the "front-office pricers" in banks. If calling the pricing function once per node in the MC simulation amounts to a considerably expensive calculation — the reduction of this cost is the focus of Chapter 15 — computing a collection of sensitivities, where each sensitivity consists of at least two calls to the pricing function, represents a much larger computational cost.

17.1.3   Computational cost

As we mentioned before, dynamic sensitivities are a desired feature of MC simulations. Consider a reference MC simulation consisting of 10,000 paths and 100 time points in the future. The computational complexity of computing a set of present values (PVs) on these scenarios is $\mathcal{O}(10^6)$. This represents, for example, the typical computational load of a CVA calculation — such as the ones presented in Chapter 15. In the case of dynamic sensitivities, however, where a set of sensitivities must be computed per scenario, the computational cost is much higher. If we assume an average of 10–100 sensitivities per trade, the cost has order between $\mathcal{O}(10^7)$ and $\mathcal{O}(10^8)$. This cost is prohibitively high, more so considering the already large number of risk calculations that need to be done on a regular basis in most financial institutions.

17.1.4 Methods available

The substantial computational load associated with the computation of dynamic sensitivities has forced practitioners to look for alternative ways to model them. Most of these come in the form of algorithmic solutions. Any potential solution should ideally have the following three properties. It should be accurate — we want to be able to replicate the sensitivities within the MC simulation to a high degree of accuracy. It should be efficient to build and evaluate — the cost involved in using the technique should not exceed the cost of using the pricing functions within the risk engine to simulate sensitivities. Finally, its implementation and maintenance should be as simple as possible — ideally, it should be a feature easily added to existing MC engines.

The first method to be aware of is the one that uses pricing functions to compute sensitivities via finite differences. As mentioned before, this is the method we use as benchmark; we will evaluate our solution in terms of speed and accuracy against this. The cost of this approach amounts to between $\mathcal{O}(10^7)$ and $\mathcal{O}(10^8)$. Note that the officially approved pricing functions in a financial institution are designed for accuracy and not always speed. This means that computing dynamic sensitivities this way gives accurate values. However, the cost of obtaining them is significant — often impossible given the computational power available and natural time constraints of the business.

When it comes to the topic of sensitivities computed dynamically within an MC simulation, one of the most famous methods is Adjoint Algorithmic Differentiation (AAD). This is a very powerful yet complicated technique. It has the advantage of computing sensitivities to their exact value. Moreover, its computational cost is unaffected by the number of sensitivities to compute.

AAD comes with two challenges. It has a sizeable computational cost, generally estimated to be between 5 and 10 times that of a typical CVA calculation, but easily up to 20 times if the implementation is not done carefully — this equates to between $\mathcal{O}(10^7)$ and $\mathcal{O}(10^8)$, assuming an MC simulation with 1,000,000 nodes. Another problem is that its implementation is often very difficult. The challenges presented are not just technical in nature, but considerable implementation effort puts a load on project management, budget approval and timely delivery. These issues make AAD sometimes impossible to implement, especially in already existing systems.

In Section 17.2, we present the method that we find ideal to significantly accelerate the computation of dynamic sensitivities with hardly any practical loss of accuracy, and with a computational burden of $\mathcal{O}(10^5)$. Also, one aspect that will be evident from the description is that its implementation is much simpler than that of AAD, especially in existing MC engines.

17.2 THE SOLUTION

What we want to do — as is the case in all applications we present in this book — is replicate the sensitivity function to be used for the computation with a proxy that is accurate and much faster to evaluate. The usual proxies we consider are DNNs and CTs. In order to optimise the calculation, we propose a combination of the Composition Technique presented in Chapter 5 and function approximation technique (DNN or CT).

The instance of the Composition Technique that constitutes the basis for the solution we propose makes use of the RFE models that drive the MC simulation. This falls into the instance of the Composition Technique described in Section 5.1. As we will see in Section 17.4, when implemented correctly, this technique gives very high levels of accuracy at the level of dynamic sensitivities.

To fully understand the solution presented, we need some details about RFE models. These have been covered in other sections of the book, but for the sake of completeness we cover the essential elements here, relying on the notation presented in Section 5.1. Unless the reader is familiar with these models, we recommend reading Section 5.1.

Without loss of generality, we work with an HW one-factor model. Although simple, it has all the elements we need from an RFE model. What we describe from now on is equally valid for any other RFE model.

The stochastic differential equation of the HW model is given by

$$dr_t = a(b - r_t)dt + \sigma dW_t. \tag{17.1}$$

The model parameters are $\theta = (a, b, \sigma)$ and its only stochastic variable W. The space of model risk factors $\mathcal{R}$ is the space spanned by the short rate r. Using the notation in 5.1, we say that this model has one degree of freedom, or dimension $k = 1$. Other models may have different degrees of freedom; the HW model itself can be extended to two degrees of freedom, $k = 2$. Other models may have larger values of k. However, in the context of MC simulations for XVA, IMM or PFE, k tends to be small.

RFE models need to be calibrated first. This means that parameter values need to be specified, typically based on current market quotes or historical data. Once this has been done, they remain fixed throughout the simulation.

RFE models come equipped with the ability to generate market risk factors; the space of market risk factors was denoted by $\mathcal{S}$ in Section 5.1. As mentioned before, in the case of the HW one-factor model, the short rate r (more generally, the model risk factors) fully determines the market risk factors. For example, given a value of the short rate, this determines, along with the values of the model parameters identified at calibration, a full swap rate curve with as many tensors as needed. Other examples of market risk factors are interest rates in general, spreads, volatilities and so on. The space of market risk factors has high dimension, sometimes in the hundreds (e.g. collections of swap rates and implied volatility surfaces). We denote the dimension of the market space by n.

Using the notation from Section 5.1, let g be the parametrisation of the market risk factors in terms of model risk factors

$$\underset{\mathbb{R}^k}{\text{Model Space}} \quad \xrightarrow{\;g\;} \quad \underset{\mathbb{R}^n.}{\text{ISDA Sensitivities Space}} \tag{17.2}$$

In the case of the HW one-factor model, g is given by

$$\left(S(t, T_1), \ldots, S(t, T_n)\right) = \left(A(t, T_1)e^{B(t,T_1)r(t)}, \ldots, A(t, T_n)e^{B(t,T_n)r(t)}\right)$$

where $S(t, T)$ denotes an interest rate between t and T, $r(t)$ is the short rate, T_i a time point ahead of t, and where A and B only depend on the parameters θ and today's yield curve. The definition of A and B can be found in Section 5.1.

The crucial point to note — as always with the Composition Technique — is that functions like g are analytic for most RFE models used in finance and hence lend themselves very well to be approximated with CTs or DNNs.[1] Therefore, composing g with a function P (often a pricing function, but in our present case a sensitivities or greek function) yields a function f (Equation 5.1) with an input domain of dimension k, where k is often small, which can be efficiently replicated by the approximating methods presented in Part I. This is regardless of the value of n — that is, the number of tensor points on the yield curve.

17.2.1 Hybrid method

In what follows we show how we build proxies to compute sensitivities within an MC simulation. As an example, we use a foreign exchange swap. This is one of the trade types for which results are presented in Section 17.4. Whatever is said equally applies to any other trade type.

Example

Let the pricing function of an FX Swap be P. This function takes market risk factors as inputs. These are swap rates (for two different currencies and two curves per currency) and the exchange rate. Notice we are after the sensitivities of P with respect to each of these market risk factors. Say there are n risk factors in total. In our example of the FX Swap $n \sim 100$, say between 20 and 30 points per curve and a single exchange rate. The number of market risk factors n affecting a pricing function can vary substantially; the variation can go from less than 10 to the thousands.

---

[1]See Definition 3.2.1 for what it means to be analytic and Section 13.1 for a discussion on pricing functions and the property of being analytic.

Consider a single time point within the MC simulation. The sensitivity of P to each market risk factor must be computed at each scenario. As an example, let the i-th swap rate be s_i. Consider the sensitivity function

$$S_i = \frac{\partial P}{\partial s_i}.$$

Applying the Composition Technique to S_i, via the parametrisation g of the risk factor generating model, gives f.

$$\mathbb{R}^k \xrightarrow{\ g\ } \mathbb{R}^n \xrightarrow{\ S_i\ } \mathbb{R} \tag{17.3}$$

$$\underbrace{\phantom{\mathbb{R}^k \xrightarrow{\ g\ } \mathbb{R}^n \xrightarrow{\ S_i\ } \mathbb{R}}}_{f}$$

Note that g is the result of putting together all the parametrisations that affect the trade in question. Likewise, k is the sum of the dimensions of the input domains of such parametrisations. In the case of the FX Swap, there are five models: each currency has two yield curves, one for forward projections and one for discounting. In the numerical tests (results of which are shown in Section 17.4), each curve was simulated using a two-factor Gaussian model as an RFE model. Additionally, the FX rate was simulated with a one-factor log-normal Brownian motion model. This gives a total of $k = 9$.

By definition, the function f gives the value of the partial derivative of P with respect to s_i at each node of the simulation. This means that any method used to replicate f replicates the sensitivity. Each node of the simulation is generated by the parametrisation g. That is, for every set of market risk factors s, in the MC simulation, there is a unique set of model risk factors r, such that $s = g(r)$. Therefore, the composition described in Equation 17.3 reduces the dimension of the approximation problem that we need to deal with most substantially, without introducing any error.

The description given so far has made the assumption that the only variables of interest when defining f are the model risk factors. We should take a closer look at this, which is what we do next.

Variables at play

Just like in previous applications, where the Composition Technique has been used, we need to identify the variables at play to determine how to build the approximation architectures presented in Part I. As Section 13.2 explains, there are different types of parameters that affect pricing functions — in this case, sensitivities functions — namely RFE model parameters, market quotes, model stochastic factors and trade-specific parameters.

As is the case with many of the applications we present, the pricing functions considered are calibrated before the calculation in question, and the RFE model parameters obtained from this calibration remain fixed throughout the calculation. These parameters, therefore, do not need to be considered as part of the domain of f, unless we want to create a replica of f that works for a range of RFE model parameters. This, however, complicates the problem substantially. We therefore assume that f is calibrated once more whenever those parameters change.

Section 17.2.1 describes the Composition Technique we employ to reduce the dimension of P from n, which tends to be high, to k, which tends to be much lower. What we are after is the evaluation of P with respect to its market risk factors. The composition in Equation 17.3 changes the domain of P that is given in terms of market risk factors to the domain of f given in terms of model risk factors. It is important to include *all* the model risk factors in the domain of f. This is because the market state of each scenario in each time point of the MC simulation is fully determined by the value of the model factors at that node. Therefore, this is all that is needed (and nothing else) to capture the risk.

When it comes to trade-specific parameters, the only variable that could potentially have an impact is time to maturity. All others remain fixed throughout the calculation. Notice this means the strike of each trade in question is fixed. Therefore, whichever approximating method is used to replicate the function f that results from the Composition Technique replicates the instance of the trade determined by the strike of the trade.

As mentioned, time to maturity can be considered as one of the variables that defines the function f. This increases the dimension of f by one, which may be a suitable thing to do in some cases but not all.

If time to maturity is included, one must identify singularity points along this dimension. For example, one must identify payment dates defined by the trade. In the presence of singularity points, one must work with splines (see Section 3.8). Otherwise, one can include time to maturity within the domain of f without further considerations.

Including time to maturity in the domain of f can help (especially in the absence of singularities) increase computational gains. Also, it allows us to increase the number of time points in the MC simulation considerably, since the approximators are very fast to evaluate and the vast majority of the computational overhead comes from the calibration of the proxy function — once the approximator has been built, we can use it as often as we want without incurring major computational overheads.

If time to maturity is not included in the domain of f, then we build a replica of f for each time point in the simulation. This may be particularly suited if one is not interested in many time points for the MC simulation, or if the number of singularity points along the time dimension is such that building splines becomes inconvenient.

Possible proxies

Once the Composition Technique (Equation 17.3) has been applied, we need to decide which approximation method to use. By construction, the dimension k of the input domain of f is low. Therefore, f lends itself very well to be approximated by CTs, as the quasi-exponential convergence means that very few evaluations of f are needed to achieve high degrees of accuracy. This is what we did in the tests, the results of which are presented in Section 17.4. However, a DNN or any other approximating object of choice could have been used, at the expense of relinquishing the exponential convergence that

CTs offer, which, to our knowledge, offers the best possible balance between accuracy and number of sample points.

Let us consider the case where we create a proxy function per MC time point. To build a CT for f, one does the following. Take the minimum and maximum value of each of the model space variables at the time point in question of the MC simulation. For example, in the case of the HW one-factor model, this would consist of the minimum and maximum values of the short rate. These values determine the hyper-rectangle — one-dimensional interval, in the case of HW one-factor model — in which f needs to be evaluated. Notice, the hyper-rectangle just mentioned is contained in $\mathbb{R}^k$. Next, build a Chebyshev grid on this hyper-rectangle. Finally, call the function f on the points of the Chebyshev grid.

Once the hyper-rectangle in $\mathbb{R}^k$ is ready, one must decide how to build the CT: either directly, by evaluating each grid point, obtaining a full Chebyshev Tensor, or by using one of the Tensor Extension Algorithms. The latter requires evaluating f only on a fraction of the total grid points. This information is then extended to the whole grid as explained in Chapter 6. In our experience, if k is between 1 and 4, one can build a full CT. For example, if the trade is an interest rate swap, where each yield curve is modelled with a one- or two-factor model, then the resulting tensors have two or four dimensions. If k is greater than 4, one ought to consider the use of the Tensor Extension Algorithms.

17.3 AN IMPORTANT USE OF DYNAMIC SENSITIVITIES

We have already mentioned that the sensitivities of a netting set or portfolio are regularly computed for a range of purposes. One that has gained particular attention in recent years is the computation of initial margin (IM).

CCR is the area within risk management that studies the impact of one counterparty defaulting on another. Specifically, if there are two counterparties — A and B — that have sold derivative contracts to one another, CCR studies the impact that a default of counterparty B would have on counterparty A.

To mitigate CCR potential losses, the industry has adopted — through a mix of practice and regulation — a series of measures to try to prevent the impact of this risk, namely, variation margin (VM) and IM. VM covers potential default-related losses from today's netting set value. IM covers potential losses from changes in the netting set value from the moment in which a default happens until the netting set at risk can be liquidated or hedged. IM can be perceived, intuitively, as a VaR number, as it tries to measure (for example) the worst 99% of the losses over a 10-day liquidation or rehedging period.

Both VM and IM carry risks and costs to the institutions posting them, for example, liquidity risk and funding cost. Their purpose is to reduce (basically, to nearly wipe out) CCR, bringing CVA, PFE and CCT capital to a very low number. Other calculations like MVA (the present value of funding cost of future IM in a portfolio) or the upcoming CVA-FRTB capital are also affected by IM.

In order to price IM into these numbers, one has to simulate it dynamically in an MC engine. This is the challenge we tackle now, because the IM calculation is often based on sensitivities, so an immediate application of dynamic sensitivities is being able to simulate IMs dynamically — that is, to simulated *Dynamic Initial Margin* (DIM).

In the next section, we are going to test the methods proposed in previous sections for dynamic sensitivities in the context of DIM. For this, the version of IM we use is the Standard Initial Margin Model (SIMM) proposed by ISDA and by now an industry standard.

17.4   NUMERICAL TESTS

This section presents the results of a set of tests run on two trade types — an FX Swap and a European Spread Option. The idea is to explore the accuracy and computational gains obtained with the techniques previously presented, compared to the benchmark approach. We compute IM profiles as it is market standard.

Two different MC simulations were run: one for the FX Swap, the other for the European Spread Option. In both cases, we use a combination of the Composition Technique and CTs, as presented in Section 17.2. Given the different characteristics of the trades, we built a full CT per time point and sensitivity in the case of the FX Swap, while only one CT per sensitivity, using the Tensor Extension Algorithms (Chapter 6), in the case of the spread option.

The accuracy of the technique is measured with respect to the benchmark. The latter is obtained by computing dynamic sensitivities using the original pricing functions, either through finite differences in a brute-force fashion — as was the case for the FX Swap — or directly as a result of the pricing routine — as was the case for the spread option based on MC simulations. The time taken using CTs in each case is measured and compared to the time taken to perform the benchmark calculation.

Note that IM profiles should be computed at netting set level. Our tests considered only a couple of trades, each constituting its own netting set. The technique employed naturally extends to a netting set with multiple trades by applying it trade by trade and aggregating the sensitivities.

The tests were done in MATLAB, on a standard laptop with i7 cores. Calculations were parallelised whenever possible, in particular for the benchmark calculations, given their high computational cost.

17.4.1   FX Swap

The FX Swap was between USD and EUR, at-the-money and had 5 years to maturity. The pricing routine used was the one implemented in the swapbyzero function in MATLAB, which is analytic. Sensitivities were obtained by finite difference using this pricing routine.

The MC simulation used consisted of 10,000 paths and 11 time points, covering the full lifespan of the trade.

The sensitivities we compute are the ones specified by ISDA required for the computation of SIMM. These risk factors consist of a collection of swap rates in two currencies (USD and EUR) and the exchange rate. Each currency has two yield curves: one for forwarding and one for discounting. Each of the yield curves were diffused using a two-factor Gaussian model. The exchange rate was diffused using Geometric Brownian Motion.

FX Swaps have payment dates. These create discontinuities in the pricing function along the time dimension. One way to deal with these discontinuities is to use Chebyshev Splines (Section 3.8), splitting the domain of approximation at the points determined by the payment dates. However, we opted to simply build a CT per time point in the simulation. Note that by doing so, time to maturity is a constant parameter for each CT.

Given the RFE models used and the market risk factors involved, the tensors had dimension 9. The domain over which they were built was determined by the range (minimum and maximum in each dimension) of the model space risk factors diffused at each time point of the simulation. Four points per dimension were used to build the Chebyshev grid. This gives a grid with 262,144 points. This tensor would take a long time to build directly. Therefore, the Sample Adaptive Algorithm presented in Chapter 6 was used, which only used between 300 and 500 pricing function evaluations to build the CT in TT format. For more details on the parameters used for the Sample Adaptive Algorithm and its performance, we refer to Appendix E.1.

The following figures show relative error distributions of the CTs built to compute dynamic sensitivities for two risk factors at three different time points of the simulation. Figure 17.1 shows the errors for the first swap rate of the USD forwarding yield curve. Figure 17.2 shows the errors for the exchange rate. Note that the vast majority of the errors are well under 1%. In fact, for all the risk factors considered, the maximum error was always below 1.5% (see Table 17.1).

Define EIM as the expected initial margin and PFIM as the potential future initial margin at 95% confidence level, at each future time point. Figure 17.3 shows EIM and PFIM profiles obtained with the benchmark and with CTs. As can be seen in Figure 17.3 and Table 17.1, the errors are all below 0.34%.

17.4.2 European Spread Option

A European Spread Option is an option between the spread of two spot underlyings (e.g. two equities). The chosen trade had one year to maturity. The pricing routine used is based on the spreadsensbyls function in MATLAB and is MC based. That is, we have a nested MC simulation. The outer simulation, for sensitivities and DIM, consisted of 10,000 paths. The inner simulation, for the local pricing routine, consisted of 1,000 paths.

The inner simulation was run with antithetic variates, and the average evaluation time was 0.5 seconds per sensitivity. Given the evaluation time and the size of the MC simulation for the computation of dynamic sensitivities, a full benchmark calculation took, even with parallelisation, up to 10 hours for each risk factor.

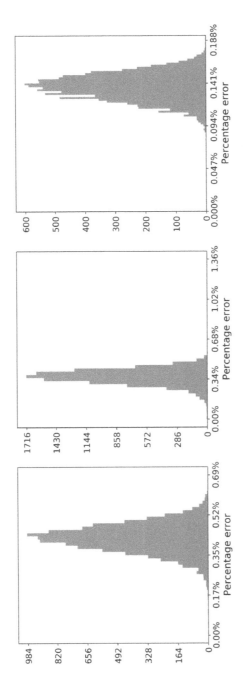

FIGURE 17.1 Percentage relative errors of CTs for sensitivity to the first swap rate of the USD forwarding yield curve. Histograms correspond from left to right, to the second, sixth and eleventh time point in the simulation.

285

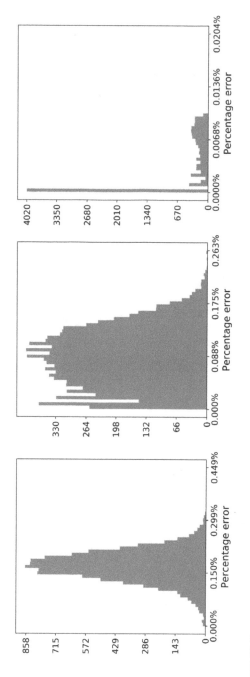

FIGURE 17.2 Percentage relative errors of CTs for sensitivity to the USD/EUR exchange rate. Histograms correspond from left to right, to the second, sixth and eleventh time point in the simulation.

TABLE 17.1 Maximum relative percentage error for market sensitivities, EIM and PFIM (95% quantile) profiles for the FX Swap.

FX Swap	ISDA sensitivities	EIM	PFIM
Maximum relative error	1.5%	0.34%	0.32%

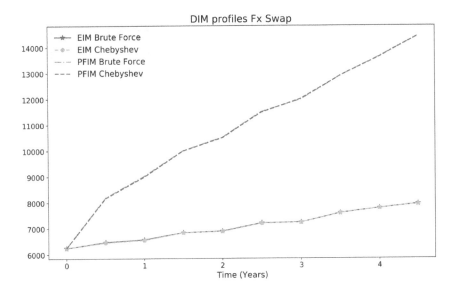

FIGURE 17.3 IM profiles — expectation and 95% quantiles — for FX Swap obtained with the benchmark (brute force) and with CTs.

Given the number of times the pricing routine was called for the benchmark calculations, the number of paths within the pricing routine had to be kept reasonably low for practical reasons. With 1,000 paths, the 95% quantile of the noise of spot sensitivities (i.e. the delta) was measured at 7.4%. Reducing the noise by half would require (roughly) increasing the number of paths by an order of magnitude, from 1,000 to 10,000. This would take the benchmark computation of dynamic sensitivities, for spot, from 10 hours to several days. Therefore, it was decided to stick to 1,000 paths.

The situation was worse for the sensitivities of the remaining risk factors (i.e. non-spot risk factors). For Vega sensitivities, the 95% quantile of the noise was measured at 32.7%; for swap rates, it was measured at 11.23%. Correcting this would increase computational times considerably. Therefore, only delta dynamic sensitivities are presented.

Ideally, we would like to report results also for an American-style option. However, due to the time it would take to produce benchmark results, this is not possible. This is due to two reasons. First, the American-style pricing function takes about five times longer than its European equivalent for the same number of paths. Second, the numerical noise of the American-style pricer is far greater than its European equivalent for the same number of paths. As a result, the number of paths in the American-style pricer needed to be increased considerably in order to obtain a reasonable numerical noise. Consequently, we could only run numerical tests on a European-style option.

However, as was highlighted in Section 13.1, the type of payoff does not hinder the approximation properties of the CTs. It is therefore expected that, with enough computational power, similar results would be obtained for the American version of this trade.

The MC simulation for the computation of dynamic sensitivities consisted of 10,000 paths and 11 time points in the future, covering the full lifespan of the trade.

No discontinuities are present along the time dimension for this trade. Therefore, the CTs built included time to maturity as a variable. This means that only one tensor per market risk factor was built.

The spread option takes two spot underlyings, two volatilities (one for each underlying) and a yield curve. The underlyings were diffused using the Heston model, which diffuses both the spot and the volatility stochastically. The yield curve was diffused using an HW one-factor model. Given the dimensions of the RFE models just mentioned and that time to maturity was considered a variable, the tensors built had six dimensions: five for the model space variables diffusing market risk factors, and one for the time to maturity.

The tensor domains were built by considering the minimum and maximum values attained by the model space variables diffused in the MC simulation, along with the time to maturity of the trade. Six points per dimension were chosen for the grid. This gives a total of 46,656 grid points. Once again, the Sample Adaptive Algorithm was used to obtain a CT in TT format that approximates the sensitivities needed. Only 12,000 random grid points were used to run the Sample Adaptive Algorithm. For more details on the parameters used for the Sample Adaptive Algorithm and its performance, we refer to Appendix E.2.

Figure 17.5 shows relative error distributions of the CT built to compute dynamic sensitivities for one of the spot underlyings in the spread option at three different time points of the simulation. Note that most errors measured are within the noise of the delta function presented in Figure 17.4.

Figure 17.6 shows equity delta margin profiles, as defined by SIMM, at expectation level (EIM) and 95% quantiles (PFIM) obtained with the benchmark and with CTs.

The maximum error for market sensitivities was 10.7%. However, the vast majority of the errors were below 5%, as the ones presented in Figure 17.5. The maximum errors at the level of delta margin profiles were 8.1% and 3.1%, for EIM and PFIM, respectively (Table 17.2). Given the noise presented in Figure 17.4 for the benchmark calculation, the main source of error in the EIM and PFIM comes from the noise intrinsic in the approximated function itself.

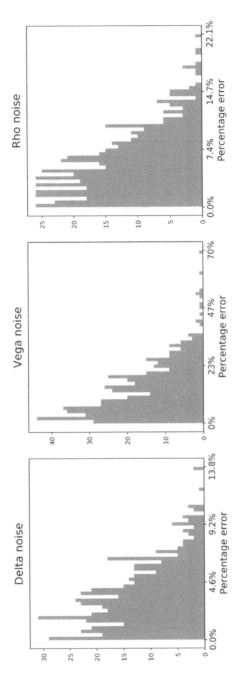

FIGURE 17.4 Noise distribution for the MC-based spread option pricing function. Histograms correspond from left to right to the noise for Delta, Vega and Rho.

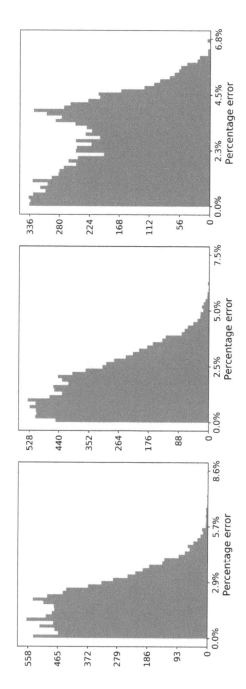

FIGURE 17.5 Percentage relative errors of CTs for the first spot. Histograms correspond from left to right, to the second, sixth and eleventh time point in the simulation.

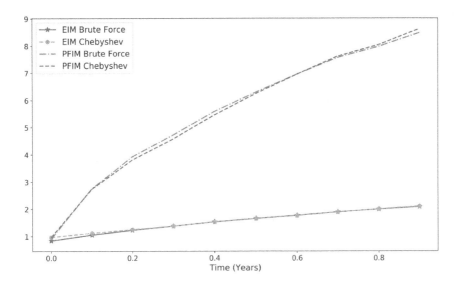

FIGURE 17.6 Equity delta margin profiles — at expectation and 95% quantiles — for the European spread option obtained with the benchmark (brute-force) and with CTs. The difference between the benchmark and Chebyshev profiles is mostly attributed to the MC noise in the benchmark pricing function.

TABLE 17.2 Maximum relative percentage error for market sensitivities, EIM and PFIM delta margin profiles for the spread option. EIM profile corresponds to expected IM, while PFE to 95% quantile. Most of these errors are attributed to the noise present in the approximated function itself.

Spread option	Market sensitivities	EIM	PFIM
Maximum relative error	10.7%	8.1%	3.1%

17.5 DISCUSSION OF RESULTS

This section discusses the performance gains obtained with the tested techniques. Granular details of how the gain metrics are obtained can be found in Appendix E.

For the FX Swap, the level of accuracy for dynamic sensitivities was high all the way through the simulation and for all risk factors. The highest relative error for sensitivities measured at 1.5%. However, for almost all risk factors, the maximum relative error was below 1%. This translated into small errors at the level of DIM profiles where both EIM and PFIM had maximum relative errors less than 0.35% (see Table 17.1).

These results were expected. The pricing function is analytic and the lack of optionality makes the trade fairly linear; few Chebyshev points are needed to approximate the sensitivities to a high degree of accuracy. This is not only reflected in the high accuracy values but also in the short training times of the Sample Adaptive Algorithm (see Table 17.3)

TABLE 17.3 Computational savings obtained by using CTs in TT format to compute dynamic sensitivities compared to benchmark method for the FX Swap. Note that the extra computational costs that come from training and evaluating the CT tensors is very small compared to the brute-force approach. Computational gains essentially come from the difference between total evaluations via brute force and number of samples needed to calibrate the CT.

Brute-force (benchmark) evaluations	Sampling evaluations	Reduction of calls to function	Extra comp. cost	Comp. savings
20,000	300 ~ 500	98.00%	3.53%	96.46%

Given that the technique used is applied identically regardless of sensitivity and time point in the simulation, computational savings are estimated for a single sensitivity and at a time point of the MC simulation. The results are presented in Table 17.3. Computing benchmark sensitivities, for a single risk factor, on a single time point, requires 20,000 calls to the pricing function — remember we use finite differences that require two calls to the pricing function per sensitivity, and there are 10,000 nodes at each time point. The Sample Adaptive Algorithm needed between 300 and 500 calls. This represents a reduction of around 98.00% in the number of times the pricing function has to be called. There are extra computational cost overheads that comes from the training of the Sample Adaptive Algorithm and the evaluation of the CT tensors on the 10,000 nodes. This amounts to 3.53% of the brute-force effort. When all components are considered, we get computational savings of 96.46%. For more details on the different components involved in the estimation of computational gains, we refer to Appendix E.1.

The spread option uses an MC-based pricer. In this case, the accuracy achieved by the single CT built to approximate delta is within the noise reported in Figure 17.4 (see Figure 17.5 and Table 17.2). This accuracy translates into similar accuracy levels at the level of delta margin profiles, as can be seen in Figure 17.6 and Table 17.2.

For the spread option, computing the benchmark dynamic sensitivities for a single risk factor, within the whole MC simulation, required 110,000 calls to the pricing function (10,000 paths, 11 time points). The Sample Adaptive Algorithm needed only 12,000. This represents a reduction of 89.10% in the number of times the pricing function is called. The computational cost relating to the training of the Sample Adaptive Algorithm and evaluation of CT tensors on all nodes represents only 0.49% of the computational cost associated with the brute-force approach. For the MC simulation used, which had only 11 time points, the computational gains come to 88.60%.

In a more realistic simulation with 100 time points, CTs would have been built in the same way since time to maturity was included in the domain of approximation of the CT. Results are presented in Table 17.4. In this case, the reduction on the number of times the pricing function has to be called stands at 98.80%, extra computational costs are 0.25% of the brute-force approach and total computational gains come to 98.55%. For more details on the different components involved in the estimation of computational gains, we refer to Appendix E.2.

TABLE 17.4 Computational savings obtained by using CTs in TT format to compute dynamic sensitivities compared to benchmark method for the spread option. Note that the extra computational cost coming from training of the CTs in TT format and their evaluation is negligible compared to the computational cost of the brute-force approach. Most of the computational gains come from the difference between total evaluations via brute force and number of samples needed to calibrate the CT.

Brute-force (benchmark) evaluations	Sampling evaluations	Reduction of calls to function	Extra comp. cost	Comp. savings
1,000,000	12,000	98.80%	0.25%	98.55%

The levels of accuracy are such that CTs should price MVA stably and provide good measures of MVA sensitivities, allowing for sound hedging. Also, the high levels of accuracy should make this DIM model easily approved by regulators, reducing IMM capital without the need of any extra capital buffers.[2] Moreover, dynamic sensitivities simulations can be used for hedging, VaR and SA-FRTB. It can also be used inside portfolio optimisation routines in order to minimise future IM funding costs.

17.6 ALTERNATIVE METHODS

The results presented in Section 17.4 were obtained using the techniques described in Section 17.2. In this section, we introduce and give references to another two techniques that can be used in the computation of dynamic sensitivities and that also use the Composition Technique. The first we call the *market state approach* to dynamic sensitivities. The second, presented in [12], relies on using the Jacobian of the parametrisation g in Equation 17.2 and orthogonal projections.

The main attractive element behind these two approaches is that their computational burden is smaller than that of the technique presented in Section 17.2, used to obtain the results in Section 17.4. However, these two new approaches have limitations that can put them in second place depending on the context and requirements.

The details of the market state approach in the computation of dynamic sensitivities are given in Appendix F. In that section, we also show numerical results that support the use of this technique. Its main limitation — which comes in the form of the range of dimensions on which it can be currently used — is also discussed there, along with research avenues that need to be explored to enhance the technique.

The details of the Jacobian Projection Technique are given in Chapter 8. The technique is presented as a way of obtaining market sensitivities from model sensitivities. Numerical tests of dynamic sensitivities within an MC simulation obtained by applying this technique, together with its shortcomings, are then presented in Appendix G.

---

[2]It is market practice to apply capital buffers on top of computed capital numbers to account for lack of accuracy in the underlying models.

17.7 SUMMARY OF CHAPTER

- **Computational load in the computation of dynamic sensitivities**. Financial institutions would benefit substantially from being able to simulate trade and portfolio sensitivities dynamically in CCR Monte Carlo simulations. Applications range from forward-simulating initial margin requirements, hedging strategies, sensitivity-based capital calculations and so on. It is a highly complex calculation, as it requires a finite difference "bump-and-revalue" calculation for every sensitivity at every Monte Carlo simulation node. Apart from the methods discussed in this chapter, the only robust way to simulate sensitivities is via AAD, which comes with its own range of implementation difficulties.

- **Solution**. The solution proposed consists of applying the Composition Technique to the sensitivity functions of the trades involved. The parametrisations used to reduce the dimension of the problem are, just like in the case of CCR applications, the ones that come with the risk factor diffusion models used to simulate future market scenarios. Once the dimension of the sensitivity functions has been reduced, CTs are built to replicate them. For the tests considered in this chapter, CTs were always built with the help of the Tensor Extension Algorithms. However, if the dimension of the diffusion models is low, they are not needed and tensors can be built directly.

- **Accuracy**. When the sensitivity function was obtained through a pricing function expressed analytically, the accuracy of the sensitivity profiles had an error of less than 1%. When the sensitivity function was Monte Carlo based, the accuracy was within the noise of the pricing function.

- **Computational gains**. Computational gains for a full Monte Carlo simulation with 10,000 paths and 100 time points in the future were estimated at more than 95% in all cases. This assumes calibration of the proxy functions in each Monte Carlo run. If they are reused, the computational gains exceed 99%.

## CHAPTER 18

Pricing model calibration

Pricing models are central to financial institutions. The outputs of these models depend on a set of inputs that must be specified. Some of these inputs can be directly read from the market while some others cannot. The ones that cannot are specified through calibration exercises. These exercises consist of finding the combination of parameter inputs to the pricing model that let the model replicate market characteristics as best as possible.

There is a whole range of pricing models that have been developed over the years. Unfortunately, some of the ones that best replicate market characteristics tend to be computationally speaking very expensive to run. Pricing models need to be calibrated on a regular basis. Calibrations rely on optimisation routines that call the pricing function a significant number of times. Therefore, a computational bottleneck is created especially for the most interesting pricing models. This is a problem in practical settings where there are time constraints, forcing practitioners to choose less sophisticated models.

In this chapter, we give details of how to use the techniques in Part III to reduce the computational bottleneck associated with the calibration of pricing models without compromising accuracy. This opens up the possibility of using some of the most advanced pricing models in real-life calibrations, which would otherwise be difficult.

18.1 INTRODUCTION

Let P be the pricing function of a given derivative trade $\mathcal{D}$. As explained in Section 13.2, the parameters that affect the pricing functions fall into three categories. The first set of parameters are $\Theta \subset \mathbb{R}^n$, the parameters of the model $\mathcal{M}$ that governs the dynamics of derivative underlyings. The second set consists of the market factors $\mathcal{S} \subset \mathbb{R}^m$; these are exogenous factors needed for pricing, such as spot values and interest rates. The third are the trade parameters $\mathcal{T} \subset \mathbb{R}^k$, which specify the instance of the trade $\mathcal{D}$, for example, time to maturity, strike and payment dates of the trade.

Once values in $\theta \in \Theta$, $s \in \mathcal{S}$ and $t \in \mathcal{T}$ have been specified, the function $\mathcal{P}$ returns the price $P(\theta, s, t)$ of the trade $\mathcal{D}$.

Given a trade type — say an option — market quotes come in a range of maturities and strikes. Strictly speaking, the price is expressed as monetary value. However, quotes are often expressed as implied volatilities.[1]

---

[1] Implied volatilities give a better indication of relative value. Therefore, options are often quoted as implied volatilities rather than prices.

To obtain the implied volatility from a price, one must invert a pricing function in the following way. Starting from a price, maturity, strike, and other exogenous factors, the implied volatility is the volatility that recovers the given price under the pricing function chosen. Given its mathematical tractability and ease of use, a common choice of function for the computation of implied volatilities is the Black-Scholes pricing model. From now on, we assume this model for the computation of implied volatilities.

Pricing functions compute prices. However, as mentioned, market quotes are often expressed as implied volatilities. Therefore, to compare the output of a pricing function $\mathcal{P}$, with market quotes, we need to express the prices obtained by $\mathcal{P}$ as implied volatilities. To do so, we consider the following composition

$$\varphi(\theta, s, t) : \mathbb{R}^{n+m+k} \xrightarrow{P} \mathbb{R}^n \xrightarrow{P_{BS}^{-1}} \mathbb{R} \tag{18.1}$$

where P is a pricing function that depends on the three families of parameters $\Theta, \mathcal{S}, \mathcal{T}$; and P_{BS} is the Black-Scholes pricing function used to invert prices (monetary value of trade) to implied volatilities. From now on, we refer to φ as a pricing function, too.

In view of the function defined, we have the following definition:

Definition of calibration exercise

Calibration consists of finding a set of values in Θ so that the implied volatilities obtained via φ (Equation 18.1) approximate market quotes as closely as possible.

To measure how well φ approximates market quotes, a loss or cost function is used. The following is a typical example of a loss function and the one we use to obtain the numerical results presented in Section 18.4:

$$L(\theta, s, t) = \sum_{i=1}^{N} \omega_i (q_i - v_i(\theta, s, t))^2, \tag{18.2}$$

where there are N market quotes that constitute the implied volatility surface — different maturities and strikes contained in $\mathcal{T}$ — q_i is the i-th implied volatility obtained from market quotes, v_i the i-th implied volatility obtained with the pricing model (Equation 18.1) and $\{w_i\}$ a set of weights.

In terms of the loss function in Equation 18.2, calibration consists of finding the set of values $\theta^* \in \Theta$ that minimise it. That is

$$\theta^* = \underset{\theta \in \Theta \subset \mathbb{R}^n}{argmin} \ L(\theta, s, t). \tag{18.3}$$

The minimisation of the loss function rarely has an analytic solution, therefore optimisation routines must be employed. These generally consist of trial-and-error exercises. At each trial, an implied volatility surface is produced by Equation 18.1

and compared to market quotes. Typically, optimisation routines involve hundreds if not thousands of these trials. Therefore, the pricing function of the model is called thousands if not tens of thousands of times.[2]

The pricing problem in pricing model calibration

Notice that the large number of calls to the pricing function during the optimisation routine is what constitutes the *pricing problem in calibration exercises*. Like in every other application considered in this book, there will be pricing functions for which the pricing step will not constitute much of a problem. However, for some pricing models, the pricing function is slow enough so that calling it thousands of times constitutes a challenging task from a computational point of view. In particular, as we will discuss next, some of the most interesting and powerful pricing models are unfortunately the slowest and the ones for which the pricing step in calibration exercises is the most challenging.

A range of optimisation routines can be used in calibration exercises. There are optimisation routines that use the gradient of the function to minimise, while others do not. The ones that use the gradient of the function tend to be faster. However, they do not guarantee a global solution and may return a local minimum. Popular examples of these routines are SLSQP, L-BFGS-B and Levenberg-Marquardt.

Gradient-free optimisers have gathered a lot of attention in recent times. They tend to be slower than the gradient-based ones, but are better at finding global solutions (see [61]). Moreover, they are able to deal with a mix of variables (discrete and continuous) and large dimensions in the space being explored. Popular examples of these are COBYLA, Nealder-Mead and genetic algorithms.

The choice of which routine to use in a given context depends on a number of factors, such as the loss function used and the computational time that it takes to run. However, the solutions to the pricing problem in calibrations presented in Section 18.2 are hardly affected (if at all) by the choice of optimisation routine.

18.1.1 Examples of pricing models

Since its presentation in 1973, the Black-Scholes pricing model has been widely used for a variety of purposes. Part of its appeal is its mathematical tractability and simplicity. For example, prices can be computed analytically. However, over the years it became apparent that it lacks the power to describe market quotes. In particular, markets violate one of the main premises of the model: deterministic constant volatility.

In an attempt to correct the shortcomings of the Black-Scholes model, more powerful models have since been developed. Two widely used ones are the Heston

---

[2]Note that each iteration of the optimisation routine involves the generation of a full volatility surface, where each volatility surface involves the evaluation of the pricing function many times: one for each maturity and strike.

(see [38]) and the SABR model (see [35]) — along with their generalisations — which model volatility in a stochastic manner. Although these models capture some features of market-implied volatilities, such as smile and skew, they still fail to replicate other aspects, such as the exploding power law nature of volatility skew as time goes to zero (see [28]). Despite these and other limitations, their mathematical tractability made them very popular among practitioners.

Rough volatility models lie at the opposite side of the spectrum to Black-Scholes. Introduced in [22], these models have received a lot of attention in recent years. One of their main strengths is their ability to model some of the more complex intricacies displayed by market-implied volatilities (see [10], [44]). However, these models are less tractable, requiring slow Monte Carlo simulations for their use. This makes them, computationally speaking, very expensive to calibrate, making them difficult to use in practical applications on a regular basis.

One of the most popular rough volatility models is the rough Bergomi model. The rough Bergomi model $\mathcal{M}$, has parameter space $\Theta = (\tilde{\xi}, \eta, \rho, H)$. The stochastic differential equation that governs the dynamics of the asset is

$$dS_t = -0.5V_t dt + \sqrt{V_t}dW_t, \quad \text{for } t > 0, \quad S_0 = 0,$$

$$V_t = \tilde{\xi}(t)\varepsilon\left(\sqrt{2H}\eta \int_0^t (t-s)^{H-0.5}dZ_s\right) \quad \text{for } t > 0, \quad V_0 > 0, \tag{18.4}$$

where $\tilde{\xi}$ is the initial forward variance curve (see [5] Section 6), ε the stochastic exponential ([19]), $\eta > 0$ the volatility of V_t, H the Hurst parameter in $(0, 1)$, and ρ a correlation parameter in $[-1, 1]$ that relates the two stochastic drivers Z and W.

For numerical calculations, the curve $\tilde{\xi}$ is approximated by a piece-wise constant term structure. Along with the rest of the parameters η, ρ and H, these constitute Θ in $\mathbb{R}^n$, for some $n \in \mathbb{N}$.

For general details on rough volatility models and their numerical simulations, we refer the reader to [3].

In recent years, the rough Bergomi model has received a lot of attention. It has the modelling advantages and computational challenges of a rough volatility model. This was the model chosen for the numerical tests, results of which are presented in Section 18.4.

18.2 SOLUTION

The solution to the pricing problem in calibration consists of using some of the techniques presented in Part III to replicate the pricing function φ in Equation 18.1 and use the proxy built in the calibration exercise, that is, in the optimisation routine used to solve Equation 20.4.

The techniques presented in Part III offer high-accuracy proxies for φ that have very high speeds of evaluation. When these proxies are used in the calibration routines instead of φ, calibration times can be reduced by more than 10,000 times — see Section 18.4 and [41]. When these proxies are built correctly, the accuracy of approximation of the pricing function φ is high — see Section 18.4 and [41]. Therefore, calibrations are performed at only a fraction of the cost and give essentially the same results compared to the ones obtained using the original pricing model.

As has been the case in other applications presented in this book, the solution has two parts: a building and an evaluating part. The building part can be thought of as an offline part; it can be done on the side, outside of live risk systems. The evaluating part — or online part — is when the built proxies are deployed in the optimisation routine to do the live calibration. One of the main advantages of splitting the process is that existing calibration systems do not need to be modified. The proxies built for φ become an added tool for the practitioner to test pricing models and run fast calibrations whenever needed.

18.2.1 Variables at play

Given the definition of calibration presented in Section 18.1, the variables in the input domain of the function to be replicated are those in the parameter space Θ of the pricing model $\mathcal{M}$, along with maturity and strike. Market factors such as spot, volatility and interest rate curves are kept fixed. Therefore, the dimensionality of the problem is driven by the parameters of the pricing model $\mathcal{M}$ along with the strike and maturity.

Not all models have the same number of parameters. Most typically have less than 10 and rarely more than 20. Notice that unlike the applications in CCR (Chapter 15) and market risk (Chapter 16), there is no need to apply the Composition Technique (Chapter 5). The dimension of the problem already lends itself to directly applying CTs or DNNs without the need of further considerations.

18.2.2 Possible proxies

There are two possible proxies that can be used to approximate φ from Equation 18.1: CTs and DNNs.

CTs can be built in two ways. The first is by evaluating every grid point with the pricing function φ. We call these tensors Full Chebyshev Tensors. The second is building Chebyshev TT tensors using one of the Tensor Extension Algorithms presented in Chapter 6, and it builds TT-format Chebyshev Tensors.

The choice of CT depends on the input dimension of the function being replicated, φ in our case. If the dimension is between 1 and 5, it is normally optimal to build a full CT. Beyond dimension 5, the situation should be considered more carefully; there will be times when a full CT can be built, others where we will need to make use of the Tensor Extension Algorithms and build a TT-format CT. When it comes to DNNs, there is no choice to be made. The dimensions normally encountered mean that DNNs can be built without much trouble.

The advantage of using CTs comes from the fact that they enjoy the exponential convergence properties discussed in Section 3.3.7. This is a very important property in many of the applications in this book, as it means that a small number of the function φ evaluations are needed to build a CT that replicates φ very closely. The disadvantage comes in the form of the curse of dimensionality. Beyond certain dimensions (which varies depending on the case, but it's usually between 5 and 10), it becomes impractical to build a full tensor due to its sheer size.

As mentioned before, the Tensor Extension Algorithms described in Chapter 6 allow us to build CTs of higher dimensions by evaluating the pricing function only on a small proportion of the full Chebyshev grid. This comes at the cost of reduced accuracy (at least theoretical) compared to full CTs. This is because the Tensor Extension Algorithms return TT-format CTs that are approximations to the full CTs. However, it is worth pointing out that the results in Section 18.4 do not show, for the example considered, any major difference in accuracy between the TT-format and the full CT.

The main advantage of DNNs, at least in the applications in this chapter, is that they are applied the same way regardless of the dimension of the input space of the function φ being replicated. The input dimension of functions such as φ usually oscillates from less than 10, to less than 20, dimensions that are well managed by a DNN. However, their main disadvantage, especially compared to full CTs, comes in the lack of convergence power and the hyper-parameter optimisation problem that affects Deep Learning algorithms in general.[3]

18.2.3   Domain of approximation

There is an important comment to make regarding the domain over which CTs and DNNs approximate the function φ. The results that constitute the mathematical backbone of CTs are valid within their domain and not outside. Also, DNNs generalisation capability is tested within that domain, but not outside of it.

For the applications presented so far in this book — for example, CCR and market risk — this was not an issue as the scenarios that need to be evaluated by the replica function (CT or DNN) are known a priori. For example, in CCR the scenarios to be priced by pricing functions are generated beforehand by the RFE models. In market risk, the scenarios that need to be priced in the calculations of ES — more generally VaR-like calculations — are collected historically and hence are also known in advance. This means the domain of approximation for the replica function is defined by these scenarios. In doing so, we know there will not be a scenario to be evaluated that lies outside this domain.

In the application discussed in this chapter, we do not have a predetermined domain where all the evaluations will be done. This is because the pricing function — or replica built for it — is evaluated on points of its domain determined by the optimisation routine used for calibration. In principle, there is no way of knowing the areas that will be explored by the optimisation routine. Therefore, one must be careful when choosing the ranges that define the domain over which the CTs or DNNs generate a replica of the function φ.

One way to get round this problem is to identify suitable domains based on historical calibrations along with optimisation routines that admit domain restrictions. There are plenty of optimisation algorithms that admit these, for example, SLSQP, L-BFGS-B and least squares. If, for some reason, one must use an optimisation algorithm with no

---

[3]For a discussion on the problems of hyper-parameter optimisation, we refer the reader to Section 1.4.3.

domain restrictions, one can opt for a mix of replica and original pricing function calls. In this case, the replica function returns implied volatilities only when the parameter explored by the optimisation algorithm is within the domain of approximation. When it is not, the pricing function is used.

This should be an effective approach as the domain of the replica function can be chosen large enough to reduce the chances of having to evaluate parameters outside this domain. As mentioned, one can, for example, use parameters from historical calibrations to identify suitable domains. Notice that, when the replica function is a CT, increasing the domain of approximation should barely affect their accuracy given the quasi-exponential convergence presented in Theorem 3.3.10.

18.3 TEST DESCRIPTION

This section presents the details of the numerical tests run on the calibration of the rough Bergomi model, where its corresponding pricing function φ, from Equation 18.1, was replaced by CTs.

In Section 18.5, we discuss the results found in the literature obtained on similar exercises to the ones presented in this section, where the proxy used to replace φ was a DNN. The results in the literature (for example, [41] and [9]) are complete enough; we saw no reason to reproduce the results therein.

18.3.1 Test setup

The pricing model used to generate the results presented in this section is the rough Bergomi model (see Equation 18.4). This was used to compute European call option prices. Two variants were considered based on the number of dimensions used for the forward variance parameter $\tilde{\xi}$. The first set of tests assumed constant forward variance. The second considered a term structure with eight points.

Note that the solution to the pricing problem in model calibration presented in Section 18.2 is general enough so that it can be applied to any pricing model $\mathcal{M}$ and any payoff. The rough Bergomi model was chosen because it has attracted attention in recent times — due to its modelling capabilities — and because it presents a challenging calibration from a computational cost standpoint.

Chebyshev Tensors Built

As mentioned before, two cases for the forward variance parameter $\tilde{\xi}$ were considered. When the forward variance is assumed constant, the dimension of the tensor to build is 6 — 4 from the parameters Θ and 2 from maturities and strikes. In this case, given the dimension, it is possible to build a full CT as well as a TT-format CT using the Tensor Extension Algorithms.

When the forward variance was modelled using 8 points, the tensor to build had dimension 13 — 11 from Θ and 2 from maturities and strikes. In this case, it is not possible to build a full tensor and only TT-format CTs were built.

In order to build the tensors, the domain for each of the input variables needs to be set. The ranges chosen for each of the model parameters were

$$(\tilde{\xi}, \eta, \rho, H) \in [0.01, 0.16] \times [0.5, 4] \times [-0.95, -0.1] \times [0.025, 0.5], \tag{18.5}$$

while the maturities and strikes that considered were

- maturities = { 0.3, 0.6, 0.9, 1.2, 1.5, 1.8, 2.0 }
- strikes = { 0.7, 0.75, 0.8, 0.85, 0.9, 0.95, 1.0, 1.05, 1.1, 1.15, 1.2, 1.25, 1.30 }.   (18.6)

Note that when the forward variance $\tilde{\xi}$ was modelled with a term structure, the interval $[0.01, 0.16]$ was used for every point on the term structure. The maturities are in years and the underlying for the European option is assumed to have value 1.

The ranges selected for these parameters were based on what is reported in the literature for similar calibration exercises (for example, [41]). These ranges, however, can be adjusted if necessary. As mentioned in Section 18.2.3, one can use historical calibrations of the same model to estimate parameter ranges that contain all or the vast majority of the points explored by the optimisation routines used at calibration.

Measuring the accuracy of Chebyshev Tensors

The fundamentals of the method being discussed in this chapter consist of replacing the heavy-to-compute φ by its CT replica when calibrating the model. Hence, once the CTs have been built, the accuracy of CTs as replicas of φ should be checked; if the accuracy is good, we know we are on the right track. Otherwise, we know the model calibration via CTs will highly likely yield suboptimal results.

To test the accuracy, 1,000 synthetically generated implied volatility surfaces were obtained by specifying 1,000 random combinations of the parameters in Θ. For each fixed set of values $\theta = (\tilde{\xi}, \eta, \rho, H)$, φ was evaluated on the collection of strikes K and maturities T specified in Equation 18.6.

$$\varphi(\theta) : K \times T \longrightarrow \mathbb{R} \tag{18.7}$$

The 1,000 parameter combinations needed to generate 1,000 implied volatility surfaces were obtained by randomly sampling (assuming a uniform distribution) the parameter domain of the rough Bergomi model within the domains given in Equation 18.5.

In order to measure the accuracy of the CTs when replicating φ, the 1,000 implied volatility surfaces generated via the full evaluation of the rough Bergomi model were compared with the corresponding surfaces obtained by the CTs. The comparison of surfaces yields a distribution of 1,000 errors for each maturity and strike in the surface. The mean and maximum errors were computed for each of these surface points.

Measuring the accuracy of calibration

Once the appropriate accuracy of the CTs had been established, we proceeded to testing them as proxies in the calibration of the rough Bergomi model under different market conditions. For this, the existing 1,000 volatility surfaces were used as market quotes. The model was calibrated against each of these surfaces (that is, 1,000 calibrations).

The accuracy of each calibration was measured using the root-mean-squared error (RMSE), defined in Equation 18.8.

$$\text{RMSE} = \sqrt{\frac{1}{NM} \sum_{i=1}^{N} \sum_{j=1}^{M} (q_{ij} - v_{ij})^2}, \tag{18.8}$$

where the index i runs through maturities, j through strikes, q_{ij} is the (synthetically created) market implied volatility corresponding to the i-th maturity and j-th strike and v_{ij} is the corresponding implied volatility generated by the calibration exercise with the CT.

Given that there were 1,000 calibrations performed — one per each synthetically generated implied volatility surface — we are able to compute metrics on the distribution of RMSEs.

Measuring computational gains

In addition to the accuracy of the proxies built — both in terms of function approximation and calibration — we are interested in the computational gains obtained with the available techniques.

The computational gains are obtained by comparing the time an average calibration takes using the pricing function of the rough Bergomi model to the time it takes to run the calibration using the proxies built. This essentially boils down to comparing the average evaluation time of the pricing function of the rough Bergomi model with the average evaluation time of the proxy used.

Although the computational gains in absolute terms depend on the systems used, the results obtained give a very good indication of the relative speed gains one would expect to obtain regardless of the system.

Technical specification

The implementation of the rough Bergomi model pricing routine used is based on the one mentioned in [9], available on github and implemented in C++.[4] It is a Monte Carlo–based pricing routine; 60,000 paths were used to generate the prices in our tests as these reduce the noise in the pricing function down to less than 1%. Once prices are obtained, these are turned into implied volatilities.[5]

Full CTs were built in Python using the MoCaX Library.[6] In this case, the optimisation routine used for calibration was the SLSQP algorithm available in SciPy for Python.

---

[4]The code can be found in https://github.com/roughstochvol.
[5]Implied volatilities are obtained using functions in https://github.com/roughstochvol, and rely on the Newton-Ralphson method implemented in boost.
[6]Available at https://www.mocaxintelligence.com/.

CTs built using the Rank Adaptive Algorithm used the MATLAB implementation described in [69]. The calibration exercises used the least squares optimisation algorithm in MATLAB.

The results presented next were obtained using a standard PC computer, with $i7$ cores; no parallelisation nor GPUs were used.

18.4 RESULTS WITH CHEBYSHEV TENSORS

As explained, two separate tests were done for the rough Bergomi model depending on the term structure for $\tilde{\xi}$. The first assumed constant forward variance. The second assumed a term structure with eight points. The dimension of the input domain of the CTs is different in each case. This required building CTs in different ways. In this section, we present the results for each of these cases. We present the building cost, accuracy and speed of the techniques used.

18.4.1 Rough Bergomi model with constant forward variance

The rough Bergomi model with constant forward variance defines a pricing function φ with six dimensions. Four of these dimensions come from the parameters in Θ; these are $(\tilde{\xi}, \eta, \rho, H)$. The other two come from maturity (T) and strike (K). This dimension allows for full CTs to be built as well CTs in TT format through the Tensor Extension Algorithms.

Building cost

For the full CTs, a mesh of 14,400 points was used. This was obtained by using the following number of Chebyshev points per dimension: 5, 5, 3, 4, 6, 8 for $(\tilde{\xi}, \eta, \rho, H, T, K)$, respectively. The decision of how many points to use per dimension was made based on one-dimensional cross-sectional slices of the pricing function: variables with respect to which the pricer showed greater sensitivity got higher numbers of Chebyshev points; those with less sensitivity got lower (see Section 3.4 for a discussion on how to explore the relationship between the error and number of Chebyshev points). The memory footprint of this CT was 800 KB.

Although these many Chebyshev points should, in principle, translate into 14,400 calls to the pricing routine, one can reduce this to only 300 pricing calls for the specific test that we are carrying out here. In the Chebyshev mesh mentioned, there are 300 parameter combinations in Θ, coming from the first four dimensions, where the number of grid points are 5, 5, 3, 4. For each of these combinations, a Monte Carlo diffusion of the option underlying can be used to obtain all prices associated with the maturity and strike combinations given by the grid on the last two dimensions, which correspond to maturity and strike.

The Tensor Extension Algorithm used to build the TT-format CTs was the Rank Adaptive Algorithm. A total of seven Chebyshev points were chosen per dimension. This gives a grid with a total of 117,649 points. Notice that the number of grid points is significantly higher than for the full CT. One can afford this increase in number of grid points because the Rank Adaptive Algorithm allows for a much lower number of calls to the pricing routine. Therefore, one can increase the granularity of the mesh and, with it, potentially the accuracy of approximation. The function was evaluated on 10,000 randomly selected grid points, 8.5% of the total grid points. Of the 10,000 grid points evaluated, 8,000 were used for training and 2,000 for testing.

Once these 10,000 values were obtained, it took the Rank Adaptive Algorithm under 5 minutes to obtain a TT-format CT — in MATLAB.[7] The maximum rank of the TT-format CT was 12 and its memory footprint 20 KB.

It is important to note that the building cost corresponds to the offline part of the process. The building of CT can be done at any point and, if needed, in a separate module to the pricing library systems. Moreover, once the CT has been built, it can be used in as many calibration exercises as required. In principle, the tensor built should work well for many weeks or monthts in the future. Perhaps one should consider building a new one once market conditions change substantially. Other than that, the object is built once, stored in memory — something that can easily be done given its low memory footprint — and loaded to be used whenever needed.

Accuracy of proxy pricer

The accuracy of the proxies built was measured by comparing the synthetically generated implied volatility surfaces with the ones generated by the proxy. Figures 18.1 and 18.2 show heat maps of the average and maximum error of the differences between the two collections of implied volatility surfaces, that is, for each maturity and strike, the average and maximum difference between the implied volatility obtained via the full evaluation of the rough Bergomi model and the one given by the CT.

The heat maps on Figure 18.1 correspond to the errors of the full CT. Figure 18.2 shows the errors of the TT-format CT. Both proxies yield high accuracy; the average errors fall within 0.05% and 0.35%, while the maximum errors are between 0.1% and 5%, in absolute implied volatility values.

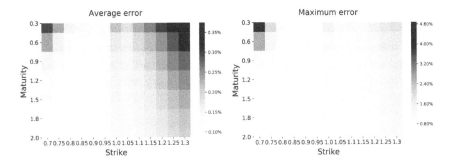

FIGURE 18.1   Average and maximum error of approximation heat map for full CTs for the rough Bergomi model. It assumes constant forward variance.

---

[7]Note that MATLAB is much slower than typical IT production setups.

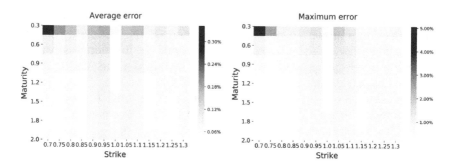

FIGURE 18.2 Average and maximum error of approximation heat map for TT-format CTs for the rough Bergomi model. It assumes constant forward variance.

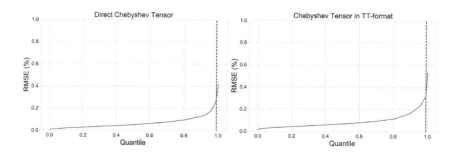

FIGURE 18.3 Quantiles for the distribution of RMSE values obtained by calibrating 1,000 synthetically generated implied volatility surfaces using CTs. The left pane corresponds to the full CT, the right pane corresponds to the CT in TT format. The vertical line on both plots corresponds to the 99% quantile.

Accuracy of calibration

The error for each calibration is measured using the RMSE. Given that 1,000 calibrations were performed using the CTs, a whole distribution of RMSEs were obtained. Figure 18.3 shows quantile values of the error distribution. The 99% quantile is marked with a vertical line. The plot on the left corresponds to the full CT; the one on the right to the TT-format CT. For both types of tensors, the 99% quantile of the RMSE is about 0.5% and the maximum RMSE value is less than 0.6%.

Computational gains at calibration

Estimating computational gains based on the tests performed is not straighforward. As mentioned in Section 18.3.1, different parts of the test were performed with different tools. For example, the average evaluation speed for the rough Bergomi pricing function was measured in C++ while the volatility surface calibrations using TT-format tensors were done in MATLAB. However, the results obtained should give an indication of the order of magnitude of the computational gains one would expect to obtain in any given system.

The average evaluation time for the pricing function — in C++, using 60,000 paths — was 2.6 seconds. The full CT had an average evaluation time of 60.5 microseconds in C++, hence, 40,000 times faster. The evaluation time for the TT-format CTs in MATLAB was 1 milliseconds. If one assumes between 10 and 100 times speed acceleration from MATLAB to C++, one would expect to have $10 - 100$ microseconds in a C++ implementation, hence, a similar evaluation time to that of the full CTs. As a result, the computational gain of the rough Bergomi model calibration via CTs is about 40,000 times faster compared to the one that uses the original pricing function.

A typical volatility calibration exercise used about 100 parameter trials. This translates — assuming 100 points on the volatility surface — into 10,000 calls to the pricer or its proxy. Given the reported time of about 60.5 microseconds per CT evaluation for a C++ object, this means 0.6 seconds spent calling the tensor during calibration. This massively contrasts with the 7.2 hours that it would take should the original pricing function be used.[8]

18.4.2   Rough Bergomi model with piece-wise constant forward variance

The rough Bergomi model with piece-wise constant forward variance defines a pricing function φ with a domain of dimension 13. Eleven of these dimensions come from the parameters in Θ; these are $(\tilde{\xi}, \eta, \rho, H)$, where $\tilde{\xi}$ has a term structure with eight tensors. The other two come from maturity and strike. This dimension requires the use of the Tensor Extension Algorithms to build a TT-format CT.

Building cost

A grid of seven points per dimension was chosen for the CT. This gives a total of 96,889,010,407 grid points. Out of these, only 20,000 were randomly chosen to be evaluated and used in the Rank Adaptive Algorithm. This represents only 2×10^{-7} of the total grid. From the 20,000 points evaluated, 16,000 were used for training and 4,000 for testing. It took the Rank Adaptive Algorithm under 8 minutes to obtain a TT-format CT — in MATLAB. The maximum rank of the TT-format CT was 9 and its memory footprint 16 KB.

Accuracy of proxy pricer

The accuracy of the TT-format CT as a proxy to the pricing function φ is shown in the heat maps from Figure 18.4. The average error is less than 0.5% and the maximum less than 3%.

---

[8]To be noted, these computational gains are being reported for a generic model calibration exercise. In the particular test that we carried out, where we were computing implied volatilities of a European option, the computational gains were lower because one Monte Carlo run of the pricing function can be used to obtain the complete volatility surface.

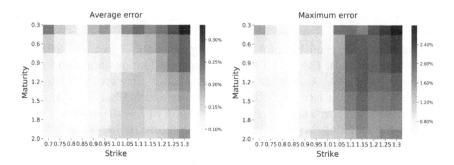

FIGURE 18.4 Average and maximum error of approximation heat map for CTs built using the Rank Adaptive Algorithm for the rough Bergomi model. It assumes piece-wise forward variance.

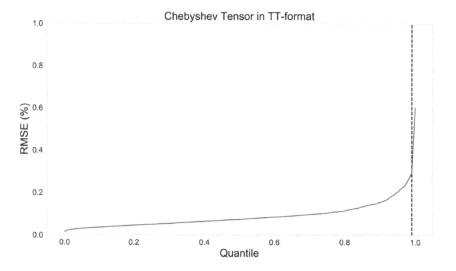

FIGURE 18.5 Distribution of RMSE values obtained by calibrating 1,000 synthetically generated implied volatility surfaces using CTs. The plot corresponds to the TT-format CT. The vertical line on both plots corresponds to the 99% quantile.

Accuracy of calibration

Figure 18.5 shows quantile values of the calibration error distribution measured using the RMSE. The 99% quantile is marked with a vertical line. Notice the maximum error is below 0.6%.

Computational gains at calibration

The evaluation time of the TT-format CT was measured at 2 milliseconds per evaluation — in MATLAB. An implementation in C++ would be expected to run between 10 and 100 times faster. It was mentioned before that the evaluation time for the pricing function was about 2.6 seconds. Therefore, the calibration routing using the

CT should be between 10,000 and 100,000 times faster than when using the original pricing function. Again, computational gains go from several hours (when using original pricing function) to a few seconds (when using CTs).

18.5 RESULTS WITH DEEP NEURAL NETS

This section presents the main results found in some of the papers within the literature where DNNs are used to accelerate the calibration of pricing models. In particular, we focus on the results in [37], [41] and [9], which provide solid evidence of the impact DNNs have in pricing model calibration. We saw no reason to reproduce the tests.

One of the first papers to discuss the use of DNNs to accelerate the calibration of pricing models is [37]. In it, the calibration of the HW model is accelerated by training a DNN that learns the whole calibration exercise. That is, a DNN that takes model parameters as a function of market risk factors — the latter typically represented by implied volatilities — is trained using a large synthetically generated data set. Once trained, model parameters are obtained and given a set of market risk factors (mainly implied volatilities) in a very short period of time. As a result, the bulk of the computational load associated with the calibration routine is passed on to the training phase, which can be done offline.

Shortly after the publication of [37], several other authors (such as [71] and [26]) explored a similar approach. In general, the aim was the same: use DNNs (in some cases convolutional DNNs) to learn model parameters from market risk factors.

The way in which DNNs are used in [41] and [9] is different. Instead of training a DNN to learn model parameters from market risk factors, DNNs are used to learn implied volatilities from model risk factors. Essentially, a DNN was used to approximate or create a replica of the pricing function that takes model parameters as inputs and returns implied volatilities — the latter function essentially the one represented by Equation 18.1. Once the DNN has been trained, it can be used within the optimisation exercise that finds the optimal model parameters given a set of market risk factors. As the reader will easily identify, this is the approach we have chosen when using CTs to accelerate the calibration of the rough Bergomi model.

In [41], the model chosen to test DNNs with was the rough Bergomi model. The DNNs take model parameters as input and return a whole implied volatility surface. As such, the DNN is a function with a domain input of dimension equal to the number of model parameters considered and an output with the same number of dimensions as elements chosen in the implied volatility surface. For the rough Bergomi model, the model parameter space was the same as considered in this chapter: with dimension 6 when forward variance is assumed flat and dimension 13 when the forward variance was modelled with a non-trivial term structure. The implied volatility surface consisted of 88 different combinations of maturities and strikes.

The data used to train the DNNs in [41] was generated by sampling the model parameters space 80,000 times. For each model parameter combination, a whole implied volatility surface was generated. Given that surfaces were treated with 88 points, this translates into 7,040,000 pricing calls. The generation of these data takes a considerable amount of time to obtain. However, the advantage is that it can be done offline.

The reported training time for the DNN, however, was very low. Indeed, the architecture of the DNNs considered was relatively simple (four hidden layers, each with 30 neurons); these required minutes to train with no hyper-parameter optimisation.

The accuracy of the DNNs as function approximators was tested. The reported accuracy is good — comparable to the ones reported in Section 18.4.

The calibration errors in [41] are measured using the RMSE. This is the same metric used in Section 18.4. The RMSE values reported in [41] are very similar to the ones reported in Section 18.4.

Calibration speeds using DNNs are reported in [41] to be between 9,000 and 16,000 times faster than the brute-force approach, which is when the original pricing function (Monte Carlo–based) is used. Once more, this is very similar to what we report in Section 18.4.

It should come as no surprise to the reader that the idea of using CTs in the calibration of models such as the rough Bergomi was the result of reading [41]. We wanted to explore (with success, as shown in this chapter) if similar accuracy levels and calibration speeds could be obtained, at a fraction of the building cost, due to the quasi-exponential convergence properties of CTs.

18.6   COMPARISON OF RESULTS VIA CT AND DNN

Table 18.1 gives a comparison between some of the results obtained with CTs in the calibration of the rough Bergomi model (Section 18.4), with the results found in [41].

Note that the results in Table 18.1 are meant only as an indication of how the two approaches compare, as tests were performed on slightly different model domain ranges and, for some parts of the tests, with different programming languages, which can make speed comparisons complicated.

Regarding the accuracy of the calibration exercise, both the CT and DNN techniques deliver very similar positive results, with inaccuracies below 1%.

The offline building computational costs is where a noticeable difference is seen. CTs were able to replicate the pricing function φ with less than 20,000 sample points, while the reported DNN tests need in the order of 7,000,000 calls. This result was expected, as CTs are unbeatable at replicating (reasonably smooth) functions (such as pricing functions) as a result of the quasi-exponential convergence property that the CTs provide (Section 3.3).

TABLE 18.1   Summary and comparison of testing results for solution via CTs and DNNs.

	Chebyshev Tensors	**Deep Neural Nets**	**Comparison**
Calibration Accuracy	< 0.6%	< 1.0%	Similar
Offline building cost	< 20,000 calls	~ 1,000,000 calls	CTs 90–99% more efficient
Online running cost	10,000–100,000 times faster than brute force	~ 10,000 times faster than brute force	~ Similar

A direct comparison of the online running computational costs is difficult as tests were performed in different IT systems and with different languages. However, it is clear that both CTs and DNNs are several orders of magnitude faster to evaluate than the original function φ.

18.7 SUMMARY OF CHAPTER

- **Computational load in calibration of pricing models**. The calibration of a pricing model requires generating market quotes on hundreds of different model parameter combinations. If the pricing model is sufficiently complex — from a computational standpoint, as is the case for the rough Bergomi model — calibration may not be possible due to time constraints.
- **Solution**. Pricing functions, expressed in terms of model parameters along with maturity and moneyness, are replicated using CTs. The replicas are used in the calibration of the rough Bergomi model instead of the original pricing function. Depending on the dimension of the pricing function, CTs are either built directly (evaluating every grid point) or with the help of the Tensor Extension Algorithms.
- **Proxy accuracy**. As replicas of the pricing function, CTs achieved high levels of accuracy with respect to the implied volatility surfaces generated by the original pricing function of the rough Bergomi model.
- **Calibration accuracy**. When CTs were used to calibrate the rough Bergomi model, using synthetically generated implied volatility surfaces, the RMSE was less than 1% across all surfaces tested.
- **Calibration speed gains**. Compared to the calibration of the rough Bergomi model that uses the original pricing function, CTs accelerated the calibration routine by about 10,000 to 100,000 times. Compared to DNNs, the tests suggest that the calibration results are similar, but the computational effort to build the CTs can be a few orders of magnitude more efficient due to their exponential convergence.

## CHAPTER 19

Approximation of the implied volatility function

I n 1973, Fischer Black and Myron Scholes presented one of the most important pricing models in finance [23]. A few years later the work would be expanded by Robert Merton who named the pricing formula associated with the model, the Black-Scholes (or Black-Scholes-Merton) formula.

One of its revolutionary ideas was the introduction of a theoretical framework under which a European-style option has a unique price regardless of the expected return and risk of the underlying asset. This paved the way to a significant increase in option trading and a general mathematical sophistication in financial models. Since then, many more complex pricing models have been developed using part of the theoretical framework set by Black, Scholes and Merton. In fact, the work of Robert Merton and Myron Scholes has been considered so influential that they were awarded the Nobel Memorial Prize in Economic Sciences in 1997.

Under this framework, the price C of a call option is given by

$$C(S_0, K, T, r, \sigma) = N(d_1)S_0 - N(d_2)Ke^{-r(T)}$$

$$d_1 = \frac{1}{\sigma\sqrt{T}}\left[\ln\left(\frac{S_0}{K}\right) + \left(r + \frac{\sigma^2}{2}\right)(T)\right] \qquad (19.1)$$

$$d_2 = d_1 - \sigma\sqrt{T}$$

where $N(\cdot)$ is the cumulative distribution function of the standard normal distribution, S_0 the spot price of the underlying asset, r the risk-free rate, T the time to maturity, K the strike, and σ the volatility of returns of the underlying asset. Out of the five variables the formula depends on, all can be found in the market (spot price S_0 and risk-free rate r) or the option definition (maturity T and strike K). The only variable that cannot be readily or unambiguously obtained is the volatility σ.

The Black-Scholes formula has an important characteristic. If spot, risk-free interest rate, maturity and strike are fixed, then the formula defines an invertible function between price and volatility. Therefore, given a price, there is a unique volatility, called the *implied volatility* that under the formula and all other variables fixed recovers the price given, that is, there is a bijective relationship between price and volatility.

If options in markets are given by their price (monetary value), why would anyone be interested in computing the implied volatility of an option? It so happens that implied volatilities are used instead of prices in a wide range of cases. In general, they are better suited than prices to measure relative value. We illustrate with the following example.

Trading desks face the following problem. Consider options on an underlying S with value, today, of $S_0 = 100$. Say the trading desk is offered to buy an OTM call option with strike $K_1 = 150$ and maturity $T_1 = 1$ year at a price of $C_1 = \$1.59$. Assume the desk is also offered to buy an ITM call option with strike $K_2 = 75$ and maturity $T_1 = 2$ years at a price of $C_2 = \$27.08$. Clearly the OTM trade has a much lower price than the ITM trade (generally, the more OTM a trade is, the lower its price, while the more ITM, the higher its price). However, this does not give an insight as to whether the OTM trade is underpriced (cheaper) or overpriced (more expensive) than the ITM trade, which can be crucial for the trading desk's strategies.

To better compare trade prices, trading desks compute the implied volatility of the prices in question. The corresponding implied volatilities help normalise values (even across assets), allowing for more effective comparisons. Doing it for the prices in the example, we obtain $\sigma_1 = 30\%$ and $\sigma_2 = 15\%$ (assuming $r = 1\%$). This information is very valuable to trading desks as it gives them insights into relative values between trades with very different prices. In this case, the \$ price given for the OTM option indicates riskier (higher volatility) underlying dynamics than those determined by the price of the ITM option. Hence, it is said that the OTM option is more expensive than the ITM option, even though $\$1.59 < \$27.08$.

In general, working with only prices is deemed insufficient in a wide range of situations. Volatilities give information that in some cases is more useful. Volatilities have become so ubiquitous in the market that they are used in market risk, stress testing, model calibration and so on. They are central to financial institutions and have become synonymous to price in option markets.

Computing implied volatilities presents several challenges in practice. A typical situation where this arises is when there is a need to compute the implied volatility of a large number of liquid options in the market, which are given by their price. This is often the case for trading desks and hedge funds, which need to compute a large number of implied volatilities in a very short period of time.

Another situation where they are typically needed is when we want to extend the information from points (K, T) of high liquidity in the market (where K represents the strike and T time to maturity) to points where the market provides limited or no information. This extension needs to be done in a manner that is consistent with the fundamental derivative no-arbitrage laws.

In this chapter, we are going to deal with the first of the two problems mentioned, that is, how to evaluate the implied volatility function in a computationally efficient manner, for the widest range of option prices. The second problem is not within the scope of this book.

19.1 THE COMPUTATION OF IMPLIED VOLATILITY

As mentioned before, the Black-Scholes formula defines an invertible function between prices and volatilities when the remaining variables are fixed. The formula presented in Equation 19.1 is a closed-form expression that defines one direction of this invertible function: given a volatility, it returns a price. However, there is no closed-form expression for the inverse. That is, there is no closed-form expression that returns the implied volatility of a given price.

Numerical approximations of the implied volatility function should ideally cover the practical needs faced day to day by practitioners. For example, options in the market are traded for a range of maturities and moneyness. This range depends on the option traded. Options for the S&P 500 will not have the same range of maturities and moneyness as options on VIX. Any method that computes implied volatilities should work for as many products as possible. Therefore, the numerical approximation should be able to compute implied volatilities for the widest possible range of maturities and moneyness.

Speed and accuracy are highly desirable characteristics for any method that computes implied volatilities. These are paramount in some applications. For example, in algorithmic trading, there is the need to convert a very large set of prices into implied volatilities both accurately and in a very short period of time. Another example where accuracy and efficiency are important is in pricing model calibration. Calibrations are done daily and often several times a day. In some cases, the pricing function of the model is in itself the bottleneck (case presented in Chapter 18). What we do not want is the implied volatility function to be an additional overhead, nor possible inaccuracies to decrease the quality of the calibration.

Finally, but not least, the method employed should ideally be easy to implement and maintain.

19.1.1 Available methods

Over the years many numerical approximation methods have been developed to compute implied volatilities. These can be separated into two types. The first consists of iterative root finders. The second are non-iterative approximation methods. As we will see next, each method has advantages and disadvantages. The aim of this chapter is to describe the method presented in [30], based on CTs, which approximates the implied volatility function and has all the desired properties mentioned in Section 19.1.

Some of the iterative root finding methods exhibit high degrees of accuracy but can be slow to run. This is particularly problematic in some applications, such as algorithmic trading, where speed is a priority. A good example is the Newton-Ralphson algorithm as applied in [64]. Although efficient for certain choices of parameters, the number of iterations grows considerably for others.

The Brent-Decker iterative scheme is another well-known example used, for instance, in the implementation of the blsimpv function in MATLAB. Although useful for small data sets, its efficiency suffers significantly for large data sets.

A third example of an iterative scheme used to compute implied volatilities is the one proposed by Jäckel in [45], which was then improved in [46]. This method is fast, accurate and covers a wide range of options in terms of maturity and moneyness. Its implementation, however, is complex enough that it can give rise to maintenance issues.

More generally, iterative methods do not give closed-form expressions of the function they represent and their implementation can be complicated and difficult to maintain.

Relevance of Jäckel's implied volatility function

This method is particularly relevant to the solution presented in this chapter. Not only are some of the ideas behind this method used in the CT solution put forward but also the function defined by Jäckel in [46] is the one approximated by CTs.

The idea of approximating Jäckel's implied volatility function with CTs is to obtain an efficient closed-form expression of the implied volatility function, with a simple and easy-to-maintain implementation, that inherits the accuracy and the wide range of options covered by Jäckel's implied volatility.

The non-iterative approximation methods have different characteristics. They are fast, easy to implement and maintain, and are given by closed-form expressions that are easy to interpret. All these are characteristics we are after. However, these methods either rely on series expansions at the at-the-money region of the implied volatility surface or on rational approximations of the surface. As a consequence, accuracy tends to deteriorate as we move away from the at-the-money region, or we end up with very restrictive domains of approximation, leaving out regions where market options appear in practice.

Well-known examples of non-iterative approximation methods for the implied volatility function that rely on series expansions can be found in [8], [14] and [53]. Two good examples that rely on rational approximations are [50], [54] and [13].

19.2   SOLUTION

This section describes the way in which CTs are used to approximate Jäckel's implied volatility function described in [46].

As mentioned in Section 19.1.1, the implied volatility function in [46] is accurate and covers a wide range of options that appear in practice, both in terms of maturity and moneyness. Its main downside is its complex implementation and consequent maintenance issues. The aim of replicating this function with CTs is to obtain a simple closed-form expression of the function in [46] that is efficient and stable to evaluate and inherits its accuracy and range of options covered.

First we describe how the problem is simplified by modifying the function to approximate to a two-dimensional function. This improves the efficiency of the replication with CTs. Then we describe the optimal type of CTs to be used. These tensors, described in [2], are unique to dimension 2.[1]

Particular attention will be paid to the choice of domain over which the replication takes place. As the reader will see, this is a crucial aspect that explains the efficiency of the method presented in [30].

In what follows, we focus on replicating the implied volatility associated with the Black-Scholes model. However, implied volatility is not unique to this model. The

---

[1]These tensors have not been discussed so far in this book.

Chebyshev method proposed in [30] can also be used to replicate the implied volatility models such as Laplace. For details we refer to [30].

19.2.1 Reducing the dimension of the problem

The Black-Scholes function for call options presented in Equation 19.1 is a function defined over a domain of dimension 5. The variables are spot S_0, strike K, risk-free rate r, time to maturity T and volatility σ. Fixing all these variables but σ defines a one-dimensional injective function of price in terms of volatility:

$$C_{S_0,K,r,T}(\sigma) : \mathbb{R}_{\geq 0} \longrightarrow \mathbb{R}_{\geq 0}. \tag{19.2}$$

As the function defined in Equation 19.3 is invertible for any choice of S_0, K, r and T, there is a corresponding function of volatility in terms of price:

$$\sigma_{S_0,K,r,T}(c) : \mathbb{R}_{\geq 0} \longrightarrow \mathbb{R}_{\geq 0}. \tag{19.3}$$

It is the collection of the functions given in Equation 19.3 that we want to approximate using CTs.

Notice the approximation just mentioned is given for any given combination of variables S_0, K, r and T. Therefore, in principle, the approximation is over a five-dimensional function. However, the solution to this problem can be reduced to the approximation of a function with domain in dimension 2. To introduce this two-dimensional function, we first introduce the normalised call price function

$$c(x,v) = e^{x/2} N\left(\frac{x}{v} + \frac{v}{2}\right) - e^{x/2} N\left(\frac{x}{v} - \frac{v}{2}\right)$$
$$x = \log(S_0 e^{rT}/K) \tag{19.4}$$
$$v = \sigma\sqrt{T}.$$

The function N is the cumulative distribution function of the normal distribution. The variable x represents the *moneyness* of the forward spot value, while v the *time-scaled volatility*. Notice that an option is out-of-the-money when $S_0 < K$. As rT is small for typical values of r and T, $S_0 e^{rT}$ is close to S_0. This means $x < 0$ for out-of-the-money options. Likewise, $x > 0$ for in-the-money options.

The normalised call function has a domain of dimension 2. Just like with the Black-Scholes function in Equation 19.1, given a price c and a fixed moneyness x, there is a unique time-scaled volatility v that under $c(x,v)$ gives c. This means that the following one-dimension function

$$c_x(v) : \mathbb{R}_{\geq 0} \longrightarrow \mathbb{R}_{\geq 0} \tag{19.5}$$

defined for fixed x, which relates time-scaled volatility and price, is invertible. The inverse of this function is given by

$$v_x(c) : \mathbb{R}_{\geq 0} \longrightarrow \mathbb{R}_{\geq 0}. \tag{19.6}$$

Notice the function in Equation 19.6 is a one-dimensional function defined for a fixed x. What we want is to approximate the two-dimensional function v, which given moneyness x and price c, returns the time-scaled implied volatility $v(x, c)$. From now on, we will focus on the approximation of the function v using CTs.

Important properties of normalised call price

There are a two important properties of Equation 19.4. These are the properties that justify working with it to solve the problem of approximating the implied volatility function. The first is that the normalised call function and the Black-Scholes call function are related as follows:

$$c(x, v) = \frac{C(S_0, K, T, r, \sigma)}{\sqrt{S_0 e^{-rT} K}}. \tag{19.7}$$

Therefore, given a price C, we can recover the price of the normalised call pricing function. If we have a CT that approximates the time-scaled implied volatility function, we can obtain the time-scaled implied volatility from the normalised call. Once we have the time-scaled implied volatility, we can recover the implied volatility function using the definition of the time-scaled implied volatility $v = \sigma\sqrt{T}$, noting that T corresponds to the maturity of the option with the price C we started off with.

The second property is that the normalised price of the in-the-money options can be recovered from the out-of-the-money via

$$c(-x, v) = c(x, v) + e^{-x/2} - e^{x/2}. \tag{19.8}$$

Therefore, the approximation of the normalised call function can be restricted to values for $x < 0$.

The first property mentioned justifies working with the normalised call price to solve the problem of approximating the implied volatility function using CTs. This is an important step as approximating a function with domain in dimension 2 is much easier than approximating a function with dimension 5, more so in light of the fact that the tool used to approximate the two-dimensional function $v(x, c)$ is specific to dimension 2. As we will see in coming sections, this, along with a careful choice of approximation domain, results in low building costs and very high levels of accuracy.

19.2.2 Two-dimensional CTs

The two-dimensional CTs chosen in [30] to approximate the implied volatility in [46] are the ones introduced in [2]. These CTs are not the ones we have used so far in the book. However, for the remainder of this chapter, we stick to the type of CTs in [2] to follow the explanation in [30] as close as possible. This section touches on the main characteristics of CTs in [2], highlighting similarities and differences with respect to the ones we have used so far.

The following result on approximation of continuous functions with a domain of dimension 2 is the starting point. This is given by the *Karhunen-Loève* or *Singular Value Decomposition* (SVD) expansion (see [67]). It says that given a continuous function $f : [-1,1]^2 \longrightarrow \mathbb{R}$, then the following holds

$$f(x,y) = \sum_{j=1}^{\infty} \sigma_j \phi_j(x) \psi_j(y) \tag{19.9}$$

where $\{\sigma_1, \ldots, \sigma_j, \ldots\}$ is a sequence of non-increasing real values and the sets $\{\phi_1, \ldots, \phi_j, \ldots\}$ and $\{\psi_1, \ldots, \psi_j, \ldots\}$ are orthonormal functions.[2]

Each function ϕ_j and ψ_j is a function defined over $[-1,1]$, which has dimension 1. Therefore, each term $\phi_j(x)\psi_j(y)$ in the series of Equation 19.9 defines a function on $[-1,1]^2$. These terms are known as "outer" products of one-dimensional functions, or two-dimensional functions of rank 1.

There are two main elements exploited by the approach in [2]. The first is that the smoother f is, the faster the convergence of the SVD expansion. This means that for a given level of accuracy ε, there is a natural number k — small for smooth f — such that

$$|f(x,y) - \sum_{j=1}^{k} \sigma_j \phi_j(x) \psi_j(y)| < \varepsilon. \tag{19.10}$$

The partial sum

$$\sum_{j=1}^{k} \sigma_j \phi_j(x) \psi_j(y)$$

is called the *partial SVD sum of rank k*. These partial sums are used to approximate f.

The second important characteristic is that the series in Equation 19.9 is given in terms of functions $\phi_j(x)\psi_j(y)$ that are products of one-dimensional functions. Therefore, each of these functions can be approximated to a high degree of accuracy with very few evaluations, using one-dimensional CTs.

The algorithm used in [2] to approximate the finite series in Equation 19.10 is called Gaussian Elimination (GE) with pivoting. Next, we describe the main ideas behind how the approximation is done. We avoid the details of how these ideas are implemented in practice. These are beyond the scope of this book and can be found in [2]. The notation we use is the same as found in [2].

Gaussian elimination with complete pivoting

Let f be a function as the one in Equation 19.9 defined over $[-1,1]^2$. The first thing is to find the point on $[-1,1]^2$ where the maximum of the absolute value of f is attained (assume this is possible). Call this point a pivot point and denote it by (x_0, y_0). Two lines are then drawn through this point, one horizontal and one vertical, as shown on the

---

[2]In the Hilbert space $L^2([-1,1])$.

left pane of Figure 19.1. The function f can be restricted to each of these lines defining functions of dimension 1. We denote the one running horizontally by $r_1(x) = f(x, y_0)$ and the one running vertically by $c_1(y) = f(x_0, y)$. We then take the outer product of these two functions $r_1(x)c_1(y)$ and divide it by $d_1 = f(x_0, y_0)$, the maximum attained by f. What we have produced is $d_1 r_1(x)c_1(y)$, a rank 1 function that we use to approximate f

$$f(x, y) = d_1 r_1(x)c_1(y) + e_1(x, y). \tag{19.11}$$

Note that as both r_1 and c_1 are functions defined over a domain of dimension 1, each can be approximated using CTs of dimension 1 attaining high levels of accuracy with only a few evaluations. What we have obtained is an approximation of $f(x, y)$, using only CTs of dimension 1.

The function e_1 in Equation 19.11 is essentially the error of approximation when using the rank 1 function $d_1 r_1(x)c_1(y)$ as a proxy to f. Notice that one thing that has been achieved is that at (x_0, y_0), the error $e_1(x_0, y_0)$ is 0, that is, the value where f attained its maximum is now 0. We are left with a function $e_1(x_0, y_0)$, that by construction has a maximum value that is less than the maximum value of f.

The starting point for the next iteration of the algorithm is e_1. We then apply to e_1 the same process applied to f. What this does is add another summand to Equation 19.11, which gives a more accurate proxy to f. By repeating the process iteratively, we hunt down the points where the error at each iteration attains its maximum and reduces it to zero at the next iteration. In doing so, we obtain a sum of rank 1 function that gradually approximates f. After k steps of this process, we have

$$f(x, y) = d_1 r_1(x)c_1(y) + \cdots + d_k r_k(x)c_k(y) + e_k(x, y). \tag{19.12}$$

Once the maximum error of the error function $e_k(x, y)$ is below a desired level, the process stops. Notice that one-dimensional CTs are built for the cross-sections of $e_i(x, y)$

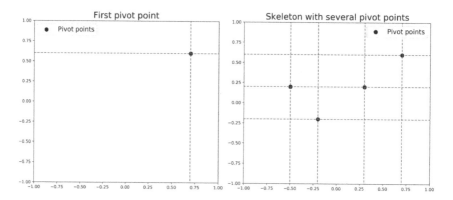

FIGURE 19.1 Left-hand pane shows first pivot point and both horizontal and vertical lines that define functions of dimension 1 to approximate with one-dimensonal CTs. The right-hand pane shows a collection of pivot points and the skeleton that is built to approximate f with a sum of rank 1 functions.

defined by its pivot point (x_i, y_i). These cross-sections may look like the ones represented on the right pane in Figure 19.1. It is only along these horizontal and vertical lines that we consider Chebyshev grids of dimension 1. At no point are two-dimensional Chebyshev grids considered. As the reader will surely have noted, the method presented in [2] heavily relies on the one-dimensional Chebyshev machinery and, of course, on the convergence described in Equation 19.10.

Advantages and disadvantages

One of the virtues of the method presented in [2] is its aggressiveness at reducing the error of approximation. In general, this method has proven to be more efficient at reaching machine precision than the one presented in Chapter 3, which is used in most of the applications discussed in this book.

One of its downsides, however, is that it relies on being able to evaluate the function to approximate many times, a luxury we do not always have in the applications presented in this book. Evaluating pricing functions is in fact something we want to avoid in most cases. Also, the method described in [2] relies on evaluating the function at different stages of the process. This approach is impractical in most settings within financial institutions as the interaction between risk systems and pricing libraries is often slow. Therefore, calling pricing functions in a dynamic manner at different stages in a process can be a problem. Finally, the method in [2] is specific to dimension 2, which limits its applicability.

The method in [2] is, however, ideal for situations such as the one described in this chapter, where a two-dimensional function is to be approximated and the building step can be done offline with virtually no time restrictions.

The remainder of this chapter assumes two-dimensional CTs as described in this section. We assume that all functions f for which we build such tensors are defined over $[-1, 1]^2$. Functions defined on more general domains $[a, b] \times [c, d]$ can be transformed to functions on $[-1, 1] \times [-1, 1]$ through scaling.

19.2.3 Domain of approximation

When choosing the domain of approximation for the function $v(x, c)$, we need to bear two things in mind. First, we want to cover the widest range possible. We should remind the reader that some of the most efficient methods to approximate the implied volatility function fail at this: these methods cannot compute the implied volatility for a considerable number of options in the market. The second is that we want to avoid points where the function $v(x, c)$ is not analytic. This is particularly relevant to the approach put forward in [30], as it relies on CTs; their approximation rates of convergence are unequalled, but these rates rely on the smoothness of the function at each point of its domain.

There are two variables to consider when deciding the domain of approximation. The moneyness variable x is easily dealt with. In Section 19.2.1, we saw that the price of in-the-money options can be expressed in terms of those out-of-the-money. Therefore, it is enough to consider $x < 0$ and x_{max} can be taken as 0. Establishing the lower bound x_{min} is not complicated either. The authors of [30] chose $x = -5$, as this covers the moneyness of the vast majority of options encountered in practice. If for some applications this is too large or too small, it can be changed without altering the method.

Establishing the range for the time-scaled volatility v, however, presents some challenges. To identify a suitable range, let us take a look at the behaviour of $c(x, v)$. By inspecting Equation 19.4, one can see that for any fixed x, $c(x, v)$ tends to 0 as v tends to 0. Likewise, as v tends to infinity, $c(x, v)$ tends to $e^{x/2}$. Moreover, given the nature of these limits, the inverse function — the time-scaled implied volatility — is not analytic at 0 and $e^{x/2}$. Figure 19.2 shows the function $c(x, v)$ and its inverse $v(x, c)$, for $x = -1$. Here one can see how $v(x, c)$ has singular points at $c = 0$ and $c = e^{x/2}$.

The existence of singular points is particularly relevant given the method of approximation we want to use. The convergence properties of CTs is one of the reasons why they were selected in [30] to approximate the implied volatility function. We know from Chapter 3 that if the function is analytic, convergence is quasi-exponential (Theorem 3.2.6). This makes CTs very efficient approximators: very few evaluations are needed to achieve high degrees of accuracy. Therefore, it is essential that the domain of approximation for the time-scaled implied volatility is restricted to values $c_{min} > 0$ and $c_{max} < e^{x/2}$.

We just mentioned that removing singular points from the domain of approximation is essential to secure the convergence properties of CTs. However, even when removed, we are faced with the following dilemma. On the one hand, the wider the range $[c_{min}, c_{max}]$, the closer the domain is to singularities and hence the slower the convergence. Note the convergence rate is still quasi-exponential, but it will be slower (still within this rate), compared to when singular points are far from the domain.

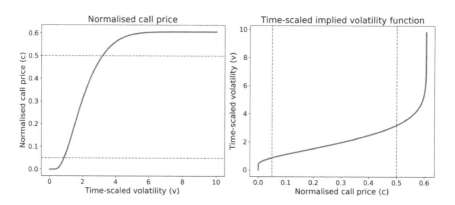

FIGURE 19.2　Left-hand pane shows the normalised call price (Equation 19.4) in terms of the time-scaled volatility for $x = -1$. The horizontal dashed lines mark the points on the normalised call price domain that define regions D_1, D_2 and D_3. The right-hand pane shows the inverse of the normalised call price for $x = -1$. The vertical dashed lines once again determine the points at which the normalised price domain is split into regions D_1, D_2 and D_3.

From this point of view, one may be tempted to take a narrow range $[c_{min}, c_{max}]$. On the other hand, the narrower the range, the fewer options one covers. As both efficiency and range of option prices covered are paramount considerations for the solution proposed in [30], one needs to be careful with the choice of endpoints c_{min} and c_{max}.

19.2.4 Splitting the domain

In the previous section, we mentioned that we want to select a wide range $[c_{min}, c_{max}]$ subject to $0 < c_{min}$ and $c_{max} < e^{x/2}$. However, choosing a wide range increases the building effort due to the proximity of singularity points. To counteract the building effort introduced by a wide range, the authors of [30] decided to split the domain into different regions. Upon scrutinising the behaviour of the time-scaled implied volatility function, they decided to split the domain into four parts.

The idea is to split the domain into regions where the behaviour of the function is homogeneous. As can be seen from Figure 19.2, the time-scaled implied volatility function is very steep on low- and high-volatility regions of c. The dashed vertical lines in Figure 19.2 represent an example of how to split the c domain of $v(x, c)$ into low-, medium- and high-volatility areas. These define three of the regions. The fourth is a subdomain of the low-volatility region obtained by splitting the moneyness domain x.

After the domain has been split into four regions, a CTs is built on each of them, reducing the overall building effort, thereby increasing the efficiency of the method.

The low-, medium- and high-volatility regions are defined by points $c_{min}(x) < c_1(x) < c_2(x) < c_{max}(x)$. We denote the low-volatility region by D_1, the medium-volatility region by D_2 and the high-volatility region by D_3. The fourth region is a subdomain of D_1, along the x dimension, that we denote by D_1'. These regions can be seen in Figure 19.3.

Note that the definition of the points that define the regions D_i, for $i = 1, 2, 3$ depends on the value of x. The idea is that regardless of x, we always end up splitting the regions according to where the function is steep and where the function is flat. We therefore end up with three ranges given by $D_1 = [c_{min}(x), c_1(x)]$ and $x < \tilde{x}$, $D_1' = [c_{min}(x), c_1(x)]$ and $x > \tilde{x}$; $D_2 = [c_1(x), c_2(x)]$; and $D_3 = [c_2(x), c_{max}(x)]$. Once CTs have been built over each region, given a point (x, c), the time-scaled implied volatility is computed by evaluating the CT that covers the part of the domain where c is found.

Defining domain split points

The authors of [30] suggest the following formulas for the points at which to split the regions. For practical reasons, they are first defined on the domain of the time-scaled volatility v. As $c(x, v)$ is monotone increasing, the points on v determine corresponding points in the domain of the normalised price c, which inherit the existing order of the points in v.

(continued)

(continued)

The first point, v_{min} and its corresponding c_{min}, are defined by

$$v_{min}(x) = 0.001 - 0.03x.$$

The points v_1 and v_2 defined by

$$v_1(x) = 0.25 - 0.4x, \qquad v_2(x) = 2 - 0.4x.$$

Finally, $v_{max} = 6$.

The corresponding points on the c domain are obtained by evaluating $c(x, v)$ on the points defined. For example, $c_1(x) = c(x, v_1(x))$.

The splitting along the moneyness dimension x determines the regions D_1 and D_1'. First, both regions have the same range along c, that is, $[c_{min}(x), c_1(x)]$. However, along x we have the following. The interval for x considered initially for all regions was $[-5, 0]$. To define D_1 and D_1', we take the point $\tilde{x} = -0.0348$. The region D_1 is defined by $[-5, -0.0348]$. The remaining part $[-0.0348, 0]$ defines D_1'. Notice that regions D_2 and D_3 cover the whole of $[-5, 0]$ along the moneyness dimension x.[3]

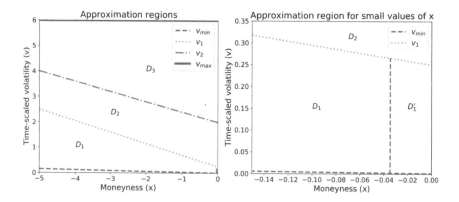

FIGURE 19.3 Domain of the normalised call pricing function is split into four regions D_1, D_1', D_2 and D_3. The plot on the left-hand side shows the whole domain split into the four regions. The plot on the right-hand side shows a close-up look at the area within the domain where region D_1' is found.

It is important to note that the choice of the formulas is partly guided by the fact that they split the domain around the area where we are interested, but also by the simple expression they have. Having a simple expression is very important for the application

---

[3]The splitting at $\tilde{x} = -0.0348$ was chosen by the authors of [30] because empirical results show an increase in the efficiency of the method.

in question, as every time the proxy is used, one must identify which CT to call. This is done by identifying whether $c < c_1$, $c_1 < c < c_2$ or $c_2 < c$. If computing c_1, c_2 is slow, then this adds an overhead to the evaluation of the proxy that we do not want to have.

To speed the part of the process that verifies where a given point (x, c) lies within the domain of approximation, the authors of [30] suggest approximating the boundary regions defined by the formulas using a one-dimensional CT. For example, given that $c_1(x)$ is defined by $c(x, v_1(x))$, which is analytic, it can be approximated very efficiently by a one-dimensional CT. Not only will it be very accurate but also tests such as $c_1(x) < c$ and $c < c_1(x)$ — needed to verify which region D_i the point (x, c) lies in — can be done very efficiently.

19.2.5 Scaling the time-scaled implied volatility

CTs converge quasi-exponentially to functions that are analytic. This is in practice the highest convergence rate one can expect and it translates into very high levels of accuracy through the evaluation of the function in question on a small set of points. Given this situation, one normally does not need to modify the function to make it more amenable to approximation. However, if the domain of the function is close to singular points, the speed of convergence — although it remains quasi-exponential — can be slower than when the singular points are nowhere in sight.

The time-scaled implied volatility function, restricted to the domain described in Section 19.2.4, is an example of a function that poses a challenge even to CTs. The approximation with these tensors is still the most efficient out of all the approximating methods normally available. The question, however, is whether we can make the approximation more efficient — that is, whether we can obtain equivalent levels of accuracy by evaluating the time-scaled implied volatility a smaller number of times.

The authors of [30] explore this possibility by splitting the domain of approximation into regions where CTs are built more efficiently. This was described in Section 19.2.4. By doing this, the complicated behaviour of the function is isolated in two regions (low volatility and high volatility). Then, by using carefully chosen transformations, the steepness of the function in these regions (see Figure 19.2) is changed to something akin to linear. As linear functions are approximated by CTs without any difficulty, these transformations make the approximation of the time-scaled implied volatility function, even in the regions of low and high volatility, a very easy exercise. This results in far fewer Chebyshev points needed to reach very high degrees of accuracy. Next we present these transformations.

Before covering the difficult regions — that is, D_1, D_1', and D_3 — we deal with D_2, the easy case. This region has been, by design, chosen for its lack of steepness and is the farthest from the two singular points affecting $v(x, c)$. As such, it is the one that is bound to be approximated by CTs without much trouble. Therefore, a two-dimensional CT is used, in the way described in Section 19.2.2, to approximate the time-scaled implied volatility function over this region.

The region D_1 and D_1', where $v(x, c)$ has low volatility is the closest to the singular point at 0. In Section 19.2.4, we described how the authors of [30] define c_{min}. The choice was made based on two reasons. On the one hand, we need c_{min} to be greater than 0 to avoid the point where the function is not analytic. On the other hand, we want it to be close to 0 to cover a wider domain of approximation and include market options that appear in practice. However, the closer we get to zero, the steeper $v(x, c)$ is and, hence, the more difficult it is to approximate that part of the function with a CT. This is why composing the function $v(x, c)$ with a transformation to change steepness for linearity (or something close to it) is paramount.

The steepness of the function $v(x, c)$ on the region of high volatility D_3 is dealt with in a similar manner. This time the singularity point is a pole and it is found at $e^{x/2}$. Once again, the bound c_{max} is defined to be less than $e^{x/2}$ to avoid the singularity. At the same time, we want it to be close to it to include as many market options as possible.

In Section 19.2.4, we mentioned that c_{max} was defined in [30] as $c(x, v_{max})$, where $v_{max} = 6$. The authors of [30] argue this choice is good enough as it includes high volatility values and long maturities. This, of course, can be changed if deemed necessary.

Just like in the low-volatility case, the aim is to correct the steepness of $v(x, c)$ on D_3. This is done once more by composing $v(x, c)$ with a transformation that changes steepness for something approximately linear.

Next we present the transformations used on the regions D_1, D_1', D_2 and D_3. The discussion of how these transformations are obtained is beyond the scope of this book. The details can be found in [30] and references therein.

There are two important things to bear in mind about these transformations. The first is that, when needed, they change the steepness of $v(x, c)$ — which hinders Chebyshev approximation efficiency — for quasi-linear behaviours that are easily approximated by CTs. The second is that they scale the domains of the different regions to $[-1, 1]^2$, over which the CTs presented in 19.2.2 can be built.

In the coming sections, we stick, as much as possible, to the notation in [30].

Low-volatility regions D_1 and D_1'

The transformation applied over the region D_1 requires the following functions:

$$\tilde{\phi}_{D_1, x} : [0, c_1(x)] \longrightarrow [-1, 1], \quad c \longmapsto \begin{cases} 2(h(c, x, \delta))^{1/2} & c > 0 \\ -1 & \text{else} \end{cases} \tag{19.13}$$

where $\delta > 0$ is used to correct problems when $x = 0$, $c_1(x)$ is defined in Section 19.2.4, and

$$h(c, x, \delta) = -\frac{2}{(x - \delta)^2} \log(c) + \frac{2}{(x - \delta)^2} \log(c_1(x)) + 1.$$

The inverse of $\tilde{\phi}_{D_1, x}$ is given by

$$\tilde{\phi}_{D_1, x}^{-1} : [-1, 1] \longrightarrow [0, c_1(x)], \quad \tilde{c} \longmapsto \begin{cases} c_1(x) e^{g(x, \tilde{c})} & \text{if } \tilde{c} > -1 \\ 0 & \text{else} \end{cases} \tag{19.14}$$

where

$$g(x, \tilde{c}) = -\frac{2(x - \delta)^2}{(\tilde{c} + 1)^2} + \frac{(x - \delta)^2}{2}.$$

The function defined in Equation 19.14 is the transformation that changes the steepness of $v(x, c)$ on D_1 for something approximately linear. Notice, however, that the image of this function is $[0, c_1(x)]$, which includes 0, a point where $v(x, c)$ is not analytic and we want to avoid. We therefore precompose the function in Equation 19.14 so that it has the same domain $[-1, 1]$ but with image $[c_{min}(x), c_1(x)]$. The latter transformation is a simple scaling given by

$$l : [\tilde{\phi}_{D_1,x}(c_{min}(x)), 1] \longrightarrow [-1, 1], \quad c \mapsto 2 \cdot \frac{c - \tilde{\phi}_{D_1,x}(c_{min}(x))}{1 - \tilde{\phi}_{D_1,x}(c_{min}(x))} - 1. \tag{19.15}$$

This defines

$$\phi_{D_1,x}^{-1}(\tilde{c}) = \tilde{\phi}_{D_1,x}^{-1}\left(l^{-1}(\tilde{c})\right) : [-1, 1] \longrightarrow [c_{min}, c_1(x)], \tag{19.16}$$

which we use to transform $v(x, c)$, by taking $\tilde{v}_1(x, \tilde{c}) = v(x, \phi_{D_1,x}^{-1}(\tilde{c}))$. The function $\tilde{v}$ is close to linear on $\tilde{c}$, defined on $[-1, 1]$, and hence we approximate it with a two-dimensional CT. Notice the same composition is used to define $\tilde{v}_1'(x, \tilde{c})$, the scaled implied volatility function on D_1'. The only difference between $\tilde{v}_1$ and $\tilde{v}_1'$ is the range of values x they take.

Note that the function used to scale $v(x, c)$ is defined using the inverses $\phi_{D_1,x}^{-1}$ and l^{-1}. The functions $\phi_{D_1,x}$ and l will be important when evaluating the proxy generated for the time-scaled implied volatility function. Specifically, given a point (x, c) to evaluate, it must first be sent to the domain of the corresponding CTs to then be evaluated. This is done using $\phi_{D_1,x}$ and l.

Medium volatility region D_2

The steepness of $v(x, c)$ over D_2 presents no problems. As can be seen in Figure 19.2, the time-scaled volatility function is rather flat over this region. Moreover, the domain is the farthest of the four from the singluarity points. Therefore, there is no need to scale the function.

The domain D_2, however, must be scaled to $[-1, 1]^2$ so that we can build a CT of dimension 2, as defined in Section 19.2.2. The scaling transformation is given by

$$\phi_{D_2,x} : [c_1(x), c_2(x)] \longrightarrow [-1, 1], \quad c \mapsto 2 \cdot \frac{c - c_1}{c_2(x) - c_1(x)} - 1$$

with inverse

$$\phi_{D_2,x}^{-1} : [-1, 1] \longrightarrow [c_1(x), c_2(x)], \quad \tilde{c} \mapsto c_1(x) + \frac{1}{2}(\tilde{c} + 1)(c_2(x) - c_1(x)).$$

The inverse $\phi_{D_2,x}^{-1}$ is used to build the CT, as it changes the domain of $v(x, c)$ from $[c_{min}, c_1(x)]$ to $[-1, 1]$. The function we end up with is $\tilde{v}_2(x, \tilde{c}) = v(x, \phi_{D_2,x}^{-1}(\tilde{c}))$. The function $\phi_{D_2,x}$ is used when evaluating the proxy.

High-volatility region D_3

Similar to the way in which the transformation was defined for D_1, we first focus on changing the steepness of the function $v(x, c)$ on D_3, and then adjust the domain of the transformation to avoid the singular point $e^{x/2}$. The first transformation to consider is

$$
\tilde{\phi}_{D_3,x} : [c_2(x), e^{x/2}] \longrightarrow [0, \infty], c \mapsto \begin{cases} \left(-8\log\left(\frac{e^{x/2}-c}{e^{x/2}-c_2(x)}\right)\right)^{1/2} & \text{if } c < e^{x/2} \\ \infty & \text{else} \end{cases} \tag{19.17}
$$

and its inverse

$$
\tilde{\phi}_{D_3,x}^{-1} : [0, \infty] \longrightarrow [c_2(x), e^{x/2}], \tilde{c} \mapsto \begin{cases} e^{x/2} - (e^{x/2} - c_2(x)) e^{-\tilde{c}^2/8} & \text{if } \tilde{c} < \infty \\ e^{x/2} & \text{else.} \end{cases} \tag{19.18}
$$

Notice the image of $\tilde{\phi}_{D_3,x}^{-1}$ contains $e^{x/2}$, a point where $v(x, c)$ is not analytic. Therefore, we restrict $\tilde{\phi}_{D_3,x}^{-1}$ to $[0, \tilde{c}_{max}(x)]$, where $\tilde{c}_{max}(x) = \tilde{\phi}_{D_3,x}(c_{max})$. This gets rid of the singular point. Then we scale the domain $[0, \tilde{c}_{max}(x)]$ to $[-1, 1]$ by precomposing it with the following function:

$$
l : [0, \tilde{\phi}_{D_3,x}(c_{max}(x))] \longrightarrow [-1, 1], \quad c \mapsto \frac{2c}{\tilde{\phi}_{D_3,x}(c_{max}(x))} - 1. \tag{19.19}
$$

Finally, the transformation $\phi_{D_3,x}^{-1}(\tilde{c}) = \tilde{\phi}_{D_3,x}^{-1}(l^{-1}(\tilde{c}))$ is the one we use to transform the steepness of $v(x, c)$ on D_3, to something close to linearity. The transformed function is $\tilde{v}_3(x, \tilde{c}) = v(x, \phi_{D_3,x}^{-1}(\tilde{c}))$, which can very easily be approximated by a two-dimensional CT.

Once more, just like in the case of D_1, the functions $\phi_{D_3,x}$ and l are used at evaluation.

The importance of transforming the time-scaled implied volatility function

The following is a point that should be highlighted once more. The reason behind applying the transformations presented to the time-scaled implied volatility function is not to make something that cannot be approximated into something that can. The function $v(x, c)$, defined over the domains mentioned in Section 19.2.4 is analytic and hence can be approximated quasi-exponentially by CTs. The transformations are introduced to make the approximation much more efficient. For example, on D_1, after the function has been transformed, we need 3,634 points to reach a medium accuracy level (Section 19.3). Had the transformation not been done, we would have required many more points.

19.2.6 Implementation

This section gives the details of the implementation suggested in [30]. It uses the regions defined in Section 19.2.4 and the scaling transformations from Section 19.2.5.

Offline part — building of CTs

The domain of approximation for $v(x, c)$ is split into four regions as described in Section 19.2.4. The aim is to build a CT on each of these regions approximating Jäckel's method ([46]).[4] To improve efficiency, the function $v(x, c)$ is scaled as described in Section 19.2.5. The resulting functions $\tilde{v}_i(x, \tilde{c})$, for $i = 1, 2, 3$ (and $\tilde{v}'_i$), are defined over $[-1, 1]^2$ and have characteristics similar to that of linear functions. Therefore, a CT can be built for each of them achieving high degrees of accuracy without having to evaluate the function many times.

Details such as the number of evaluations used to build CTs for the functions $\tilde{v}_i$, and the accuracy achieved by these tensors are presented in Section 19.3.

Online part — evaluation of proxy

The following steps describe what needs to be implemented to evaluate the implied volatility function σ (Equation 19.3), given the price of a market option, using the CTs built in the offline phase.

A market option has a strike K, maturity T and a price C, the last quoted in the market. The remaining factors required by the implied volatility function σ can also be read from the market. These are the spot of the option underlying S_0 and the risk-free rate r (see Equation 19.3).

- **Normalisation** — The CTs were built for the normalised time-scaled implied volatility function v and not the implied volatility function σ. Therefore, the first step is to transform the data we start off with (S_0, K, T, r and C) to moneyness x and normalised price c. This is done using the formulas in Equations 19.4 and 19.7. If the moneyness of the option x is positive, then we use Equation 19.8 to obtain the corresponding normalised price c for $x < 0$.
- **Region identification** — Once the moneyness x and normalised price c have been obtained for the option in question, we can evaluate the point (x, c) with one of the CTs built during the offline phase. To do this, we need to identify the region where (x, c) lies. The authors of [30] suggest to first check whether $c \leq c_{max}(x)$. If this holds, then check $c \leq c_2(x)$, then $c \leq c_1(x)$ and finally $c \geq c_{min}(x)$. If at any point one of these tests is false, the remaining ones are not performed.

  Remember that c_{max} is a function of dimension 1 (just like $c_2(x)$, $c_1(x)$ and $c_{min}(x)$) and the authors of [30] recommend approximating with a one-dimensional CT. Therefore, the inequality tests above can be done very efficiently.[5]
- **Transformation** — Once the region where the point (x, c) lies has been identified, we evaluate (x, c) by the appropriate scaling function ϕ_{D_i} (defined in Section 19.2.5).

---

[4]The implied volatility function in [46] is the industry benchmark in terms of accuracy and domain covered.

[5]The only boundary that is not approximated with a one-dimensional CT is $c_{min}(x)$. Given its proximity to the singular point $x = 0$, such approximation can be problematic. The verification in this case can be done using the normalised call price in [46]. Note that this will not affect the efficiency of the method too much as $c_{min}(x)$ is the last of the boundaries to be tested, hence the one that is called the least.

Just as an example, assume (x, c) is in D_1. This means $\phi_{D_1,x}(c)$ is in $[-1, 1]^2$, the domain of the CT built for region D_1.

■ **Evaluation of CTs** — Once the point (x, c) has been transformed under the appropriate ϕ_{D_i}, the corresponding CT evaluates it.

■ **Recovery of implied volatility** σ — The CT evaluated returns a value v that corresponds to the time-scaled volatility given the input (x, c). To obtain the implied volatility σ, we use $v = \sigma\sqrt{T}$ from Equation 19.4.

19.3   RESULTS

This section reports the main results in [30].

19.3.1   Parameters used for CTs

There are three parameters that are specified in the building of CTs. The first is the rank k of the SVD partial sum used to approximate the function in question (see Section 19.2.2). The greater the k, the higher the accuracy but the longer it takes to build and evaluate.

The other two parameters are the number of Chebyshev points in each dimension. These are denoted by N_1 and N_2, for the first and second dimension, respectively. Once more, the higher the values of N_1 and N_2, the higher the accuracy but the longer it takes to build and evaluate the CT.

Using a combination of the parameters mentioned, the authors of [30] built three proxies to the time-scaled implied volatility. The idea was to have proxies with different levels of accuracy: low (1×10^{-6}), medium (1×10^{-9}) and high (1×10^{-12}). Each of these proxies consists of four CTs, one per region over which the time-scaled implied volatility is defined (see Section 19.2.4).

The parameters for the CTs built in each of the proxies, along with their corresponding accuracy, are shown in Table 19.1.

Notice, from Table 19.1, that to increase the level of accuracy of a CT, the rank k and the number of Chebyshev points N_1 and N_2, are increased. Also notice that not all regions have the same parameters even for a given degree of accuracy. The idea behind the choice of parameters was to obtain the same level of accuracy across all regions. For example, low accuracy was chosen to have a maximum error of about 1×10^{-6}. The

TABLE 19.1   Parameters used to build CTs. Parameter k denotes the rank k of the SVD partial sum, the parameters N_1 and N_2 the number of Chebyshev points in the first and second dimension, respectively.

Region	Low accuracy	Medium accuracy	High accuracy
D_1	$k = 10, N_1 = 25, N_2 = 36$	$k = 16, N_1 = 46, N_2 = 79$	$k = 22, N_1 = 67, N_2 = 122$
D_1'	$k = 9, N_1 = 27, N_2 = 18$	$k = 16, N_1 = 51, N_2 = 39$	$k = 23, N_1 = 77, N_2 = 57$
D_2	$k = 6, N_1 = 21, N_2 = 20$	$k = 11, N_1 = 36, N_2 = 33$	$k = 14, N_1 = 51, N_2 = 47$
D_3	$k = 5, N_1 = 11, N_2 = 9$	$k = 7, N_1 = 17, N_2 = 14$	$k = 9, N_1 = 23, N_2 = 19$

parameters were then chosen, over each region, so that the CT would have this level of accuracy.

19.3.2 Comparisons to other methods

In the introductory section, we explained the main aim of the method to which this chapter is dedicated. The aim is to build a function that approximates the implied volatility function with the following characteristics: it should have a high degree of accuracy; it should be fast to evaluate; it should cover a wide range of options that appear in real markets; finally, it should have a closed-form expression that can be easily implemented and maintained. To put these characteristics to the test, the authors of [30] carried out the following tests.

Accuracy and speed

First, the accuracy and speed of the Chebyshev method was tested. This was done by comparing it to three other methods. The first is the one presented in [46], by Jäckel, as explained in Section 19.1.1, the most complete, other than the Chebyshev one, and the one used as the benchmark to build CTs. The second method used for comparison is the implementation of the Newton-Ralphson method (an iterative root-finding method) presented in [64]. The third and last, the non-iterative approximation method by Li ([50]), of which there are two versions, one more accurate but slower than the other. These were chosen as they have desirable properties and constitute well-known methods for computing the implied volatility.

The tests for accuracy and speed were done in two different domains. The first, a small domain A_1 where all the methods mentioned can be compared (see Figure 19.4). The Chebyshev method, Jäckel's ([46]) and the Newton-Ralphson ([64]) all cover a much larger domain than A_1. However, the method by Li ([50]), although fast at evaluation, only works on A_1. Therefore, A_1 was chosen to compare all methods.

The second set of tests for accuracy and speed were done over the domain the proxy built out of CTs is defined on. Let us denote this domain by A_2 (see Figure 19.4). As we just mentioned, both the method by Jäckel ([46]) and the Newton-Ralphson method ([64]) can be used over this domain, hence, results can be compared. The method by Li ([50]) was excluded from these tests.

The accuracy of each of the methods is measured in the following way. First a grid of $1,000 \times 1,000$ is generated on the chosen domain of the normalised call price $c(x, v)$, either A_1 or A_2. As an example, consider A_2. Remember this domain is given by $[-5, 0]$ along the moneyness dimension and by $v_{min}(x) = 0.001 - 0.03x$, $v_{max}(x) = 6$, along the time-scaled volatility variable. As this is not rectangular, we first take an equidistant grid with 1,000 points on $[-5, 0]$. Then, for each point on this grid, a grid with 1,000 along the time-scaled implied volatility in the range $[0.001 - 0.03x, 6]$. This establishes the mesh over A_2. Denote, for illustration purposes, a generic point on this grid by (x_i, v_i).

The normalised call price function $c(x, v)$ is then applied to the whole grid defined. This defines a grid of points on the domain of the time-scaled implied volatility function $v(x, c)$, the domain over which this function was approximated with CTs. The grid just defined over the domain of $v(x, c)$ is then evaluated by a given proxy p.

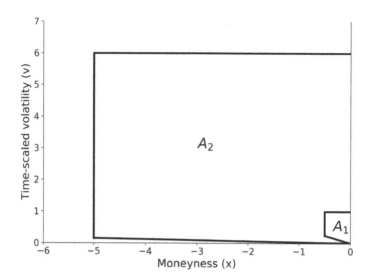

FIGURE 19.4 Domains over which the tests were performed. Domain A_1 is the small domain over which all the methods can be compared. Domain A_2 is the larger domain over which the method by Li has to be excluded from the comparison.

If we start with a grid point (x_i, v_i) and apply $c(x, v)$, we obtain $c_i = c(x_i, v_i)$. Given that $v(x, c)$ is the inverse of $c(x, v)$, then $v(x_i, c_i) = v_i$. Therefore, a way of measuring the accuracy of any proxy p to $v(x, c)$ is to consider $|p(x_i, c_i) - v_i|$, which measures how close the proxy is to being the inverse of $c(x, v)$. This is what the authors of [30] define as $|\Delta \sigma|$.

The second way in which accuracy was measured in [30] was the following. Denote $p(x_i, c_i)$ by p_i. Then we can define $|\Delta c|$ by $|c(x_i, p_i) - c(x_i, v_i)|$.

The speed of evaluation of each method is expressed in Tables 19.2, 19.3 and 19.4 as a proportion of the time it takes to evaluate the Newton-Ralphson.

The following table shows the accuracy and speed of the methods compared over domain A_1.

As can be seen from Table 19.2, the low-accuracy version by Li is the fastest. However, it comes with the smallest precision of all the methods. The high-accuracy version by Li is however slower than the low-accuracy Chebyshev method. On the high-accuracy end of the spectrum, the Chebyshev method is faster than the Newton-Ralpshon and Jäckel method. Jäckel's method, however, is the one with the highest accuracy.

The following table shows the accuracy and speed of the methods compared over domain A_2.

The Newton-Ralpshon and Jäckel methods cover the same domain as the Chebyshev method. The Chebyshev method is faster than the other two for both medium and high accuracy.

Jäckel's method, considered the benchmark, reaches the highest levels of accuracy and is twice as fast as the Newton-Ralphson method. The advantage of

TABLE 19.2 Errors (time-scaled implied volatility and and normalised price) and runtimes for all methods compared over region A_1.

Method	max $|\Delta\sigma|$	mean $|\Delta\sigma|$	max $|\Delta c|$	mean $|\Delta c|$	Runtime
Jäckel	2.80×10^{-14}	4.57×10^{-16}	1.67×10^{-15}	9.99×10^{-17}	1.39
Li (low accuracy)	3.26×10^{-3}	3.42×10^{-4}	2.15×10^{-4}	9.43×10^{-5}	0.12
Li (high accurate)	2.02×10^{-5}	6.12×10^{-9}	1.10×10^{-6}	3.89×10^{-10}	0.63
Newton-Ralphson	2.05×10^{-10}	6.32×10^{-14}	2.91×10^{-11}	1.00×10^{-14}	1
Chebyshev (low accuracy)	1.52×10^{-5}	1.40×10^{-6}	4.91×10^{-6}	3.94×10^{-7}	0.40
Chebyshev (medium accuracy)	3.20×10^{-8}	2.17×10^{-9}	3.52×10^{-9}	5.92×10^{-10}	0.55
Chebyshev (high accuracy)	4.88×10^{-11}	4.78×10^{-12}	1.51×10^{-11}	1.41×10^{-12}	0.67

TABLE 19.3 Errors (time-scaled implied volatility and and normalised price) and runtimes for all methods compared over region A_2.

Method	max $|\Delta\sigma|$	mean $|\Delta\sigma|$	max $|\Delta c|$	mean $|\Delta c|$	Runtime
Jäckel	5.30×10^{-13}	5.35×10^{-15}	2.55×10^{-15}	7.10×10^{-17}	0.52
Newton-Ralphson	8.34×10^{-8}	6.64×10^{-12}	1.94×10^{-11}	1.28×10^{-15}	1
Chebyshev (low accuracy)	2.55×10^{-5}	1.85×10^{-6}	4.63×10^{-6}	1.42×10^{-7}	0.14
Chebyshev (medium accuracy)	4.42×10^{-8}	2.38×10^{-9}	4.02×10^{-9}	1.36×10^{-10}	0.16
Chebyshev (high accuracy)	1.66×10^{-10}	1.32×10^{-11}	1.52×10^{-11}	4.83×10^{-13}	0.20

the Chebyshev method in this respect is that we can choose three different levels of accuracy. This lets the practitioner choose the accuracy level depending on the application and possibly benefitting from the speed gains obtained by choosing lower accuracy. Even the Chebyshev proxy with the highest level of accuracy is faster than Jäckel's method. If lower levels of accuracy are appropriate for the application in question, we gain further evaluation speed. For example, for the medium accuracy level, the Chebyshev method is 3.2 times more efficient than Jäckel's.

Covering real option prices

Two of the strengths of the method by Li ([50]) are its speed and simple expression. We have already shown that the Chebyshev method is fast (Tables 19.2 and 19.3). Also, given that it is based on CTs, it has a closed-form expression and is simple to implement and maintain. On top of this, the Chebyshev method is defined over a much larger domain.

The last test done in [30] is to see whether the Chebyshev method covers real-life options typically present in markets. They used real market data from the S&P 500 index traded on 17 July 2017. They computed the time-scaled implied volatility using the Chebyshev method, the Newton-Ralpshon method ([64]) and Jäckel's method ([46]). Errors were measured the same way as when just testing accuracy and speed. Table 19.4 shows the results.

All three methods covered the whole set of market options.

TABLE 19.4 Errors (time-scaled implied volatility and and normalised price) and runtimes measured on S&P market data.

Method	max $|\Delta\sigma|$	mean $|\Delta\sigma|$	max $|\Delta c|$	mean $|\Delta c|$	Runtime
Jäckel	8.05×10^{-16}	1.40×10^{-16}	2.11×10^{-15}	2.43×10^{-16}	0.89
Newton-Ralphson	1.78×10^{-10}	2.91×10^{-12}	7.72×10^{-12}	2.22×10^{-13}	1
Chebyshev (low accuracy)	1.57×10^{-5}	2.95×10^{-6}	4.44×10^{-6}	4.78×10^{-7}	0.37
Chebyshev (medium accuracy)	4.19×10^{-8}	3.87×10^{-9}	3.45×10^{-9}	3.98×10^{-10}	0.48
Chebyshev (high accuracy)	1.73×10^{-11}	2.21×10^{-12}	2.70×10^{-12}	2.91×10^{-13}	0.58

In terms of speed, the Chebyshev method was the fastest of the three (the other ones being Jäckel's and the Newton-Ralphson method), even when using the high-accuracy version of the Chebyshev method.

The Chebyshev method uses Jäckel's method ([46]) for the evaluation of the implied volatility at Chebyshev points. This means that the levels of accuracy achieved with the Chebyshev method will never surpass those achieved in [46]. However, this should not be seen as a limitation, as the method in [46] reaches machine precision, accuracy that is matched by the Chebyshev method when built with high accuracy.

When it comes to accuracy, the Chebyshev method has a flexibility advantage over Jäckel's method. As can be seen in Table 19.1, CTs can be built with different degrees of accuracy. Moreover, as we lower the accuracy, the tensors increase their evaluation speed. This makes the Chebyshev method more widely applicable as they cover the cases where machine precision is needed, while offering increased speed in cases where lower levels of accuracy suffice.

On top of the speed and accuracy tuning capabilities of the Chebyshev method, it is the only one of the three with a closed-form expression and the simplest to implement and maintain.

19.4   SUMMARY OF CHAPTER

- **The challenge.** There is a considerable collection of methods available to compute implied volatilities. These methods have both strengths and weaknesses. For example, the most efficient methods tend to cover small areas. The most accurate tend to be slower to compute. In this chapter, we use CT of dimension 2 (as defined in [2]) to obtain an approximation of the implied volatility function of the Black-Scholes pricing model, which has the strength of most (if not all) of the methods available.

- **Speed and accuracy.** The method based on CTs offers a very good balance between accuracy and speed. For the lowest levels of accuracy presented (1×10^{-6}), the speed was very high. For the highest levels of accuracy (machine precision), speed remained well within the needs of most applications.

- **Domain range.** CTs are generated by replicating the method in [46], which is the one with the widest domain.

- **Simplicity.** Out of all the accurate methods that cover a wide domain, the one relying on CTs is the easiest to implement and maintain.

## CHAPTER 20

Optimisation Problems

In other chapters of Part IV, we have seen how the correct use of function-replicating techniques, either via CTs or DNNs, can lead to a substantial improvement in the computational cost of several heavy calculations. Computational gains range from 90% in the worst case seen in the applications, up to in excess of 99.9% in some cases. This means that a computation that was taking hours now takes only minutes, seconds or less.

This enables a new paradigm for risk management. Often, risk managers need to find ways to optimise a portfolio. This means maximising or minimising some risk metric (e.g. IMM capital, future funding cost). If the calculation of the risk metric to be optimised takes, say, a few hours, the reality is that the risk manager is only able to try, by hand, a few intuition-based scenarios, compute the new risk metrics, and in that way gain some (very limited) view of the sensitivity of the risk metric to these scenarios. If, by contrast, the risk metric calculation takes, say, one second, the number of things the risk manager can now do to optimise it opens up substantially.

To start with, the risk manager will be able to try, if only by hand, lots of combinations of different scenarios, and obtain in this way a deeper and better sense of the risks being managed. Additionally, one can now insert the risk calculation inside an optimisation engine, so we can find the optimal set of inputs for the risk metric under study, subject to possible constraints given by the optimisation problem itself.

In this chapter, we are going to see a few examples of these.

20.1 BALANCE SHEET OPTIMISATION

A few months before this book went to press, we were approached by a software vendor that specialises in banking book balance sheet management. We were asked if the CTs or DNNs that we were applying to risk calculations could be used to optimise a balance sheet. This section describes the tests we carried out.

A bank's balance sheet

A bank's balance sheet is a very complex financial instrument that sometimes requires computationally heavy calculations to compute. It has a vast number of inputs and outputs.

Banks are always interested in exploring possible changes to the balance sheet that will increase the profitability of the business. For example, what is the optimal proportion of US treasuries? What is their optimal term structure? Typically, the answer to this question is obtained based on intuition and only a few slow manual tests are done due to the amount of time each balance sheet calculation takes.

The idea to exploit this: can we create a replica of the balance sheet via a CT or a DNN and use this fast-to-compute replica inside an optimisation routine in order to find the input values that optimise the balance sheet?

In this exercise, there are four key aspects to be defined. First, we need to define a single number, a metric, that is to be optimised. This metric can be a direct output of the balance sheet or a combination of them. We are going to refer to such a metric as ψ. The metric to be optimised for this exercise was chosen to be the net interest income (NII), a metric that reflects the difference between the revenue and expenses from interest-bearing assets and liabilities.

Second, we must define a number of balance sheet input variables that are to be navigated by the optimiser in order to find the optimal value of ψ. We are going to refer to these variables as x. Which variables to choose is central for the success of the optimisation exercise. The following aspects need to be considered:

- The number of variables must not be too low nor too high. If the number is too low, the exercise will be of limited use for the risk manager. If the number is too high, the computational cost associated with obtaining the metric on all sample points needed to calibrate the CT or DNN architecture could be prohibitively high.
- The variables chosen must be meaningful to the risk manager. They must be variables that can be modified by the risk manager, for example, the number of treasuries in the balance sheet. Moreover, the modification of such variables should change the profitability of the balance sheet.

We are going to refer to the number of these input variables as n, that is, $x \in \mathbb{R}^n$. We denote by f the balance sheet calculation that maps each combination of input variables to the target output metric, $\psi = f(x)$. Note that the balance sheet calculation generally takes many more than n input variables. However, for the purpose of this exercise, all other variables not in x are left constant.

In principle, any variable that is an input to the balance sheet is a candidate to be part of the input variables x. Both continuous and discrete variables can be considered but for simplicity we will focus on continuous variables. Variables to be considered include balance sheet composition, tensor term structures of assets and liabilities, level of charges passed on to clients and so on. For the purposes of the test being run, the first round of candidate inputs considered in x are shown in Table 20.1.

The third aspect to be considered is the restriction we want to impose on the input variables x when looking for the optimal ψ. In the working example, the restrictions were that the balance sheet manager could not change any item in the asset and liabilities by more than 1%, that the aggregated change in total assets should be zero (the same for the aggregated change in total liabilities), and that the balance sheet manager was not allowed to change A6 (other assets), L7 (other liabilities) nor L8 (equity).

TABLE 20.1 Balance sheet input variables for the optimisation routine.

Assets

A1. Cash and balance with Central Bank
A2. Interbank deposits
A3. HQLA level 1
A4. Retail loans
A5. Wholesale loans
A6. Other assets

Liabilities
L1. Interbank borrowings
L2. Retail NMD
L3. Real term deposits
L4. Wholesale NMD
L5. Wholesale term borrowings
L6. Long term borrowings / bond issuance
L7. Other liabilities
L8. Equity

If we name $a_1, \ldots a_6$ and $l_1, \ldots l_8$ the percentage changes to each respective item in the balance sheet, the restrictions just mentioned translate into

$$a_1, \ldots, a_5, l_1, \ldots, l_6 \in [-0.01, 0.01]$$
$$a_6, l_7, l_8 = 0$$
$$a_1 + a_2 + a_3 + a_4 + a_5 = 0 \tag{20.1}$$
$$l_1 + l_2 + l_3 + l_4 + l_5 + l_6 = 0.$$

Given the restriction in Equation 20.1, a_5 can be expressed in terms of $a_1, \ldots, a_4$ and l_6 in terms of $l_1, \ldots, l_5$. Hence the domain in which we need to explore f is given by $x = (a_1, \ldots, a_4, l_1, \ldots, l_5)$. In the running example $n = 9$, and the domain is restricted to $x \in X$, where X is the domain that results from the conditions expressed in Equation 20.1.

Finally, the fourth aspect to be considered relates to restrictions imposed by other outputs of the balance sheet. We denote the set of restrictions of this kind by $\gamma = g(x)$, where γ is an m-dimensional vector, $\gamma \in \mathbb{R}^m$, and g represents the balance sheet calculation that outputs γ. In the working example, the balance sheet manager could do changes to the balance sheet as long as the liquidity coverage ratio (LCR) was greater than 120%, the net stable funding ratio (NSFR) greater than 105% and the capital adequacy ratio (CAR) greater than 12%. That is, $\gamma = (\text{LCR}, \text{NSFR}, \text{CAR})$, and the solutions need to be restricted to $\gamma \in \Gamma$, where $\Gamma = (\text{LCR} > 120\%, \text{NSFR} > 105\%, \text{CAR} > 12\%) \subset \mathbb{R}^3$.

The Optimisation

We want to find the optimal input values x^* that give the maximum target output, ψ^*, where

$$\psi^* = \underset{x \in X, \gamma \in \Gamma}{argmax} \; f(x) \qquad (20.2)$$

where X is the domain determined by the constraints in Equation 20.1, and Γ the constraints on the balance sheet outputs.

In our working example, a CT of nine dimensions was built with six Chebyshev points per dimension. A full Chebyshev grid with these parameters would have 10,077,696 points. If the full tensors is to be used, the balance sheet function f would need to be evaluated on all those points and the resulting values stored. As this is computationally very costly, if doable at all, only 300 from the 10,077,696 were randomly selected. The balance sheet function f was then evaluated on these 300 points and the Rank Adaptive Algorithm run to produce a TT-format CT that replicates f (see Chapter 6).

The optimal input x^* was found using a sequential quadratic programming (SQP) optimiser, in which the TT-format CT, which is very fast to evaluate, was used instead of the full balance sheet function.

By construction, the starting point of the optimiser was $x = 0$. After a number of iterations, the optimal point was found at

$$x^* = (-0.66, 0.13, -0.13, 0.66, -0.77, 0.42, 0.75, -0.42, 0.46).$$

The optimal NII, ψ^*, is plotted in Figure 20.1 together with eight manual balance sheet calculations that the balance sheet manager ran in an attempt to find the maximum NII.

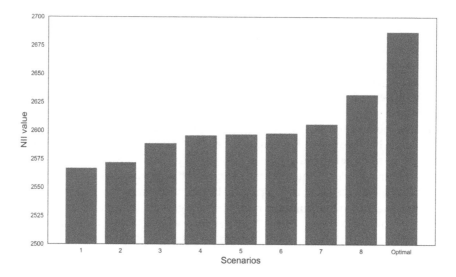

FIGURE 20.1 NII values for different input scenarios. Bars 1 to 8 are manual attempts to find the maximum NII. The last "optimal" bar corresponds to the value found by the optimiser.

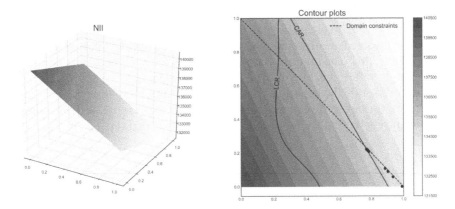

FIGURE 20.2 A 3D plot on the left pane showing the surface of NII in terms of the two high-quality assets. On the right, a contour plot showing the optimisation of NII in terms of the high-quality assets, along with the restrictions imposed on the asset values and balance sheet metrics.

A most valuable tool that can now be used by the balance sheet manager is a 3D and contour plot that provides a visual aid of the effects that changes in the input have on the output ψ. For example, a separate but similar exercise was done with only two variables in x, where the x_1 and x_2 were the proportion of two types of high-quality assets in the balance sheet. The variables were allowed only to take values in the range $[0, 1]$, and there was a further input constraint given by $x_1 + x_2 \leq 1$. There were also output constraints (just like the ones before) imposed on LCR and CAR. After the optimisation was done, the following plots, shown in Figure 20.2, were obtained.

The right pane on Figure 20.2 shows the LCR, CAR and domain constraint lines. The starting point was $x = (1, 0)$, and the risk manager wanted to obtain the optimal proportion of assets 1 and 2 that would maximise NII. The plot illustrates clearly how the LCR is less of a problem than CAR, because the CAR limit will be crossed before the LCR limit from the starting point. The optimiser found that the point of optimal NII was $x = (0.77, 0.23)$, that is, transferring 23% of the high-quality asset 1 to asset 2.

20.2 MINIMISATION OF MARGIN FUNDING COST

Another example of an optimisation problem is the minimisation of funding costs derived from margining.

As intended by the regulation, the introduction of mandatory margining between financial institutions in recent years has had the effect of reducing the CCR between them. In the event of a default, the surviving entity has a variation margin (VM) to cover losses coming from the exposure at the time of default, and an initial margin (IM) to cover potential close-out losses during the margin period of risk (MPoR).[1] This

---

[1]The time it takes the surviving entity to close out the netting set hedging positions and/or reallocate the trades in the defaulted netting set.

framework reduces CCR at the expense of the funding cost and the liquidity risk that arises from the cost of financing the purchase of collateral and from the potential lack of liquidity that the needed collateral may suffer from. An important part of that funding cost comes from IM.[2] The minimisation of this cost is the focus of this section.

The margin value adjustment (MVA) is an XVA price designed to measure the cost coming from IM. It is the expected present value of future funding cost derived from IM. There are various formula frameworks for it. For the purpose of this section, and without losing any generality, we use the following simplified version

$$MVA_i = \int_0^T c(u) \cdot S_i(u) \cdot EIM_i(u) \cdot du, \tag{20.3}$$

where it is assumed that we are the financial institution suffering MVA as a cost, i refers to one of our counterparties, c is the net rate of funding cost for the collateral, S_i is the risky discount factor (that accounts for the joint survival probability of ourselves and counterparty i), EIM_i is the expected IM in the netting set under consideration with counterparty i and T is the time to maturity of the netting set.

A counterparty may have several netting sets. MVA is computed per netting set and added up at counterparty level. Without loss of generality, we assume for the remainder of this section that each counterparty has one single netting set.

The EIM is, computationally speaking, a challenging quantity to obtain, as it requires heavy Monte Carlo simulations. Indeed, we dedicate a big part of Chapter 17 to it. In that chapter, we see how the MVA calculation can be accelerated by orders of magnitude and without any relevant loss of precision with the help of certain approximation frameworks — in particular, with CTs. Important for this section, most of the computational cost associated with the calculation of MVA comes from the calibration of the CTs; once calibrated, subsequent MVA calculations can be done at hardly any computational cost.

Computational Strategies for MVA

That last point will become important later in this section, so it is worth discussing it in more detail.

In the computational strategy developed in Chapter 17, we first calibrate a CT per individual trade and sensitivity. This builds replicas based on CTs for each sensitivity of the trade.[3] Then, the sensitivities of the trades that need to be simulated can be obtained by evaluating the corresponding CT at each Monte Carlo node.

To be noted, a netting set is composed of several trades. Sensitivities are additive, so we can sum up the sensitivities of all trades to produce the aggregated sensitivities of the netting set, at each Monte Carlo node. Then, subsequent calculations (for example, IM) are done with the netting set sensitivities.

---

[2]VM can typically be re-hypothicated, while IM cannot in many cases. This creates a significant added cost in IM.

[3]This could be done with one CT per Monte Carlo time point, or one single CT for the whole simulation. The points discussed in this section are valid for either approach.

From the computational standpoint, the vast majority of the effort comes from the generation of the CTs, as they require the evaluation (a limited but not negligible number of times) of the typically slow-to-compute pricing function for each trade. This can be done in an off-line process, before the evaluation of the sensitivities on each Monte Carlo node, that results in all the CTs needed for the Monte Carlo simulation.

Once simulation is launched and the sensitivities for each trade of a portfolio have been evaluated via the CTs, they can be stored in two-dimensional memory grids that span all Monte Carlo time steps and scenarios. In this way, the simulated sensitivities can be accessed in the future when needed. If all we need in a given calculation is the *portfolio* sensitivities, we can add the grids that contain the sensitivity of each trade into a portfolio grid, and access this portofolio grid when needed.

An alternative approach is to serialise the CTs instead of the sensitivity grids. Let us recall that CTs are very light in memory, typically a few kilobytes each. In this way the storage cost of the IT systems is greatly reduced. This is quite relevant in large investment banks with big portfolios of derivatives. When a simulation of sensitivities is needed, the serialised CTs can be evaluated at hardly any computational cost.

Also, it must be noted that CTs are additive (see Sections 3.9 and 6.1.3) and so the CTs of each single trade can be added to obtain a single CT for the portfolio. In this way, the evaluation of a sensitivity in a netting set can be reduced to one single evaluation of a CT. When this happens, if a netting set has, say, 1,000 trades, this strategy will accelerate the repeated evaluation of the sensitivities an additional 1,000 times (on top of the acceleration coming from the use of CTs compared to full revaluation).

The Use Case

Let us say we are a financial institution with a portfolio of derivatives, divided in a number of netting sets, distributed amongst several counterparties. MVA is a quantity computed for every netting set so that the total MVA is the sum of all MVAs across all netting sets, that is, $MVA = \sum_i MVA_i$.

MVA is a cost for any financial institution operating in the market. As such, it must be reduced as much as possible to optimise the profitability of the trading unit. One way to do so is by adding new trades to the netting sets in a way that the *EIM* is reduced, and hence MVA, too.

It is important to note that reducing only *today's* IM may be suboptimal, because future IM requirements may increase as a result of actions that may decrease today's IM due to future netting effects. In order to minimise MVA via the introduction of new trades into a netting set, one must take a broad view and look at the impact on IM up to maturity T.

With this in mind, let us consider the following strategy. Could we find pairs of *mirroring* positions (i.e. two identical trades, one long and one short, or one payer and one receiver) traded with two different counterparties that have the overall effect of reducing portfolio MVA? This strategy is self-financing by construction and will have zero impact on the market risk of the portfolio.[4]

---

[4]The bid offer spread of the mirror trades would be the only cost. We neglect this cost in this analysis. Also, to have zero market risk impact under the IMA-FRTB framework, both trades must belong to the same trading desk. Impact in other XVAs is not considered in this analysis.

This exercise can be done by manually choosing (based on experience) the mirroring trades. However, this will be slow and clearly suboptimal as only a handful of trials are possible. Alternatively, if we have a way to compute MVA fast enough, we could insert the MVA computation into an optimisation routine and let it find the optimal pair of mirroring trades that minimise MVA.

The optimisation

We ran the test described next. It follows a method similar to the one proposed in [49].

Sixteen theoretical counterparties were created, one netting set per counterparty. One hundred randomly selected but realistic IR swaps were generated for each counterparty. The random components were the direction of the trade (whether it was paying or receiving), the maturity (between 5 and 30 years), and the notional (between $1 and $20 million). MVA was then computed using the method described in Section 17.4, using 10,000 paths, time steps every three months and using the Brownian Bridge Sobol sequence. The interest rate diffusion was done using a one-factor HW model calibrated to typical market conditions. Interest rates, survival probabilities and costs of funding were also calibrated to typical market conditions.

The candidate MVA-reducing mirroring trades were IR swaps defined by their notional, time to maturity, the counterparties to which they are allocated to and their directionality (payer/receiver) relative to each counterparty. The problem of finding an optimal pair of mirroring trades that would minimise MVA was tackled using the Differential Evolution for Integer Programming Problems optimiser.

This test only considered vanilla IR swaps. However, if the portfolios have optionality in them (a more realistic case), more sophisticated candidate mirroring trades (e.g. swaptions) could be used applying the same fundamental methodology described here.

The objective function in the optimiser was $f(x) = MVA(x)$, and the parameter space to be explored by the optimiser is $x = (N, T_{mat}, (i,j), p)$ where N is the notional of the mirror trades, T_{mat} is their maturity, (i,j) are the two counterparties to which the mirroring trades are allocated and p represents the counterparty that gets the payer trade. The aim of the optimisation exercise is to find the x that minimises MVA. If we denote the minimum MVA by MVA^*, then

$$MVA^* = \underset{x \in X}{argmin} \; f(x) \tag{20.4}$$

where X denotes the domain with all possible solutions: notionals between $1 and $30 million, swap maturities up to 30 years and the mirroring trades allocated to two of the 16 counterparties. To be noted, two of the exploration parameters are continuous, notional and maturity, while the other two are discrete.

Due to the large number of trials normally done by optimisers, the optimisation exercise can be run efficiently only if we have a fast way to compute the objective function $f(x) = MVA(x)$. For that, the methods described in Section 17.4 were used, which are based on CTs. As discussed in Chapter 17, similar approaches with DNNs could be considered, too.

In the tests we ran, the CTs used for the MVA calculation were created per Monte Carlo time point. We saw in Section 17.4 that this avoids having to do splines of CTs to deal with the discontinuity points introduced by the payment dates of the swaps.

At each iteration of the optimiser, the MVA of the base portfolio (the one constituted by all 16 counterparties with their corresponding 100 swaps each) with a candidate pair of mirroring trades is computed. The information obtained at this iteration is used by the optimiser to decide which pair of trades to test next. The MVA is then computed for the base portfolio with the new pair of trades chosen. This iterative process continues until the optimiser is satisfied with the MVA value found. The specific details of how the optimiser works — for example, when it decides to stop — are beyond the scope of this chapter; the reader is referred to [77] for more information.

The MVA calculation at each iteration requires the simulation of the sensitivities of the existing portfolio plus the pair of candidate mirroring trades. As explained in Chapter 17, this is the bottleneck of the computation. Given that the optimiser needs to compute MVA lots of times, this step must be accelerated. To be noted, the RFE step of the Monte Carlo simulation could be done once, stored and reused by all the MVA calculations to extra-accelerate each MVA computation.[5]

In each MVA computation, two components need to be considered:

1. **Existing portfolio**. As discussed before, the sensitivities simulation of the swaps in the existing or base portfolio could be done very efficiently because the CTs that replicate the sensitivities for each of the 16×100 swaps could be stored in memory, via grids or via the CTs, and hence they do not need to be recomputed at each iteration of the optimiser.
2. **Candidate mirroring trades**. These mirroring trades change at every iteration of the optimising algorithm, so the CTs that replicate the sensitivities for each of them need to be created and evaluated at each iteration.[6]

In this way, we can compute the MVA of the existing portfolio plus a new candidate pair of mirroring trades very fast. This means the optimiser can find a solution within a reasonable time frame.

Figure 20.3 shows how the MVA with a given counterparty can change when one of the two mirroring swaps is allocated to it. It can be seen how, in this case, the maximum effect is produced with large maturity and notional.

When the optimiser finds the minimum MVA, it will output the optimal pair of mirroring trades: notional, maturity, to which counterparties they are to be allocated and which of them will have the payer/receiver swap.

Obviously, once an optimal first pair of mirror trades has been found, the exercise can be repeated again on the portfolio with the new pair of trades. By running the same exercise again, we want to find another pair of mirroring trades with different counterparties to further reduce MVA. This optimisation routine can be done repeatedly until

---

[5]This step, however, is usually not very expensive.
[6]Appendix H discusses how this step can be further optimised.

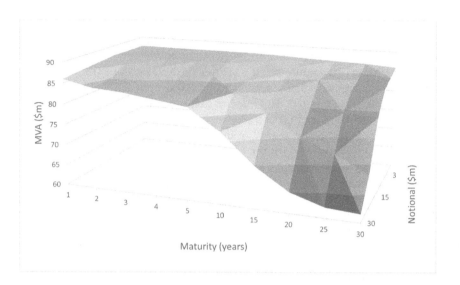

FIGURE 20.3 MVA with a given counterparty, when one of the new payer swaps is allocated to it. The horizontal axis corresponds to the maturity and notional of the new swap.

the MVA reduction is small enough that introducing more IR swaps will not make a difference.

Results

These tests were run on a standard laptop computer, with code in C++, using the QuantLib IR swap pricer. The optimiser took on average one minute to find the solution. We saw that the portfolio MVA could be decreased between 10% and 30% in different tests run.

Implementing this type of calculation in the systems of a financial institution could be highly beneficial as it optimises the portfolio's funding cost coming from IM. In a bank, this type of optimisation calculation would take notably longer than a few minutes, but they could be done periodically (e.g. daily, weekly) so that the MVA cost is always kept at a minimum. For example, they could be run over every weekend so trading desks receive every Monday the candidate mirroring trades to be executed during the week, which will decrease MVA.

Needless to say, these tests were carried out in the context of MVA, but similar approaches could be considered to optimise CVA, FVA, KVA and so on. The fundamental idea is to run the XVA calculation (or other risk calculation to be optimised) via fast pricing (CTs or DNNs), that once generated can be stored and reused, so the XVA calculation is fast enough to be evaluated repeatedly by an optimiser in order to find the optimal portfolio composition.

Further computational enhancement

Appendix H describes how this MVA optimisation can be further enhanced from a computational standpoint.

20.3 GENERALISATION – CURRENTLY "IMPOSSIBLE" CALCULATIONS

The introduction of efficient function replication computational architectures, either via CTs or DNNs, opens the gate for a new range of calculations that, without them, seem impossible. In this chapter, we saw two of them: balance sheet and MVA optimisation. Also, the methodology described for balance sheet optimisation is fundamentally the same as the method described in Chapter 18 for calibration of sophisticated models, another example of an optimisation problem substantially accelerated via function replication architectures.

Historically, the computation of risk calculations has been a cumbersome task. The calculation of XVAs, VaR, IMM capital, PFE, simulation of sensitivities and balance sheet calculation, among others, has traditionally been computationally slow at best, easily taking hours for large and sophisticated portfolios. As a result, any computation that requires the evaluation of these slow calculations many times (e.g. XVA optimisation) was seen as an impossible calculation, hence out of sight for trading units and risk managers.

The introduction of algorithmic solutions like the ones described in this book, together with high-performance computing from a hardware standpoint, enable us to compute many of these risk metrics in seconds instead of hours. As a result, this new computational environment opens the gate for a new generation of risk calculations and creates a new paradigm.

The general idea is that if we are able to locate the steps in a risk computation that create a computational bottleneck, and if we are able to accelerate them a few orders of magnitude via function replication computational architectures, without any relevant loss of precision, a door that was closed before is now open: we are able to plug the risk computation into an optimisation routine to find the inputs to the risk computation that output the optimal risk metric.

The examples described in this chapter show ways to optimise the composition of a balance sheet in order to maximise the net interest income in a banking book or to minimise the MVA cost in a trading book. We are sure that, as time goes by, banks will design more and more optimisation calculations that will be beneficial to their business.

For instance, reverse stress testing is a most valuable analysis tool. It tries to find which market events or conditions could trigger particular negative outcomes for the bank; for example, which market events will bring a given risk metric like VaR, CVA or capital above a certain number that is typically perceived as a seriously bad event.

As a specific example, consider some major currencies to which our business is very sensitive (e.g. USD, EUR, JPY, GBP and CHF), consider parallel shifts for them and study how the risk metric of interest (e.g. profit & loss) reacts to these events. This can be efficiently and comprehensively done by exploring the five-dimensional space defined by the currencies and running an optimiser to find the scenarios that make the bank go into default.

When the only way of computing the risk metrics in question is through slow, computationally expensive routines, we are restricted to only a few iterations of the risk optimisation exercise, typically manually selected. However, if we are able to accelerate the computation of the risk metric with CTs or DNNs, we can now run a vast number of iterations of this exercise through an optimiser. Clearly the latter approach will yield much better results than the former.

All in all, the point we are trying to make is that the acceleration of risk calculations via CTs and DNNs opens a plethora of analytic tools via risk metric optimisation that were impossible to consider without them. We are sure that the quantitative community can make use of them to design many new useful optimisation frameworks in the future.

20.4   SUMMARY OF CHAPTER

- **New paradigm for risk management**. One of the main aims of the solutions presented throughout this book is to resolve the computational bottlenecks present in a wide range of risk calculations. Being able to compute these metrics in a very short period of time lets practitioners run a series of exercises that were not possible before. For example, one can explore *automatically* a considerable number of portfolio configurations with the aim of adjusting specific risk metrics to the appetites of the financial institution. At present, most institutions can only do this exercise manually, if at all.
- **Possible applications**. This chapter presented the results of exercises performed for balance sheet optimisation and the minimisation of margin funding cost. However, these optimisation exercises can be extended to a whole range of metrics such as XVA values, VaR, IMM capital, PFE and sensitivity simulations, among others.

## CHAPTER 21

Pricing Cloning

The reality of IT systems in financial institutions tends to be far from ideal. In an optimal IT setup, risk systems and pricing libraries live inside an umbrella architecture in a way that they communicate and interact with each other seamlessly. However, leaving exceptions aside, quantitative engines in financial institutions tend to have been built over the years in a fairly disconnected manner. Also, sometimes the addition of third-party software from vendors adds complexity. As a result, banks often have an amalgamation of computing systems with cumbersome interaction between them.

Reportedly, some large institutions have tried to create new global systems from afresh to overcome these challenges. In general, this has come with limited success. The computation requirements, system complexities, regulatory necessities and different needs of units within a bank make having a fully integrated system a remarkably challenging task.

One particular common suboptimal feature is that pricing libraries are separated from risk engines. By pricing libraries it is meant libraries to price financial derivatives under risk-neutral assumptions — the often so-called front office (FO) pricers. By risk engines it is meant systems to compute CCR and market risk metrics such as the XVAs, VaR and expected shortfalls, as well as stress testing, among others.[1]

The calculation of risk metrics by risk engines requires the revaluation of large portfolios at many scenarios; from a few hundred up to several million of them. In a world with infinite computing resources, we would want to use the front office pricers in all risk calculations. However, as discussed, often they are not easily available to the risk engine.

In this chapter, we are going to discuss how the methods discussed throughout this book can be used to improve the current situation in IT systems within financial institutions and the positive side effects they bring, as well as the challenges.

21.1 PRICING FUNCTION CLONING

A common theme throughout this book is how to replicate functions for the effective computation of risk calculations. As a solution to these challenges, we suggest ways to

---

[1]Strictly speaking, some of the XVAs are risk-neutral prices (e.g. CVA). However, the complexity of calculation is orders of magnitude higher than traditional risk-neutral pricing models, and they share lots of characteristics with risk engines. Hence, we consider XVA engines risk systems for the purposes of this book.

replicate the pricing function in a manner that delivers identical or substantially the same result, but with an (also substantial) decrease in the computational cost. This is achieved by sampling the pricing function in a number of specific ways — depending on the problem at hand — so that with relatively little information we are able to create an approximation to the pricing function that is both accurate and fast to compute.

The original mindset we had when designing those solutions was generally to decrease the computational load of the risk calculation. However, the solutions created unexpected beneficial side effects, one of which is what we call *function cloning*, which became apparent after a number discussions with bank's quants and IT managers.

Let us illustrate the situation with the discussion we had with the head of XVA IT in a leading European bank. They developed their XVA engine about 2010, before the algorithmic solutions we discuss in this book had been developed. In order to accelerate the calculation, they invested a considerable amount of resources in developing the platform for GPUs. This meant they had to develop specific pricing functions (written in CUDA) for all major trade types. This was quite a task.

There were two groups of trades that could not be priced in the Monte Carlo simulation of the XVA engine. In the first group, the pricing function for a number of trade types could not be developed in CUDA, because it was too complicated to do in an economical manner. Instead, the XVA engine was calling the corresponding front office pricers of these trades running them on CPUs. This was very slow, but it was better than nothing.

The second group was a number of equity trades. They were not being considered by the XVA engine at all. The reason was not only that the pricers were too complex to code in CUDA with reasonable effort, but that the equity pricing library for them was sitting in a system to which, for some reason, the XVA engine could not connect. As a result, this part of the business was being penalised with a punitive XVA contribution from those trades.

As discussed with this head of XVA IT, the CCR methods we explain in Chapter 15 not only could be used to accelerate substantially the pricing step of the trades being priced in CPUs and GPUs — a very interesting step forward in the engine — but the equity trades could now be incorporated into the XVA engine.

His thinking was the following: *"we cannot call those equity pricing libraries dynamically as the XVA engine runs, but we can (semi-automatically) pass a number of scenarios in a flat file to the equity IT team and ask them to return the prices of the trades at those scenarios. We cannot, however, pass millions of these scenarios, only a handful of them. Therefore, if that information is enough for us to construct a pricing function in our XVA system that replicates the equity library pricing function ... we are in business"*.

What this XVA IT manager said was that the methods of Chapter 15 could be used to *clone* the pricing functions from the equity pricing library to the XVA system. That is, leaving aside the (also beneficial) computational improvement of the methods, this cloning feature was most valuable in itself, within his context.

The Cloning

The interaction would work as follows.

Let us summarise the solution described in Section 15.2.2. First, a function f is created via the Composition Technique as described in Equation 21.1.

$$\mathbb{R}^k \xrightarrow{\;g\;} \mathbb{R}^n \xrightarrow{\;P\;} \mathbb{R}, \tag{21.1}$$

$$\underbrace{\phantom{\mathbb{R}^k \xrightarrow{\;g\;} \mathbb{R}^n \xrightarrow{\;P\;} \mathbb{R}}}_{f}$$

where $\mathbb{R}^k$ is the model space of the RFE model that drives the XVA calculation. The number k, which is the dimension of the model space, is a relatively low number, typically between 1 and 10. Each dimension in $\mathbb{R}^k$ represents a stochastic model factor (e.g. a factor in an HW model).

The market space is represented by $\mathbb{R}^n$. This is where market scenarios generated by the RFE live. The market space is formed of yield curves, volatility surfaces and so on. The dimension n of the market space tends to be relatively high — it can be in the several tens or several hundreds. Each dimension in $\mathbb{R}^n$ represents a market factor like a swap rate, a volatility and so on.

The function g is given by the RFE. This is the parametrisation that creates a market scenario from a given element in the model factor space. The function P represents the pricing function of a given trade; this function evaluates market scenarios. In our current context, g resided in our XVA engine, while P sits in the remote pricing library.

Systems interaction

The interaction between both systems would work as follows. As an illustrative example, a two-factor equity Heston model is assumed as RFE (that is, $k = 2$).

1. As a first step, the RFE model diffuses the equity spot and volatility factors, generating N nodes made of the simulation paths and time points. The distribution of model factors just diffused establishes the domain of the model space in $\mathbb{R}^2$ where we need to evaluate the function f, as described in Section 15.2.
2. The points where we need the values of f in order to generate its replica are calculated. If CTs are used for replication, these must be Chebyshev points. If DNNs are used instead, then these points can be randomly generated. Later we elaborate which of these two options is ideal in a given context. Let us denote by M the number of sampling points where f needs to be evaluated.
3. Once we have the sampling points in the model space, we evaluate them with g. This results in M calibrating market scenarios of equity price, volatility surfaces, dividend yield curves perhaps, interest rate curves and so on.
4. All operations up to this point have been done in the risk system — the XVA engine in the working example. Now, we pass the M market scenarios from the risk system to the pricing system. This can be done, for example, via a flat file.
5. The pricing system computes the value of the portfolio at each sampling scenario. These M values per trade are returned to the risk system.
6. The risk system has all the sampling points and values of the trades on the sampling points; hence, the replica of the pricing function can be calibrated in the risk system using the techniques described in Section 15.2 and illustrated in Section 15.3.

7. The risk system evaluates the calibrated replica of f on each of the N Monte Carlo nodes previously generated in the model space, hence computing the price of the trade for the whole simulation.

In this way, we have "cloned" the pricing function from the pricing library into the risk system.

Generic implementation

Figure 21.1 illustrates the pricing cloning method within a generic risk system. Without pricing cloning, the risk system needs to obtain the price of the portfolio on all the scenarios using its pricing functionality (e.g. $N = 5,000$). With a pricing cloning, the risk system generates the calibrating scenarios (e.g. with only $M = 100$). These are then passed to the pricing library for the portfolio to be priced on them. The resulting M values are then passed back to the risk system, where the replica functions are generated. The replica functions are then used to price the portfolio on the original $N = 5,000$ scenarios.

Flexibility and performance

The reader may have already thought of variations of the described methodology. These modifications give flexibility to the setup but can affect the performance of the solution. Let us review some of them.

The Composition Technique is central to this computational strategy. Otherwise, the dimensionality of the input space of the function P to be replicated is huge. This in turn would mean that the sampling or exploration of its input domain can become unmanageable, mainly due to the curse of dimensionality.

For example, in the interest rate world, it does not make sense to explore the pricing function in areas where the one-year and three-year swap rates are 1%, but the

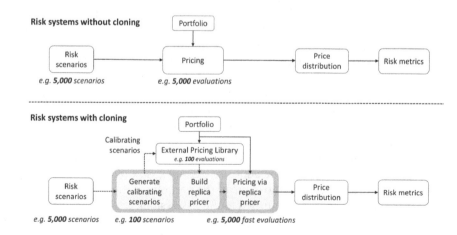

FIGURE 21.1   Illustration of a generic risk system with and without pricing cloning.

two-year swap rate is −0.1%, due to no-arbitrage conditions. What the Composition Technique does is to optimise the constraints we make on the exploration of the function P by restricting ourselves to the regions in the market space $\mathbb{R}^n$ that are relevant to the specific risk calculation; that is, restricting the exploration to the regions of the market space in $\mathbb{R}^n$ that are relevant and that are fully determined by the model space in $\mathbb{R}^k$.

Another source of flexibility comes from the choice of using CTs or DNNs as the function replication method. Typically in the type of IT settings we are considering, we want the interaction between the systems to be as efficient as possible. First, because it is costly to transfer data. Second, because P is typically expensive to run; therefore, we want the number of function sampling points to be as small as possible.

As discussed in Chapter 14, CTs are optimal in this sense as their quasi-exponential convergence is unbeatable in terms of the accuracy achieved for a given number of sampling points. If k is low enough, full CTs are best (that is, the ones that store a value per grid point). As k increases, the Tensor Extension Algorithms allow us to manage the effects of the curse of dimensionality that CTs suffer from (Chapter 6). If k is too large, then we can use DNNs or sliders (Chapter 7), as they can deal with lots of variables in the input domain of f. However, note that, in this case, sliders are in principle preferred, if possible, to DNNs, because they require substantially fewer calibrating scenarios, a critical feature that determines the success of the cloning technique.

When designing the method and architecture for the proxy pricer, all the drivers of the risk in the risk system (i.e. the factors in the model space) should be included.[2] Then, we could build a proxy function per individual trade. However, let us say that the portfolio has lots of quasi-identical trades, for example, options that are equal to each other except for having a different strike. In this case, we could consider adding one dimension to the input domain of f, which now lives in $\mathbb{R}^{k+1}$, where this extra dimension is the option strike. This is going to increase the number of sample points for the exploration of f, so it will be beneficial depending on the number of quasi-identical trades that exist in the portfolio. If there are only a few of them, we will be generally better off not including this extra dimension to the input domain of f, but if the number of trades is high, it may be worth the extra effort of calibrating f with the extra dimension. This topic is discussed in more detail in Section 15.2.3.

Also, we may want to consider some flexibility for the RFE model parameters (e.g. Vol-of-vol in the Heston model). In the previous explanation, these parameters were implicitly ignored. That could be done because they are constant throughout the whole risk simulation. Those parameters are driven by market-implied and historical calibrations that tend to be recomputed daily. This means that, in principle, the proxy functions need to be regenerated daily, or whenever the RFE model parameters are changed. However, those parameters tend to change very little day to day, so we could think of generating the proxy pricers from time to time (e.g. weekly) and ignore the minor error that the change in the model parameters introduce on f. Alternatively, if one is not happy with ignoring this source of error in one or some of the RFE parameters, they could be introduced in the input domain of the function f, so that the proxy to f can

---

[2]In some cases some factors can be left out, and assumed to be constant, if they are known to have a small effect on the risk of the portfolio at hand.

operate without loss of accuracy in the desired range of RFE model parameters. This, of course, will increase the exploration cost when creating the proxy function. This topic is also discussed in more detail in Section 15.2.3.

An extra source of flexibility is given by the possibility of generating one proxy function per simulation time step or one for the whole Monte Carlo simulation that covers all time points. The pros and cons of each approach are discussed in detail in Section 15.3.

Finally, in some risk calculations the function g is not immediately available or it is not obvious. In these cases, it must be created. Sections 15.2.7 and 16.3.2 elaborate on how this can be managed in the context of CCR and market risk, respectively.

It must be noted that an XVA engine was used in this explanation as an example, but the same ideas can be applied to many, if not all, risk calculations. Indeed, the test results shown in Section 16.4 in the context of FRTB were run cloning the front office pricing functions in the market risk engine.

21.1.1 Other benefits

As it can be appreciated from the explanation given so far, one of the benefits of this type of interaction between systems is that no major changes in the systems need to be done to have it up and running. For example, we did a test with a consulting client, in which we played the role of the risk system with no access to the model factors in $\mathbb{R}^k$, and they played the role of the pricing library. The interaction was done via email.

We were given the market scenarios in $\mathbb{R}^n$ on all Monte Carlo nodes by the client. Using these market scenarios, we constructed the parametrisation g as explained in Section 15.2.7. Then the sampling scenarios using Chebyshev grids were generated. These sampling scenarios were then sent via email back to the client. They evaluated the portfolio on the sampling points received and sent them to us. With these values we built CTs to evaluate the price of the portfolio on all Monte Carlo nodes. These prices were then compared to the prices they had obtained via full revaluation. The minimum accuracy (that is, maximum error) per node was $1e^{-3}$.

An added benefit is that, if this type of solution is implemented in a risk engine, all pricing functions cloned have the same evaluation formula (for example, the barycentric interpolation formula in the case of CTs, Equation 3.17), regardless of the complexity of the pricing function. This means that the software development and maintenance effort of this solution in the risk engine is very small — the affected trade-type pricing functions do not need any specific development in the risk engine.

21.1.2 Software vendors

One particular group of beneficiaries from the discussed cloning functionality are the risk systems software vendors.

It is a current trend in the industry to unify all pricing functions. Historically, the front office would use one set of pricing libraries, often considered the official ones. Market risk would price via Taylor expansions (i.e. sensitivity based), CCR via their own pricing functions or some form of basic Linear Regression. This range of pricing functions for the same trade creates a perceived operational risk that auditors and regulators do not feel comfortable with. As a result, there is a push in the industry for unified pricing within organisations. This means that all pricing in the organisation should be done either using the official pricing functions or accurate approximations of them. The existence of the P&L attribution test in IMA-FRTB is an example of this, as it forces the market risk engine to use either front office pricers or something that approximates them to a high degree of accuracy.

This creates a challenge for software vendors, as they tend to use the pricing functionality built into the systems they provide, which is generally different from the front office official pricing functions. However, the pricing cloning functionality discussed in this chapter helps in this regard, as it provides a way to transfer the front office pricing functions that a bank has into the system the vendor provides.

A clear example would be IMA-FRTB. Software vendors may provide all the data management, scenario generation and post pricing functionality that an IMA-FRTB solution requires, but the bulk of the computational burden is the large amount of portfolio revaluations needed in the expected shortfall calculation. The P&L attribution test imposes tight restrictions on any proxy pricing function to be used. However, we show in Section 16.4 how to clone the pricing functions into an IMA-FRTB risk systems. Using this method, the vendor would only ask the client for the price of the portfolio on a relatively low number of calibrating scenarios, from which the client's pricing functions can be cloned into the FRTB vendor system. A similar approach could be used for CCR.

21.2 SUMMARY OF CHAPTER

- **IT systems are rarely well connected**. IT systems in most financial institutions have been developed over a long period of time under the guiding eye of different groups. As a result, IT systems often do not enjoy efficient communication between its different constituent parts. In particular, risk systems in an area of an IT infrastructure may not have direct and efficient access to the pricing libraries it needs for its calculations, which sit in a different area of the bank. This creates a substantial challenge for the computation of risk (and other) metrics, being very difficult to obtain fast and efficiently.

- **Proxy pricers help bridge this gap**. The proxy pricers that lie at the heart of the solutions proposed throughout this book are serialisable and very light in memory. This means they can easily be stored in memory grids and efficiently transmitted to other areas of the bank without the need of sophisticated communication systems. If properly built, these proxy pricers can be used in a wide range of calculations for days to come. By doing this, pricing routines are effectively cloned and used in other systems. This affects not only financial institutions with disjointed IT systems but also software vendors that would benefit from access to the proprietary pricing routines of a bank, without being given full access to the bank's systems.

## CHAPTER 22

XVA sensitivities

The focus of Chapter 15 was the computational challenge associated with the calculation of CCR metrics obtained using Monte Carlo simulations. An important family of CCR metrics is the XVA family associated with a portfolio of trades. As we saw in Chapter 15, these metrics are slow to compute. In practice, practitioners often wait long periods of time to obtain them or simply work with the ones they can compute given the time constraints of the business.

XVA values represent the price of credit risk, funding costs and capital costs in books of derivatives. As a result, it is current market standard to include some of the XVA values in the trading book balance sheet (e.g. CVA, FVA). As the P&L associated with XVA values can be substantial, financial institutions have the incentive to manage and hedge this P&L to market conditions. Therefore, it is extremely valuable to compute the sensitivities of XVA values with respect to market parameters.

In this chapter, we discuss different ways in which the techniques described in Chapter 15 can be used to accelerate the computation of XVA sensitivities.

22.1   FINITE DIFFERENCES AND PROXY PRICERS

A direct and accurate way of computing sensitivities using the pricing functions of a risk engine involves using finite differences. Finite differences consist of computing the change in the value of a function f that results from changing the value of the input variables. This is normally used to estimate the partial derivatives of f. Therefore, if s is the variable with respect to which we are interested in estimating the sensitivity of f, one normally takes a small change in s, fixing all other variables, and evaluates f before and after the "bump" of s.

Let us give an example relevant to our context. Suppose f is the function that computes CVA for a portfolio of Bermudan Swaptions. As explained in Section 15.1, to compute a CVA value, we first have to calibrate the RFE models to a fixed set of market factors (e.g. yield curves and swaption volatilities). Denote today's values for these market factors by $(s_0, s_1, \ldots, s_n)$. Once the RFE calibration is done, many market factor scenarios are obtained at future time points within a Monte Carlo simulation. The portfolio at stake is then priced at each market factor scenario. Finally, these prices are used to obtain the expected exposure profiles and, subsequently, the CVA value in question. For the purpose of CVA values, we think of f as given in terms of $(s_0, s_1, \ldots, s_n)$, that is, $CVA = f(s_0, s_1, \ldots, s_n)$. Therefore, we compute $f(s_0, s_1, \ldots, s_n)$ and the CVA sensitivities we consider are with respect to $(s_0, s_1, \ldots, s_n)$.

Say we are interested in the CVA sensitivity with respect to the first swap rate with value s_0. Using finite differences, we are interested in computing $f(s_0 + \varepsilon, s_1, \ldots, s_n) - f(s_0, s_1, \ldots, s_n)$, where ε is a small quantity; in the case of swap rates, this may be one basis point.[1]

Notice that the sensitivity, computed through finite difference, involves calling f twice: once for today's values $(s_0, s_1, \ldots, s_n)$, the other after the bump has been applied to the market factor in question. If we are interested in 100 sensitivities, this requires the evaluation of f 100 times, which is 101 CVA calculations.

As we know, these are the CCR MC simulations that were the focus of Chapter 15, that are in themselves computationally challenging. As XVA values are sensitive to a wide range of market factors — easily hundreds of them — the computation of XVA sensitivities is a much bigger computational challenge than the computation of XVA itself.

Given that the computational burden of an XVA sensitivity via finite differences comes from the evaluation of the XVA function f, one possible way of accelerating the computation of XVA sensitivities is to obtain the required values of f — that is, $f(s_0 + \varepsilon, s_1, \ldots, s_n)$ and $f(s_0, s_1, \ldots, s_n)$, in the example — using the techniques presented in Section 15.2. We consider two ways in which this can be done, each with advantages and disadvantages. But first, we briefly remind the reader what it means to use the techniques presented in Section 15.2 in the computation of an XVA value $f(s_0, s_1, \ldots, s_n)$.

22.1.1 Multiple proxies

As explained before, the computation of an XVA value means: calibrating RFE diffusion models with respect to a fixed set of market factors; diffusing market factors scenarios; pricing the portfolio at these scenarios; using prices obtained to compute the XVA value. The computational bottleneck tends to reside in the pricing step, so the techniques in Section 15.2 essentially consist of building proxy pricers in a very efficient manner and using them, instead of the pricing functions, at the pricing step at each node of the simulation.

The first way in which proxy pricers (such as the ones described in Section 15.1) can be used to accelerate the computation of an XVA sensitivity is by building proxy pricers at both evaluations of f, that is, for $f(s_0 + \varepsilon, s_1, \ldots, s_n)$ and $f(s_0, s_1, \ldots, s_n)$. Therefore, one incurs the building cost of these proxy pricers twice: once for $f(s_0 + \varepsilon, s_1, \ldots, s_n)$, another for $f(s_0, s_1, \ldots, s_n)$. Given that the use of these proxy pricers can accelerate the computation of XVA values substantially (e.g. 99%), with essentially no loss of accuracy (see Section 15.3), we obtain the same computational gains with no loss of accuracy in the computation of XVA sensitivities.

The computational savings just mentioned mean that if one is normally able to compute 100 XVA sensitivities using the pricing functions in an existing risk engine, then with the help of the techniques presented in Section 15.2 as described, one would be able to compute about 10,000 XVA sensitivities.[2]

---

[1] A basis point corresponds to 0.01% or equivalently 0.0001 in decimal values.

[2] It is assumed that the bulk of the computation is taken by the pricing step in the CCR MC simulation.

22.1.2 Single proxy

The increased computation capability for XVA sensitivities just presented assumes the building of proxy pricers every time the XVA function f is called. An alternative approach, which further increases the computational capability, is the following.

Assume we build the proxy pricers to compute $f(s_0, s_1, \ldots, s_n)$. As shown in Chapter 15, this accelerates the computation of $f(s_0, s_1, \ldots, s_n)$ significantly with no loss of accuracy in practice. The memory footprint of these proxy pricers is very small so they can be serialised and loaded into the XVA engine to be used whenever needed. The missing component so far is the value of $f(s_0 + \varepsilon, s_1, \ldots, s_n)$. In the approach suggested, one needs to build proxy pricers for the new market factors conditions, that is, for $(s_0 + \varepsilon, s_1, \ldots, s_n)$. However, one can also simply just use the proxy pricers built for the conditions given by $(s_0, s_1, \ldots, s_n)$.

The main advantage of reusing the proxy pricers built for the computation of $f(s_0, s_1, \ldots, s_n)$ in the computation of $f(s_0 + \varepsilon, s_1, \ldots, s_n)$ is that most of the computational cost associated with the use of these proxy pricers comes from the building phase (i.e. the generation of the pricing replica functions) while the evaluation of these proxy pricers takes virtually no time. Therefore, the computation of $f(s_0 + \varepsilon, s_1, \ldots, s_n)$ is most efficient once the proxy pricers for $f(s_0, s_1, \ldots, s_n)$ have been built. Note, most important, that this can also be applied when we bump any other risk factor s_i. That is, all values of the form $f(s_0, \ldots, s_i + \varepsilon, \ldots, s_n)$, and hence all sensitivities, can be obtained with essentially the computational effort of obtaining $f(s_0, s_1, \ldots, s_n)$.

The main downside of this approach is that the proxy pricers used in the computation of every "bumped" XVA value, that is $f(s_0, \ldots, s_i + \varepsilon, \ldots, s_n)$, were built using risk factors $(s_0, \ldots, s_n)$. This means the value $f(s_0, \ldots, s_i + \varepsilon, \ldots, s_n)$ may not necessarily be as accurate as if it were obtained with proxy pricers gotten for the corresponding risk factors values $(s_0, \ldots, s_i + \varepsilon, \ldots, s_n)$. How much accuracy is lost depends on a few factors. Practitioners should be aware of this and test the conditions under which there could be a meaningful loss of accuracy.

It is important to note that for some risk factors, there is no difference between rebuilding proxy pricers for the bump and reusing the ones already built on today's values, when no risk factors have been bumped. Let us illustrate with the following simple example. Say we have a European option defined over some underlying s. Assume s is diffused using a GBM model, which assumes constant volatility σ. The pricing function of the European option (and hence the XVA value) is sensitive to both s and its volatility σ. Hence, an XVA on a netting set that contains this trade is also sensitive to both s and σ.

Say we compute an XVA value for this European option using today's values s_0, σ_0.[3] The proxy pricers built will take into account s within their domain of approximation but not necessarily σ as the latter is fixed throughout the simulation. Therefore, each proxy built corresponds to the pricing function of the European function for the fixed volatility value σ_0. Therefore, when we compute the XVA sensitivity with respect to s, the bump $s + \varepsilon$ will not affect the pricing function used in the calculation of the new

---

[3]There will be other factors with respect to which the XVA value is sensitive, but we have omitted them for simplicity.

XVA value, and hence the already built proxies work just like newly created ones. With the volatility, the situation is different, as the volatility passed to the pricing function will be $\sigma_0 + \varepsilon$, whereas the proxies were built assuming σ_0.

For the sensitivity with respect to s, the same proxy pricers can be used with no loss of accuracy. For the sensitivity with respect to σ, one must estimate if the loss of accuracy is material enough to require the overhead of building new proxy pricers.

When having to decide between the two methods presented so far (i.e. multiple or single proxies), one should always consider the context. Building proxy pricers every time the XVA function f is called gives high accuracy. However, depending on the computational power available, one may not be able to compute all the sensitivities needed, despite the computational gains obtained already with the first method. If the loss of accuracy coming from the second method is negligible, or we are happy to put up with some degree of inaccuracy for the benefit of obtaining a larger number of sensitivities, then one should consider using the second approach for some or all sensitivities.

22.2 PROXY PRICERS AND AAD

In terms of accuracy, the state-of-the-art technique to compute sensitivities is Adjoint Algorithmic Differentiation (AAD). With it, XVA sensitivities can be obtained, to a high degree of precision, in about 10 times what it takes to compute a single XVA value. The main downside of AAD is its implementation difficulty. In fact, financial institutions often do not implement it, given the magnitude of this difficulty. However, if the risk engine in question has AAD or is designed to incorporate AAD, it also benefits from the use of the techniques presented in Section 15.2.

There are two main benefits that result from combining AAD with the proxy pricers used for the solutions in Section 15.2. The first is that the calculation of XVA sensitivities enjoys the same benefits as any other CCR calculation — that is, high levels of accuracy at a small proportion of the computational cost. With AAD alone, XVA sensitivities are calculated in about 10 times what a single XVA value takes using the benchmark approach (original pricing functions). The techniques in Section 15.2 increase the speed of a single XVA value by about 10–100 times compared to the benchmark approach. Therefore, the combination of AAD and the proxy pricers presented allow the user to perform an XVA run with AAD around 10–100 times more efficiently.

The second advantage relates to the implementation and maintenance effort of AAD. Part of the complication associated with AAD relates to the fact that one must obtain the adjoint of all the operations embedded in the code. The more code, the more work one typically has to do; the higher the complexity of the code, the more complex the implementation of AAD becomes. The advantage of using the proxies presented in Section 15.2 in conjunction with AAD is that their adjoints are much simpler to obtain compared to the adjoint of most pricing routines. One could implement the adjoint of the generic proxy pricing routine and use it to obtain the adjoints of all pricing functions we are interested in. The result could be a significant reduction in the implementation and maintenance effort of the AAD engine.

## CHAPTER 23

Sensitivities of exotic derivatives

T rade and portfolio sensitivities (greeks) are fundamental to the risk management of all financial institutions. Sensitivities give traders and analysts valuable information regarding how financial instruments change in value given certain market moves. This information is used in multiple functions within financial institutions, ranging from hedging and VaR calculations to asset allocation and so on.

It is market practice to do at least one sensitivities calculation of first order, for the whole portfolio, every day. Some portfolios require second-order sensitivities. Additionally, some functions need to constantly recompute the sensitivities during the day, in a matter of minutes or, ideally, seconds.

In this chapter, we discuss how CTs (Chapter 3) can be used to obtain sensitivities for trades and portfolios, on a single market scenario, in a numerically stable manner, and at a reduced computational cost compared to the finite difference method.[1]

Notice that in Chapter 17 we saw how to use the hybrid techniques presented in Part III to compute the sensitivities of a portfolio of trades inside a Monte Carlo simulation. This is done with high accuracy and at a small fraction of the computational cost of the chosen benchmark computation that consisted of using the sophisticated pricing functions in a risk engine. However, although the sensitivities being computed in that chapter and in the present one are the same, the context under which these are computed is very different. In this chapter, we are interested in the sensitivities of a trade "now", given the current market conditions; in Chapter 17, we are interested in the simulation of future sensitivities inside a Monte Carlo simulation.

This highlights the importance of the context under which calculations are performed. The relevance of the approximation methods used is clear — without them we would not be able to create accurate proxy objects for the values we want to compute. However, the approximation methods can be tailored and optimised for the calculation of a single sensitivity (this chapter) or dynamic sensitivities (Chapter 17) by combining them with the right techniques given the particular environment and conditions under which the calculation of interest is performed.

It must be said that the motivation to write this chapter came only a few weeks before sending the book to press. It is the result of a series of conversations we had with the authors of [1] about the research and results reported in that paper.

---

[1]Also called "bump and reval". The sensitivity is computed by fully revaluing the trade after having bumped the market factor under consideration a small amount.

In this chapter, no numerical results are shown; the reader is referred to [1] for that. However, the details provided should give a clear outline of what steps are needed to start exploring the different ways in which CTs can help with the daily and intra-day sensitivities calculations.

23.1 BENCHMARK SENSITIVITIES COMPUTATION

The sensitivity of a trade with respect to a risk factor at a particular state of the market is often performed using finite differences with the so-called front office pricing functions. To make this more precise, assume the trade has an associated pricing function P and that we are interested in computing its sensitivities with respect to market factor s on market conditions S. Notice that the market conditions S consist of all those market parameters that affect the pricing function P. Therefore, s, the market scenario with respect to which we compute the sensitivity, is contained in S.

The sensitivity with respect to s, at a fixed market scenario (i.e. a state of the market) S_0, computed through finite differences, is obtained as follows. First a small positive displacement for the market risk factor s is chosen. Denote this displacement by ε. This displacement (or bump) is appropriately chosen depending on the type of risk factor. For example, if the risk factor is an interest rate, a displacement of the order of a basis point (0.0001%) is often chosen.

Once the displacement has been selected, two sets of market scenarios or conditions are chosen. The first is the base market scenario S_0. Denote by s_0 the value of the risk factor s at S_0. The second is the market scenario S_ε that has exactly the same values as S_0 for all risk factors except s, which now is $s_0 + \varepsilon$. That is, all risk factor values remain the same and only the market risk factor of interest s is bumped. Finally, these two market scenarios, S_0 and S_ε, are evaluated under P and their difference computed. That is, the sensitivity of P, with respect to market factor s, is $P(S_\varepsilon) - P(S_0)$.[2]

The finite difference method just described can also be used to compute sensitivities of higher orders. For second-order derivatives, we use the same market factor displacement ε, but instead of computing the price of the trade at S_0 and S_ε, we compute the first-order derivative of P with respect to s, at S_0 and S_ε.

The first-order derivative described requires two pricing function calls. Second-order derivatives require two calls to the first-order derivative. Given that the first-order derivative is obtained with two calls, we get a total of four calls to P for second-order derivatives. However, two of the four prices needed are obtained by evaluating P on the same set of market factors. This reduces the number of calls down to three. In general, to compute a derivative of order N via finite difference, we need $N + 1$ calls to the function.

Unfortunately, computing sensitivities via finite differences can in some cases come with numerical noise and a considerable computational burden. This is a problem as it makes the values computed this way not just difficult to obtain from a computational standpoint but useless if the noise present in the values is high. Next we describe such contexts.

---

[2]Or $\frac{P(S_\varepsilon) - P(S_0)}{\varepsilon}$, depending on the context.

Many of the trades in the portfolios of financial institutions are complex products that rely on Monte Carlo simulations for the computation of their price. This not only makes them expensive to evaluate but also it means that the price obtained contains noise. The noise present in the price trickles down to the sensitivities when these are computed through finite differences. In order to reduce this noise, the number of paths in the Monte Carlo simulations used must be increased. However, as the noise in a Monte Carlo simulation is only reduced in proportion to the square root of the number of paths, to achieve adequate numerical stability at the level of sensitivities, one must increase the number of paths considerably — especially if one is interested in computing second-order derivatives, which in some applications are fundamental. When the sensitivity calculation needs to be done quickly (e.g. for dynamic hedging), or when a portfolio contains lots of trades, this computational task becomes a problem.

An alternative to finite differences, in the computation of sensitivities, is AAD. This technique has been mentioned at several points throughout the book. Its main advantages are the estimation of sensitivities to a high level of accuracy and the fact that the computational burden associated with the computation of a single sensitivity is the same as that of computing a large number of them — something very useful if a significantly large set of sensitivities are needed. However, the computational cost associated to the calculation of sensitivities via ADD, in this context, for a given trade, is roughly around 10 times that of a single price of the trade in question. Although not humongous, it is a computational burden that should not be neglected. On top of this, there are considerable complications associated with the implementation of AAD. Finally, AAD is very good at giving first-order derivatives but in practice not so effective for second-order derivatives.

In the next section, we will see how CTs can be used to achieve numerical stability in the computation of sensitivities, while also reducing the computational burden associated with the calculation of such sensitivities via finite differences.

23.2 SENSITIVITIES VIA CHEBYSHEV TENSORS

In Section 23.1, we saw that the use of finite differences to compute the sensitivities of a trade (and hence portfolios) can in some important cases come with two big problems. The first is the large computational burden associated with the calculation. The second is the numerical noise inherited by the sensitivities calculation from the noise intrinsic to the Monte Carlo simulations used to price the trade. In this section, we argue that the use of CTs can help control the numerical noise as well as help reduce the computational load just mentioned.

As an illustration, we focus on the computation of the delta of an exotic equity option, that is, the first-order derivative with respect to the underlying spot of the trade, which trading desks often need updated many times during the day for hedging purposes. However, everything that is said about the computation of delta is also valid for sensitivities of any order, regardless of the risk factor considered.

As we have mentioned, the numerical noise forces us to increase the number of Monte Carlo paths. To give a concrete example, the number may have to be increased substantially, for example to 1,000,000 paths. Therefore, total computational burden associated with the finite difference sensitivity calculation (our benchmark) is of the order of 2,000,000 Monte Carlo paths. Notice that even with a large number of paths, we may still have noise in the delta value. This noise becomes particularly acute as we go to second-order derivatives, for example gamma, the derivative of delta. The reason is that gamma is obtained by applying finite differences to delta which itself is obtained through finite differences.

An example of why stable sensitivities are important

The lack of sensitivities stability is problematic for trading desks. Imagine that we are hedging a portfolio of derivatives. We build our hedges from the sensitivity values. However, if we recompute the sensitivities one minute later and we get quite a different value, which should the trader use?

A common trick used by many in the industry is to fix the seed for the random number generator in the Monte Carlo simulation. With this we make the sensitivities more stable. However, this is sometimes not possible due to system configuration reasons, and also some may argue that that is not a solution but a patch to the problem — by fixing the seed we just turn a blind eye to the inherent noise within the Monte Carlo simulation. On top of this, sometimes the source of the noise also comes from the payoff (e.g. in the case of barriers), and so fixing the seed may not solve the problem in all cases.

The method we propose to reduce the noise and computational burden associated with the use of finite differences uses CTs. However, it must be noted that other types of tensors could be used, too. What we need from these approximation methods is very fast convergence (this reduces the computational burden associated with their use as much as possible) and for their derivatives to be accurate and efficient to compute. As mentioned in Appendix A, other tensors enjoy these properties, too. However, CTs are unique when it comes to the combination of strong mathematical properties and the ease with which these can be implemented in practical settings. Therefore, they are the optimal choice for problems like the one described in this chapter.

Denote the pricing function of the equity option considered by P. We remind the reader that P relies on running a Monte Carlo simulation to return a price. Say that we are interested in computing the delta at a set of market states S, where s denotes the risk factor with respect to which we compute delta.

The objective is to build a one-dimensional CT of the pricing function P along the direction determined by the risk factor s. Once that is done, we can compute the derivative to the order needed, following Section 3.7, and evaluate it at S_0. We know this is done very efficiently and that its accuracy is very high, as shown in Section 3.7. Therefore, the only thing remaining is to review how to build, in this context, the one-dimensional CT.

The point of interest is S_0. The variable considered, the market factor s. Along s, the pricing function P may have singular points — after all we are assuming P corresponds to a complex trade which may have barriers and complex payoffs along this dimension. For simplicity, we choose the interval over which the CT is built narrow enough so that it does not include singular points. This removes the need for Chebyshev Splines (Section 3.8). However, if for whatever reason singularities must be included within the range, then Chebyshev Splines should be considered.

Once the interval has been chosen, Chebyshev points must be specified. From experience (and what has been reported by quant analysts), seven Chebyshev points give good results in these applications. At each Chebyshev point, the function P is called. This is all the information needed to build the tensor. The derivative of the tensor built can be computed very efficiently as described in Section 3.7. The evaluation of such derivative also relies on the barycentric interpolation formula, hence, delta is obtained in no time whatsoever. Higher order derivatives are also easy to compute using the tensor just built.

Noise smoothing and computational improvement

Although the pricing function P used to build the CT has noise coming from the Monte Carlo simulations, CTs tend to smooth out the noise. This is something that interpolants, splines and regression models generally do. This is a very useful property that is taken advantage of in this particular context: this is precisely the element that introduces the stability of the sensitivity calculated. This is illustrated in Figure 23.1. On the left, we see the price of an American option that uses Monte Carlo as the evaluation method. On the right, we see its CT version. It can be seen that the Monte Carlo noise of the original Monte Carlo pricer becomes smoother in the CT version.

Moreover, in the CT, the noise is attenuated to such degree that P does not need the number of Monte Carlo paths used when finite differences are used. In the cases reported, the number of paths used was around 200,000 — five times less than the 1,000,000 used in finite differences.

The total computational cost in the calculation of sensitivities via CTs comes entirely from the number of times P is called to build the tensor. This is because the time it takes to compute the derivative of the tensor and its evaluation at S_0 is negligible

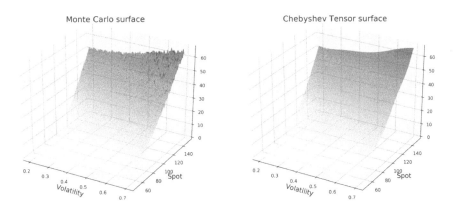

FIGURE 23.1 The left pane shows the noisy spot-vol surface generated with a Monte Carlo pricer. On the right, we have the smoothed surface obtained with a CT that replicates the Monte Carlo pricer.

compared to the Monte Carlo simulations needed to compute values for P. Notice we assumed seven Chebyshev points. This translates into seven calls to P, where P only uses 200,000 Monte Carlo paths. This gives a total computational burden of 1,400,000 Monte Carlo paths. Compared to the 2,000,000 paths used to compute delta using finite differences, this corresponds to a 30% computational gain as a result of using CTs.

When it comes to higher-order derivatives such as gamma, the situation is similar. CTs are built in the same way as done for delta. The only difference is that the CT must be differentiated twice. However, this extra operation introduces no extra overhead via the Chebyshev method. As explained in Section 3.7, this reduces down to a matrix multiplication that is performed very efficiently. Once more, noise stability is obtained even with a reduced number of Monte Carlo paths, due to the properties of the CT. For the case of gamma, computational gains are even higher, as the benchmark requires three calls to P with an increased number of Monte Carlo paths. If we assume 1,000,000 Monte Carlo paths, the computational cost associated with the benchmark consists of the order of 3,000,000 Monte Carlo paths. Building the CT tensor only requires seven Monte Carlo runs each with 200,000 paths. The computational gain, therefore, stands at 53%.

We find it quite remarkable, even counter-intuitive, that when computing sensitivities of Monte Carlo–based pricers via CTs, they become both more stable and computationally efficient under the conditions discussed here, as explained by our colleagues in our conversations.

Final comments

This chapter discussed the basic arguments put forward by practitioners who have been exploring CTs as a tool with which to improve the quality and efficiency in the calculation of trade and portfolio sensitivities. As the reader probably realises, many variants of the approach presented can be explored and tuned.

## CHAPTER 24

Software libraries relevant to the book

In this chapter, we comment on the libraries that have been used in the implementation of the solutions described in this book.[1] In the first section, we give a list of (and comment on) the most important libraries used. In the second section, we describe in detail the suite we have developed, called the MoCaX suite.

24.1   RELEVANT SOFTWARE LIBRARIES

The two main approximation frameworks for the solutions presented throughout this book are based on DNNs and CTs. Next we mention some of the most popular open source libraries that implement these frameworks.

Deep Learning libraries

There are several open source libraries that offer Deep Learning functionality. The following are some of the most popular ones:

- **TensorFlow.** This is one of the most famous open source platforms for ML. Its main focus is on the training and inference of Deep Neural Nets. It was developed by the Google Brain team. It is available at https://www.tensorflow.org/.
- **Keras.** This is an open source Python interface to the TensorFlow Library. Keras was the library used for the Deep Learning functionality in the solutions presented throughout this book. It is available at https://keras.io/.
- **PyTorch.** Although not used in the implementation of the solutions and tests in this book, we think it is important to mention it as it has become in recent years one of the most used libraries for Deep Learning. PyTorch is the Python interface to the Torch library, an open source ML library. It was developed by Facebook's AI Research lab. It is available at https://pytorch.org/.

Chebyshev Tensor libraries

The following are the two libraries used to implement the Chebyshev functionality component of the solutions used in the applications of Part IV in this book.

---

[1]All libraries mentioned here are open source.

- **MoCaX suite.** This consists of two libraries developed by us. It offers all the Chebyshev functionality needed for the solutions described throughout this book. It was developed with a focus on the application of risk calculation. It is available in Python and C++ and can be freely downloaded from https://www .mocaxintelligence.org/.[2]
- **Chebfun.** The Chebfun project was initiated by Professor Trefethen of Oxford University, who leads one of the most important research groups in approximation theory. Chebfun has been developed in MATLAB and offers a substantial range of functionality for CTs in dimensions 1, 2 and 3. Available at https://www .chebfun.org/.

Other relevant libraries

Other libraries were used in both the implementation and testing of the solutions presented throughout this book. Some of the important ones in Python were Numpy, Pandas, Scipy, matplotlib and Seaborn.

The quantitative finance components needed for many of the tests run relied on the open source software for quantitative finance QuantLib, which can be found at https://www.quantlib.org/. Others relied on the financial toolbox in MATLAB.

24.2 THE MoCaX SUITE

The MoCaX Library is the first of the two libraries developed by the authors. It has been designed to build objects that represent *full* CTs of any specified dimension. Several methods have been incorporated within its various classes that let the user perform the main operations possible with these tensors. This part is available in Python and C++. It basically implements most of the methods described in Chapter 3.

The following sections present examples of how to use the functionality within the MoCaX Library for the version in Python. Along with the examples, we sometimes add descriptions of how the methods were implemented.

24.2.1 MoCaX Library

Full CTs, discussed in detail in Chapter 3, are represented by MoCaX objects in the MoCaX Library. Instantiating MoCaX objects is straightforward. In this section, we will see the parameters that need to be specified.

The basic construction of full CTs (that is, MoCaX objects) requires specifying the dimension of the object, the domain of approximation, the number of points that constitute the Chebyshev grid and the values of the function (f) on the Chebyshev grid.

---

[2]At the time of this book going to press, all functionality is available in Python and a good amount (but not all) in C++.

The dimension of the object and the domain of approximation are defined in the following way:

```
import mocaxpy

# Number of dimensions
num_dimensions = 3

# Domain of approximation in three dimensions
dom_values = [
    [-1.0, 1.0],
    [-4.0, 1.0],
    [1.0, 3.0]
]

domain = mocaxpy.MocaxDomain(dom_values)
```

Listing 24.1: Dimension and domain specification.

Notice the package mocaxpy has been imported in the code. This package contains all the classes and methods of the MoCaX Library implemented in Python. Normally, it will be assumed that any code example presented in this book is a fragment of a longer script that imports the package mocaxpy, regardless of whether `import mocaxpy` appears or not in the example.

Also notice the parameter that specifies the domain of approximation, named domain, is an object of a type MocaxDomain. This is defined within mocaxpy and is instantiated by passing a list of lists named dom_values in Listing 24.1. Each entry in dom_values consists of a list with two entries. The list with two entries defines the interval over which the Chebyshev approximation is to be done along the dimension determined by the entry. That is, the values [-1.0, 1.0], which appear as the first entry in dom_values, specify the approximation interval along the first dimension. The values [-4.0, 1.0] determine the interval over the second dimension, and so on.

However, the variable that specifies the dimension of the MoCaX object is simply a variable holding an integer value greater than zero.

To specify a Chebyshev grid, we do the following:

```
# Chebyshev grid
grid_pts = [10, 8, 4]
ns = mocaxpy.MocaxNs(grid_pts)
```

Listing 24.2: Chebyshev grid specification.

The object that contains the information for the Chebyshev grid is of type MocaxNs. This type is defined within mocaxpy. To instantiate an object of this type, a list with integer values must be passed to the initialiser of MocaxNs. In the example shown in Listing 24.2, the list is the variable grid_pts. It must have the same number of entries as the dimension of the MoCaX object to be built (dimension 3 in our example). Each entry of grid_pts corresponds to one of the dimensions in the object and determines the number of Chebyshev points along that dimension. For example, the first entry in grid_pts has value 10. This means that we are asking for 11 Chebyshev points along the first dimension.[3]

So far, the only information missing to define a CT, or equivalently, a Chebyshev interpolator, is the set of values of the function to be approximated f, on the Chebyshev points. There are two ways of making this information available to the MoCaX objects.

The first is to pass the function f as a parameter to the MoCaX object instantiator. In this case, the MoCaX object calls f on each Chebyshev point, finalising the building of the MoCaX object. This is what we call the one-step building process. This, however, requires the function f to have a specific signature.

```
def funct(x1, x2, x3):
    return math.sin(x1) + math.sin(x2) + math.sin(x3)

def wrapped_funct(x, additionalData):
    return funct(x[0], x[1], x[2])

mocax_obj = mocaxpy.Mocax(wrapped_funct, num_dimensions,
                          domain, None, ns)
```

Listing 24.3: MoCaX object built by passing function f.

If the function f of interest is implemented by funct, as in Listing 24.3, it would need to be wrapped into function wrapped_funct. The latter function has the signature required by the initialiser of the MoCaX class.

Alternatively, the MoCaX object can be built in two steps, the first where all the required parameters are passed with the exception of the values of f on Chebyshev points. This is done in the following way:

```
mocax_obj = mocaxpy.Mocax(None, num_dimensions, domain, None, ns)
```

Listing 24.4: MoCaX object partial build. First step.

Notice that wrapped_funct has been replaced by None in Listing 24.4. The object returned, mocax_obj, is an object that is only partially built. It still needs the values of f on Chebyshev points so that it can evaluate points within its domain, the way a tensor or interpolant would. What it can do, however, is return the Chebyshev points that need to be evaluted by f. This is done by calling the following method:

```
eval_pts = mocax_obj.get_evaluation_points()
```

Listing 24.5: Obtaining Chebyshev grid.

---

[3]Remember that counting always starts from 0. Hence, if $n = 10$, then there are 11 points.

By calling the method `get_evaluation_points`, a list of points, denoted by `eval_pts` in Listing 24.5, is obtained. This list consists of the Chebyshev points that define the tensor grid. These points can then be transformed into whichever format the function f takes as input. Once the values associated with the grid points have been obtained and transformed into a list of real values, say with name `funct_grid_vals`, these can be passed to the object `mocax_obj` to finalise the building of the object, as shown in Listing 24.6.

```
mocax_obj.set_evaluation_points(funct_grid_vals)
```

Listing 24.6: Setting values on Chebyshev points within MoCaX object.

This way of building the MoCaX object is particularly suited to situations where modifying f appropriately is complicated. In fact, financial functions (such as pricing functions) implemented within the engines of financial institutions, typically depend on all sorts of attributes within different objects that often sit in different files, containers, and possibly even systems. This complicates the definition of wrappers, such as the one in Listing 24.3, making the two-step approach just described much more amenable.

The user can now build full CTs. In subsequent sections, we review a number of useful operations and functionalities that are useful or necessary for the applications described in this book.

Accuracy management

In this section, we describe the way in which the ex ante error estimation algorithm, presented in Section 3.4, is used in the MoCaX Library. There are two places where it plays a prominent role. The first is when the estimation of the error of an already existing MoCaX object is needed. The second is when a MoCaX object with a specified accuracy wants to be built. This functionality is grounded in the methods described in Section 3.4.

Say a MoCaX object has been built. Getting the error estimate is as simple as calling the method `get_error_threshold` as is done in Listing 24.7. This provides an estimation of the *maximum* error that the CT incurs in the domain of approximation.

```
error_estimate = mocax_obj.get_error_threshold()
```

Listing 24.7: Error estimate method.

In Section 24.2.1, we saw how a MoCaX object was built by specifying the number of Chebyshev points in each dimension (Listing 24.4). If, however, one wants to build a MoCaX object by specifying its level of accuracy, this can also be done. The MoCaX Library has an algorithm that determines the number of grid points needed to achieve this level of accuracy.

The algorithm goes as follows. First, consider a sequence of nested Chebyshev points. This can be obtained, for example, by considering Chebyshev grids with $2^n + 1$ number of points. For each of these grids, the function in question f can be evaluated and the error estimated. The algorithm first does this for the smallest Chebyshev grid.

Say the one defined by $2^1 + 1$. If the error estimate is below the accuracy threshold specified, the algorithm stops and the tensor corresponding to this grid is built. If the error estimate is above the error threshold, the algorithm considers the Chebyshev grid defined by $2^2 + 1$ points. The process continues until it finds a Chebyshev grid for which the error estimate is below the accuracy threshold specified.

Notice the requirement of nested Chebyshev grids is there so that f is called the least number of times. Every time a new Chebyshev grid is considered, the values of f on the previous grid can be used once again.

To build a MoCaX object this way, one does the following:

```
error_threshold = 1e-4
mocax_obj = mocaxpy.Mocax(wrapped_funct, num_dimensions, domain,
                          error_threshold, None)
```

Listing 24.8: MoCaX object built with error threshold.

In Listing 24.8, the variable `error_threshold` holds a real value that specifies the desired level of accuracy. This variable has replaced what before was a **None** value, while the variable ns of type `MocaxNs` has been replaced by None. Notice that the building of this object is done in one step: the function to be approximated is made available to the initialiser of the MoCaX class. The reason is that the algorithm has to dynamically decide which Chebyshev grids are to be evaluated and does not know a priori how many times it will need to call the function. The most efficient way of doing this is by giving it access to the function so the latter is called whenever necessary.

Evaluation of MoCaX objects

This section describes how to call the barycentric interpolation formula to evaluate MoCaX objects (Section 3.6.2).

The barycentric interpolation formula presented in Equation 3.18 was chosen as the algorithm to evaluate MoCaX objects created by the MoCaX Library due to its strong mathematical properties: mainly its efficiency, numerical stability and the fact that it can be called with only Chebyshev points and the values of the function on these points. This formula is run by calling the method `eval`.

```
pt = [0.1, 0.3, 1.7]
val = mocax_obj.eval(pt)
```

Listing 24.9: Evaluating a MoCaX object using the barycentric interpolation formula.

The points to be evaluated by the object need to be defined using lists. In the example presented in Listing 24.9, a list with name pt is defined. It represents a point within the domain of the MoCaX object `mocax_obj`. This list is passed to the method **eval**. Under the hood, the barycentric interpolation formula is used to return a value corresponding to the value of the tensor or interpolant on pt.

Note that, if we try to evaluate the MoCaX object at a point that lies outside of the domain of approximation, the method will raise an exception. The reason is that convergence outside the domain is not guaranteed when working with CTs. In practice, to avoid evaluating points outside the domain of the CT in the applications of interest to this book, we choose domains that are large enough so that all evaluations, at least to a high degree of certainty, will lie within the domain. Given the quasi-exponential convergence of CTs, only a few extra grid points are needed to keep accuracy high, as we increase the domain of approximation.

Derivative computations with the MoCaX Library

The computation of the Chebyshev matrix $\mathcal{D}$, presented in Theorem 3.7.2, has been implemented within the MoCaX software. The order of the derivative needed is specified with the parameter `max_derivative_order`. This parameter must be passed to the initialiser of the MoCaX object during the build phase as follows:

```
max_der_ord = 2
mocax_obj = mocaxpy.Mocax(None, num_dimensions, domain, None, ns,
                    max_derivative_order = max_der_ord)
```

Listing 24.10: Build MoCaX object that can approximate derivatives.

In the example shown in Listing 24.10, the derivative order specified is 2. This means that the MoCaX object built will be able to evaluate a tensor corresponding to the original function f, along with tensors that approximate its derivatives up to order 2. If the MoCaX object built has dimension 3, then the object would have tensors corresponding to all partial derivatives of f of order 1, f_x, f_y, f_z, along with tensors corresponding to the second-order derivatives $f_{xx}, f_{yy}, f_{zz}, f_{xy}, f_{xz}$, etc.

The algorithm operates as follows. The generation of the Chebyshev matrix $\mathcal{D}$ (along with its powers, needed for derivatives of orders higher than 1) is done at build time. Once these have been built and multiplied by the values of the function f on the Chebyshev grid, all the elements needed to evaluate any of the required tensors are ready.

The evaluation of any of the derivatives is done by calling the method **eval**. Listing 24.11 shows how to specify the required tensor.

```
pt = [0.1, 0.3, 1.7]

derivative_id = mocax_obj.get_derivative_id([0, 1, 0])
mocax_obj.eval(pt, derivative_id)
```

Listing 24.11: Evaluate derivative of MoCaX object.

The derivative of interest is specified with a list such as `[0, 1, 0]`. Each entry corresponds to a dimension. The integer in each entry specifies the order of derivative needed with respect to that variable. If the list is `[0, 1, 0]`, it corresponds to f_y. If the list is `[1, 1, 0]`, it corresponds to f_{xy} and so on.

This list is then passed to the method `get_derivative_id`. This returns a derivative identification number that the MoCaX objects uses to identify the tensor that needs to be evaluated. Note that if no derivative identification number is passed, the MoCaX object evaluates the tensor corresponding to the function f.

Splines of Chebyshev with MoCaX objects

Splitting the domain of approximation, and creating splines of CTs, is very easy with the MoCaX Library (see Section 3.8). This is done in the following way:

```
# Specifying list of lists specifying discontinuities
disconts = [[0.5, 0.7], [0.3], []]
mocax_special_pts = mocaxpy.MocaxSpecialPoints(disconts)

mocax_obj = mocaxpy.Mocax(None, num_dimensions, domain, None, ns,
                          special_points = mocax_special_pts)
```

Listing 24.12: Specifying spline points (e.g. for discontinuities and points of inflection in f) when building a MoCaX object.

An object of type `MocaxSpecialPoints` has to be instantiated and passed to the MoCaX object instantiator as the `special_points` parameter. The object named `mocax_special_pts`, of type `MocaxSpecialPoints`, is built in the following way. First a list or container has to be defined. This list, named `disconts` in Listing 24.12, contains a collection of lists. Each of these sub-lists specify the points where the domain must be split. For example, in the code in Listing 24.12, the variable `disconts` is `[[0.5, 0.7], [0.3], []]`. The first list within it, `[0.5, 0.7]`, specifies two discontinuities or special points, as they are called in the MoCaX Library, along the first dimension. Clearly, these points must be within the domain specified by the parameter `domain`, otherwise an exception will be raised. The second list in `disconts` contains only one element, `[0.3]`. The third entry in Listing 24.12 is `[0.3]`. This means there are no special points defined in the third dimension. As `disconts` only has three sub-lists, this means the MoCaX object to be built has dimension 3. If the object's dimension and the number of sub-lists in `disconts` does not coincide, an exception is raised.

Addition and scalar multiplication of MoCaX objects

The operators $*$ and $+$ have been overloaded in the MoCaX Library to define multiplication by scalars and addition of MoCaX objects (see Section 3.9). Given a real scalar value c and two MoCaX objects, `mocax_obj_1` and `mocax_obj_2`, the multiplication and addition of MoCaX objects is done as shown in Listing 24.13.

```
# Scalar value for multiplication
c = 0.3

# Scalar multiplication
mocax_obj_scaled = c*mocax_obj

# Addition of MoCaX objects
mocax_obj_add = mocax_obj_1 + mocax_obj_2
```

Listing 24.13: Multiplication and addition of MoCaX objects.

Note that, in the running example, both `mocax_obj_1` and `mocax_obj_2` have been defined with the same domain instance, `domain`, and Chebyshev grid configuration instance, `ns`. However, adding MoCaX objects does *not* require the same instance of these two types of variables. The only condition is that the domains need to intersect as explained in Section 3.9. When this occurs, the resulting sum object will have the domain given by the intersection. Also, if the number of grid points is different in each tensor being summed, for a given tensor dimension, the algorithm will take the maximum of the two for the sum.

MoCaX Sliders

Sliders of CTs have been discussed in detail in Chapter 7. As a brief reminder for the reader, a Chebyshev Slider is a collection of full CTs joined at a point (called pivot point), that evaluate points of the input domain by adding the values obtained when each full CT evaluates the portion of the input domain it is assigned to. They are implemented, along with the methods needed in practical applications, in the class `MocaxSliding`, defined within the MoCaX Library.

We show how to instantiate an object of type `MocaxSliding` by building the object in two steps. Just as objects of type `Mocax` can be built either in one step (Listing 24.3), or two (Listing 24.4), the building of objects of type `MocaxSliding` can be done in these two ways. Next, we present how to build them in two steps. The example presented should be enough, along with Listing 24.3 to show how they can be built in one step.

As said, a Chebyshev Slider is a collection of full CTs. Each of the constituent full CTs is called a *slide*.

The basic construction of a Chebyshev Slider requires specifying the parameters presented in Listing 24.14. First we need to specify the number of slides along with their dimension. This is done through the list `dimensions_per_slide`, which specifies the number of slides through its length (2 in the example) and the dimensions of each constituent slide (1 and 2 in the example) in its entries.

In Listing 24.14, the slider has two slides: the first has dimension 1, the second dimension 2. Note this implicitly says the function f to be approximated has an input domain of dimension 3, because the sum of the number of dimensions in each slide adds up to the total number of dimensions in the input space of f. To illustrate this clearly, in this example the function is $f(x, y, z)$, which has an input domain of dimension 3. With this slider, we are saying that $f(x, y, z) \sim f_1(x) + f_2(y, z)$, where f_1 and f_2 are each of the slides.

The second parameter that needs to be specified is the one that specifies the domain of approximation. This is specified in exactly the same way as it is done for objects of type `Mocax` — see Listing 24.1.

The third parameter specifies the number of points in the Chebyshev grid per dimension. Listing 24.14 specifies a value of 10 for the first slide (f_1 has dimension 1), and values 8 and 4 for the second slide (f_2 has dimension 2).

Then comes the pivot point around which the approximation of the function f takes place (details of the role played by the pivot point can be found in Chapter 7). The pivot point, given by the variable `pivot_point` in Listing 24.14, is a point within the domain of approximation of f.

The slider object, represented by `slider_obj` is instantiated as shown in Listing 24.14. Once the object has been instantiated, the first stage of the building process has been finished.

As a second step, we must pass the value of the function f at each of the Chebyshev points of each slide to the object. These points can be obtained by calling the method `get_evaluation_points`, just as in the case of MoCaX objects. Once we have these values, we pass them to the slider object `slider_obj` using the method `set_evaluation_points`. This finishes the building process, just as it is done with MoCaX objects as shown in Listing 24.6.

The evaluation of objects of type `MocaxSliding` is done exactly in the same way as it is done for objects of type `Mocax` — see Listings 24.9 and 24.11 — with the method **eval**.

```
import mocaxpy

# Number of dimensions for each slide.
dimensions_per_slide = [1, 2]

# Domain
dom_values = [
    [-1.0, 1.0],
    [-1.0, 1.0],
    [1.0, 3.0]
]

domain = mocaxpy.MocaxDomain(dom_values)

# Chebyshev grid
n_values = [10, 8, 4]
ns = mocaxpy.MocaxNs(n_values)

# Pivot point
pivot_point = [0.0, 0.0, 2.0]

# Partial build
slider_obj = mocaxpy.MocaxSliding(None,
                                  dimensions_per_slide,
                                  domain,
                                  ns,
                                  pivot_point)


# Get Chebyshev grid to evaluate on
eval_pts = slider_obj.get_evaluation_points()
```

```
# Setting values on grid (funct_grid_vals reprents values on eval_pts)
slider_obj.set_evaluation_points(funct_grid_vals)

# Evaluate on point pt
pt = [0.5, 0.2, 2.1]
val = slider_obj.eval(pt)
```

Listing 24.14: Instantiation of slider object.

Slicing and Extrusion of MoCaX objects

There are another two operations that can be performed on MoCaX objects that are useful. These have been incorporated into the MoCaX Library and are called slicing and extrusion. Slicing reduces the dimension of a MoCaX object, while extrusion increases it.

Slicing

Given a MoCaX object `mocax_obj`, we can slice it by simply specifying a value along a chosen dimension. What this does is restrict the domain of `mocax_obj` so that along the chosen dimension it always has the specified value. This defines a hyper-plane of one dimension lower than the dimension of `mocax_obj`.

With this method, a new Chebyshev grid can be defined, which can be seen as a slice (hence the name) of the original domain; for example, using the grid of `mocax_obj` restricted to the sliced domain. Finally, the MoCaX object `mocax_obj` can be evaluated on this grid to produce a new MoCaX object.

This type of operation may be useful in the following context. Suppose there is a large collection of MoCaX objects, not all of the same dimension but with a common set of variables. If we reduce the MoCaX objects down to the set of variables they share, we can then add them to generate a single MoCaX object. If the collection of MoCaX objects had to be evaluated on a distribution of scenarios that only involve the set of variables in common, it is much more efficient to evaluate the addition of these MoCaX objects than each of them individually.

Multiple slicing operations can be performed with one instruction using the MoCaX Library in the following way:

```
# Specifying slice
hyper_plane_slices = [(1, 0.3), (3, 0.6)]

# Specification of hyper-planes to slice along
mocax_obj_sliced = mocax_obj.slice(hyper_planes_slice)
```

Listing 24.15: Slicing of a MoCaX object.

The variable `hyper_plane_slices` specifies a set of pairs, each with the dimension to remove and the point at which we slice `mocax_obj`. In Listing 24.15, the variable `hyper_plane_slices` specifies that two slicings must be performed; the first fixing the second dimension at the value 0.3, the second on the fourth dimension at the value 0.6. The slicing is then performed by calling the **slice** method.

Extrusion

The extrusion operation does the opposite of slicing. It extends the dimension of an existing MoCaX object mocax_obj along a chosen dimension. To do so, an interval is defined for the new dimension to be created. A set of Chebyshev points are specified on this interval. This extends the original tensor grid, along the new dimension, at each Chebyshev point of the new dimension. For each of these grids, we take the same values that mocax_obj has.

This can be useful, for example, if we want to add two tensors that share some but not all variables. If we extrude both tensors to include the variables of the other tensor that they do not have, then these two tensors can be added.

The instructions to extrude an existing MoCaX objects are the ones in Listing 24.16.

```
# Extrusion parameter
extrusion_params = [(1, [0,5])]

# Extrusion
mocax_obj_extruded = mocax_obj.extrude(extrusion_params)
```

Listing 24.16: Extrusion of a MoCaX object.

Extrusion is performed by calling the extrude method. The only parameter that needs to be passed consists of a set of pairs. In Listing 24.16, this parameter is denoted by extrusion_params. Each pair consists, firstly, of the dimension along which the extrusion is performed. Secondly, the range of the variable along which the extrusion takes place. In the example in Listing 24.16, extrusion_params indicates that we must extrude mocax_obj along the second dimension on the range [0, 5]].

Serialisation and deserialisation

Once built, MoCaX objects can be serialised to be stored (as a file or in memory grids) or transmitted through a computer network. The idea is that these objects can be reconstructed at a later time without having to build them again by having to evaluate the function at Chebyshev points. The appropriate methods have been incorporated into the MoCaX Library so that MoCaX objects can be serialised and deserialised.

For serialisation, the following is done:

```
# Serialize the object to a file.
mocax_obj.serialize("mocax_obj_serialised.mcx")
```

Listing 24.17: Serialisation of a MoCaX object.

To serialize an existing MoCaX object, the `serialize` method must be called as is done in Listing 24.17. The parameter passed is the name of the file where the serialised object is stored.

To load a serialised MoCaX object, one must call the static method `deserialize` as shown in Listing 24.18, passing to it the name of the file where the object is stored.

```
import mocaxpy

# Deserialize the object from a file.
file_name = "mocax_obj_serialised.mcx"
loaded_mocax_obj = mocaxpy.Mocax.deserialize(file_name)
```

Listing 24.18: Deserialisation of a MoCaX object.

24.2.2 MoCaXExtend Library

The MoCaXExtend Library is the second library within the MoCaX suite. It provides a Python implementation of the Completion Algorithm and the Rank Adaptive Algorithm presented in Chapter 6.

As a reminder of the contents in that chapter, the CT in TT format that we construct with these algorithms is an approximation of the full CT, calibrated using only a subgrid of the full tensor. Its benefit is that, given that it needs a reduced (often very reduced) grid of points compared to the full tensor, we reduce the number of points where the function to be approximated needs to be evaluated. Under certain conditions (relevant to our applications), the created CT in TT format is a very good approximation of the full CT.

Creating the main object

The main object of this library is an object of type MoCaXExtend. This object handles all the information and methods needed to run the Rank Adaptive Algorithm, which generates CTs in TT format, using only a subgrid of the full tensor.

Listing 24.19 shows how to instantiate the class MoCaXExtend. In this example, we assume that the function we want to build a CT in TT format for is the Black-Scholes pricing function, with an input domain of dimension 5.

There are three parameters that are needed to create the object of type MoCaX-Extend. The first is the dimension of the tensor we want to build. In this case, the dimension is 5, which corresponds to the variables we model: spot, strike, interest rate, volatility and time to maturity.

The second specifies the size of the Chebyshev grid. For this parameter we have, in Listing 24.2.2, a list with five values each set at 10. Each value is used to determine the number of Chebyshev points for its corresponding dimension. However, note that the value assigned to each dimension gives the order of the Chebyshev polynomial whose extrema (maxima and minima) defines Chebyshev points. As the polynomial of degree n has $n + 1$ extrema, the value 10 in each dimension in Listing 24.2.2, determines 11 Chebyshev points per dimension.[4]

The third specifies a list of variable ranges. In Listing 24.19, we see the ranges corresponding to the spot ([50,150]), strike (same as spot), interest rate ([0.01, 0.1]), etc.

These three parameters are passed to the instantiator as shown in Listing 24.19, to create the object.

```
from mocaxextendpy import mocax_extend as me


# -- Parameters needed
dimension = 5
n = dimension * [10]
variable_ranges = [[50, 150],
                   [50, 150],
                   [0.01, 0.1],
                   [0.2, 0.7],
                   [1.0, 3.0]]


# -- Object instance
obj = me.MocaxExtend(dimension,
                     n,
                     variable_ranges)
```

Listing 24.19: Instantiation of a MoCaXExtend object.

Generating subgrid for Chebyshev Tensor building

In order to obtain the CT in TT format that approximates the full CT, through the Rank Adaptive Algorithm, we need to specify a subgrid of the full CT.

There are three ways in which the MoCaXExtend Library allows one to do this. Listing 24.20 shows how to call these three methods. The first is subgrid_by_number. A parameter with the number of grid points required is passed (in the case of Listing 24.20 it is num_scenarios set to 1,000 grid points). This returns a randomly selected Chebyshev subgrid.

---

[4]The reader should note that, at the time of the book going to press, the library only allows for the same number of Chebyshev points in each dimension (i.e. a symmetric grid, 11 points in the example). In principle, we see no reason why the algorithms explained in Chapter 6 should work differently with a different number of Chebyshev points in each dimension (i.e. asymmetric grids). However, we have found that the convergence of the algorithm is negatively affected when asymmetric grids are used. Also, there is little mention in the literature regarding asymmetric grids when tests have been performed ([29] and [69]). Furthermore, the MATLAB code in the public domain that implements these algorithms only considers symmetric grids. The possibility of using asymmetric grids is one that will be considered in future projects. If anyone is interested in this particular problem, please contact the authors.

The second way is implemented in the method subgrid_by_percent. To call it, we must pass a value between 0 and 1, denoted by percent in Listing 24.20. This specifies the size of the subgrid as a percentage of the total grid. Once again, the subgrid is randomly generated and the subgrid returned once the method is called. In the example shown in Listing 24.20, we want 1% of the total grid.

The third method does not generate a subgrid, but rather allows the user to impose a subgrid of choice. The method called is set_subgrid. One must pass the subgrid chosen. The method then stores the subgrid within the object of type MoCaXExtend.

```
# -- Subgrid creation


# Specifying the number of grid points
num_scenarios = 1000
random_cheb_pts = obj.subgrid_by_number(num_scenarios)



# Specifying the percentage of the total grid that we want to keep
percent = 0.01
random_cheb_pts = obj.subgrid_by_percent(percent)



# Setting the subgrid manually
obj.set_subgrid(subgrid_points)
```

Listing 24.20: Generating subgrid required for the building of the CT in TT format.

Setting subgrid values

Once the subgrid of the CT is known, one needs to obtain the value of the function we want to approximate on the grid. These values must then be passed to the object of type MoCaXExtend.

Listing 24.21 shows how to pass the values of the function on the subgrid to the object of type MoCaXExtend. In the example shown, the function is the Black-Scholes pricing function with 5 variables. This function is represented by funct, which evaluates the Chebyshev subgrid random_cheb_pts to obtain vals_subgrid. These values are then stored in the object of type MoCaXExtend by calling set_subgrid_values.

```
# -- Black Scholes function
def funct(x): return [bs.blackScholes("C", *pt) for pt in x]

# -- Function evaluation on subgrid
vals_subgrid = funct(random_cheb_pts)

# -- Incorporate data to rank adaptive object
obj.set_subgrid_values(vals_subgrid)
```

Listing 24.21: Passing the values of the function on the subgrid to approximate to the object of type MoCaXExtend.

Generating training and validation data

Once the Chebyshev subgrid and values of the function to approximate on these are stored within the object of type MoCaXExtend, we generate the training and validation data sets used to run the Rank Adaptive Algorithm. To generate both data sets, we must call the method gen_train_val_data, as shown in Listing 24.22. This method has an optional parameter specified in the example below by percent. This indicates the percentage that should be used for training, the remaining part being assigned to validation. In the example in Listing 24.22, we have specified 0.7, which means 70% percent of the total data passed to the object — that is, the Chebyshev subgrid and function values on it — should be used for training and the remaining for validation. If the parameter percent is not passed, then a default of 0.8 is used.

As the reader may guess from Listing 24.22, the methods get_tensor_size and get_subgrid_size return the size of the full tensor and the reduced tensor (i.e. the subgrid) respectively.

```
# -- Generate training and validation data sets
percent = 0.7
obj.gen_train_val_data(percent)


# -- Size comparison of original grid with subgrid
original_grid_size = obj.get_tensor_size()
subgrid_size = obj.get_subgrid_size()
```

Listing 24.22: Generate the training and validation sets needed to run the Rank Adaptive Algorithm.

Running Rank Adaptive Algorithm

Once the training and validation sets have been generated (Listing 24.22), the Rank Adaptive Algorithm is ready to be run.

Listing 24.23 shows how to do this. The method called is run_rank_adaptive_algo. A series of optional parameters can be passed. These are contained in the dictionary named rank_adaptive_params in Listing 24.23. Next, we briefly mention what they do. For more details, we recommend reading Chapter 6 and reading the documentation included in the MoCaXExtend Library.

The parameter tolerance is the error of approximation beyond which the algorithm stops. The user should specify the desired degree of accuracy for the CT in TT format as a proxy to the function being approximated using this parameter.

The parameter rel_tolerance is used to stop the Completion Algorithm — the routine that is run at every iteration of the Rank Adaptive Algorithm — when progress is slow. The value specified in Listing 24.23 of 11×10^{-8} means that if the error of approximation is improved by less than this value at any iteration of the Completion Algorithm, then it should be stopped and another iteration of the Rank Adaptive Algorithm should be run; for more details on this, see Chapter 6.

The parameter max_iters specifies the maximum number of iterations the Completion Algorithm should run every time it is called.

The parameter `max_rank` specifies the maximum rank we want for the CT in TT format we are building. The algorithm will stop if such rank is surpassed by any of the matrices that constitute the tensor in TT format.

The parameter `print_progress` allows the user to see the progress of the training performed by the Rank Adaptive Algorithm. Training and testing errors are printed and the parameters of the tensors in TT format explored in training shown.

The parameter `max_rounds` specifies the maximum number of times we are willing to try to increase the rank of all the matrices that determine the tensor in TT format without success. If this value is reached, then the algorithm stops.

```
# -- Parameters needed
rank_adaptive_params = {"tolerance": 1e-3,
                        "rel_tolerance": 1e-8,
                        "max_iters": 100,
                        "max_rank": 10,
                        "print_progress": True,
                        "max_rounds": 5}


# -- Building of Chebyshev Tensor in TT format
obj.run_rank_adaptive_algo(**rank_adaptive_params)
```

Listing 24.23: Running the Rank Adaptive Algorithm.

Evaluating Chebyshev Tensor in TT format

Once a CT in TT format has been built, it is ready to be evaluated.

In order to evaluate the CT on a collection of points, the method `cheb_tensor_evals` should be called. Listing 24.24 shows that the collection of points on which we want to evaluate the CT is the only parameter passed.

Upon calling the method `cheb_tensor_evals`, we obtain the values of the tensor on the collection of points passed. Note that if the object of type `MocaxExtend` does not have a trained CT in TT format stored as an attribute, the evaluation method will raise an exception.

```
# -- Evaluate Chebyshev Tensor in TT format on collection of points
vals = obj.cheb_tensor_evals(pts)
```

Listing 24.24: Evaluation of the CT in TT format on a collection of points.

The reader should note that the `run_rank_adaptive_algo` method can be called more than once. Every time it is called, a new CT in TT format will be obtained. Even if the parameters used to run the algorithm are the same, the tensors obtained in different runs may not be the same as the algorithm explores the space in search of optimal tensors generating random numbers at different parts of the process.

Serialisation and deserialisation

Just like the MoCaX objects, MoCaXExtend objects can be serialised and deserialised. This means that once the MoCaXExtend object has been built and a CT in TT format built, we can serialise the object. This allows us to use the object at a future date without having to build it again. Note that the object obj stores the last TT tensor (cheb_tensor_tt) trained as an attribute with name trained_tt_tensor. The serialisation and deserialisation of objects of type MocaxExtend is shown in Listing 24.25.

```
import mocax_extend as me

# -- Serialization
obj.serialize("MocaxExtend_obj.pickle")

# -- Deserialization
obj_des = me.MocaxExtend.deserialize("MocaxExtend_obj.pickle")
```

Listing 24.25: Serialisation and deserialisation of MoCaXExtend objects.

Appendices

Families of orthogonal polynomials

Chapter 3 focused on Chebyshev grids and tensors defined over these grids, their associated polynomial interpolants and the remarkable mathematical properties they have as approximating objects. However, Chebyshev polynomials are just one of many families of *orthogonal polynomials*, some of which also enjoy strong mathematical properties.

A family of polynomials p_k defined on the interval $[-1, 1]$, where $k = 0, 1, 2, \ldots$, is said to be orthogonal if

$$\langle p_i, p_j \rangle = \int_{-1}^{1} p_i(x)p_j(x)w(x)dx = 0 \tag{A.1}$$

when $i \neq j$. The function w is called the *weight* or *measure* function, which makes the function defined in Equation A.1 an inner product — hence, why p_i is said to be orthogonal to p_j. There is a vast collection of families of orthogonal polynomials, each defined by their own weight function.

The roots of these polynomials are grid points of interest when it comes to interpolants. For some of these families, the polynomial interpolants do not have good properties as function approximators. However, for others, such as Chebyshev polynomials, their convergence properties are remarkable, as discussed extensively in Chapter 3.

For each family of orthogonal polynomials, one can define a potential associated with it, either by considering their roots or the points where they attain their extrema, as charges in space. In that section, we also saw the strong connection between potential theory and function approximation and how, from all the possible ways in which points can be distributed, the energy-minimising distribution of points is the one that minimises interpolation errors.

When the family of orthogonal polynomials are the Chebyshev polynomials, the energy associated with the potential field defined by the points where these polynomials attain maxima and minima is as low as it can be. This means that the interpolants and tensors defined over these points (Chebyshev points) converge exponentially, which is as good as one can hope for in practice. Other families of polynomials have similar convergence properties, for example, Legendre, Jacobi and GegenBauer (see [72]).

385

In particular, the roots of these families of polynomials also define potential fields with low energy levels and, hence, high degrees of accuracy are obtained by their corresponding interpolants and tensors.

Even when, from a mathematical point of view, there is no difference between the convergence of Legendre, Jacobi, Gegenbauer and Chebyshev interpolants, there are other properties that only Chebyshev interpolants have, which can have a big impact in contexts where practicality matters. For example, the expression of the barycentric interpolation formula simplifies considerably when Chebyshev points are used. Also, in the case of Chebyshev interpolants, going from its expression in terms of Lagrange polynomials (expression that only needs the values of the function on the grid, as can be seen in Equation 3.15) to its expression in terms of Chebyshev polynomials, only takes an effort proportion to $\mathcal{O}(nlog(n))$ through the Fast Fourier Transform. This helps a lot, for example, in estimating the accuracy of the approximation in an efficient way (see Section 3.4).

The examples just mentioned may not be relevant from a mathematical point of view. However, they are paramount in practical applications such as the ones presented in Part IV. In general, any application brings all sorts of challenges, independent of the mathematical objects used. In the spirit of Occam's razor, it is always better to keep the tools and methods used to solve problems as simple as possible.[1]

---

[1]Occam's razor normally associated with the idea that "the simplest solution is most likely the right one".

Exponential convergence of Chebyshev Tensors

I n Section 3.6.3, we described how to use the barycentric interpolation formula — which evaluates CTs of dimension 1 in an efficient and numerically stable manner — to evaluate CTs of dimension greater than 1.

We remind the reader that the expression of the barycentric interpolation formula when the grid chosen is given by Chebyshev points is given by

$$p_n(x) = \sum_{j=0}^{n} {}' \frac{(-1)^j v_j}{x - x_j} \Big/ \sum_{j=0}^{n} {}' \frac{(-1)^j}{x - x_j}. \tag{B.1}$$

We have that $p_n(x) = v_j$ if $x = x_j$, where v_j is the value of the function f being approximated by the CT at the Chebyshev point x_j. Also note the symbol ' means the summation is multiplied by 0.5, when $j = 0, n$. We will refer to the formula in Equation B.1 as the 'formula' during this chapter.

Notice that when the formula is used on a CT of dimension 1, the inputs to the formula v_j are the exact value of the function f being approximated. The output of the formula is the value of the Chebyshev interpolant, which is an approximation to f, hence it carries an error.

When the formula is used to evaluate CTs of dimension greater than 1 (as explained in Section 3.6.3), the formula is called several times along each dimension. When called on the first dimension, the input to the formula is the exact value of the function f being approximated. However, when we move to the remaining dimensions, the input to the formula corresponds to the output of the formula in the previous dimension. This means that the input to the formula for these dimensions contains an error if compared to the value of the function f. The question here is how this error accumulates as we call the formula repeatedly, dimension after dimension. In this appendix, we see how this error decreases exponentially as we increase the number of Chebyshev points in every dimension.

To simplify the exposition, we assume a two-dimensional CT. The reader should easily see how the arguments presented extend to any dimension.

The mesh of the two-dimensional CT to be evaluated is represented by Figure B.1. This figure also shows the way we group horizontally running Chebyshev points into

CTs of dimension 1. These are the first ones to be evaluated whenever a point such as **X** in Figure B.1 has to be evaluated. The resulting values of evaluating the horizontal CTs are marked by circles. These values constitute a CT of dimension 1 running vertically. The formula uses these values as input to evaluate the value at **X**. As we mentioned before, the values represented by the circles are not the values of the function f at the circles, but the approximations of them given by the output of the formula at each horizontal CT of dimension 1.

Take a generic point (x, y) in the domain of the tensor. Its value under f is given by $f(x, y)$. If the values on the circles in Figure B.1 are denoted by $\tilde{v}_j$, for $j = 0, 1, \ldots, n$, then the error between the output of the Chebyshev Tensor of dimension 1 running vertically and the function f, is given by

$$\left| \sum_{j=0}^{n} \tilde{v}_j \ell_j(y) - f(x, y) \right|,$$ (B.2)

where the expression on the left is the Chebyshev interpolant expressed in terms of Lagrange polynomials, and we have assumed $n + 1$ Chebyshev points running vertically.

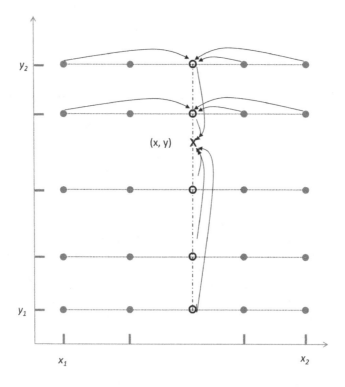

FIGURE B.1 Chebyshev Tensor evaluation in dimension 2.

Given that $\tilde{v}_j$ is the output of the formula when evaluating horizontally running CTs, these can be expressed as $v_j + \varepsilon_j$, where v_j is the *exact* value of f on the circles in Figure B.1. Therefore, Equation (B.2) can be expressed as

$$\left| \sum_{j=0}^{n} (v_j + \varepsilon_j) \ell_j(y) - f(x, y) \right|.$$

This in turn can be expanded and bounded as follows, using the triangle inequality

$$\left| \sum_{j=0}^{n} v_j \ell_j(y) - f(x, y) + \sum_{j=0}^{n} \varepsilon_j \ell_j(y) \right| \leq$$

$$\left| \sum_{j=0}^{n} v_j \ell_j(y) - f(x, y) \right| + \varepsilon \sum_{j=0}^{n} |\ell_j(y)| \tag{B.3}$$

Notice that, as a result of Theorem 3.2.6, the first term in (B.3) tends to zero exponentially as n tends to infinity — that is, as the number of Chebyshev points along the vertical dimension in Figure B.1 tends to infinity.

The term on the right-hand side consists of a value ε, which is the maximum of all the ε_j. As the values ε_j are the errors of the formula when applied horizontally, these also decay exponentially as the number of Chebyshev points along the horizontal dimension tends to infinity.

The only remaining expression to account for is

$$\lambda(y) = \sum_{j=0}^{n} |\ell_j(y)|$$

which is known as the Lebesgue function. Its supremum Λ_n, is known as the Legesgue constant

$$\Lambda_n = \sup_{y \in [-1,1]} \lambda(y).$$

When the grid over which the Lebesgue constant is obtained consists of Chebyshev points, it is known that it diverges logarithmically (see Chapter 15 in [72]). As ε decreases exponentially, the expression in Equation (B.3) decreases quasi-exponentially as the number of Chebyshev points in each dimension tend to infinity.

Chebyshev Splines on functions with no singularity points

Most applications that concern this book are characterised by the need to reduce the number of calls to a given function within a computation. For example, CCR risk calculations often require calling a pricing function hundreds of thousands if not millions of times. One of the main advantages of CTs for these types of calculations stems from the fact that high levels of accuracy are obtained by calling the function a much reduced number of times.[1]

There are times, however, that even a further reduction in the number of calls to the function is required. This is another setting where the use of Chebyshev Splines brings advantages. By introducing knots in the domain of approximation, thereby building Chebyshev Splines, a further reduction in the number of calls to the function can be obtained.

The following is an example of a test done on the Black-Scholes pricing function in the specific case in which time to maturity is small. As the maturity decreases, the curvature of the Black-Scholes pricing function around the strike becomes more pronounced. If we normally need 10 Chebyshev points (along the dimension of the option underlying) to reach an accuracy of 10^{-4} when the maturity is more than a year, shortening the maturity to only a few days may force us to increase the number of Chebyshev points needed considerably. To be noted, a few days from maturity the Black-Scholes function is still analytic, so the CT converges exponentially. However, the rate (although exponential) is lower compared to when the option has a year until expiry. Therefore, as the option approaches maturity, we may need, say, 100 Chebyshev points to achieve the same accuracy. This is a good example of where, for the applications of interest to this book (Part IV), we want to further reduce the number of calls to the function.

For this illustrative example, all variables but one (spot) were kept fixed, thereby yielding a one-dimensional function to be approximated.

Two approximating objects were built. The first was a global or single CT. The second a spline of Chebyshev interpolants consisting of three CTs. This means that two

---

[1] In fact, using CTs reduces the calls to the pricing function more than any other approximation framework that relies on sampling the pricing functions due to the quasi-exponential convergence they have. See Theorem 3.3.10.

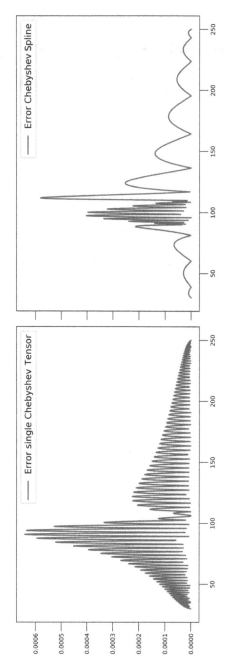

FIGURE C.1 Reduction in the number of calls to pricing function through the use of Chebyshev Splines.

knots were specified. The locations of the knots were chosen given the characteristics of the function. The Black-Scholes function has most of its curvature concentrated on the strike. The aim is to isolate this region and build a Chebyshev interpolant for this part of the function approximating it to a high degree of accuracy with a reduced number of points. Therefore, one knot was placed before the strike, the other after the strike. The two remaining parts of the function are much easier to approximate and require a small number of Chebyshev points.

The plot on the left-hand side of Figure C.1 shows the absolute value of the differences between the Black-Scholes function and a *single* CT, built over a grid with 95 points. The error is of the order of 10^{-4}. The plot on the right-hand side corresponds to a spline of three Chebyshev approximators, applied to the same instance of the Black-Scholes pricing function. The first spline was built with 5 points, the second with 12 and the third with 8, giving a total of 25 grid points. Compared with the 95 points used with a single CT, this decrease represents a reduction of 74% in terms of the computational cost, for the same order of accuracy.

Deciding where to place the knots for the splines requires a bit of heuristics. The following is a useful guiding rule. We could place the knots at the points where the second derivative of the pricing function (i.e. the Black-Scholes gamma) is smaller than a chosen (small) value. In this way, we separate the domain of approximation into a region of significant curvature and two with little curvature that can be resolved with few Chebyshev points.

It is to be noted that the case of Black-Scholes is easy because we have an expression for the gamma function. If we are dealing with a pricing function for which we do not have such expression, we could obtain such function numerically in a one-off exercise.

Computational savings details for CCR

In this appendix, we present granular information regarding the computational gains presented in Section 15.3. In particular, we consider the number of times pricing functions have to be called both for the benchmark approach and the proxy technique used, as well as training (whenever present) and evaluation times of the proxy objects built. All simulations were run on a standard laptop with i7 intel cores. The time reported are obtained with no parallelisation. Absolute times will be different in different systems (e.g. production systems in banks), but relative gains should be similar; hence, we focus mostly on such relative performance improvements.

D.1 BARRIER OPTION

The pricing function used for the Barrier option was the one found in QuantLib. The pricing routine is based on Monte Carlo simulations and is implemented in C++. The Chebyshev Spline was built using the MoCaX software in C++.

The pricing function had an average evaluation time of 0.8 seconds. This translates into 8,000 seconds on the 10,000 evaluations needed per time point. However, the Chebyshev Spline evaluated 10,000 notes in 0.01 seconds, which is 800,000 times faster than the pricing function. The Chebyshev Spline built is a full tensor and hence no training is needed. Using all this information, we arrive at a total computational savings of 99.04%, as seen in Table D.1.

D.2 CROSS-CURRENCY SWAP

The pricing routine used for the cross-currency swap was the one implemented in the swapbyzero function in MATLAB. The Sample Adaptive Algorithm used to build tensors in TT format is also implemented in MATLAB[1]. Therefore, a direct comparison

---

[1]At the time when these tests were performed, the MoCaXExtend Library (Section 24.2.2) had not been developed yet; hence, the tests were performed on a prototype MATLAB version.

TABLE D.1   Computational gain of running the CCR calculation for Barrier options with a CT as a proxy. Note that the compute time of the CT is negligible compared to the Barrier option evaluation. The computational gain essentially comes from the difference between total evaluations via brute force and number of samples needed to calibrate the CT.

	Brute-force (benchmark) evaluations	Sampling evaluations	Avg. training time	Cheb. Tensor evaluations	Comp. savings
Number of evaluations	10,000	96	NA	10,000	99.04%
Time (seconds)	9,000	86.4	0	0.01	

TABLE D.2   Computational costs and savings obtained by using TT-format CTs to compute PV profiles — at expectation and 95th percentiles — and CVA, for a cross-currency swap.

	Brute-force (benchmark) evaluations	Sampling evaluations	Avg. training time	Cheb. Tensor evaluations	Comp. savings
Number of evaluations	10,000	$300 \sim 700$	NA	10,000	91.75%
Time (seconds)	700	~ 30	<30	9.5	

between the evaluation time taken by the pricing function and its proxy (CT in TT format) can be made.

The Sample Adaptive Algorithm was restricted to a maximum of 700 pricing function samplings. Also, the accuracy threshold was set to 1×10^{-3}, and the number of iterations of the Completion Algorithm (running underneath the Sample Adaptive Algorithm) was set to 50.[2]

To estimate the computational savings obtained by using CTs in TT format, we need to account for the cost at each step of the process. The MC simulation run consisted of 10,000 paths and 10 time points. At every time point of the simulation, the brute-force approach has the same computational cost (10,000× cost of one cross-currency swap evaluation), and the Composition Technique is applied in the same way. Therefore, we only have to estimate the computational cost of a single time point to estimate the overall computational gain.

Table D.2 shows the different components that play a role in the estimation of the computational savings for the pricing step in a CCR computation. Some of these values are averages taken over the 10 time points of the MC simulation.

---

[2]For more details on Tensor Extension Algorithms and its parameters, we refer to Chapter 6.

At each time point, the brute-force approach involves 10,000 calls to the pricing function. These 10,000 calls took an average of 600 seconds. However, the Sample Adaptive Algorithm only used between 300 and 700 calls to the pricing function, equivalent to around 30 seconds. In the case tested, the running of the Sample Adaptive Algorithm (after pricing function evaluation) never took longer than 30 seconds to return a CT in TT format — sometimes this process took only seconds. The average time taken by the CT to evaluate 10,000 scenarios was 9.5 seconds. Taking all these elements into account, the computational savings were estimated to be about 90%.

D.3 BERMUDAN SWAPTION

There were three different simulations run with Bermudan Swaptions. The first involves using full CTs, the second CTs in TT format, the last one DNNs. In all simulations, the pricing function for the Bermudan Swaption, which was tree based, was taken from QuantLib, implemented in C++.

The simulation run consisted of 10,000 paths and 20 time points. Given that time to maturity was included within the domain of approximation of all proxies considered (full CT, CT in TT format and DNN), one can use these proxies in MC simulations with as many time points as needed, as long as these are within the maturity of the trades considered in the simulation. Therefore, we can easily extrapolate computational gains to MC simulations with any given number of time points. The computational gains reported for each proxy assumes a MC simulation with 10,000 paths and 100 time points, which reflects a typical CCR MC simulation.

D.3.1 Using full Chebyshev Tensors

The full CTs were built using the C++ version of the MoCaX software.

There is a total of 1,000,000 nodes in the MC simulation assumed that need to be evaluated by the pricing function (brute-force approach) and by the full CT (fast technique). A total of 86,436 pricing function samplings were needed to build the full CT. No training was needed as full CTs are built with only the sampling values.

The brute-force approach would take a total of 175,000 seconds to run. The building of the full CT took 15,126 seconds. The evaluation of the CT tensor on the 1,000,000 nodes would take 250 seconds. The total computational gain came to 91.21%, as can be seen in Table D.3.

D.3.2 Using Chebyshev Tensors in TT format

The Sample Adaptive Algorithm was implemented in MATLAB.[3] A maximum of 50 iterations were used for the Completion Algorithm (running underneath the

---

[3] At the time when these tests were performed, the MoCaXExtend Library (Section 24.2.2) had not been developed yet; hence, the tests were performed on a prototype MATLAB version.

TABLE D.3   Computational gain of running the CCR calculation with a CT as a proxy for Bermundan Swaptions. Note the evaluation of the CT is negligible compared to the Bermudan Swaption evaluation. The computational gain essentially comes from the difference between total evaluations via brute force and number of samples needed to calibrate the CT.

	Brute-force (benchmark) evaluations	Sampling evaluations	Avg. training time	Cheb. Tensor evaluations	Comp. savings
Number of evaluations	1,000,000	86,436	NA	1,000,000	91.21%
Time (seconds)	175,000	15,126	0	250	

TABLE D.4   Computational gain of running the CCR calculation for a Bermudan Swaption with a CT in TT format as a proxy. Note that the training and compute time of the CT is negligible compared to the Bermudan Swaption evaluation, this despite the former being implemented in MATLAB and the latter in C++. The computational gain essentially comes from the difference between total evaluations via brute force and the combination of sampling and training needed to build the CT in TT format.

	Brute-force (benchmark) evaluations	Sampling evaluations	Avg. training time	Cheb. Tensor evaluations	Comp. savings
Number of evaluations	1,000,000	5,000	NA	1,000,000	98.97%
Time (seconds)	175,000	875	30	900	

Sample Adaptive Algorithm) to reduce the training time. We set the accuracy threshold to 1×10^{-3}.

The Sample Adaptive Algorithm took about 30 seconds to find a CT in TT format with a relative error of less than 1×10^{-3}. The tensor obtained took an average of 9 seconds to evaluate all 10,000 scenarios at each time point.

The brute-force approach took 35,000 seconds on the simulation run (200,000 nodes). For this particular MC simulation, the computational gains stand at 97%. A more realistic production simulation would have about 100 time steps. Remember that for 100 time points we would build the TT-format CT in the same way since we are including the time to maturity as an input variable in the function f obtained after applying the Composition Technique. The only difference would be that 1,000,000 scenarios would be evaluated by both the pricing function (brute-force approach) and the CT in TT format. Table D.4 summarises the different components involved in the computational cost for the brute-force approach and the TT-format CT approach, considering an MC simulation with 100 time points.

Note that the implementation used to run Chebyshev TT tensors was written in MATLAB while the brute-force pricing function in C++. Calculations typically run

TABLE D.5 Computational gain of running the CCR calculation for a Bermudan Swaption with a DNN. Note that the time for training and evaluation of the DNN is negligible compared to the Bermudan Swaption evaluation, this despite the former being implemented in Python and the latter in C++. The computational gain essentially comes from the difference between total evaluations via brute force and the combination of sampling and training needed to build the DNN.

	Brute-force (benchmark) evaluations	Sampling evaluations	Avg. training time	Cheb. Tensor evaluations	Comp. savings
Number of evaluations	1,000,000	5,000	NA	1,000,000	99.17%
Time (seconds)	175,000	875	180	400	

much faster in C++ compared to MATLAB — in some cases by more than an order of magnitude. This puts the evaluation of CT tensors in TT format and, hence, the technique based on proxy pricing, at a disadvantage when a direct comparison with the benchmark is made. Even when this was the case, computational gains were still as high as 98.97% (see Table D.4).

D.3.3   Using Deep Neural Nets

The DNNs built for this simulation were obtained using Keras. The training of the DNN took 120 seconds. The evaluation of this DNN on the MC simulation with 100 time points would take a total of 400 seconds. The DNN was trained and run in Python. This puts the training and evaluation of the DNN at a disadvantage when compared to the computational cost incurred by the benchmark, which is in C++. Nevertheless, computational savings stand at 99.17%. This is summarised in Table D.5.

D.4   AMERICAN OPTION

The portfolio considered for the simulations run with American options consisted of three trades. The trades had different moneyness and less than one year to maturity. The pricing routine is the one in QuantLib which is MC based and implemented in C++.

Two simulations were done. The first involved the use of CT tensors in TT format as part of the fast technique. The second, a DNN. Both simulations consisted of an MC simulation with 10,000 paths and 11 time points, giving a total of 110,000 nodes to be evaluated.

Notice that the strike of the trade has been included as one of the factors in the domain input of the proxy built — either a DNN or a CT in TT format. This means that the single proxy built is able to return the prices needed for the CCR metrics for any American option with a strike and time to maturity within the ranges considered in the building of the proxy. This means we can easily extrapolate computational savings for much larger portfolios and MC simulations. The computational savings, presented next, reflect a portfolio with 100 trades and an MC simulation with 10,000 paths and 100 time points.

D.4.1 Using Chebyshev Tensors in TT format

The Sample Adaptive Algorithm used to build CT tensors in TT format was implemented in MATLAB.[4] As was done in other tests, a limit of 50 iterations for the Completion Algorithm and a stopping accuracy criteria of 1×10^{-3} were used.

The Sample Adaptive Algorithm took about 120 seconds to find a CT in TT format with a relative error of less than 1×10^{-3}. The tensor built in TT format took an average of 9 seconds to evaluate the 10,000 nodes in each MC time point, for each trade in the portfolio. Note the TT tensors used in these tests were implemented and run in MATLAB. Had they been implemented and run in C++, times would be much lower. Despite this, computational gains are still significant (see Table D.6).

The average evaluation time for the pricing function of the American option was 0.87 seconds. This translates into 287,100 seconds on the 110,000 nodes in the MC simulation (total number of nodes coming from 11 time points and 10,000 nodes at each time point), when the three trades in the portfolio are considered. For this specific MC simulation, computational gains stand at 72.6%. If 100 time points had been considered in the MC simulation (a number that reflects more accurately the number of time points in a CCR MC simulation), the TT-format CTs would have been built in the same way as we did, and the computational gains would be 96.9%. If the portfolio consists of 100 American options, then the computational gains stand at 99.81%, as Table D.6 shows.

TABLE D.6 Computational gain of running the CCR calculation for American options with a CT in TT format as a proxy on a portfolio with 100 trades and 100 time points. Note that the training and evaluation time of the CT is negligible compared to the American option evaluation, despite the former being implemented in MATLAB and the latter in C++. The computational gain essentially comes from the difference between total evaluations via brute force (benchmark) and the evaluations needed to build the CT in TT format.

	Brute-force (benchmark) evaluations	Sampling evaluations	Avg. training time	Cheb. Tensor evaluations	Comp. savings
Number of evaluations	100,000,000	90,000	NA	100,000,000	99.81%
Time (seconds)	87,000,000	78,300	120	90,000	

---

[4]At the time when these tests were performed, the MoCaXExtend Library (Section 24.2.2) had not been developed yet; hence, the tests were performed on a prototype MATLAB version.

TABLE D.7 Computational gain of running the CCR calculation for American options with a DNN on a portfolio with 100 trades and 100 time points. Note that the compute time of the DNN is negligible compared to the training and evaluation time of the portfolio of American options, despite the former being implemented in Python and the latter in C++. The computational gain essentially comes from the difference between total evaluations via brute force (benchmark) and the sampling needed for training.

	Brute-force (benchmark) evaluations	Sampling evaluations	Avg. training time	Cheb. Tensor evaluations	Comp. savings
Number of evaluations	100,000,000	100,000	NA	100,000,000	99.72%
Time (seconds)	87,000,000	87,300	120	160,000	

D.4.2 Using Deep Neural Nets

The DNN built used the Keras implementation in Python. The training of the DNN took 120 seconds. The evaluation of the DNN on 110,000 nodes took 176 seconds.

The computational savings presented in Table D.7 correspond to an MC simulation with 100 time points and a portfolio with 100 American options. The training of the DNN would take the same 120 seconds. The evaluation of the DNN on 1,000,000 nodes (coming from 10,000 paths and 100 time points) for all the trades in the portfolio would take 160,000 seconds. The brute-force approach would require 100,000,000 evaluations, which translated into 87,000,000 seconds in the setup used for the tests. This gives a total of 99.72% computational savings.

Note that the DNN was trained and evaluated in Python, which is slower than C++, the language in which the benchmark pricing routine was implemented. Despite this, computational gains are still significant, as can be seen in Table D.7.

Computational savings details for dynamic sensitivities

This appendix presents more granular information regarding the computational gains from Chapter 17. The simulations were run on a standard laptop with i7 intel cores using MATLAB. The time reported are obtained with no parallelisation.

E.1   FX SWAP

The pricing function used to price the FX Swap tested is the one implemented in the swapbyzero function in MATLAB. At each time point of the MC simulation, a Chebyshev grid of dimension 9 was built. Four points were used per dimension, giving a grid with 262,144 points.

The Sample Adaptive Algorithm was used to build CTs in TT format. The algorithm started with 300 points for training and 50 for testing; that is, 350 function evaluations. As the algorithm increases the number of points automatically if a level of precision is not reached — which in turn increases the number of required function evaluations — a maximum number of evaluations needs to be set. This was fixed at 1,000. For most risk factors and time points, 300 points were enough to reach an accuracy at both training and testing of $5e^{-3}$. In some cases, the number of points needed was 500. This represents a reduction on the number of times the pricing function has to be called to build the CTs of about 99.8%. Once the values were obtained, the algorithm was very fast to train, never taking more than 1 minute to train; in some cases, just seconds.

The computational savings for the FX Swap are summarised in Table E.1. Computing benchmark sensitivities, for a single risk factor, on a single time point, requires 20,000 calls to the pricing function. The Sample Adaptive Algorithm needed between 300 and 500 calls. The training of the algorithm took seconds in most cases. The evaluation of the CTs on the 10,000 scenarios took an average of 15.5 seconds. Compared to the cost of the benchmark calculation, for each risk factor and each time point — measured at 2,000 seconds — the training and evaluation times reported for CTs are negligible. The computational savings are therefore about 96.46%.

TABLE E.1   Computational savings obtained by using CTs in TT format to compute dynamic sensitivities compared to benchmark method for the FX Swap. Note that the time it takes to train the Sample Adaptive Algorithm and run CT tensors on 10,000 nodes is negligible compared to the FX Swap pricing evaluation. The computational gain essentially comes from the difference between total evaluations via brute force and number of samples needed to calibrate the CT.

	Brute-force (benchmark) evaluations	Sampling evaluations	Avg. training time	Cheb. Tensor evaluations	Comp. savings
Number of evaluations	20,000	300~500	NA	10,000	96.46%
Time (seconds)	2,000	~40	<30	15.5	

TABLE E.2   Computational savings obtained by using CTs in TT format to compute dynamic sensitivities compared to benchmark method for the Spread Option. Note that most of the computational gains come from the difference between total evaluations via brute force and number of samples needed to calibrate the CT.

	Brute-force (benchmark) evaluations	Sampling evaluations	Avg. training time	Cheb. Tensor evaluations	Comp. savings
Number of evaluations	1,000,000	12,000	NA	1,000,000	98.55%
Time (seconds)	499,800	5,998	120~180	1,110	

It must be appreciated that the tests were carried out using MATLAB on a standard laptop computer.[1] The computational times could be far smaller in a bank's optimised pricing library. However, the relative gains the technique brings should be the same.

E.2   EUROPEAN SPREAD OPTION

The pricing function used to price the European Spread Option is the one implemented in the spreadsensbyls function in MATLAB. The evaluation of this pricing function is Monte Carlo based; hence, it has a relatively high degree of numerical noise.

A single CT was built for the whole MC simulation — that is, including time to maturity as a variable input. The Chebyshev grid considered for each sensitivity had dimension 6. Six points were used per dimension, giving a grid with 46,656 points.

---

[1]At the time when these tests were performed, the MoCaXExtend Library (Section 24.2.2) had not been developed yet; hence, the tests were performed on a prototype MATLAB version.

The Sample Adaptive Algorithm was used to build CTs in TT format. It used 12,000 randomly selected Chebyshev grid points; 10,000 were used for training and 2,000 for testing. After 2–3 minutes, the algorithm typically reached an error of $5e^{-3}$, comparable to the noise level of the pricing function.

The pricing function took around 5,000 seconds to return the sensitivities with respect to one risk factor on 10,000 scenarios. The CT built to approximate this sensitivity function took an average of 11.1 seconds on the same 10,000 scenarios. If we assume an MC simulation with 100 time points, this gives a computational gain of 98.55%, once all computational costs are considered. Results are shown on Table E.2.

Dynamic sensitivities on the market space

The solution presented in Section 17.2, to alleviate the computational bottleneck in the calculation of dynamic sensitivities within a Monte Carlo (MC) simulation, relies on applying the Composition Technique and approximating the resulting function f with a CT. In this case, the Composition Technique involves pre-composing the sensitivity functions of a trade, for which we want to compute dynamic sensitivities, with the parametrisation g that RFE models use to model market risk factors (normally many of them; at times in the hundreds) in terms of model risk factors (normally a handful; usually less than 10).

The main reason behind applying the Composition Technique using parametrisations coming from RFE models is that we reduce the dimension of the input domain of the sensitivity functions. We take advantage of the fact that the market scenario at each Monte Carlo (MC) node is fully determined by its corresponding point in the model space. This means that no information is lost by using the Composition Technique. By doing this, we can then approximate the sensitivities using CTs, taking full advantage of the quasi-exponential convergence, which in turn means a low number of evaluations of the approximated function (f) to achieve high levels of accuracy. As a result, the Composition Technique in combination with CTs provide very accurate proxy functions, as can be seen from the numerical results presented in Section 17.4.

In this section, we describe an alternative technique to further reduce the computational bottleneck of dynamic sensitivities simulations. This technique, however, is less robust than the one presented in Chapter 17, at least in the present form — we believe future research may improve this technique.[1] Just like the solution in Section 17.2, it uses the Composition Technique and the resulting function f is approximated with a CT. However, the parametrisation used is different.

The motivation is the following. There are cases when we do not have access to the parametrisations from the risk factor diffusion models. Say, for example, we sit in the

---

[1] The results presented in this section were obtained from a research project that we believe can be enhanced and extended. What appears in this section is what had been obtained at the time this book went to press. Potential future paths for research have been highlighted. Readers are welcome to contact us via social media (e.g. LinkedIn) should they want to discuss their thoughts on the topic.

front office where we have control over pricing functions but not over the RFE models that generate the scenarios in the MC engine; these scenarios are given to us without any details of how they were obtained. In these cases, if we want to apply the Composition Technique, we would have to generate our own parametrisation g (see Equation 17.3).

Another possible situation where we may want to generate our own parametrisation is when the number of model risk factors in the risk factor diffusion model is very large. Remember it is this dimension, the one that determines the dimension of the input of f, for which we build CTs. If the dimension of f is too great, its approximation with CTs may not be as efficient; a different parametrisation with lower input domain would solve this problem.

In either of these cases, the aim is to parametrise the market risk factors using a low-dimensional space independent of the model used to simulate risk factors. The new parametrisation function (let us call it h) would be an approximation to the way in which g models the dynamics of the diffused risk factors. The challenge is to control the error being introduced. If successfully done, not only will we be able to apply the Composition Technique, yielding good results, but also we will have removed the dependency on the risk factor diffusion model. This would be a desirable feature in practical settings within banks.

F.1 THE PARAMETRISATION

First we start with the characteristics that the parametrisation h needs to have. The key thing to bear in mind is that we want to use the parametrisation to reduce the dimension of the input domain of the sensitivity functions as much as possible, while losing the least amount of information possible. This parametrisation will then be used in the same way g was in the instance of the Composition Technique described in Section 17.2.

For illustration purposes, assume the trade for which we want to compute dynamic sensitivities is an interest rate swap. The market risk factors that constitute the inputs to the pricing function (and hence sensitivity function) of this trade are curves of swap rates. Each of these curves will consist of n swap rates (n is any natural number). Remember that we apply the Composition Technique for each sensitivity function. For the example of the swap, we apply the Composition Technique to each sensitivity function S_i, where i denotes the i-th swap rate.

The parametrisation, corresponding to the i-th swap rate, is given by h_i

$$h_i : \mathbb{R}^k \longrightarrow \mathbb{R}^n. \tag{F.1}$$

This function takes values in $\mathbb{R}^k$ and returns them in $\mathbb{R}^n$. In our example, each point in $\mathbb{R}^n$ is a curve of swap rates. That is, h_i parametrises each swap rate curve in terms of values in $\mathbb{R}^k$. Notice that since we want to use h_i for the Composition Technique, we want k to be lower than n, in fact, in some cases much lower.

The main requirement we impose on h is that its image should contain all swap rate curves given by the simulation at the time point in question. That is, if the swap rate curve $(s_1, \ldots, s_n)$ has been generated by the MC simulation, then there must be an $x = (x_1, \ldots, x_k)$ such that $h_i(x) = (s_1, \ldots, s_n)$.

With this characteristic not only do we reduce the dimension of the input domain of the sensitivity function S_i, but also (very importantly) we do not lose any information on the risk factors generated by the MC simulation.

It is important to note that if the (unknown) RFE model has $\tilde{k}$ factors (that is, the domain of its corresponding parametrisation g has dimension $\tilde{k}$), and we define h to have a domain with dimension k, where $k < \tilde{k}$, then there is a good chance that h will not be able to capture the dynamics of the RFE model. Therefore, the closer k is to $\tilde{k}$, the better results we expect to obtain with h.

$$\mathbb{R}^k \underset{f_i}{\overset{h_i}{\longrightarrow}} \mathbb{R}^n \overset{S_i}{\longrightarrow} \mathbb{R}. \tag{F.2}$$

A possible parametrisation h

Without loss of generality, fix a time point in the simulation. At that time point, we have a collection of simulated yield curves $\{s_{1,j}, \ldots, s_{n,j}\}$, with n tensors, and where $j \in \mathbb{N}$ ranges from 1 to m, the number of scenarios. Assume we are interested in simulating the sensitivity to the i-th swap rate.

Suppose (for now) that $k = 1$. The question we ask is, can we use any of the variables from the simulated yield curves as a model parameter to parametrise the simulated yield curves?

An obvious candidate is the i-th swap rate. We denote by h_i the parametrisation we want to define. Assume its input parameter is given by x, which represents the i-th swap rate. Next we show how to define h_i at Chebyshev points.

The i-th swap rate, at the time point in question (of the MC simulation), has simulated values $\{s_{i,1}, \ldots, s_{i,m}\}$. This collection has a minimum and a maximum, $s_{i,min}$ and $s_{i,max}$. This means any scenario we are interested in evaluating with S_i has its i-th swap rate value between $s_{i,min}$ and $s_{i,max}$. The Chebyshev points are trivial to compute in the interval $[s_{i,min}, s_{i,max}]$; all we need is a natural number N, as per Section 3.3.3. Denote the first N Chebyshev points in $[s_{i,min}, s_{i,max}]$ by $\{x_c\}_{c=0}^{N-1}$.

What we want is to define a yield curve $h_i(x_c)$, given a Chebyshev point x_k. Once we have this, we can compute the sensitivity S_i on $h_i(x_k)$, for example, using finite differences. This will give values for f on Chebyshev points, where $f = S_i \circ h_i$ is the function we want to approximate. As per Section 3.6.2, this is all the information we need to build a one-dimensional CT for f, which can then be evaluated by a barycentric interpolation formula on any value in the range $[s_{i,min}, s_{i,max}]$.

For the Chebyshev points corresponding to $c = 0$ and $c = N - 1$, the yield curve $h_i(x_c)$ is trivial since these Chebyshev points correspond to $s_{i,min}$ and $s_{i,max}$ — these are points in the simulation and hence have an associated yield curve given by the simulation.[2] However, for Chebyshev points that are not part of the simulated values, we do not

---

[2]For Chebyshev points that happen to be part of the simulation, we often have one of the two values needed for finite differences from other CCR calculations (CVA, IMM, PFE, etc.).

have an obvious choice of yield curve $h_i(x_c)$. This yield curve, which we call *Chebyshev scenario* or *Chebyshev yield curve*, can be defined as follows.

Definition of the h function

If x_c is the $c - th$ Chebyshev point, where $0 \leq c \leq N - 1$, then denote by $(s_{1,cheb_c}, \ldots, s_{N-1,cheb_c})$ the yield curve given by $h_i(x_c)$. For the i-th swap rate of $h_i(x_c)$, that is $s_{i,cheb_c}$, we simply take x_c. The other swap rates are defined as follows:

1. Sort the simulated i-th swap rates $\{s_{i,1}, \ldots, s_{i,m}\}$ in increasing order.
2. Identify where the Chebyshev point x_c lies within this ordered set.
3. Take the yield curves that correspond to the i-th swap rates immediately below and above x_c, $\{s_{1,blw}, \ldots, s_{n,blw}\}$ and $\{s_{1,abv}, \ldots, s_{n,abv}\}$.
4. To define the i'-th tensor or swap rate, where $i' \neq i$, interpolate the values of the i'-th tensor that correspond to the yield curves immediately below and above

$$s_{i',cheb} = s_{i',blw} + \frac{s_{i',abv} - s_{i',blw}}{s_{i,abv} - s_{i,blw}}(x_c - s_{i,blw})$$

Note we have used linear interpolation, but could have used other interpolation frameworks.

This description defines the yield curve $h(x_c)$ at the c-th Chebyshev point. As mentioned before, the sensitivity S_i at $h_i(x_c)$ can then be computed by finite differences, hence obtaining the value of f on the Chebyshev point x_c. This can be done for every Chebyshev point yielding the CT that replicates the sensitivity function.

Notice we have defined h_i as a function with input domain of dimension 1, since $k = 1$. Later in Section F.3, we discuss possible parametrisations h_i for $k > 1$.

Also note that the definition of h_i on Chebyshev points given above immediately generalises to any point in interval $[s_{i,min}, s_{i,max}]$. Therefore, one can also build DNNs on any given collection of points, instead of CTs.

If we want to compute n sensitivities at each node of the MC simulation using the parametrisation just defined, we need to create n replicating objects — DNNs or CTs — of dimension one per time point in the MC simulation. Each of these approximating objects is evaluated at each node of the time point generating the sensitivities we need.

F.2   NUMERICAL TESTS

In this section, we present numerical results obtained by applying the technique described in Section F.1. The aim was to compute the sensitivities of a European Swaption at each node of an MC simulation. The MC simulation consisted of 10,000 paths and 10 time points in the future, covering the whole maturity of the trade.

Once the dynamic sensitivities were obtained, these were used to compute Dynamic Initial Margin (DIM), that is, Initial Margin (IM) at each node of the simulation.[3] With the distribution of IM values in the MC simulation, we then computed IM profiles.

The swaption used had a year to expiry. The market risk factors that constitute its inputs and that are relevant in the computation of IM are a curve of swap rates and a surface of implied volatilities. There were more than one hundred market risk factors. These were generated in the MC simulation by one-factor models.

With the pricing function P of the swaption, we define the sensitivity function with respect to any risk factor by using finite differences. This constitutes the benchmark with respect to which we compare our technique in terms of accuracy and speed. The Composition Technique was then applied to each sensitivity function S_i using the parametrisation h_i presented in Section F.1. The resulting functions f_i are one-dimensional functions that were approximated with one-dimensional CTs. A total of seven Chebyshev points were used for each tensor. Needless to say, there is no need for the Tensor Extension Algorithms because k is very low in this case, and so full tensors were defined.

Figure F.1 shows Expected Initial Margin (EIM) and Potential Future Initial Margin (PFIM) at 95% confidence level obtained with the benchmark (finite differences) and with full CTs. As can be seen in Figure F.1 and Table F.1, the errors are all below 0.45%.

The CTs built for each MC simulation time point had dimension 1 with only seven tensor points. These are full CTs; therefore, no training as such in the DNN sense is

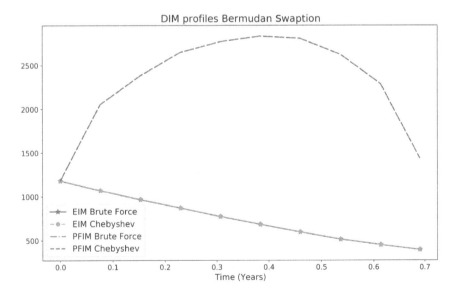

FIGURE F.1   DIM profiles — expectation and 95% quantiles — for a European Swaption obtained with the benchmark (brute-force) and with CTs.

---

[3]The version of IM used is SIMM, proposed by ISDA, which is based on sensitivities and by now the standard in the industry.

TABLE F.1 Maximum relative percentage error for EIM and PFIM (95% quantile) profiles for the European Swaption.

European Swaption	EIM	PFIM
Maximum relative error	0.45%	0.26%

TABLE F.2 Computational savings obtained by using full CTs to compute dynamic sensitivities compared to benchmark method for the European Swaption.

	Brute-force (benchmark) evaluations	Sampling evaluations	Avg. training time	Cheb. Tensor evaluations	Comp. savings
Number of evaluations	20,000	14	NA	20,000	99.9%
Time (seconds)	100	0.07	0	0.001	

needed to build the replicating objects; all that is needed are the Chebyshev points and the values of the sensitivity function on these. As each sensitivity requires two pricing function evaluations, a total of 14 pricing function evaluations are needed to build the proxy object.

The average evaluation time of the one-dimensional CTs on the full set of 10,000 scenarios corresponding to a single time point in the MC simulation was 0.001 seconds. As the benchmark approach requires 20,000 pricing function evaluations (two evaluations per sensitivity given we use finite differences) per sensitivity per time point, the total computational gain stands at 99.9%. This is shown in Table F.2.

Both the levels of accuracy and the computational gains are very high. The main reason is that we were able to reduce the dimension of the input domain of the sensitivity functions from more than 100 to just one. With dimension one, CTs need very few points to reach high levels of accuracy. Moreover, as they are full CTs, no extra time is spent running the Tensor Extension Algorithm. Finally, the time it takes to evaluate one-dimensional CTs is minimal, even on millions of scenarios.

F.3   FUTURE WORK... WHEN $K > 1$

So far, we have presented the progress obtained in this piece of research up to the point of this book going to press. Next, we outline possible next steps.

The tests in Section F.2 work well because the underlying RFE dynamics are given by a one-factor model. As a result, one-dimensional parametrisations stand a chance of capturing the dynamics of the yield curves — the results presented in Section F.2 are evidence of this.

We believe that if the RFE model has k factors, where $k > 1$, then there must be a way of defining a parametrisation h with input domain of dimension k that gives good results. The question is how to define such h.

The reader may have noted that the domain of the function h defined in Section F.1 is the one determined by the simulated swap rate with respect to which we want to compute the sensitivity. However, given that yield curve RFE models tend to have parallel shifts of the yield curve as the main driver of the dynamics, we could have used any other tensor in the yield curve to define the domain of h. For example, we could have used the five-year swap rate as the x variable for all sensitivities and we would expect to obtain results as good as the ones presented in Section F.2.

As said, yield curve models tend to use parallel shifts of the curve as the main driver of the dynamics. Curve rotations are typically the second driver and curve flattening the third.[4] Therefore, we think that if the underlying RFE model has two factors, then two tensor points in the curve (for example, the one-year and the 10-year points) should be able to parametrise the curve dynamics with high precision; if the underlying RFE model has three factors, then three points in the curve should do a good job. What one would then need to do is specify an interpolation similar to the one proposed in Section F.2 in order to define the h. We believe this can work very well and give results just as good as the ones displayed for the one-factor case in Section F.2.

One of the main benefits of defining a parametrisation such as h is that we do not need any specifics of the underlying RFE model beyond the number of factors it uses. We do not present results using this approach in the computation of sensitivities. However, we tested a similar idea in the context of price simulation. This is discussed in Section 15.2.7, which we briefly describe next.

We were given a full IMM CCR simulation (many time steps and paths, a market snapshot at each node of the simulation). We applied PCA to the set of yield curves from each time point. Using the first three principal components and the inverse of the PCA projection (see Section 5.2.1), we built a CT with a three-dimensional domain ($k = 3$); the domain variable x given by the first three principal components. The CTs were used to price the portfolio. The results obtained were very good despite the fact that the RFE that generated the yield curves had many factors. The reason was that the first three principal components captured 99% of the variance and with it, the curve dynamics. We see no reason why this technique should not work for sensitivities, too.

The ideas presented in this section have not been tested in the context of sensitivity simulation. We believe this approach could be fruitful. Therefore, we encourage anyone interested in pursuing this line of research to get in contact with us, for example, through LinkedIn.

---

[4]There can be more than the three factors mentioned, but we use the first three that are normally used.

Dynamic sensitivities and IM via Jacobian Projection technique

Here we present numerical results obtained by applying the technique presented in Chapter 8 to the computation of dynamic sensitivities. The test was done using a European Swaption. A Monte Carlo (MC) simulation was run with 10,000 paths and 10 time points in the future, covering the whole maturity of the trade. At each node of the MC simulation, a set of sensitivities to the swaption were computed using the technique in Chapter 8.

Once sensitivities were obtained at each node of the MC simulation, these were used to compute Initial Margin (IM) at each node (see Section 17.3). The resulting distribution of IMs is known as Dynamic Initial Margin (DIM).[1] With the distribution of IM values in the MC simulation, we then computed IM profiles.

The swaption used for the test was the same as the one used to obtain the results presented in Appendix F. That is, the trade had a year to expiry.

The market risk factors that serve as input to the pricing function and that are relevant to the computation of IM are a curve of swap rates and a surface of implied volatilities. The total number of market risk factors are more than one hundred. Each of these (i.e. swap rates and implied volatilities) were generated in the MC simulation by one-factor models.

The benchmark used to compute dynamic sensitivities is based on finite differences. That is, the sensitivity of the trade with respect to any of its risk factors at any of the nodes of the MC simulation is obtained by using the pricing function P of the trade and doing a finite difference approximation of the sensitivity.

To obtain sensitivities using the technique presented in Chapter 8, we first apply the Composition Technique. This consists of composing, at each time point of the MC simulation, the pricing function P with the parametrisation g that comes with the models used to diffuse risk factors within the MC simulation. The resulting function f can

---

[1] The version of IM used is SIMM, proposed by ISDA, which is based on sensitivities and by now the standard in the industry.

be easily replicated with high accuracy with a CT. Note that since there are two families of risk factors involved — swap rates and implied volatilities — and we use one-factor diffusion model for each family, we end up with a function f that has a domain input of dimension 2. For more details on the Composition Technique, see Chapter 5.

The function f is then approximated with a two-dimensional CT. Only 5 Chebyshev points per dimension were used given the quasi-exponential convergence of CTs (see Section 3.3), giving a total of 25 points on the Chebyshev mesh, equivalent to 25 calls to the pricing function. Once these 25 calls are made, the CT is built and ready to be used (see Section 3.6).

The CT, as a function proxy, has a domain of dimension 2, the variables of which are the model risk factors of the RFE models used in the MC simulation. Therefore, it is very easy to obtain the values of the partial derivatives of f with respect to model risk factors using the built CT (see Section 3.7). Finally, once the partial derivatives of f are obtained using the CT, we apply the Jacobian Projection technique presented in Chapter 8 to obtain estimates for the partial derivatives of P with respect to market risk factors.

Figure G.1 shows Expected Initial Margin (EIM) and Potential Future Initial Margin (PFIM) at 95% confidence level obtained with the benchmark (finite differences at each MC node) and with the Jacobian Projection technique. As can be seen in Figure G.1 and Table G.1, although maximum errors are high, reaching 53.2% for the EIM, most errors are much smaller, something that is reflected on the mean errors.

Computing sensitivities using the Jacobian Projection technique involves two steps. The first consists of obtaining sensitivities with respect to model factors. The second

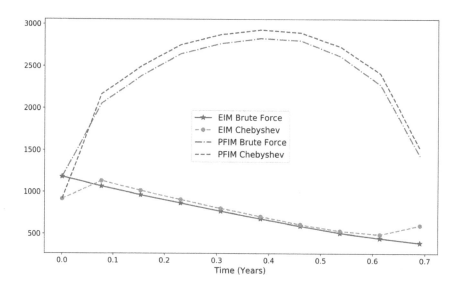

FIGURE G.1   DIM profiles — expectation and 95% quantiles — for a European Swaption obtained with the benchmark (brute force) and with the Jacobian orthogonal projection technique.

TABLE G.1 Maximum relative percentage error for EIM and PFIM (95% quantile) profiles for the European Swaption.

European Swaption	EIM	PFIM
Mean relative error	11.8%	6.4%
Maximum relative error	53.2%	22.2%

TABLE G.2 Computational savings obtained by using full CTs to compute dynamic sensitivities built using the Jacobian of g, compared to benchmark method for the European Swaption.

	Brute-force (benchmark) evaluations	Sampling evaluations	Avg. training time	Cheb. Tensor evaluations	Comp. savings
Number of evaluations	2,000,000	25	NA	2,000,000	99.99%
Time (seconds)	10,000	0.125	0	0.001	

involves using these sensitivities to estimate the sensitivities with respect to market factors.[2] The second step is computationally very fast and gives all sensitivities with respect to market risk factors in a very short period of time. Therefore, once sensitivities with respect to model risk factors are obtained, we obtain, with little extra effort, the sensitivities with respect to all market risk factors.

With this in mind, we can estimate computational gains obtained using this technique. If we assume 100 sensitivities and 10,000 nodes per time point in the MC simulation, we need 2,000,000 calls to the pricing function to compute all sensitivities at each time point via brute force, which is our benchmark — remember each sensitivity is obtained by calling the pricing function twice.

Obtaining all market risk factor sensitivities via the Jacobian Projection technique requires only one CT per time point. The CTs in the tests had dimension 2 and had a total of 25 tensor points. These are full CTs; therefore, no training is needed to build the proxy objects; all that is needed to build the CT and be able to use it is the Chebyshev points and the values of the pricing function on these. Therefore, the total computational gain stands at 99.99%, as shown in Table G.2.

As we can see from the results, one of the main advantages of the Jacobian Projection technique is the huge computational gain obtained with it. Out of the three techniques presented in this book for the computation of dynamic sensitivities (Chapter 17.2, Appendix F and this appendix), it is the most efficient, computationally speaking.

---

[2]See Chapter 8.

Its downside is the lack of accuracy control it has. From Figure G.1 and Table G.1 we can see that although the overall errors are relatively high, there are many time points in the MC simulation at which the error is low. This is also confirmed by the tests presented in [12].

The lack of error control comes from the very definition of the estimate of the market factor sensitivity encapsulated in Equation 8.9. The estimate is the result of removing the second component in Equation 8.8, which is not readily available (computationally speaking). When this component is small, Jacobian Projection technique is highly accurate. When it is large, the estimation is potentially poor. Reducing or controlling this error is left for future research.

MVA optimisation — further computational enhancement

In the methodology described in Section 20.2, each iteration of the optimiser uses the sensitivities simulation for the existing portfolio. This sensitivities simulation only need to be computed once. They can then be re-used at every iteration of the optimisation exercise. This can be achieved by either storing the sensitivities in memory grids — to then be loaded whenever needed — or by serialising the CTs built for the sensitivities simulation; these CTs can then be loaded whenever the optimisation exercise is run, generating the sensitivities needed in a very short period of time. Therefore, the only new CTs that must be built at each iteration of the optimisation exercise are the ones associated with the candidate mirroring trades. Once built, these CTs are evaluated at each Monte Carlo node, which then allows for the simulation of IM and subsequent MVA value of the portfolio with the new mirroring trades.

We have seen extensively throughout many of the applications in Part IV that, when performing a risk calculation using the solutions proposed, the vast proportion of the computational overhead is taken by the generation of the proxy object; the evaluation of the objects built — based either on CTs or DNNs — is nearly always very fast.

Therefore, a way to further improve the methodology in Section 20.2 could be to generate the CTs for the candidate mirroring trades before the optimisation exercise is run. In this way, they would not have to be generated at each iteration of the optimisation routine. The challenge, however, is that we do not know the candidate trades the optimiser will choose during the optimisation process before the exercise beings. Next, we describe a way around this problem.

The optimisation routine searches the space of parameters that define the mirroring IR swaps. Notice that the parameters considered are only the ones that vary, which are notional, maturity and direction. The MVA optimisation described in Section 20.2 consists of building a proxy object per pair of mirroring swaps being tested at each iteration of the optimisation algorithm. Consider, for illustration purposes, the same portfolio of IR swaps as in Section 20.2. The aim is to reduce the MVA value of the portfolio by introducing pairs of mirroring swaps. Candidate pairs of mirroring swaps are added to the netting sets of the 16 theoretical counterparties in each loop of the optimiser to compute a new candidate MVA value. Each counterparty is assumed to have one single netting set, each with 100 swaps.

To avoid having to build a proxy object at each iteration, we include all the parameters of the IR swaps into the input domain of the proxy object. In our case, this means incorporating time to maturity in the input domain of the function to approximate with CTs. This enables us to build the proxy object offline, which can then be used throughout the optimisation exercise. Moreover, no other proxy object needs to be built during the optimisation exercise. As the evaluation of such objects is very efficient, the optimisation routine will be very fast. This allows for such what-if types of exercises, even in situations where time is significantly constrained.

Note that by incorporating the parameters that define the possible incoming trades, the dimension of the proxy object (for example, CTs) will be higher than when built at each iteration of the optimisation algorithm. In the case just presented, the dimension only increases in value by 1; in other cases, if we consider parameters for the set of possible incoming trades, the dimension increase would be higher. Increasing the dimension of the input domain of the proxy object increases its building computational cost. Therefore, the practitioner must bear in mind that for this approach to work, the number of parameters over which the optimisation exercise is run should not be too large.

In exercises like the one just discussed, the practitioner must weigh advantages and disadvantages before deciding whether to build proxy objects at each iteration or a single one offline. On the one hand, increasing the number of trade parameters over which we select pairs of mirroring swaps gives the optimisation algorithms more freedom to explore trades that could potentially reduce the MVA value of the portfolio. On the other hand, keeping the number of parameters reasonably low enables us to build a single proxy offline, which significantly increases the speed of the optimisation.

Bibliography

1. S. Scoleri A. Maran A. Pallavicini. *Chehyshev Greeks: Smoothing Gamma without Bias.* 2021. URL: https://arxiv.org/abs/2106.12431.
2. L.N. Trefethen A. Townsend. "An Extension of Chebfun to Two Dimensions". In: *SIAM Journal on Scientific Computing* 35(6) (2013), pp. C495–C518.
3. A. Muguruza B. Horvath A. Jacquier. *Functional Central Limit Theorems for Rough Volatility.* 2017. URL: arXiv:1711.03078.
4. A.R. Barron. "Approximation and Estimation Bounds for Artificial Neural Networks". In: *Machine Learning* 14(1) (1994), pp. 115–133.
5. L. Bergomi. *Stochastic Volatility Modeling.* Chapman & Hall/CRC, 2015.
6. S. Bernstein. "Sur l'Ordre de la Meilleure Approximation des Fonctions Continues par des Polynomes de Degré Donné". In: *Mém. Acad. Roy. Belg.* (1912).
7. BIS. *Basel Committee on Banking Supervision. 2016. Minimal Capital Requirements for Market Risk.* 2016.
8. M. Brenner M.G. Subrahmanyan. "A Simple Formula to Compute the Implied Standard Deviation". In: *Financial Analysts Journal.* 44(5) (1988), pp. 80–83.
9. B. Stemper C. Bayer. *Deep Calibration of Rough Stochastic Volatility Models.* 2018. URL: https://arxiv.org/abs/1810.03399.
10. J. Gatheral C. Bayer P. Friz. "Pricing under Rough Volatility." In: *Quantitative Finance* 16(6) (2015), pp. 1–18.
11. A. Curtis C. Clenshaw. "A Method for Numerical Integration on an Automatic Computer". In: *Numer. Math.* 2 (1960), pp. 197–205.
12. H. Plank C. Kappen. *Simulation of Future Initial Margin along Low-Dimensional State Spaces.* 2017. URL: https://papers.ssrn.com/sol3/papers.cfm?abstract_id=3001424
13. O. Salazar Celis. "A Parametrized Barycentric Approximation for Inverse Problems with Application to the Black-Scholes Formula". In: *IMA Journal of Numerical Analysis.* 38(2) (2017), pp. 976–997.
14. C.J. Corrado T.W. Miller. "A Note on a Simple, Accurate Formula to Compute Implied Standard Deviations". In: *Journal of Banking & Finance.* 20(3) (1996), pp. 595–603.
15. R. Courant F. John. *Introduction to Calculus and Analysis, Volume I.* Springer, 1988.
16. G. Cybenko. "Approximation by Superpositions of a Sigmoidal Function". In: *Mathematics of Control, Signals, and Systems* 2(4) (1989), pp. 303–314.
17. T. Wiesel D. Hubel. "Receptive Fields of Single Neurones in the Cat's Striate Cortex". In: *J. Physiol.* 148(3) (1959), pp. 574–591.
18. L. Ba D. Kingma. *Adam: A Method for Stochastic Optimization.* 2014. URL: https://arxiv.org/abs/1412.6980.
19. C. Doléans-Dade. "Quelques applications de la formule de changement de variables pour les semimartingales". In: *Wahrscheinlichkeitstheorie ver-wandte Gebiete* 16 (1970), pp. 181–194.
20. J. Duchi E. Hazan Y. Singer. "Adaptive Subgradient Methods for Online Learning and Stochastic Optimization". In: *JMLR* 12 (2011), pp. 2121–2159.
21. M. Dupuy. "Le calcul numérique de fonctions par l'interpolation barycentrique". In: *Compt. Rend. Acad. Sci* 226 (1948), pp. 158–159.

22. J. Vives E. Alòs J.A. León. "On the Short-Time Behavior of the Implied Volatility for Jump-Diffusion Models with Stochastic Volatility." In: *Finance and Stochastics* 11(4) (2007), pp. 571–589.

23. M. Scholes F. Black. "The Pricing of Options and Corporate Liabilities". In: *The Journal of Political Economy* 81 (3) (1973), pp. 637–654.

24. G. Faber. "Über die interpolatorische Darstellung stetiger Funktionen". In: *Jahresber. Deutsch. Math.* 23 (1914), pp. 192–210.

25. R. Ferguson A. Green. *Deeply Learning Derivatives.* 2018. URL: https://arxiv.org/abs/1809 .02233.

26. D. Röder G. Dimitroff C.P. Fries. *Volatility Model Calibration with Convolutional Neural Networks.* 2018. URL: https://papers.ssrn.com/sol3/papers.cfm?abstract_id=3252432.

27. M. Gaß et al. "Chebyshev Interpolation for Parametric Option Pricing". In: *Finance Stoch.* 22 (2018), pp. 701–731.

28. J. Gatheral. *The Volatility Surface: A Practitioner's Guide.* Wiley, 2011.

29. K. Glau D. Kressner F. Statti. *Low-Rank Tensor Approximation for Chebyshev Interpolation in Parametric Option Pricing.* URL: https://arxiv.org/abs/1902.04367.

30. K. Glau et al. *The Chebyshev Method for the Implied Volatility.* 2017. URL: https://arxiv.org/abs/ 1710.01797.

31. I. Goodfellow Y. Bengio A. Courville. *Deep Learning.* http://www.deeplearningbook.org. MIT Press, 2016.

32. L.A. Grzelak. *Sparse Grid Method for Highly Efficient Computation of Exposures for xVA.* 2021. URL: https://arxiv.org/abs/2104.14319.

33. L.N. Trefethen H. Behnam. "Chebfun in Three Dimensions". In: *Preprint* (2016).

34. K. Zeller H. Ehlich. "Auswertung der Normen von Interpolationsoperatoren". In: *Math. Ann.* 164 (1966), pp. 105–112.

35. P.S. Hagan et al. "Managing Smile Risk". In: *The Best of Wilmott* 1 (2002), pp. 249–296.

36. T. Hastie et al. *The Elements of Statistical Learning: Data Mining, Inference, and Prediction.* New York: Springer, 2001.

37. A. Hernandez. "Model Calibration with Neural Networks". In: *Risk* (2017).

38. S. Heston. "A Closed-Form Solution for Options with Stochastic Volatility with Applications to Bond and Currency Options". In: *The Review of Financial Studies* 6(2) (1993), pp. 327–343.

39. N. Higham. "The Numerical Stability of Barycentric Lagrange Interpolation". In: *IMA J., Numer.* (2004), pp. 547–556.

40. G. Hinton N. Srivastava K. Swersky. *Neural Networks for Machine Learning - Lecture 6.* 2012. URL: https://www.cs.toronto.edu/~tijmen/csc321/slides/lecture_slides_lec6.pdf.

41. B. Horvath, A. Muguruza, and M. Tomas. *Deep Learning Volatility.* URL: https://arxiv.org/abs/ 1901.09647.

42. B. Huge and A. Savine. *Differential Machine Learning.* 2020. URL: https://arxiv.org/abs/2005 .02347.

43. ISDA. *Methodology, version R1.3. (Effective Date: April 1, 2017).* URL: //www2.isda.org/ attachment/OTIzMQ==/ISDA%5C%20SIMM%5C%20vR1.3%5C%20(PUBLIC).pdf.

44. M. Rosenbaum J. Gatheral T. Jaisson. "Volatility Is Rough." In: *Quantitative Finance* 18(6) (2018), pp. 933–949.

45. P. Jäckel. "By Implication". In: *Wilmott* 26 (2006), pp. 60–66.

46. P. Jäckel. "Let's Be Rational". In: *Wilmott* 75 (2015), pp. 40–53.

47. C.G.J. Jacobi. *Disquisitiones Analyticae de Fractionibus Simplicibus.* 1825.

48. P. Kidger T. Lyons. *Universal Approximation with Deep Narrow Networks.* 2020. URL: https:// arxiv.org/abs/1905.08539.

49. A. Kondratyev G. Giorgidze. "MVA Optimisation with Machine Learning Algorithms". In: *SSRN* (2017).

50. M. Li. "Approximate Inversion of the Black-Scholes Formula Using Rational Functions". In: *European Journal of Operational Research* 185(2) (2008), pp. 743–759.
51. H. Lin S. Jegelka. "ResNet with One-Neuron Hidden Layers Is a Universal Approximator". In: *Neural Information Processing Systems* 30 (2018), pp. 6169–6178.
52. F.A. Longstaff Eduardo S. Schwartz. "Valuing American Options by Simulation: A Simple Least-Squares Approach". In: *The Review of Financial Studies* 14(1) (2001), pp. 113–147.
53. S. Pagliarani M. Lorig A. Pascucci. "A Taylor Series Approach to Pricing and Implied Volatility for Local-Stochastic Volatility Models". In: *The Journal of Risk.* 17(2) (2014), p. 3.
54. J. Stolte M. Pistorius. "Fast Computation of Vanilla Prices in Time-Changed Models and Implied Volatilities Using Rational Approximations". In: *International Journal of Theoretical and Applied Finance* 15(4) (2012), p. 1250031.
55. W. McCulloch W. Pitts. "A Logical Calculus of Ideas Immanent in Nervous Activity". In: *Bulletin of Mathematical Biophysics* 5 (1943), pp. 115–133.
56. M. Minsky S. Papert. *Perceptrons: An Introduction to Computational Geometry.* The MIT Press, 1969.
57. T. Mitchell. *Machine Learning.* McGraw Hill, 1997.
58. P. Fisher N. Ahmed. "Study of Algorithmic Properties of Chebyshev Coefficients". In: *Int. J. Computer Math.* (1970), pp. 307–317.
59. S. Nitish et al. "Dropout: A Simple Way to Prevent Neural Networks from Overfitting". In: *Journal of Machine Learning Research* 15(1) (2014), pp. 1929–1958.
60. I.V. Oseledets. "Tensor-Train Decomposition". In: *SIAM J. Sci. Comput.* 33 (2011), pp. 2295–2317.
61. L.M. Rios N.V. Sahinidis. "Derivative-Free Optimization: A Review of Algorithms and Comparison of Software Implementations". In: *Journal of Global Optimization* 56(3) (2013), pp. 1247–1293.
62. F. Rosenblatt. "The Perceptron—A Perceiving and Recognizing Automaton". In: *Cornell Aeronautical Laboratory* 1 (1957), pp. 85–460.
63. C. Runge. "Über empirische Funktionen und die Interpolation zwischen äquidistanten Ordinaten". In: *Z. Math. Phys.* 23 (1901), pp. 224–243.
64. G. Koehler S. Manaster. "The Calculation of Implied Variances from the Black-Scholes Model: A Note." In: *The Journal of Finance* 37 (1) (1982), pp. 227–230.
65. A. Saini. *A Formula for Justice.* 2011. URL: https://www.theguardian.com/law/2011/oct/02/formula-justice-bayes-theorem-miscarriage.
66. H.E. Salzer. "Lagrangian Interpolation at the Chebyshev Points $xn, v = cos(vpi/n)$, $v = O(1)n$; Some Unnoted Advantages". In: *Computer J.* (1972), pp. 156–159.
67. E. Schmidt. "Zur Theorie der linearen und nichtlinearen Integralgleichungen. I Teil. Entwicklung willkurlichen Funktionen nach System vorgeschriebener". In: *Math. Ann.* (63) (1907), pp. 433–476.
68. A. Smoktunowicz. "Backward Stability of Clenshaw's Algorithm". In: *BIT Numerical Mathematics* 42.1 (2002), pp. 600–610.
69. M. Steinlechner. "Riemannian Optimization for High-Dimensional Tensor Completion". In: *SIAM J. Sci. Comput.* 38 (2016), S461–S484.
70. S. Stigler. "Gauss and the Invention of Least Squares". In: *Ann. Stat.* 9(3) (1981), pp. 465–474.
71. H. Stone. "Calibrating Rough Volatility Models: A Convolutional Neural Network Approach". In: *Quantitative Finance* 20(3) (2019), pp. 379–392.
72. L.N. Trefethen. *Approximation Theory and Approximation Practice.* SIAM, 2013.
73. L.N. Trefethen. "Probably Good to Mention or Reference Six Myths of Polynomial Interpolation and Quadrature". In: *Mathematics Today* 47(4) (2012), pp. 184–188.
74. L.N. Trefethen. *Spectral Methods in MATLAB.* SIAM, 2000.

75. A. Tsantekidis et al. "Forecasting Stock Prices from the Limit Order Book Using Convolutional Neural Networks". In: *IEEE 19th Conference on Business Informatics (CBI)* (2017).

76. K. Weierstrass. "Uber die analytische Darstellbarkeit sogenannter willkurlicher Functionen einer reellen Veranderlichen". In: *Sitzungsberichte der Akademie zu Berlin* 322(10) (1885), pp. 633–639.

77. Wikipedia contributors. *Differential Evolution.* [Online; accessed 09-042021]. 2021. URL: https://en.wikipedia.org/wiki/Differential_evolution.

78. Wikipedia contributors. *Polynomial Interpolation.* [Online; accessed 2105-2020]. 2020. URL: https://en.wikipedia.org/wiki/Polynomial_interpolation.

Index

Page references followed by *f* indicate an illustrated figure; followed by *n* indicate a footnote; followed by *t* indicate a table.